Nsef Anundoya

Oracle Press™

OCP Oracle 9*i* Database: Fundamentals II Exam Guide

About the Author

Rama Velpuri

Rama Velpuri is the founder and CEO of ORAMASTERS Inc. ORAMASTERS specializes in providing online support services for Oracle users worldwide. Before founding ORAMASTERS, Mr. Velpuri worked with Oracle Corporation for more than ten years. At Oracle, he was an Executive Director of the Oracle Application Development Center. He has built two offshore development centers for Oracle, one in Bangalore, India (India Product Engineering Center), and the other in Hyderabad, India (Oracle Application Development Center). Before that, he was a Senior Manager of the Mission Critical Support Center. Mr. Velpuri has presented numerous technical papers at various International Oracle Conferences and Oracle user conferences on disaster recovery, and he has trained Oracle support personnel in 22 different countries in problem-solving techniques. You can reach him via e-mail at *rvelpuri@oramasters.com.*

Rama's Oracle Press Books:

- *Oracle8i Backup & Recovery Handbook* (ISBN 0-07-212717-1, 2001)

- *Oracle8 Backup & Recovery Handbook* (ISBN 0-07-882389-7, 1998)

- *Oracle8 Troubleshooting* (ISBN 0-07-882580-6, 1999)

- *Oracle NT Handbook* (ISBN 0-07-211917-9, 1998)

- *Oracle Troubleshooting* (ISBN 0-07-882388-9, 1997)

- *Oracle Backup & Recovery Handbook 7.3 Edition* (ISBN 0-07-882323-4, 1997)

- *Oracle Backup & Recovery Handbook* (ISBN 0-07-882106-1, 1995)

ORACLE® *Oracle Press*™

OCP Oracle 9*i* Database: Fundamentals II Exam Guide

Rama Velpuri

McGraw-Hill/Osborne

New York   Chicago   San Francisco
Lisbon   London   Madrid   Mexico City   Milan
New Delhi   San Juan   Seoul   Singapore   Sydney   Toronto

McGraw-Hill/Osborne
2600 Tenth Street
Berkeley, California 94710
U.S.A.

To arrange bulk purchase discounts for sales promotions, premiums, or fund-raisers, please contact **McGraw-Hill**/Osborne at the above address. For information on translations or book distributors outside the U.S.A., please see the International Contact Information page immediately following the index of this book.

OCP Oracle9*i* Database: Fundamentals II Exam Guide

       890 FGR FGR 0 9876
Book p/n 0-07-219544-4 and CD p/n 0-07-219545-2
parts of
ISBN 0-07-219543-6

Publisher Brandon A. Nordin	**Acquisitions Coordinator** Athena Honore
Vice-President & Associate Publisher Scott Rogers	**Technical Editor** John Watson
Acquisitions Editor Jeremy Judson	**Cover Series Design** Damore Johann Design, Inc.
Project Manager Jenn Tust	**Composition and Indexing** MacAllister Publishing Services, LLC

This book was composed with QuarkXPress™.

To the victims and their families of the September 11, 2001
World Trade Center and Pentagon tragedy

OracleCertified
Professional

About the Oracle Certification Exams

The expertise of Oracle database administrators (DBAs) is integral to the success of today's increasingly complex system environments. The best DBAs operate primarily behind the scenes, looking for ways to fine-tune day-to-day performance to prevent unscheduled crises and hours of expensive downtime. They know they stand between optimal performance and a crisis that could bring a company to a standstill. The Oracle Certified Database Administrator Track provides DBAs with tangible evidence of their skills with the Oracle database.

The Oracle Certified Professional (OCP) Program was developed by Oracle to recognize technical professionals who can demonstrate the depth of knowledge and hands-on skills required to maximize Oracle's core products according to a rigorous standard established by Oracle. By earning professional certification, you can translate the impressive knowledge and skill you have worked so hard to accumulate into a tangible credential that can lead to greater job security or more challenging, better-paying opportunities.

Oracle Certified Professionals are eligible to receive use of the Oracle Certified Professional logo and a certificate for framing.

Requirements for Certification

To become an Oracle Certified Database Administrator for the Oracle9*i* track, you must pass four tests. These exams cover knowledge of the essential aspects of the SQL language, Oracle administration, backup and recovery, and performance tuning of systems. The certification process requires that you pass the following four exams:

- Exam 1: Introduction to Oracle9*i*: SQL (1Z0-007)
- Exam 2: Oracle9*i* Database: Fundamentals I (1Z0-031)
- Exam 3: Oracle9*i* Database: Fundamentals II (1Z0-032)
- Exam 4: Oracle9*i* Database: Performance Tuning (1Z0-033)

If you fail a test, you must wait at least 30 days before you retake that exam. You may attempt a particular test up to 3 times in a 12-month period.

Recertification

Oracle announces the requirements for upgrading your certification based on the release of new products and upgrades. Oracle will give six months' notice announcing when an exam version is expiring.

Exam Format

The computer-based exams are multiple-choice tests, consisting of 50–65 questions that must be completed in 90–120 minutes.

Contents at a Glance

PART III

Test Yourself: Oracle9*i* DBA Practice Exams

Contents

PART I
Oracle Networking

PART II
Backup and Recovery

PART III
Test Yourself: Oracle9*i* DBA Practice Exams

Acknowledgments

lthough I really enjoyed writing this book, I couldn't have met the aggressive time schedules if not for the DBA team of ORAMASTERS. Specifically, I would like to thank Akhilesh Agrawal, Venkat Mandala, Yash Kapani, Veera Babu Thinnathi, Sai Prasad Tammana, and Asad Khan for their long hours of research, review, and testing, without whom the book would not have been a reality. I would also like to thank Varma P. S. K., Rajasekhar Reddy C., Shaikh Shavali, and Suresh Shanbhag for their technical reviews and feedback. Thanks to Madhusudhana Raju Alluri and Shahid Hussain for helping me with the figures in the book.

Next, a word of gratitude to the management team at ORAMASTERS—Som Sarma, Radha Mocherla and Rama Rao, and the advisory board of ORAMASTERS—Dr. Terry Gannon, Carolyn Gannon, Michael Corey, and Raj Velpuri for their support and patience. Thanks also to ORAMASTERS' partners Mutrib, Al-Sudairi, Marwan, Shareef, Syed, and Lloyd Pollock. Thanks to Shakuntala, Hanumantha Rao and Desiree—the operations team of ORAMASTERS, for their support and putting up with our schedules. Last but not least from the ORAMASTERS team, I would like to thank Srinivas Reddy, who has been my right hand person throughout this entire project. I thank him very much for his dedication, hard work, and sincerity.

Next, I would like to thank Oracle Corporation for its support in developing this book and John Watson, in particular, ensured the accuracy of the material. With real-life teaching experience, John's feedback was extremely useful and has improved the quality of the book. Also thanks to Vinay Srihari and Sujatha Muthulingam of the Oracle Kernel development team for their support.

I would like to thank Jeremy Judson of McGraw Hill/Osborne for asking me to write this book and to the rest of the team—Scott Rogers, Athena Honore, and Lisa McClain. I would also like to thank Beth Brown and the MacAllister team for their editorial and production work.

I would like to thank my parents Seetha and Lakshminarayana Velpuri, my wife Anuradha Velpuri, and my children Akhil and Manasa, for their support during this project with grueling schedules. Thanks to Kamala Reddy, Ramana and Nirmala Reddy, Ramana Gogula, Anand Adkoli, Ramana Balagani, Sunitha Balagani, Dr. Aruna, Sudha, Chandrika, Mythili, Aravinda, Agastya, and Raj Velpuri for their moral support.

This book is dedicated to the memory of the victims of the World Trade Center and the Pentagon, who lost their lives in the atrocity. I would like to convey my deepest sympathy to their families.

Introduction

he Oracle Certified Professional DBA certification exam series from Oracle Corporation is a great opportunity for you to demonstrate your expertise on the use of Oracle database software. Called OCP, it represents the culmination of many people's request for objective standards in Oracle database administration, one of the hottest markets in the software field. The presence of OCP on the market indicates an important reality about Oracle as a career path. Oracle is mature, robust, and stable for enterprise-wide information management. However, corporations face a severe shortage of qualified Oracle professionals.

The OCP certification core track for DBAs consists of four tests in the following areas of Oracle9*i*: SQL, database administration fundamentals I and II, and tuning, with the current content of those exams covering Oracle through Oracle9*i*. For professionals who are already Oracle8*i* certified, there is an upgrade exam available. Each test consists of about 60 to 64 multiple-choice questions pertaining to the recommended usage of Oracle databases. You have about 90 minutes to take each exam. Obtaining certification for Oracle9*i* through the core track is contingent on taking and passing *all* core examinations. This book will help you prepare for the third exam (database fundamentals II) in the DBA track.

Why Get Certified?

If you are already an Oracle professional, you may wonder, "Why should I get certified?" Perhaps you have a successful career as an Oracle DBA, enjoying the instant prestige your resume gets with that one magic word on it. With market forces currently in your favor, you're right to wonder. However, although no one is saying you don't know Oracle when you put the magic word on your resume, can you prove how well you *do* know Oracle without undergoing a technical interview?

If you're looking for a reason to become certified in Oracle, consider the experience of computer professionals with Novell NetWare experience in the late 1980s and early 1990s. Back then, it seemed that anyone with even a little experience in Novell could count on a fantastic job offer. Then Novell introduced its CNE/CNA programs. At first, employers were okay with hiring Novell professionals whether they had a certificate or not. As time went on, however, employers no longer asked for computer professionals with Novell NetWare *experience*—they asked for CNEs and CNAs. A similar phenomenon can be seen in the arena of Microsoft Windows NT/2000, where the MCSE has already become the standard by which those professionals are measuring their skills. Furthermore, with the latest economic downturn in the technology-driven U.S. economy comes the possibility of involuntary IT job changes. If you want to stay competitive in the field of Oracle database administration or development through those changes, your real question shouldn't be *whether* you should become certified, but *when*.

If you are not in the field of Oracle database management or if you want to advance your career using Oracle products, there has never been a better time to do so. OCP is already altering the playing field for DBAs by changing the focus of the Oracle skill set from "how many years have you used it" to "do you know *how* to use it?" That shift benefits organizations using Oracle as much as it benefits the professionals who use Oracle because the emphasis is on *skills*, not attrition.

Managers who are faced with the task of hiring Oracle professionals can breathe a sigh of relief with the debut of OCP as well. By seeking professionals who are certified, managers can spend less time trying to determine if the candidate possesses the Oracle skills for the job and more time assessing the candidate's work habits and compatibility with the team.

How Should You Prepare for the Exam?

If you spend your free time studying things like what happens when you do incomplete media recovery using the UNTIL CANCEL option, you are probably ready to take the OCP Oracle9*i* database fundamentals II exam now. For the rest of us, Oracle and other companies offer classroom- and computer-based training options to learn Oracle. Now, users have another option—this book. By selecting this book, you demonstrate two excellent characteristics—that you are committed to a superior career using Oracle products, and that you care about preparing for the exam correctly and thoroughly. By the way, the UNTIL CANCEL command enables you to apply redo till the end of each archive log, and it is on the OCP Oracle9*i* database fundamentals II exam. That fact, along with thousands of others, is covered extensively in this book to help you prepare for and pass the OCP Oracle9*i* database fundamentals II exam.

DBA Certification Past and Present

Oracle certification started in the mid 1990s with the involvement of the Chauncey Group International, a division of Educational Testing Service. With the help of many Oracle DBAs, Chauncey put together an objective, fact- and scenario-based examination on Oracle database administration. This test did an excellent job of measuring knowledge of Oracle7, versions 7.0 to 7.2. Consisting of 60 questions, Chauncey's exam covered several different topic areas, including backup and recovery, security, administration, and performance tuning, all in one test.

Oracle Corporation has taken DBA certification ahead with the advent of OCP. Their certification examination is actually four tests, each consisting of about 64 questions. By quadrupling the number of questions you must answer, Oracle requires that you have unprecedented depth of knowledge in Oracle database administration. Oracle has also committed to including scenario-based questions on the OCP examinations, and preparation material for these new questions is included in this book as well. Scenario-based questions require you to not only know the facts about Oracle, but also understand how to apply those facts in real-life situations. This guide includes hundreds of scenario-based questions and answers.

Oracle's final contribution to the area of Oracle certification is a commitment to reviewing and updating the material presented in the certification exams. Oracle-certified DBAs will be required to maintain their certification by retaking the certification exams periodically—meaning that those who certify will stay on the cutting edge of the Oracle database better than those who do not.

The Next Steps

Next, understand the test interface you will encounter on exam day. Figure I-1 contains a diagram of the actual test graphical user interface. Now we'll delve into an explanation of the interface. The top of the interface tells you how much time has elapsed and the number of questions you have answered. You can use the checkbox in the upper left-hand corner of the interface to mark questions you would like to review later. In the main window of the interface you'll find the actual exam question, along with the choices. Generally, the interface enables the user to select only one answer (unless the question specifically directs you to select more answers). In this case, the interface will enable you to select only as many answers as the question requests. After answering a question or marking the question for later review, the candidate can move onto the next question by clicking the appropriate button in the lower left-hand corner. To return to the previous question on the OCP exam, hit the next button over to the left. You can score your questions at any time by pressing the grade test button on the bottom right-hand side. The final point feature to cover is the exhibit button. In some cases, you may require the use of an exhibit to answer a question. If the question does not require the use of an exhibit, the button will be grayed out.

Once you've completed all questions on the exam, the Sylvan Prometric interface will display a listing of all the answers you selected, shown in Figure I-2. The questions you marked for later review will be highlighted, and the interface will

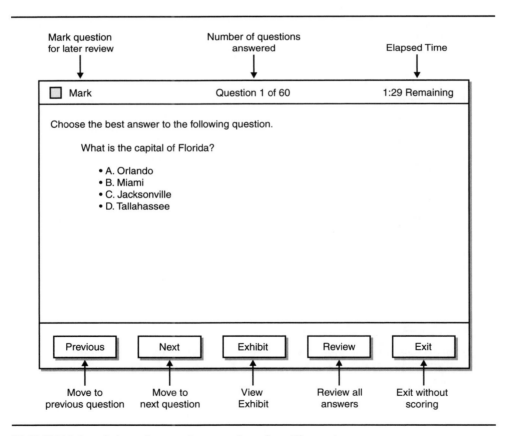

FIGURE I-1. *Sylvan Prometric exam interface illustration*

guide you through review of all those questions you marked. You can review individual questions, or simply have Sylvan Prometric grade your exam.

The free Assessment Test provided by Oracle on their Web site indicates your performance by means of a grade window, such as the one displayed in Figure I-3. It details the number of questions you answered correctly, along with your percentage score based on 100 percent. You will be shown a section-by-section breakdown of how you did according to the topics covered on the exam as published in the OCP DBA Candidate Guide from Oracle. Finally, a bar graph indicates where your performance falls in comparison to the maximum score possible on the exam. The OCP exam reports your score immediately after you exit the exam, so you will know right then whether you pass or not in a similar fashion as the assessment test. Both interfaces offer you the ability to print a report of your score.

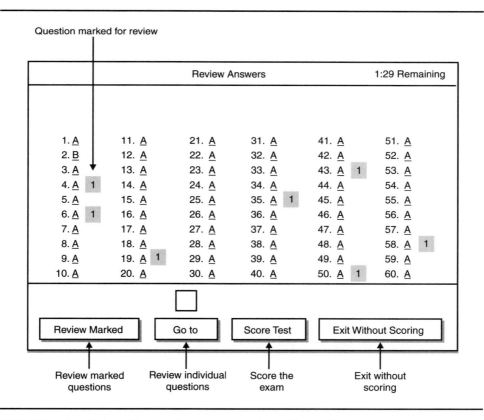

FIGURE I-2. *Sylvan Prometric answer interface illustration*

Strategies for Improving Your Score

When OCP exams were first released, the score range for each OCP Exam was between 200 and 800. However, Oracle has vacillated on whether to scale the OCP exam score, and has experimented lately with reporting only a raw score of the number of questions you answered correctly. However, the bottom line is still the same. Because there are typically 60 questions on an OCP exam, you want to make sure you get at least 75 percent, or 45 of the questions right in order to pass. Given the recent use of questions with two or even three correct answers on OCP exams, you need to be careful to select *all* correct answer choices on a question or else you will not get credit for your partially correct answer. *There is no penalty for wrong answers.*

Some preliminary items are now identified for you to take the OCP exams. The first tip is, *don't wait until you're the world's foremost authority on Oracle to*

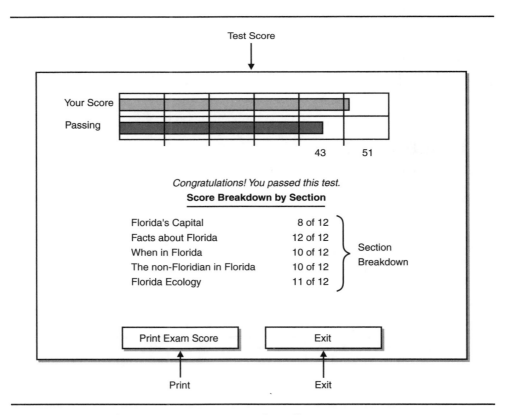

FIGURE I-3. *Sylvan Prometric score interface illustration*

take the OCP Exam. If your OCP exam is scaled as it was when the exams were first released, the passing score for most exams is approximately 650. You have to get 45 to 50 questions right, or about 75 to 80 percent of the exam. So, if you are getting about four questions right out of five on the assessment test or in Chapter 20 of this guide, you should consider taking the OCP exam. Remember, you're certified if you pass with 77 or 96 percent correct answers.

If you can't answer the question within 30 seconds, mark it with the checkbox in the upper left-hand corner of the OCP interface for review later. The most significant difference between the OCP interface and the assessment test interface is a special screen appearing after you answer all the questions. This screen displays all your answers, along with a special indicator next to the questions you marked for review. This screen also offers a button for you to click in order to review the questions you marked. You should use this feature extensively. If you spend only 30 seconds answering each question in your first pass on the exam, you will have at least an hour to review the questions you're unsure of, with the added bonus of knowing you answered all the questions that were easiest to you first.

Third, *there is no penalty for guessing*. If you answer the question correctly, your score goes up; if not, your score does not change. If you can eliminate any choices on a question, you should take the chance in the interest of improving your score. In some questions, the OCP exam requires you to specify two or even three choices—this can work in your favor, meaning you need to eliminate fewer choices to get the question right.

A Note about Updates and Errata

If you have comments about the book or would like to contact me about it, please do so by e-mail at *rvelpuri@oramasters.com*. Share with me your success story or any technical questions you have on this book.

PART
I

Oracle Networking

CHAPTER
1

Networking Overview

hat does it mean to say that the Internet has become so prominent in the last decade? It means that humans are perfecting the art of networking computers. Being part of a network helps you to access information on other computers, lets other people access your information, and allows people on the network to share devices like printers.

There are several ways to connect from one computer to another computer or to a network. A typical network connection may be a

- Link between the input/output (I/O) ports of two computers using a single cable.

- Private network using a modem or an Integrated Services Digital Network (ISDN) adapter or a Network Interface Card (NIC).

- Network using a Virtual Private Network (VPN) connection.

In this chapter we give you an overview of network configurations and the solutions provided by Oracle to manage networks. The topics covered in this chapter include

- Networking challenges in the business environment

- Network configurations

- Oracle's solution to networking issues

Networking Challenges in the Business Environment

Networking has changed drastically over the last few years. The importance and presence of networks are growing. With the growth of the e-commerce model, new business requirements have been created. The success of this e-commerce business depends on how business Web sites provide reliable connectivity and availability. The sites should be up and running around the clock. To meet the thousands of simultaneous Internet connections, scalability, performance, reliability, and security are key factors to be considered.

In this business model, implementing a successful networking environment is a big challenge. Many issues have to be considered before designing a network environment. A few of these issues are discussed in the following section.

Considerations for Configuring the Network Environment

Proper configuration of the network is most crucial in maintaining a network for any enterprise. Prior to setting up the network environment, you must consider various issues that would influence the design of the network. The type of network required depends on the business rules. Is it a small network with few clients or a complex network with a large number of clients and servers? The protocols supported by the environment also need to be identified. You will need to assess if your network requires a single protocol or if you would require multiple protocol support.

You must understand and plan for the future growth of your network as well. This would have a profound impact depending on whether the network would be static or expanding dynamically. The various available configuration options for setting up the network environment have to be clearly defined and the best option chosen. You should also consider the number of routers, switches, or hubs that you require for your intranet. If connecting to the Internet, you should consider the various security options.

Maintaining the Network

Estimating the growth of your network and implementing methods to successfully incorporate the changes in the network environment are key to successfully maintaining your network. You must figure out the growth of the network by understanding in advance the type of technology to be implemented: client-server (or simple), N-tier, or complex networks. You must estimate the number of clients and servers to be added to the network and further draw statistics pertaining to the frequency at which upgrades occur to the network.

Tuning the Network

Tuning the network for the better propagation of data across different nodes is an important step in successful maintenance. The process involving effective tuning, troubleshooting, and monitoring depend greatly on the number of users, transactions, and nodes; the location of the node's routers, switches, hubs; and the availability of the network.

Implementing Security in the Network

The most crucial aspect of a network is the implementation of secured links across nodes. This primarily is a business requisite. You must know the level of security that needs to be implemented and whether the transmission of data is secure depending on its sensitivity. You should be aware of the tools available to you for implementing various levels of network security.

Integrating Legacy Systems

The factors involving the integration of legacy systems with the networking environment are significant. You must be aware of the various proprietary protocols supported with the legacy systems and then work towards further integration.

All the previous issues are just a few among the many that must be considered when designing a networking environment.

Network Configurations

Depending on the business requirements, you can establish a *simple network*, an *N-tier network*, or a *complex network*. The configuration you choose should depend on your business requirements. A brief description of each of the previously mentioned network configurations is provided in this section.

Simple Network

In a *simple* network, the clients connect directly to the database server using a given network protocol. The simple network is also referred to as the *client-server architecture* or the *two-tier architecture.* The client and server should use the same network protocol. The simple network environment is best suited for an environment where the number of clients is small. With the PC revolution, the client-server architecture has become very popular with businesses.

Although it is very easy to manage a client-server environment, the simple network is not scaleable. If you add a large number of clients to the network, and all the clients are accessing the database server, the server may not be able to handle all the requests, as there will be bottlenecks. As a result, this will become an ineffective network. This is a major drawback of the simple network architecture. The simple network is still very much preferred for small businesses with a small number of clients and servers. Figure 1-1 shows the simple network architecture.

NOTE
A simple network in a large and widely distributed environment is very difficult to manage with respect to software version control, security, and configuration maintenance.

N-Tier Network

The drawback of the simple network can be overcome with the *N-tier* network architecture, as it introduces one or more servers or agents between the client and the database server. The middle tier is known as the *agent* or the *application tier.* The

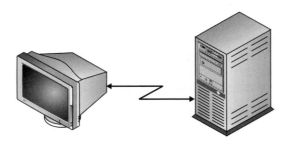

FIGURE 1-1. *Simple network architecture*

N-tier network provides for centralized maintenance. If you have an environment where hundreds or thousands of users require simultaneous connections to the server, the N-tier architecture would suit you best.

The agent in the N-tier network provides translation services to the client-server environment or acts as a bridge between protocols. The agent also acts as a transaction-processing monitor to balance the load of requests between servers and provides the intelligent agent services like mapping a request to a number of different servers, collating the results and returning a single response to the client. Figure 1-2 shows the N-tier network architecture.

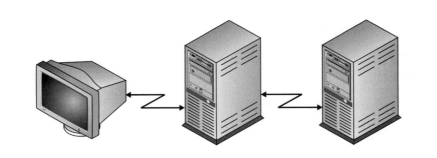

FIGURE 1-2. *N-tier network architecture*

Complex Network

If your business requirement includes the maintenance of large-scale distributed database systems, it requires different hardware and operating systems using multiple protocols, and these systems are located in different geographical locations, you will need to design a complex network. This kind of solution is suitable for large and global companies in a heterogeneous environment. Figure 1-3 show the complex network architecture.

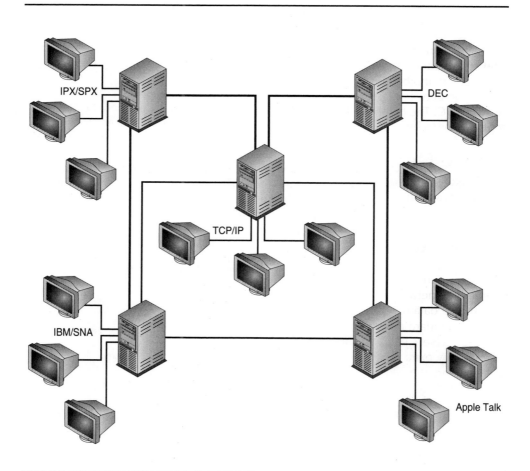

FIGURE 1-3. *Complex network architecture*

Oracle's Solution to Networking Issues

To interact with the Oracle database server from the client applications, a method of connection is required. Oracle offers *Oracle Net* to provide the connectivity solutions in a distributed, heterogeneous computing environment regardless of vendor, operating systems, or hardware architecture. It eases the complexities of network configurations, management, and performance. It also improves the diagnostic capabilities. Oracle Net should be located on each of the machines in the network. Once the network session establishes a connection between a client and server, Oracle Net acts as a data courier between the two. Oracle Net is the networking solution for Oracle9*i*.

Oracle Net also provides a data conversion facility between two national language character sets. For example, interaction between two machines that use different character sets, such as a European language on one machine and an Asian language on another machine, is possible with Oracle Net. It can also provide interaction between different computer architecture character sets, such as ASCII and EBCDIC. The extensive national-language character set enables Oracle applications to be deployed globally on any environment.

Oracle Net Features

Oracle Net sits on top of a given protocol, providing transparency to the machines that are conversing. This section discusses the connectivity, manageability, scalability, and security features of Oracle Net.

Connectivity

Oracle Net provides for transparent client-server application connectivity and includes a rich set of networking services. It is responsible for establishing and maintaining network sessions between a client and the database server and for exchanging data between them. Oracle Net provides support to most of the industry-standard network protocols.

Oracle Net's data conversion is invisible to the user and to the application. Without any extra burden on the network infrastructure, Oracle Net can interoperate across different types of computers, operating systems, and networks to transparently connect any combination of PC, UNIX, and legacy system.

Oracle Net is layered on top of a network protocol that determines how applications access the network and how data is subdivided into packets for transmission across the network.

NOTE
SPX/IPX will no longer be supported with Oracle9i.

Manageability

For easy configuration and management of networking components, Oracle Net offers a number of manageability features. This section discusses some of these features.

Location Transparency   To access an Oracle database, clients need to provide a service name to identify this database. The information about the database service and its location in the network is transparent to the client because the information needed to make a connection is stored in a repository. The repository can be represented by one or more naming methods. Oracle Net offers several types of naming methods that support a localized configuration on each client or a centralized configuration that can be accessed by all the clients in the network. Easy-to-use graphical user interfaces (GUIs) enable you to manage data stored in the naming methods.

Centralized Configuration and Management   To manage huge networking environments, administrators need to be able to easily specify and modify the network configuration in a centralized repository. To meet this requirement, Oracle Net configuration provides the capability to store information in an Lightweight Directory Access Protocol (LDAP)-compliant directory service.

   The support of LDAP-compliant directory servers provides a centralized vehicle for managing and configuring a distributed Oracle network. The directory can act as a central repository for all data on database network components, user and corporate policies, and user authentication and security, thus replacing client-side and server-side localized configuration files. To access this information, all systems on the heterogeneous network can refer to the directory.

Easy Client Configuration   The key to managing huge networks with potentially thousands of clients is to have the ability to change network preferences easily. Oracle Net provides a variety of naming solutions designed to give customers a high degree of flexibility in how they integrate Oracle services into their dynamic environments. The naming solutions for a dynamic, enterprise-wide network are Oracle Names and LDAP-based directory services.

Trace Assistant   The Trace Assistant is a diagnostic tool that decodes Oracle Net trace files and provides an analysis of the network to identify possible bottlenecks. You should use the Trace Assistant when you have problems while configuring or maintaining your networks. This tool will be obsolete in future releases of Oracle.

Internet and Intranet Scalability

Oracle Net provides scalability features that enable you to maximize system resources and improve performance. These features are described here.

Shared Server   Oracle's *shared server* (previously called Multi-threaded Server [MTS]) architecture increases the scalability of applications and the number of clients simultaneously connecting to the database. It can enable existing applications to scale up without making any changes to the application itself. Shared server is ideal for configurations with a large number of connections, the reason being that it reduces the number of processes that the server OS has to manage in contrast to a dedicated server. Shared server is well suited for both Internet and intranet environments.

Virtual Interface   The *Virtual Interface* (VI) protocol reduces the overhead of TCP/IP by eliminating intermediate copies and by transferring most of the messaging burden away from the CPU and onto the network hardware. The result is a low-latency, high-throughput interconnect protocol that reduces the amount of CPU cycles dedicated to messaging. This increases the performance between application Web servers and the Oracle databases.

Network Security

The significant factor influencing the database user in a secure network environment is granting and denying access to the database. Oracle Net enables various database access controls by enabling firewall access control and protocol access control. Oracle's Connection Manager (CMAN) can also be configured to grant or reject access to a particular database service or you can alternately implement the system firewall access control mechanism. You can enable various filtering rules by specifying the clients' or servers' hostnames or IP addresses or the database service names. For information on Connection Manger functionality, see the "Connection Manager" section later in this chapter.

Oracle Names

Oracle Names reduces the administrative overhead, which is primarily due to configuring and maintaining client-server networks. It centrally defines the service addresses, inter-database links, net service names (aliases), and client configuration profiles through the Oracle Enterprise Manager utility. Oracle Names supports hierarchical naming structures. It enables the enterprises to set up the administrative authority to be distributed among different regions. Figure 1-4 shows the Oracle Names server architecture.

Connection Manager (CMAN)

Oracle CMAN is a router that enables the propagation of requests to either the intermediate destination or to the destination server. CMAN enables the clients to take advantage of its advanced capabilities such as connection multiplexing, access control, and protocol conversion. CMAN can filter connections based on origin,

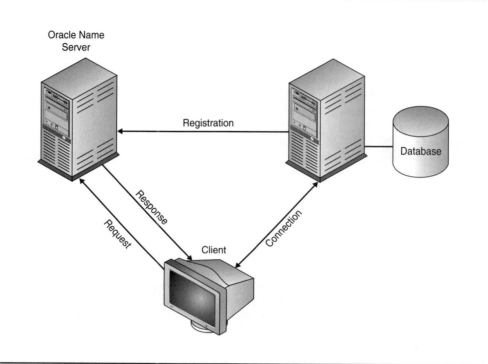

FIGURE 1-4. *Oracle Names server*

destination, or database service names. This is an important configuration feature to restrict remote access to data.

CMAN can provide access to services via the Internet while maintaining total access control using the *access control* feature. This feature enables you to control access to specific servers in a network where TCP/IP is predominant. This can be achieved by setting the appropriate "accept" rules. Clients who need to establish a connection must meet the criteria of the rules set in order to gain access to the service. Figure 1-5 shows the CMAN architecture.

NOTE
Multiplexing using CMAN is only available for TCP/IP.

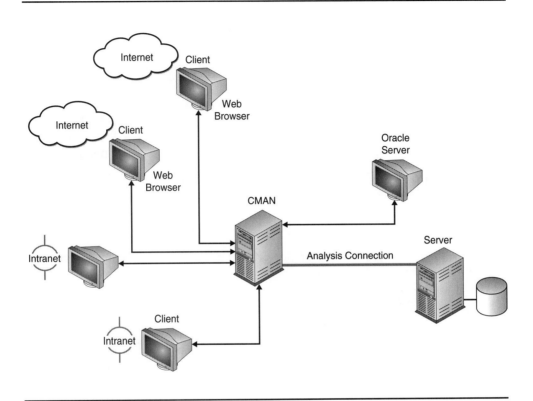

FIGURE 1-5. *CMAN*

Oracle Advanced Security

With the continuing growth of distributed systems involving numerous databases and applications comes an ever-increasing challenge of user authentication and user management. To meet this challenge of enterprise user management, Oracle provides methods of encryption, authentication, and authorization, along with integrated security and directory services, called the Oracle Advanced Security.

Oracle Advanced Security runs on top of Oracle Net to deliver security solutions to the Oracle network and beyond through the integration of industry standards for encryption, authentication, and remote access. Oracle provides security solutions by offering Secure Sockets Layer (SSL) and Remote Authentication Dial-In User Service (RADIUS) protocol adapters, enterprise user management by offering integrated security, and directory services through the Oracle Internet Directory (O*i*D).

Oracle Advanced Security provides a comprehensive suite of security features to protect enterprise networks and securely extend corporate networks to the Internet. It provides a single source of integration with network encryption and authentication solutions, single sign-on services, and security protocols. By integrating industry standards, it delivers unparalleled security to the Oracle network.

Features of the Oracle Advanced Security

Some of the features provided by the Oracle Advanced Security Option (ASO) are described in this section.

Data Privacy   Oracle Advanced Security protects the privacy of data transmissions through encryption methods like RSA encryption, DES encryption, and Triple-DES encryption. The selection of the network encryption method is a user configuration option, providing varying levels of security and performance for different types of data transfers.

Data Integrity   To guarantee that the contents of the message received were not altered from the contents of the original message sent, Oracle Advanced Security can generate a cryptographically secure message digest using MD5 or SHA encryption algorithms and include it with each message sent across a network.

Authentication   To verify the identity of a user or a device in a computer system, Oracle Advanced Security provides enhanced user authentication through several third-party authentication services as well as the use of SSL and digital certificates. Many Oracle Advanced Security authentication methods use centralized authentication. This can give you a high confidence in identifying users, clients, and servers in a distributed environment. Having a central facility authenticate all members of the network (clients to servers, servers to servers, and users to both clients and servers) is one effective way to address the threat of nodes on a network falsifying their identities.

Single Sign-On   Single sign-on lets a user access multiple accounts and applications with a single password. Once authenticated, subsequent connections to the database or applications occur transparently. Oracle Advanced Security supports Kerberos, CyberSafe, DCE, and SSL-based single sign-on authentication.

Authorization   Using the authentication methods supported by Oracle Advanced Security significantly enhances user authorization, a function of Oracle9*i* roles and privileges. For example, on certain operating systems, such as Solaris, Oracle Advanced Security supports authorization with DCE.

LDAP-Based Directory Service

Oracle Net supports a centralized, LDAP-compliant enterprise directory-service solution for managing network resources. The support for directory services, such as O*i*D, will provide a centralized vehicle for managing and configuring a distributed, heterogeneous network.

Before this chapter ends, we would like to briefly discuss a few important features that will be referred to in later chapters.

Oracle Internet Directory (O*i*D)

OiD is a standards-based LDAP directory that leverages the scalability, high availability, and security features of the Oracle database. O*i*D enables you to efficiently administer the employees, customers, suppliers, and partners that need access to your applications. The product provides a single, centralized repository for all user data. It enables sites to manage user identities, roles, authorization and authentication credentials, and application-specific preferences and profiles in a single repository.

Secure Sockets Layer (SSL)

SSL is an industry-standard protocol for secure network connections over the Internet. Oracle Advanced Security implements the SSL protocol. It secures Oracle Net connections and other protocols as well, including IIOP connections used with thin clients and Enterprise Java Beans. SSL uses digital certificates and a public key infrastructure (PKI) to provide the major pieces of security such as the authentication of people and machines, encryption techniques for privatizing, and checksums for protecting against data modification or snooping.

Remote Authentication Dial-In User Service (RADIUS)

The *RADIUS* protocol is an industry standard for remote authentication and controlled access to networks. It is widely accepted because of its flexibility, its capability to handle many devices, and its capability to provide user authentication, authorization, and accounting between a network client and an authentication server. The major benefit of RADIUS is it instantly integrates into existing systems by making the Oracle database server a RADIUS client, thereby capitalizing on the infrastructure and investment that organizations have already made. The other benefit is the authentication of Oracle users by enabling support for authentication technologies such as token cards, smart cards, and other challenging response mechanisms.

Oracle Wallet Manager

The Wallet Manager, which is part of Oracle's SSL implementation, gives users (and administrators of data servers) complete control over the contents of their wallets.

An Oracle wallet contains a user's credentials, which are used for authenticating the user to multiple services, such as data servers and application servers. The contents of the wallet are encrypted with a key based on a user-specified password. Since the wallet is encrypted, it may be stored locally on a user's disk or centrally in a directory accessible via LDAP.

The user only needs to remember one password, which opens the wallet to access his or her credentials that can then be used to authenticate the user to multiple services. And those services don't need to store and manage local passwords for users any longer.

Chapter Questions

1. **Which of the following statements is true?**

   A. Oracle Net resides only on client applications.

   B. Oracle Net resides only on client machines.

   C. Oracle Net resides on both client machines and database server machines.

   D. Oracle Net resides on the management server.

2. **As a DBA in a mid-sized company, you realize that the number of users accessing the client-server application has increased dramatically. What are your valid options to scale the application to meet this increased demand?**

   A. Implement simple network architecture.

   B. Implement N-tier network architecture.

   C. Migrate the application to a server.

   D. Migrate the application to each client.

3. **Which of the following architectures is used to support the agent or the application tier?**

   A. Simple

   B. Two-tier

   C. N-tier

   D. Client-server

4. **Which of the following options would you choose to implement controlled access using remote authentication for your networks?**

   A. O*i*D

   B. RADIUS

   C. Wallet Manager

   D. Oracle Names server

5. **Which of the following reduces the overhead of using the TCP/IP protocol?**

   A. OCI

   B. VI

   C. UPI

   D. SSL

6. **Which of the following is not part of the functionality of Oracle Names?**

   A. Securing network connections over the Internet

   B. Defining service addresses

   C. Defining database links

   D. The configuration and maintenance of client-server networks

7. **Which Oracle Net tool would you use to analyze your Oracle network trace files?**

   A. Net Manager

   B. Connection Manager

   C. Trace Assistant

   D. Net Assistant

   E. Names Server

8. **Which of the following two options would you consider when estimating the anticipated workload during the design of your networking environment?**

   A. User privileges

   B. User training

   C. Number of network administrators

    D. Number of nodes

    E. Network maintenance

    F. Number of transactions

9. **You must ensure that client requests through the network to remote servers in your N-tier architecture are handled. Which middle-tier component is placed between the client and the server to enable this?**

    A. Gateway

    B. Adapter

    C. Agent

    D. Protocol

10. **Which type of network is represented as a computational architecture with client processes communicating directly with server processes?**

    A. N-tier

    B. Complex

    C. Simple

    D. Single

    E. Middle-tier

Answers to Chapter Questions

1. C.   Oracle Net resides on both client machines and database server machines.

Explanation   To interact with the server, client machines need Oracle Net. Similarly, the server needs Oracle Net to understand the requests from the client. So, Oracle Net should reside both on the server and client machines.

2. B.   Implement a N-tier architecture.

Explanation   An N-tier architecture has an agent placed between the server and the client that can be used to load balance connection requests.

3. C.   N-tier

Explanation   Two-tier, simple networks and client-server mean the same thing; the client communicates directly with the server. Oracle Names is a method used for name resolutions. An N-tier architecture has an agent placed between the server and the client.

4. B.   RADIUS

Explanation   The Remote Authentication Dial-In User Service (RADIUS) protocol is an industry standard for remote authentication and controlled access to networks.

5. B.   VI

Explanation   Virtual Interface (VI) is introduced in Oracle 9i to reduce the overhead of TCP/IP. VI reduces the burden on TCP/IP by eliminating intermediate copies and by transferring most of the messaging burden away from the CPU and onto the network hardware.

6. A.   Securing network connections over the Internet

Explanation   The last three options are part of the functionality of Oracle Names. Securing network connections over the Internet is done using SSL.

7. C.   Trace Assistant

Explanation   The Trace Assistant is a diagnostic tool that decodes Oracle Net trace files and provides an analysis of the network to identify possible bottlenecks.

8. D. and F.   Number of nodes and the number of transactions

Explanation   The number of transactions that the servers must process and the total number of nodes that will be available provide a good estimate for future workload.

9. C.   Agent

Explanation   Agents are introduced in the N-tier architecture. They offer high scalability, request translation, and support of intelligent agent services.

10. C.   Simple

Explanation   A simple two-tier architecture is comprised of a client and a server connected through a network. In this environment both the client and the server use a similar protocol.

CHAPTER
2

Basic Oracle Net
Architecture

racle Net is the technology offered by Oracle to establish communication between the client and the database server. Oracle Net is a software layer that resides on the client and the Oracle database server. It is responsible for establishing and maintaining the connection between the client application and servers, as well as exchanging messages between them using industry-standard protocols. Oracle Net is comprised of two software components—namely, the Oracle Net foundation layer and the Oracle protocol support.

In this chapter we give you an overview of the key components of the Oracle Net architecture and explain the various methods of establishing a connection using Oracle's networking products. The topics covered in this chapter include

- Open System Interconnection Architecture
- Oracle Net layered architecture
- Oracle Net services
- Web client connections

Distributed processing and distributed databases are features of Oracle networking. In distributed processing environments, a single data transaction requires an involvement of two or more machines. For example, in a client/server environment, the client requests the data and the server provides the data. In the distributed database environment, multiple databases are located on multiple systems in a network, but all appear as a single logical database to the end users. Database links are used to perform transactions and retrieve data in a distributed database environment.

Open System Interconnection Architecture

Oracle Net is based on the *Open System Interconnection* (OSI) architecture. The OSI reference model was developed in the early 1980s by International Standards Organization (ISO) to define standards for linking heterogeneous computer systems. This model describes various principles that set guidelines to develop interconnection of computer systems in an OSI environment. The OSI model consists of seven discrete layers. The communication function is broken down into different hierarchical sets of layers that have their own sets of rules. The function of each layer was chosen to aid the definition of internationally standardized protocols. The various layers of a typical OSI protocol communication stack are shown in Figure 2-1.

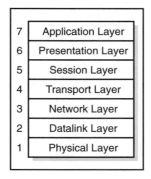

7	Application Layer
6	Presentation Layer
5	Session Layer
4	Transport Layer
3	Network Layer
2	Datalink Layer
1	Physical Layer

FIGURE 2-1. *OSI protocol communication stack*

Figure 2-1 shows the physical layer as the lowest layer and the application layer as the highest layer. Analysis of the protocol stack should always begin from layer number 1 since it is the standard denominator for all communication flow. There are various implementations that do not have some of the higher layers, but always comprise the lower most layers. All seven layers are briefly described in the following sections.

Physical Layer

The *physical layer* is primarily responsible for transmitting a stream of unstructured bits over the physical link. This layer exclusively deals with electrical interfaces, various electrical levels, and procedures for sharing bandwidth. For example, it evaluates how long a bit can be present on a physical link.

Data Link Layer

The *data link layer* is responsible for transmitting the bits over the physical layer without any errors and ensuring that the data is synchronized and the flow is correct. The input data (bits) is assembled into frames, which is thereafter transmitted sequentially.

Network Layer

The *network layer* is sometimes referred to as the communication subnet layer that controls the operation of subnets by determining how data (that is, packets) is to be routed between the subnets. It is responsible for establishing, maintaining, and terminating connections.

Transport Layer

The *transport layer* is responsible for data reliability and transparent transfer of database between two end-points. This layer accepts data from the session layer, if necessary splitting it into smaller parts and transferring it to the network layer. It also makes sure that the other end successfully receives the data. It provides for end-to-end error recovery of the data. The transport layer apart from all the above capabilities ensures that the session layer is completely shielded from changes at the lower layers.

Session Layer

The *session layer* provides a control structure for communication between applications. It is popularly referred to as "a user's interface to the network." A connection between two presentation layer processes is called a *session*. Each session has a unique addressing mechanism, which is different from the transport addressing that exists between machines. However, each session in order to establish connection through the transport layers must be able to perform conversion between the two types of addresses.

Presentation Layer

The *presentation layer* performs certain transformations on data to provide a standardized application interface. The types of transformations that this layer might perform include text compression for well-known transactions, conversion from one coding system to another, encryption and decryption, and conversion between terminal types for displaying the data on non-compatible screens.

Application Layer

The *application layer* provides services to the OSI environment. The application layer is responsible for the communication between two applications. Telnet and ftp are two of the programs that use the application layer.

Oracle Net Layered Architecture

The technology involved in distributed processing relies on the capability of computers to communicate and interact with each other. This is accomplished through a process known as *stack communications* by implementing the OSI-modeled technology. The layers in a typical Oracle communications stack are similar to those of a standard OSI communications stack and are shown in Figure 2-2.

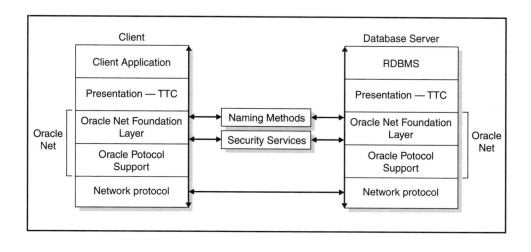

FIGURE 2-2. *Typical Oracle Net communication stack*

Client-Side Stack

The client stack is divided into five communication layers: client application, presentation, Oracle Net foundation, Oracle protocol support, and network protocol. These layers are described next.

Client Application

The *client application layer* enables all user-specific activity, such as character user display, graphical user display, screen control, data presentation, application flow, and so forth. This application identifies the commands or statements to be performed at the server end and transfers them using the OCI layer.

When a session is made with the database, the client uses the *Oracle call interface* (OCI) to interact with the database server. The OCI contains the information needed to execute SQL statements at the server end. The functionality of the OCI includes parsing of SQL statements, syntax validation, executing the statements at the server end, and fetching the results back to the client application. It is also responsible for controlling cursors and binding client application variables into the shared memory of the server.

TIP
SQL*Plus and Oracle Forms are widely used
applications of the client application layer.

Presentation

The *presentation layer* used by client/server applications is *two task common* (TTC).
The TTC layer provides conversion of character sets and datatypes between clients
and servers. This layer will be bypassed if the character sets and datatypes of the
clients and the servers are the same.

During the time of initial connection, the two task common layer evaluates
whether any differences in internal data and character set representations exist and
determines whether conversions are required.

Oracle Net Foundation Layer

The *Oracle Net foundation layer* is responsible for establishing and maintaining
the connection between the client application and database server, as well as
exchanging messages between them.

The Oracle Net foundation layer uses the *transparent network substrate* (TNS)
technology to perform these tasks. TNS provides a common interface to support the
industry standard protocols.

On the client side, the Oracle Net foundation layer receives client application
requests and resolves all generic computer-level connectivity issues, such as

■ The database destination

■ Protocols involved in the connection

■ Interrupts between client and database server

On the server side, the Oracle Net foundation layer has the same functionality
as on the client side. In addition to this functionality, the Oracle Net foundation
layer on the server side uses the listener to receive incoming connection requests.

NOTE
In addition to establishing and maintaining
connections, the Oracle Net foundation layer
communicates with naming methods to resolve
names and uses security services to ensure secure
connections.

Oracle Protocol Support

The *Oracle protocol support layer* is responsible for mapping the TNS functionality to industry standard protocols that are used in the client/server connection. This layer is the implementation of the network transport (NT) layer. Oracle provided protocols include LU6.2, Named Pipes, TCP/IP, TCP/IP with SSL, and the Virtual Interface (VI) protocol. Each of these protocols is responsible for mapping the equivalent functions between the individual protocol and TNS.

Network Protocol

The *network protocol* is the final layer on the client-side stack and is responsible for handling the machine-level connections between the client and the server. The network-specific protocol gathers the data from the client machine and passes it to the server machine, at which point the data is passed to the server-side network-specific protocol layer.

Server-Side Stack

A similar communications stack on the server side receives information passed by the network specific protocol layer on the client side. The process stack on the server side is the reverse of what occurs on the client side with information ascending through the various communication layers. The one operation unique to the server side is the act of receiving the initial connection through the listener.

The only additional component on the server-side stack is the RDBMS, which is described next.

The RDBMS layer uses the *Oracle program interface* (OPI) to perform a complementary function to that of OCI in the application layer on the client-side stack. It is responsible for responding to each of the possible messages sent by OCI. For example, an OCI request to fetch 100 rows would have an OPI response to return the 100 rows, once they have been fetched.

Oracle Net Services

Oracle Net allows connections to various services, such as Oracle databases, non-Oracle databases, gateways, and external procedures. This section focuses on Oracle Net services related to Oracle databases.

When an end user connects to a database service from across the network, a connect string identifies the service through a net service name. For example:

```
SQL> CONNECT username/password@net_service_name
```

A *net service name* accesses a service across the network by providing the network description information necessary to locate the service on the network. A net service name is resolved into

■ Network route to the service, including the listener location through a protocol address

■ Service name that is typically the *global database name*, a name comprised of the database name and the database domain, used in combination to identify the database service

The listener, through a protocol, accepts the client connection. It verifies the client information with the information it has received from the database service, as well as information it has stored in its own configuration file, the listener.ora. If the information matches, a connection is granted.

Oracle net services are comprised of the components described in the following sections.

Oracle Net

Oracle Net provides the following basic network functionality such as Connect and Disconnect operations, data operations and exception operations. These operations are briefly described next.

Connect and Disconnect Operations

In order for clients to connect to servers, Oracle Net needs to coordinate its network sessions with the help of a *listener*. The listener is responsible for detecting and routing the incoming requests to the proper destination. Users initiate a request by providing the username, password, and a service name. The *service name* is an identifier mapped to a network address contained in a connect descriptor. The *connect descriptor* contains the network route and the service name. The service name is a logical representation of the database or SID or an optional instance name.

Clients and servers use this service name to make connections. The connect description can be stored in a local names configuration file (tnsnames.ora), an Oracle names server, or an external naming service (such as NIS, DCE CDS). Once the service name is resolved, a request is sent to the listener and the listener determines where to direct the request. The listener spawns a new process or redirects the connection to an existing process that handles the communication with the Oracle database. The address of the process is handed off to the client-side process, and the client directly communicates with the server for the duration of the session without involving the listener.

Whenever a client-server transaction completes, the user can request a disconnection from the server. A server can also disconnect from a second server when all the server-to-server data transfers have been completed. When you disconnect or abort the connection without giving notice, Oracle Net recognizes the failure during its next data operation and cleans up the client and server operations, effectively disconnecting the current operation. This situation typically results in the following error message:

```
ORA-3113: end-of-file on communication channel
```

Dead connection detection allows Oracle Net to identify connections that have been left hanging by the abnormal termination of a client. You can use the parameter SQLNET.EXPIRE_TIME to set the time when a small probe packet is sent from the server to the clients. Connections that fail to respond to these probe packets are disconnected.

Data Operations
Oracle Net performs client-server data operations, such as sending data and receiving data synchronously and asynchronously. Communication in the client-server architecture is handled synchronously, and in a shared server, asynchronously.

Exception Operations
Oracle Net performs exception operations like *breaks* over the connection on user initiation (when the user presses the interrupt key) or by the database initiation. The user controls this operation. The two types of requests for a break in the connection are *in-band* and *out-band*. The in-band break transmits the request for the connection to terminate. The messages are transmitted as a part of the normal connection. Out-band breaks are connection terminated requests that are urgent. The out-band break request sends the signal outside of the normal transmission. The user-initiated exception can be either in-band or out-band. Oracle Net also performs exception operations like resetting a connection for synchronization after a break and then testing the condition of the connection for an incoming break. These are application-specific operations to resolve network timing issues.

Listener
The listener process, which is unique to Oracle database servers, is responsible for detecting and routing incoming requests from the clients. When the listener determines where to route the client's request, it spawns a new process or redirects the request to an existing process. The address of the newly spawned process or the existing process is handed over to the client process. Once this connection is made, the client and the server communicate directly. Figure 2-3 shows a listener accepting a connection request from a client and forwarding that request to an Oracle database.

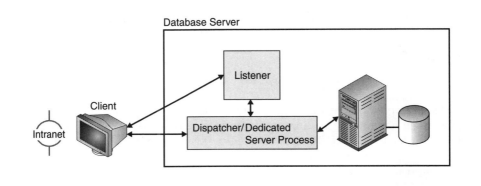

FIGURE 2-3. *Listener connection request process*

Oracle Connection Manager

Oracle Connection Manager (CMAN) is a router that enables the propagation of requests to either the intermediate destination or to the destination server. The Connection Manager enables the clients to take advantage of its advanced capabilities such as connection multiplexing, access control, and protocol conversion. Using the multiplexing feature, the CMAN enables the handling of many logical client sessions with a single transport connection. The CMAN maintains the access control by filtering the connections, based on origin, destination, or database service names. In heterogeneous network where the clients are using different protocols compared to the servers (for example the client is using like TCP/IP and server is using running with other protocol such as LU6.2), then CMAN enables transparent communication between the clients and server. This is handled by the bidirectional protocol conversion. Figure 2-4 shows the Oracle Connection Manager, the CMGW process, and the CMADMIN process.

The CMAN is required in the database environment where there are typically more than 1,000 users. CMAN will be configured as the middle tier in the three-tier architecture. For configuring the CMAN, we need not perform any modifications to the existing applications. The CMAN increases the scalability and optimizes use of the resources. To scale further we can configure multiple CMANs that will support thousands of concurrent client connections as shown in Figure 2-4. Using multiple CMANs provides automatic fault tolerance. CMAN also provides the logging and tracing feature to identify the errors, which helps you resolve problems in the multi-protocol environment.

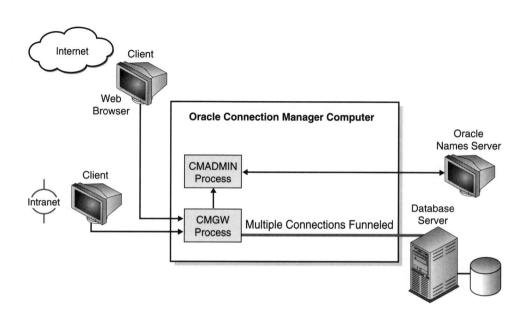

FIGURE 2-4. *Oracle Connection Manager processes*

To use the feature of the Connection Manager, you need to start the CMGW process. This process is responsible for the following tasks:

■ Registering with the CMADMIN process

■ Listening for incoming connection requests

■ Initiating connection requests to the listeners on behalf of clients

■ Relaying data between the client and database server

■ Responding to the Oracle Connection Manager Control utility

NOTE
By default, the CMGW process listens on TCP/IP with port 1630.

When you use the connection manager with the shared server, you need to start an additional process, the CMADMIN process. The CMADMIN process is responsible for the following tasks:

■ Processing the CMGW registration

■ Identifying all listeners serving at least one database instance

■ Registering source route address information about the CMGW process and listeners

■ Responding to the Oracle Connection Manager Control utility

■ Locating the Oracle Names servers

■ Monitoring registered listeners with Oracle Names servers

■ Maintaining address information in Oracle Names servers for clients

■ Periodically sending a request to Oracle Names servers to update their cache of available services

NOTE
CMGW process registers with the CMADIN process and the CMGW process handles client requests.

Networking Tools

Oracle Net Services provides graphical user interface (GUI) tools and command-line utilities that enable you to easily configure, manage, and monitor the network. Oracle Net Configuration Assistant is a GUI tool that configures basic network components after installation, including listeners, naming methods, and directory server usage.

Oracle Net Manager combines configuration capabilities with component control to provide an integrated GUI environment for configuring and managing Oracle Net Services. With Oracle Net Manager, you can fine-tune the listener and naming method configuration created with the Oracle Net Configuration Assistant. In addition, Oracle Net Manager offers built-in wizards and utilities that enable you to test connectivity, migrate data from one naming method to another, and create additional network components.

NOTE
Oracle recommends the use of the Oracle Net Configuration Assistant or the Oracle Net Manager when configuring the Net files.

Web Client Connections

Internet connections from the client's Web browsers to an Oracle database server are similar to client/server applications, except for the architecture. This connection is possible either by using the application Web server or by directly connecting to the database server.

Connections Using the Application Web Server

The architecture for a Web client application includes the Web client (browser), an application Web server, and an Oracle database server. The browser on the client uses HTTP to communicate with a Web server to make a connection request. The Web server sends the request to an application where it is processed. The application on the application Web server uses Oracle Net to communicate with the database server, which is configured with Oracle Net. The HTTP protocol is used for communicating between the Web browser and the application Web server, and the TCP/IP protocol is used for communicating between the application and Web server. The oracle Net is used to communicate with the application and the database server. Figure 2-5 shows a typical three-tier architecture configuration of a Web client connection to the database server.

The various components of the Web client architecture are explained next.

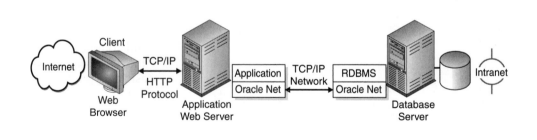

FIGURE 2-5. *Web client connection using an Application Web server*

Web Browser

The clients forward the requests using HTTP, which provides the language that enables Web browsers and application Web servers to communicate. The requests from the browser are in the uniform resource locator (URL), while the response from the Web server is typically ASCII text carrying the HTML.

Application Web Server

An *application Web server* manages data for a Web site, controls access to that data, and responds to the Web browsers. The application on the Web server communicates with the database and performs the job requested by the Web server on behalf of the clients.

NOTE
A Web application server consists of a Web listener that receives URLs and passes back pages of static HTML in response. The Web application server also acts as the front end to an application server which processes URLs that cannot be handled by the Web listener because they request dynamic information.

The application Web server communication stack is shown in Figure 2-5. From the top down, the stack is constructed with the Application and the Oracle Net layers.

The Application server can be a Java-based application server using JDBC or Java thin client to pass the requests to the databases server. The application server uses Oracle Net when using JDBC and Java Net when using the Java thin client.

NOTE
Please note that while the Web listener and the application server are separate, all communications go through the Web listener.

Database Server

The database server communication stack is shown in Figure 2-5. From the top down, the stack is constructed with the RDBMS and the Oracle Net layers

Connections Without Using the Application Web Server

Web clients can access the Oracle database directly—for example, by using a Java applet. In addition to regular connections, the database can be configured to accept HTTP and *Internet Inter-ORB Protocol* (IIOP) connections. These protocols are used for connecting to the Oracle9i *Java Virtual Machine* (JVM) in the Oracle9i instance. There are three different ways to configure the Web clients:

- Web client using a HTTP connection to access the database

- CORBA client using an IIOP connection to access the database

- Web client using a Web browser with a JDBC thin driver, which in turn uses a Java version of Oracle Net (called *Java Net*) to communicate with the Oracle database server that is configured with Oracle Net

Figure 2-6 shows three Web clients connecting to an Oracle database in three different ways. The database server shows a communication stack that includes two layers. From the top down, the stack is constructed with the RDBMS and the Oracle Net layers.

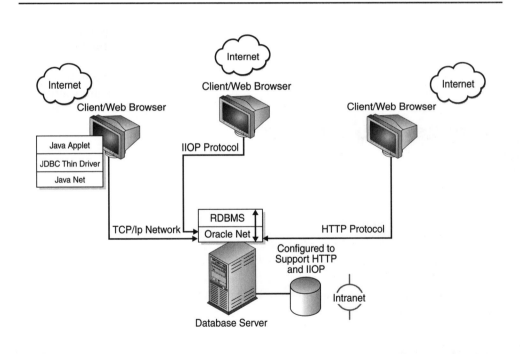

FIGURE 2-6. *Web client connection without using an Application Web server*

NOTE
The Oracle database server is also configured to support HTTP and IIOP.

In Figure 2-6, one Web browser uses the HTTP protocol to connect to the Oracle Net layer on the database server. The second Web browser uses the IIOP protocol to connect to the Oracle Net layer on the database server. The third browser uses the TCP/IP network protocol to connect to the Oracle Net layer on the database.

The Internet Inter-ORB Protocol (IIOP) has been developed by the Object Management Group (OMG) to implement CORBA solutions over the Internet. The Clients access EJBs and CORBA Servers in the database via the IIOP.

NOTE
The third Web browser shows a communication stack that is constructed using the Java applet, the Java thin driver, and the Java Net.

Chapter Questions

1. **Which Oracle Net layer component handles breaks and requests for a connection?**

   A. Client application

   B. Presentation

   C. Oracle Net foundation layer

   D. Network protocol

2. **Which Oracle Net layer is responsible for parsing of your PL/SQL statements?**

   A. Client application

   B. Oracle protocol support

   C. Network protocol

   D. Presentation

3. **Which of the following does the service name best represent?**

   A. Local address

   B. Connect descriptor

   C. Listener address

   D. Destination address

4. **Which configuration files identify the destinations for clients and distributed database servers?**

   A. init.ora

   B. sqlnet.ora

   C. listener.ora

   D. tnsnames.ora

   E. services.ora

5. **The Oracle Net architecture is based on which of the following?**

   A. OCI

   B. OSI

   C. TCP/IP

   D. SNMP

6. **Which of the following statements is false?**

   A. A connect descriptor contains the network route information.

   B. A connect descriptor contains the service name.

   C. A connect descriptor can be stored in the tnsnames.ora file.

   D. A connect descriptor can be stored in the listener.ora file.

7. **Which of the following statements is true?**

   A. Listener is responsible for transferring data between the client and server.

   B. Listener is responsible for establishing connections between the client and server.

   C. Listener is a router.

   D. Listener is a protocol converter.

8. **Which server stack communication layer corresponds to the client application layer in a distributed environment?**

   A. RDBMS

   B. Application

   C. Oracle Net foundation

   D. Network protocol

   E. Presentation

9. **When connecting from a client to a server, what happens after the listener determines where to direct the client request in a dedicated server environment?**

   A. The connect descriptor is resolved.

   B. A new process is spawned by the listener.

   C. A connect request is sent to the listener.

   D. The process address is passed to the client side.

10. **What is the default location of the Oracle Net files on Windows NT?**

   A. %ORACLE_HOME%\ora90\network\admin

   B. %ORACLE_HOME%\net90\admin

   C. %ORACLE_HOME%\admin\network\

   D. %ORACLE_HOME%\network\admin

Answers to Chapter Questions

1. C.   Oracle Net foundation layer

Explanation   The Oracle Net foundation layer receives client application requests and resolves all generic computer-level connectivity issues. The location of the database or the destination, the protocols involved in the connection, and interrupts between the client and the server are handled by this layer.

2. A.   Client application

Explanation   The Client application layer is responsible for the parsing of your SQL and PL/SQL statements against the data dictionary where as the execution plan will take over at the server side. The Client application layer uses the Oracle call interface (OCI) to interact with the database. OCI is an interface between the application and the SQL language, which is the language that the Oracle database understands.

3. D.   Destination address

Explanation   A service name is an alias for the destination address and it maps to a connect descriptor. It follows the username and password in a connect string.

4. D.   tnsnames.ora

Explanation   The tnsnames.ora file contains the addresses the user needs to connect to a particular listener on a particular node.

5. B. OSI

Explanation   The Oracle Net architecture is identical to the architecture of the Open System Interconnection (OSI). This model describes the principles for the interconnection of computer systems.

6. D. A connect descriptor can be stored in the listener.ora file.

Explanation   The first three statements are true. The connect descriptor contains the network route and the service name. The service name is a logical representation of the database or SID or optional instance name. The connect description can be stored in a local names configuration file (tnsnames.ora), the Oracle names server, or an external naming service. The connect descriptor cannot be stored in the listener.ora file.

7. B.   Listener is responsible for establishing connections between the client and server.

Explanation   Once the connection is established between the client and the server, the server interacts directly with the client and the client interacts directly with the server without the interference of the listener. Listener is neither responsible for transferring data between client and server, nor is it a router or a protocol converter.

8. A.   RDBMS

Explanation   The RDBMS layer at the server side is similar to client application layer at the client side. It is responsible for responding to each of the possible messages sent by the client application layer.

9. B.   A new process is spawned by the listener.

Explanation   The listener will either spawn a new process or redirect the request to an existing process in a dedicated server environment. The process then handles the communication with the Oracle database.

10. D.   %ORACLE_HOME%\network\admin

Explanation   The default location of the network configuration files on Windows NT is the %ORACLE_HOME%\network\admin directory. You can change this default directory by setting the TNS_ADMIN environment variable. This default location for UNIX systems is the $ORACLE_HOME/network/admin directory.

CHAPTER
3

Basic Net Server-Side Configuration

he Oracle server layer, which is the most important part of an Oracle Net environment, is primarily responsible for receiving client requests. The listener, which is present at the server end, receives the request and checks the request with its supported services. The listener can support various services, such as connection to Oracle databases, non-Oracle databases, gateways, and external procedures.

In this chapter, you will learn the purpose and functionality of the listener in the Oracle Net environment. We explain the steps involved in configuring the listener using Oracle's Net Manager. We also explain how to control the listener using the **listener control** utility and describe the dynamic service registration process. Later in this chapter, we will describe the process of configuring the listener for IIOP connections. This chapter includes the following topics:

- How the listener responds to incoming connections

- Components of the listener

- Configuring the listener using the Oracle Net Manager

- Controlling the listener using the listener control utility (**lsnrctl**)

- Dynamic service registration

- Configuring the listener for IIOP

The net service name—which is resolved into a listener location, the protocol address, and the service name using some naming method—enables the client to establish a connection with the database server. The Oracle server side of the connection receives the client requests that pass through the various layers of the Oracle Net environment. The server receives the request from the client OCI code and then resolves the SQL statements. This request is further processed and the output data or the appropriate feedback is delivered to the OPI for formatting and sent back to the client application.

When a connection is established between two servers, the layers for such connections are similar to those in a client-server environment. The client application would not be part of this setup. The servers interact through the *network program interface* (NPI), which performs the functions that are performed by OCI in a client-server environment.

How the Listener Responds to Incoming Connections

The Oracle listener is a process that resides on the server and whose responsibility is to listen and establish connections for incoming client requests. It is positioned above the Oracle Net foundation layers. Whenever a client requests a connection, the listener either spawns a new process and bequeaths the connection or forwards the connection request to an existing process. There can be multiple listeners running on a database server. Each listener is configured with one or more protocol addresses that specifies its listening port numbers. The clients must be configured with the same type of protocol addresses to converse with the listener. When a listener encounters a client's connection request, it verifies the request and forwards it to an appropriate service handler for further processing. In the process of forwarding the request, the listener determines if a database service and its service handlers are available through a service registration. Here, the background process PMON is responsible for providing information to the listener about the instance name associated with the services and service handlers, including the type, protocol address, and the maximum load. The listener process dynamically registers the listening port numbers (HTTP and IIOP). This enables the listener to direct the client requests to the appropriate service.

NOTE
The listener service should be invoked prior to starting a database instance for proper manageability of client requests.

The steps involved for a client to establish a connection with the server follow:

1. Initially, it is essential that all information about the services, instances, and the service handlers that are associated with one or multiple databases be registered with the listener.

2. The client forwards a connection request to the listener.

3. The listener then parses the client connection request and forwards it to the appropriate service handler for the database service. The request would be directed to either the shared server process through the dispatcher or the dedicated server process based on the service handler type registered.

Figure 3-1 shows how a client connects to server through the listener. While the connection is being processed at the server, the listener verifies the client information stored in the **listener.ora** file. If the information is in sync, the connection is established.

Dedicated Server Environment

In a *dedicated server* environment, a client process connects to a dedicated server process. By default, the server process is released as soon as the client closes the connection. This server process is not shareable. The background process PMON is

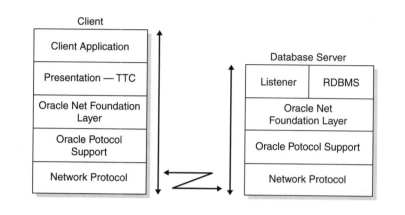

FIGURE 3-1. *Listener-connection interface between the client and server*

responsible for registering information about the dedicated server processes with the listener. Whenever a client request arrives for a connection, the listener starts a dedicated server process and passes the connection to the dedicated server process. This is known as a *bequeathed session.* In order for this method to be used, the listener must be running on the same server as the node; that is, the listener cannot bequeath a connection to another node. Once the client connection is established with the server process with the help of the listener, the client will now directly communicate with the server process. Since the client's connection with the listener is transient and its connection with the server is permanent, you can shut down the listener with out affecting the existing connections.

NOTE
Dedicated server architectures do not support HTTP and IIOP clients.

Shared Server Environment

In a *shared server* environment, the client's connection request is directed to the dispatcher and not directly to the server processes. A dispatcher enables many clients to connect to the same server without the need for a dedicated server for each client. A dispatcher is responsible for receiving client requests and directing them to the appropriate server process, depending upon their availability. The dispatcher can support multiple client connections simultaneously. The advantage of shared servers is that system overhead reduces and fewer resources are consumed by enabling users to share server processes.

NOTE
Client connections to the listener are transient, but the connections to the dispatcher are permanent.

The background process PMON registers the location and load of the dispatchers with the listener. This enables the listener to forward requests to the least loaded dispatcher.

Every client connection is bounded to a *virtual circuit*. A virtual circuit is a shared memory area. The dispatcher uses the virtual circuit to handle the connections between the client and databases. Oracle maintains a common queue of virtual circuits. On a client request, the dispatcher places a virtual circuit in that queue. The shared server process that is idle picks up the virtual circuit from the common queue, services the request, and abandons the virtual circuit to get a hold of another virtual circuit in the common queue.

Components of the Listener

The listener process runs on the database server side. It is responsible for receiving incoming client connection requests and directing them to appropriate service handlers. The listener is primarily configured with one or more listening protocol addresses, supported services, and parameters that control its runtime behavior. The configuration is stored in the file called **listener.ora**, which is located in the default directory $ORACLE_HOME/network/admin on UNIX and %ORACLE_HOME%\network\admin on Windows 2000. You can also relocate the file **listener.ora** to a different destination by specifying the path using the TNS_ADMIN environment variable or modifying its registry value.

NOTE
You can specify the listener name while configuring the listener. The default name of the listener service provided by Oracle is LISTENER. This default listener is not configured with any services upon startup and listens on the following TCP/IP protocol address: (ADDRESS=(PROTOCOL=tcp) (HOST=host_name)(PORT=1521)).

The SID_LIST in the **listener.ora** file is automatically configured for the database and external procedures. The listener configuration file describes the name of the listener, protocol addresses, services and control parameters. It is possible to configure multiple listeners, each with a unique name, in one **listener.ora** file. A sample **listener.ora** file follows:

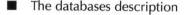

```
LISTENER=
  (DESCRIPTION=
    (ADDRESS_LIST=
      (ADDRESS=(PROTOCOL=tcp)(HOST=oramasters)(PORT=1521))
      (ADDRESS=(PROTOCOL=ipc)(KEY=extproc))))
SID_LIST_LISTENER=
  (SID_LIST=
    (SID_DESC=
      (GLOBAL_DBNAME=support.Oramasters.com)
      (ORACLE_HOME=/usr/oracle)
      (PROGRAM=extproc)
      (SID_NAME=support)
    )
  )
```

In this section, we will discuss the contents of the **listener.ora** file. The **listener.ora** file stores the following information:

- The address list
- The databases description
- The control parameter settings

Address List

The listener can be configured to listen to multiple network protocols like Transfer Control Protocol (TCP) for a Net client connection to the Oracle database, *Interprocess Communication Protocol* (IPC) for connections to external procedures, and IIOP for an IIOP client connection to the Java option. The default listener is configured to support TCP and IPC protocols. The DESCRIPTION parameter contains the listener protocol addresses. These protocols need to be specified using the ADDRESS_LIST parameter. You must initially specify the name for the listener (default name is LISTENER) with the corresponding ADDRESS_LIST. Further on, you must specify the address that would include the protocol, the host name, and the port number where the listener should listen.

The IPC protocol, if specified, would listen to connection requests from the clients and applications that reside on the node where the listener is running. The TCP protocol requires that the hostname and port number be specified. For a successful TCP connection, the client must request the connection on the same port number where the listener is listening. The listening port number will be configured in the **listener.ora** file.

Databases Description

A listener can be configured to support multiple databases. The list of all databases included in the listener is drawn under a global listener heading list, which is specified using the SID_LIST_<*listener_name*>. The SID_LIST can be configured with multiple database descriptions using the SID_DESC parameter. The SID_DESC is divided into three parts: the GLOBAL_DBNAME, ORACLE_HOME, and SID_NAME. The GLOBAL_DBNAME is the global database name for the database. The global database name is a combination of the database name and the database domain. The ORACLE_HOME is the home directory where Oracle resides. The SID_NAME is the Oracle database system identifier.

NOTE
The Oracle database is represented as a service that stores and retrieves data for clients. A database can be represented with one or more services associated with it. While the instance is compromised of the SGA and background processes, a database can have multiple instances running on different computers sharing data on one database.

Oracle8i and 9i database information can be dynamically registered with the listener during instance startup; therefore, the SID_LIST is not required unless Oracle Enterprise Manager is used to monitor an Oracle9i or Oracle8i database.

Control Parameter Settings

Several control parameters can be set in the **listener.ora** file, and these are described in the following sections.

NOTE
We use the listener name listener in the following discussion.

The ADMIN_RESTRICTIONS_*listener_name* parameter is a security feature. This parameter enables you to restrict runtime administration of the listener. This feature is useful if you are not using a password-protected listener. It does not allow you to configure the listener when it is running. That is, the listener would refuse to accept changes to the parameters, which are attempted using the SET command. To enable modifications to the listener dynamically using the SET command, initialize the parameter to the value OFF in the **listener.ora** file as shown and reload the listener settings:

```
ADMIN_RESTRICTIONS_listener=OFF
```

> **NOTE**
> *Oracle recommends securing the listener through a password. Later in this section, we show you how to configure a password for the listener.*

The SAVE_CONFIG_ON_STOP_*listener_name* parameter enables you to save any configuration done using the SET command in the **listener.ora** file, while the listener is running. These settings are saved when the STOP command is issued to stop the listener. To enable this parameter, you must set it to TRUE in the **listener.ora** file as shown:

```
SAVE_CONFIG_ON_STOP_listener=true
```

The STARTUP_WAIT_TIME_*listener_name* parameter sets the number of seconds the listener waits before responding to a START command that is issued using the *listener control utility* (lsnrctl). For example, to set a value of ten seconds for this parameter, you must set the following in the **listener.ora** file:

```
STARTUP_WAIT_TIME_listener=10
```

> **NOTE**
> *The value of ten seconds would be used only after the listener has restarted.*
>
> *The STARTUP_WAIT_TIME_listener parameter has been deprecated in Oracle9i.*

The PASSWORDS_*listener_name* parameter stores an encrypted password for the listener, so that operations performed on the listener when it is running are secure. The password can be set using the CHANGE_PASSWORD command at the listener control utility or by using the Oracle Net Manager. The password is only required to stop or shut down the listener. A sample setting of this parameter in the **listener.ora** file follows:

```
PASSWORDS_listener=(5N6M48144GF753ST)
```

The SSL_CLIENT_AUTHENTICATION parameter enables you to specify whether a client is authenticated using the secure sockets layer (SSL). The database server authenticates the client. Therefore, this value should be set to FALSE. If this parameter is set to TRUE, the listener attempts to authenticate the client, which could result in a failure. For example, to set this parameter to true, you must set the following in the **listener.ora** file:

```
SSL_CLIENT_AUTHENTICATION=true
```

The LOG_DIRECTORY_*listener_name* parameter specifies the destination directory for the listener log file. A sample setting of this parameter in the **listener.ora** file follows:

```
LOG_DIRECTORY_listener=c:\oracle\network\admin\log
```

NOTE
The default path set for logging is $ORACLE_HOME/network/log directory on UNIX, and the %ORACLE_HOME%\network\log directory on Windows NT/2000.

The LOG_FILE_*listener_name* parameter specifies the name of the log file for the listener. To specify the log file name as listoramasters.log, you must set the following in the **listener.ora** file:

```
LOG_FILE_listener=listoramasters.log
```

The LOGGING_*listener_name* parameter is used to configure the logging feature. It allows you to either enable or disable logging. To enable logging, you must set the parameter to the following in the **listener.ora** file:

```
LOGGING_listener=on
```

The TRACE_DIRECTORY_*listener_name* parameter enables you to specify the location where the listener trace files will be generated. A sample setting of this parameter in the **listener.ora** file is shown here:

```
TRACE_DIRECTORY_listener= d:\oracle\network\admin\trace
```

The TRACE_FILE_*listener_name* parameter is used to specify the name of the trace file for the listener. A sample setting of this parameter in the **listener.ora** file follows:

```
TRACE_FILE_listener=listoramasters.trc
```

The TRACE_FILENO_*listener_name* parameter specifies the number of trace files required for listener tracing. When this parameter is set along with the TRACE_FILELEN_*listener_name* parameter, trace files are used in a cyclical fashion. The first file is filled first, then the second file, and so on. When the last file has been filled, the first file is re-used.

The TRACE_LEVEL_*listener_name* parameter turns tracing on or off to a certain specified level. If the parameter is set to OFF, no trace files will be written to the trace destination. The USER level provides user trace information. The ADMIN level enables you to trace information pertaining to administration. The SUPPORT level trace generation must be enabled only when requested by Oracle Support for problem resolution. The trace generated through this level gathers information on the packets transferred and actions taken by the listener process.

For example, if the parameter is set to ADMIN as shown in the following code, Oracle will only trace information pertaining to administration.

```
TRACE_LEVEL_listener=admin
```

The TRACE_TIMESTAMP_*listener_name* parameter enables you to add a timestamp in the form of dd-month-yyyy hh:mm:ss to every trace event in the listener trace file. To add a timestamp in the trace files, you must set the parameter to true in the **listener.ora** file as shown here:

```
TRACE_TIMESTAMP_listener=true
```

Oracle Net Configuration Assistant

During the installation of the Oracle software, the Oracle universal installer enables you to configure the Oracle Net environment. You can configure the listening protocol address and services information for the Oracle databases. The default configuration would create a listener with the name *listener* and support the TCP/IP protocol. It configures the IPC protocol address for external procedures or functions.

The configuration settings will be saved in the **listener.ora** file. The Oracle Net Configuration Assistant is invoked immediately after installation, enabling you to configure various Oracle Net components. These components and their capabilities are as follows:

- **Listener** Enables you to add, delete, rename, or reconfigure an already existing listener. The settings will be stored in the **listener.ora** file.

- **Naming methods** Enables you to configure a naming method like Oracle *names*, *host names*, NDS, SUN NIS, and DCE CDS, which will allow the client to resolve connect identifiers. These settings are stored in the **sqlnet.ora** file.

- **Net service names** Enables you to add, delete, rename, and reconfigure the already existing Net service name. The settings will be stored in the **tnsnames.ora** file.

- **Directory server access** Enables you to configure directory naming and enterprise user security features.

The Oracle Net Configuration Assistant can also be invoked after the installation is completed to configure the above-mentioned components of Oracle Net. To invoke the assistant on UNIX, run the **netca** executable, which resides in the $ORACLE_HOME/bin directory. On Windows NT/2000, choose Start | Programs | Oracle-Home_Name | Network Administration | Oracle Net Configuration Assistant. Figure 3-2 shows the Oracle Net Configuration Assistant.

NOTE
The Oracle Net Configuration Assistant is written in Java, and requires X Window to run on UNIX-based platforms.

Configuring the Listener Using the Oracle Net Manager

The Oracle Net Manager is a GUI tool that enables you to manage the Oracle Net environment. You can invoke the Oracle Net Manager either by using the *Oracle Enterprise Manager* (OEM) console or as an independent application. To invoke the Oracle Net manager from the OEM console, choose Tools | Service Management | Oracle Net Manager. To start the Oracle Net Manager as an independent application on UNIX, run the **netmgr** executable from $ORACLE_HOME/bin directory. To start

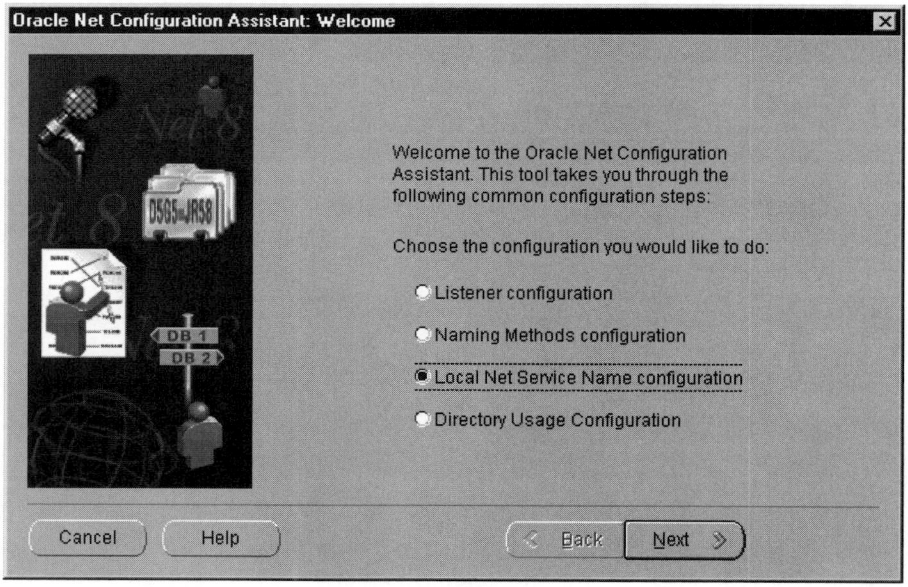

FIGURE 3-2. *Oracle Net Configuration Assistant*

the Oracle Net Manager on Windows NT/2000, choose Start | Programs | Oracle-HOME_NAME | Network Administration | Oracle Net Manager. Figure 3-3 shows the Oracle Net Manager.

The basic steps required for configuring a listener are described in the next sections.

To configure a listener, click on the listener node and then choose Edit | Create from the menu option. This will display a text window, asking you to specify the listener name as shown in Figure 3-4.

Specifying the listener name takes you to the next screen that enables you to specify the listening location for the listener. Click the Add Address button to specify the protocol, the host, and the port number. This enables you to configure the parameter ADDRESS_LIST in the **listener.ora** file. This is shown in Figure 3-5.

You must select the Database Services option from the pull-down menu. You can click the Add Database button to specify the databases. This allows you to configure the SID_LIST parameter in the **listener.ora** file. The components that you need to specify for the databases are the global

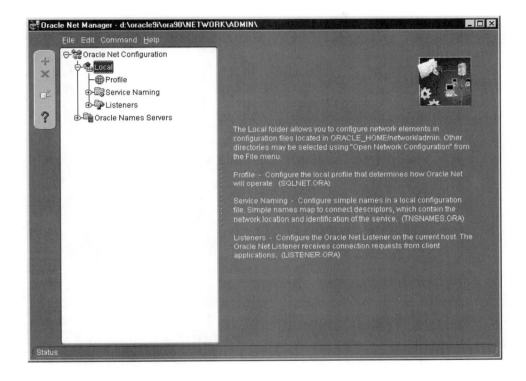

FIGURE 3-3. *Oracle Net Manager*

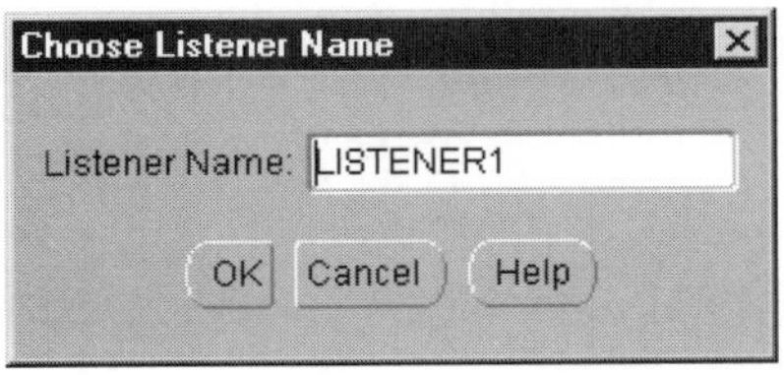

FIGURE 3-4. *Listener name*

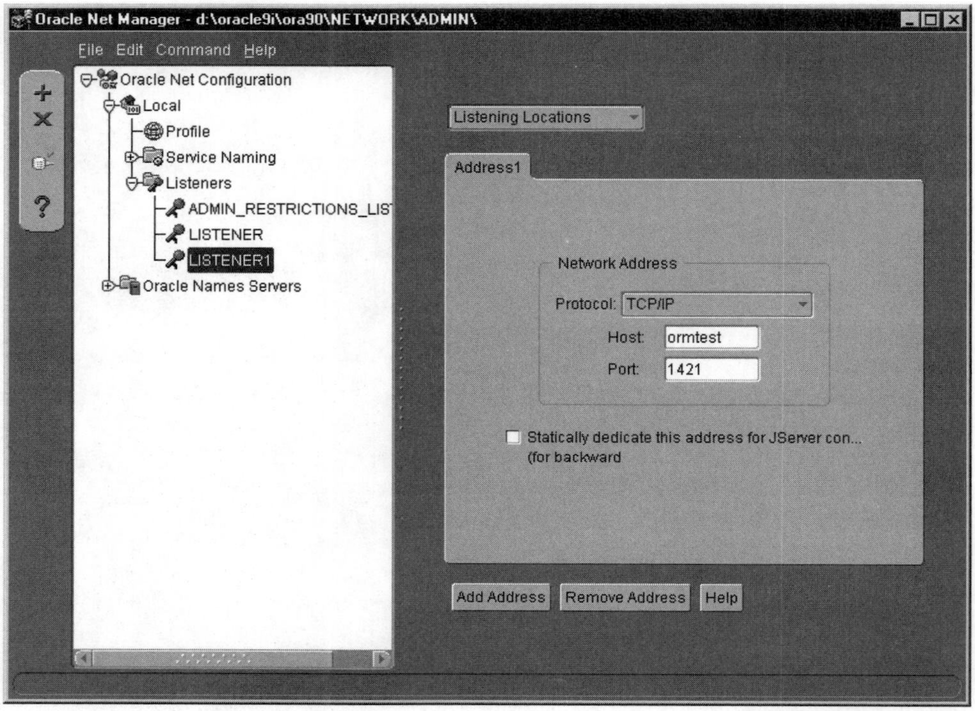

FIGURE 3-5. *Listening locations*

database name (GLOBAL_DBNAME), Oracle home directory for the database (ORACLE_HOME), and the system identifier (SID). This is shown in Figure 3-6.

You can also configure some general control parameters for the listener by selecting the General Parameters option from the pull down menu. The General tab screen enables you to configure the startup wait time (STARTUP_WAIT_TIME_*listener_name*) and save configuration on shutdown (SAVE_CONFIG_ON_STOP_*listener_name*), as shown in Figure 3-7.

The Logging & Tracing tab enables you to specify the information related to logging of the listener (LOGGING_*listener_name*) and the trace levels (TRACE_LEVEL_*listener_name*). It also allows you to specify the log file (LOG_FILE_*listener_name*) and the trace file (TRACE_FILE_*listener_name*) as shown in Figure 3-8.

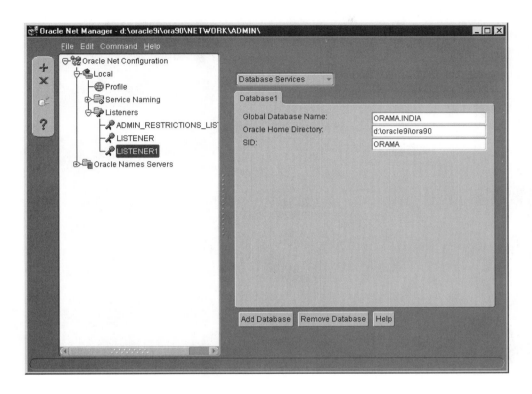

FIGURE 3-6. *Database Services*

The Authentication tab enables you to specify a password for the listener as shown in Figure 3-9.

NOTE
*To establish an encrypted password, you will need to use either the **listener control** utility's CHANGE_PASSWORD command or the Oracle Net Manager.*

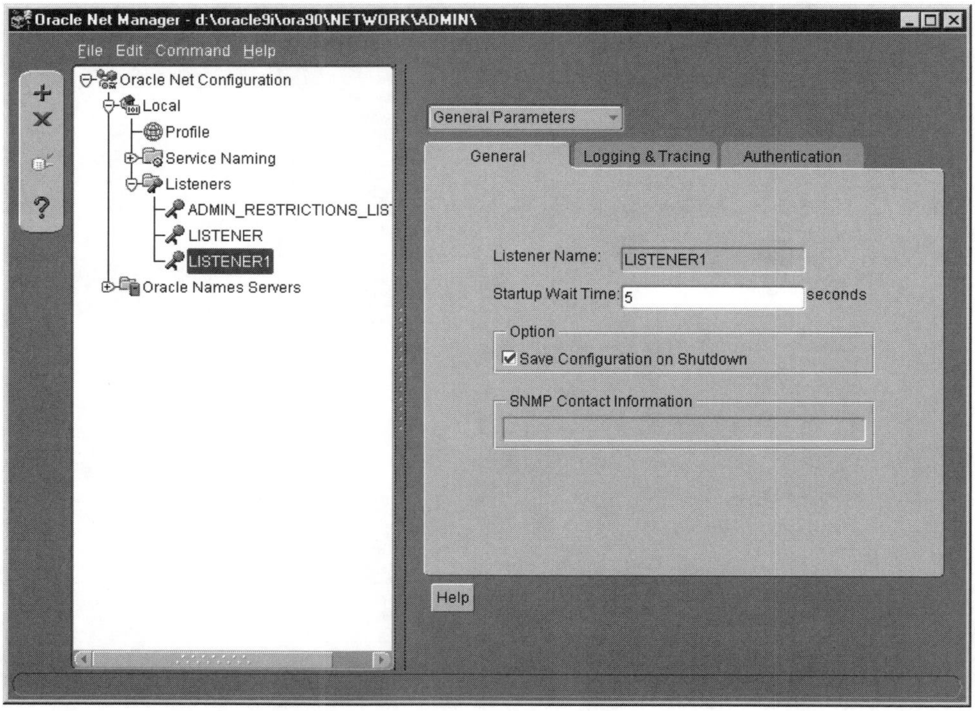

FIGURE 3-7. *General parameters*

Controlling the Listener Using the Listener Control Utility (lsnrctl)

The **listener control** utility is an application, which enables you to administer the listener at the command line. There are various options, which can be enabled dynamically using the command line utility. You can invoke the executable by issuing the following command at the command line:

```
C:\>lsnrctl
LSNRCTL for 32-bit Windows: Version 9.0.1.0.0 - Production on 27-SEP-2001
11:55:27
Copyright (c) 1991, 2001, Oracle Corporation. All rights reserved.
Welcome to LSNRCTL, type "help" for information.
LSNRCTL>
```

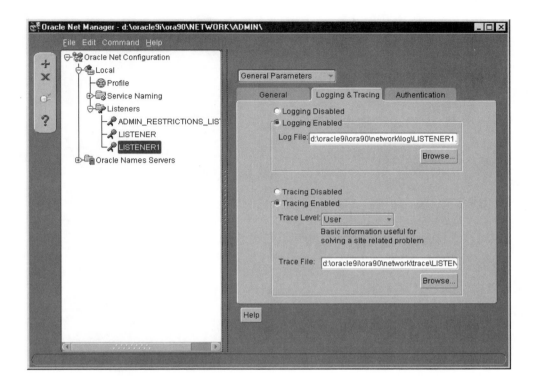

FIGURE 3-8. *Logging & Tracing*

Listener Control Commands

The following commands can either be executed at the **listener control** prompt or at the O/S command prompt. To execute the commands at the O/S command prompt, you must use the syntax given below:

```
LSNRCTL command [listener_name]
```

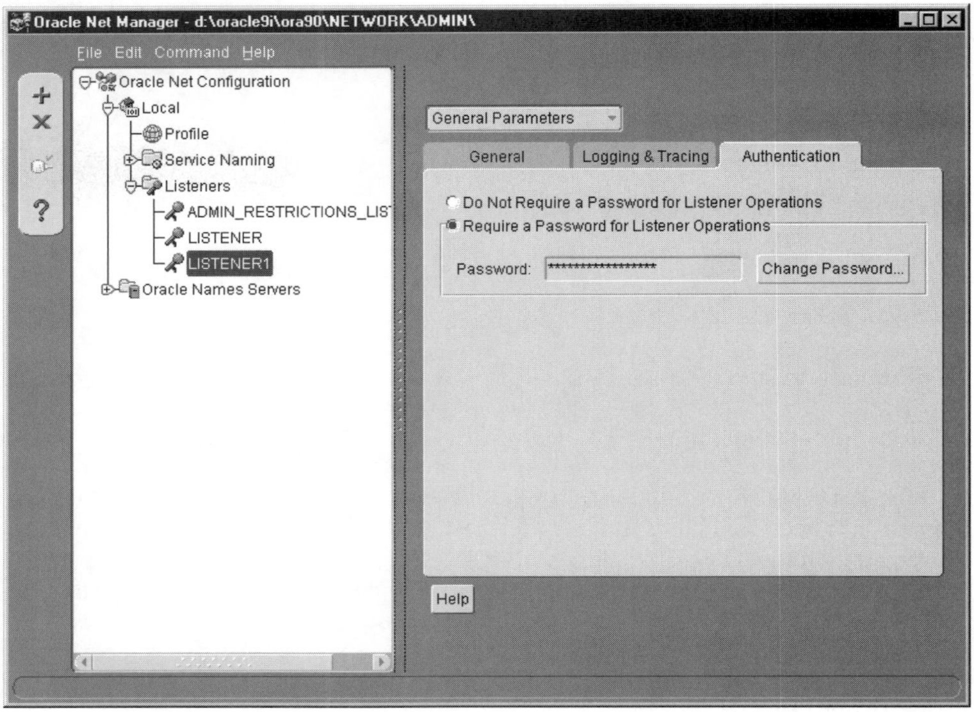

![Oracle Net Manager screen showing Listener Authentication]

FIGURE 3-9. *Listener Authentication*

NOTE
*In the following section, please note that all the
commands are being executed from the **listener
control** prompt and the name of the listener is
listener.*

All the available commands for the **listener control** utility can be obtained as
shown here:

```
LSNRCTL> HELP
The following operations are available. (An asterisk * denotes a modifier
or extended command):
```

```
start              stop              status
services           version           reload
save_config        trace             change_password
quit               exit              set*
show*
```

START, STOP, and RELOAD Commands

The control operations involving the starting and stopping of the listener must be carefully executed. You must ensure that all the database users are informed prior to stopping the listener. To start a particular listener, you must issue the following command:

```
LSNRCTL> START listener
```

Similarly, to stop a listener, you must issue the following command:

```
LSNRCTL> STOP listener
```

The RELOAD command is very helpful to DBAs. To modify any settings for the listener, you need to include the entries in the **listener.ora** file. These entries are applied only if the listener is stopped and then restarted. Oracle provides you the ability to load all the updates dynamically, thereby eliminating the need for stopping and restarting the listener by using the RELOAD command. You can do this by executing the following command:

```
LSNRCTL> RELOAD listener
```

STATUS Command

Oracle enables you to view the current status of the listener through the STATUS command. This is one of the most widely used commands by any DBA. Listed below is the sample output for the STATUS command:

```
LSNRCTL> STATUS
Connecting to (DESCRIPTION=(ADDRESS=(PROTOCOL=IPC)(KEY=EXTPROC1)))
STATUS of the LISTENER
------------------------
Alias                 LISTENER
Version               TNSLSNR for 32-bit Windows: Version 9.0.1.0.0 -
Production
Start Date            05-OCT-2001 21:58:42
Uptime                0 days 18 hr. 10 min. 41 sec
Trace Level           off
Security              OFF
```

```
SNMP                    OFF
Listener Parameter File    d:\oracle9i\ora90\network\admin\listener.ora
Listener Log File          d:\oracle9i\ora90\network\log\listener.log
Listening Endpoints Summary...
(DESCRIPTION=(ADDRESS=(PROTOCOL=ipc)(PIPENAME=\\.\pipe\EXTPROC1ipc)))
(DESCRIPTION=(ADDRESS=(PROTOCOL=tcp)(HOST=ormtest.india.oramasters.com)(POR
T=1521)))
Services Summary...
Service "MODOSE" has 1 instance(s).
  Instance "orama", status READY, has 1 handler(s) for this service...
Service "OEMREP.india.oramasters.com" has 1 instance(s).
  Instance "OEMREP", status UNKNOWN, has 1 handler(s) for this service...
Service "PLSExtProc" has 1 instance(s).
  Instance "PLSExtProc", status UNKNOWN, has 1 handler(s) for this
service...
Service "TARGET.india" has 2 instance(s).
  Instance "TARGET", status UNKNOWN, has 1 handler(s) for this service...
  Instance "TARGET", status READY, has 1 handler(s) for this service...
Service "oemdb" has 1 instance(s).
  Instance "oemdb", status UNKNOWN, has 1 handler(s) for this service...
Service "orama.india" has 2 instance(s).
  Instance "orama", status UNKNOWN, has 1 handler(s) for this service...
  Instance "orama", status READY, has 3 handler(s) for this service...
The command completed successfully
```

The STATUS command displays the following information:

- Name of the listener (alias)

- Version of the listener

- Address

- Start and up time

- Trace level in use

- Security

- Listener parameter file location

- Log and trace file locations and the database SIDs that are currently registered with the listener and for which connection requests are accepted from the clients

SERVICES Command

The SERVICES command enables you to display the registered services, names of the instances associated with the services, and the names of the service handlers (dispatcher or dedicated server).

SHOW and SET Commands

The SHOW and SET commands are frequently used to either display or configure the parameters for the listener. The SHOW command enables you to view the information pertaining to the settings done for the parameters.

The SET command enables you to dynamically set the values for the listener parameters. The values persist till the listener is stopped.

Table 3-1 list the SET command options available for use with the listener control utility.

SET Command Options	Description
SET CURRENT_LISTENER	To change the current listener.
SET DISPLAYMODE	To configure the output mode for listener control utility. The available options are NORMAL, RAW, COMPAT, and VERBOSE.
SET LOG_DIRECTORY	To dynamically change the log directory.
SET LOG_FILE	To dynamically change the log file name.
SET LOG_STATUS	To turn ON or OFF the logging.
SET PASSWORD	To set the user password.
SET SAVE_CONFIG_ON_STOP	To save the new configuration to the **listener.ora** file.
SET STARTP_WAITTIME	To set the time the listener should be ideal before responding to the initial status command.
SET TRC_DIIRECTORY	To change the location of the trace file.
SET TRC_FILE	To set the trace file name.
SET TRC_LEVEL	To set the level of the tracing.

TABLE 3-1. *SET Command Options*

CHANGE_PASSWORD Command

You can specify a new password for the listener by issuing this command. The password is stored in an encrypted form with the PASSWORDS_*listener_name* parameter in the **listener.ora** file.

```
LSNRCTL> CHANGE_PASSWORD listener
```

SAVE_CONFIG Command

If you want to save the configuration settings that have been done using the SET command, issue the following command:

```
LSNRCTL> SAVE_CONFIG
```

These settings are permanently stored in the **listener.ora** file.

VERSION Command

To view the current version of the listener control utility, execute the following command:

```
LSNRCTL> VERSION listener
```

TRACE Command

The TRACE command is used to set the tracing for the listener. You can set the tracing levels to either OFF, USER, ADMIN, or SUPPORT.

```
LSNRCTL> TRACE ADMIN listener
```

EXIT and QUIT Commands

The commands EXIT and QUIT enable the user to exit the listener control utility and return back to the O/S command prompt.

Dynamic Service Registration

Oracle's dynamic service registration feature eliminates the need for static configuration of its supported services. The background process PMON is responsible for registering the database service with the listener. The dynamic service registration does not require you to configure the **listener.ora** file manually since the information is registered with the listener. The PMON process registers the following information to the listener with the service registration:

- The service names for the running database instances

- The database instance names

- The service handlers (dispatchers and dedicated servers) that are available for each instance

There are many advantages of using the service registration. The dynamic service registration has simplified the configuration a great deal. You do not need to explicitly specify the SID_LIST parameter setting that is required for specifying the databases served by the listener in the **listener.ora** file. Since the listener always knows the state of the instances, service registration facilitates automatic failover to a different instance if one instance is down. This is known as *connect-time failover*. In contrast, for the static configuration model, a listener would start a dedicated server process and then verify whether the instance is up, which in this case would result in an error. The service registration enables the listener to forward client connect request to the least loaded instance—either to a dispatcher or to a dedicated server. This balances the load across the service handlers and the various nodes. This is known as *connection load balancing*.

NOTE
Static configuration is essential when using the Oracle Enterprise Manager. The SID_LIST_listener_name parameter is required if you are using OEM to manage the database.

Configuring Service Registration

Dynamic service registration should be configured in the database initialization parameter file. The **listener.ora** file does not require any configuration. You must configure some initialization parameters to ensure that the service registration is successful. The SERVICE_NAMES for the database service names and the INSTANCE_NAME for the instance name must be configured in the database. For example, the values of these initialization parameters must be similar to the following:

```
SERVICE_NAMES=Support.oramasters.com
INSTANCE_NAME=Support
```

Registering Information with the Default Local Listener

The background process PMON is responsible for registering service information with its local listener on the default local address (TCP/IP and port 1521). This requires the listener configuration and the database configuration to be in sync, where the protocol address of the listener must be specified in the **listener.ora** file.

Registering Information with a Non-Default Listener

You can also enable the PMON process to register the service information with the non-default local listener that does not use the TCP/IP protocol and the port 1521. The LOCAL_LISTENER parameter must be configured in the database initialization parameter file. If it is a shared server environment, you can also use the LISTENER attribute of the DISPATCHERS parameter in the initialization parameter file to register the dispatchers with a non-default local listener.

To specify the local listener with non-default settings, you need to specify the following initialization parameter:

```
LOCAL_LISTENER= listener1
```

To set the LISTENER attribute in the DISPATCHERS initialization parameter for a shared server environment, you need to specify the following initialization parameter:

```
DISPATCHERS="(PROTOCOL=tcp)(LISTENER=listener1)"
```

NOTE
The LISTENER attribute overrides the LOCAL_LISTENER parameter.

Listener1 is then resolved to the listener protocol addresses through a local naming method using the **tnsnames.ora** file on the database server, if the listener is configured to use port 1421.

The local **tnsnames.ora** should be configured as follows:

```
listener1=
  (DESCRIPTION=
    (ADDRESS=(PROTOCOL=tcp)(HOST=support-server)(PORT=1421)))
```

Configuring the Listener for IIOP

The *Internet Inter-ORB Protocol* (IIOP) is developed by the *Object Management Group* (OMG) to implement CORBA solutions over the Internet. The clients access EJBs and CORBA Servers in the database via the IIOP. In order to support IIOP, the database must be configured in shared server mode with the *General Inter-ORB Protocol* (GIOP) presentation.

IIOP Architecture

IIOP clients have different communication stacks in contrast with the Oracle Net client stacks. The IIOP clients use the GIOP as the presentation layer rather than TTC and no sessions layering rather than TNS. For clients to access the Oracle servers, the listener must be configured at the server side to accept IIOP requests. The listener must be able to redirect the requests to a dispatcher port that accepts session IIOP. A new session needs to be established for an IIOP request; this session has an independent Java VM and its own ORB.

The server side needs only a network protocol of TCP/IP and an Oracle protocol of TCP/IP or TCP/IP with SSL. The only required component of the Oracle Net is TNS.

Overview of Listeners and Dispatchers

The listeners and dispatchers are configured in such a manner that IIOP requests are redirected from the listener to the dispatcher. Each dispatcher listens on a random port number that is assigned to it when it is initiated. These port numbers are distinct for a particular database instance. The listener is configured with two listening end-points: one for TTC requests and one for IIOP requests.

Whenever the database is started, the dispatchers register with all the listeners configured within the same database initialization file. This is how the listeners know where each dispatcher is and the port that the dispatcher listens on. When an IIOP client invokes a request, the listener either redirects the request to a GIOP-specific dispatcher or hands off to a generic dispatcher.

A client sends a request to the listener. The listener recognizes the IIOP and redirects the request to a registered GIOP dispatcher. This is the default behavior that is configured during installation.

Configuring IIOP

The database supports incoming requests through a presentation. Both the listener and the dispatcher accept incoming network requests based upon the presentation that is configured. For IIOP, you configure a GIOP presentation. You configure the IIOP connection in the database initialization file by modifying the PRESENTATION attribute of the DISPATCHERS parameter. To configure an IIOP connection within the database, manually edit the database initialization file.

The following is the syntax for the DISPATCHERS parameter:

```
dispatchers="(protocol=tcp | tcps)
             (presentation=oracle.aurora.server.SGiopServer)"
```

NOTE
Use oracle.aurora.server.SGiopServer for session-based GIOP connections. This presentation is valid for TCP/IP and TCP/IP with SSL.

If you want your client to go to a dispatcher directly, bypassing the listener, you can direct your client to the dispatcher's port number. To discover the dispatcher's port number, you can either configure a port number for the dispatcher by adding the ADDRESS parameter or discover the port assigned to the dispatcher by invoking the listener control utility.

Specify the following parameter in the **init.ora** file to direct a connection bypassing the listener:

```
dispatchers="(address=(protocol=tcp | tcps)
             (host=<server_host>)(port=<port>))
             (presentation=oracle.aurora.server.SGiopServer)"
```

Configuring the Listener for IIOP

Oracle enables you to configure the listener for IIOP connections either dynamically through a tool or statically by specifying the entries in the configuration files. In order for a listener to receive an incoming IIOP request, the listener must have an IIOP end-point registered. The registration of any type of listening end-point can be done through the dynamic registration tool, REGEP. The primary objective of dynamically registering a listener end-point is that you do not need to restart your database for the listener to be IIOP enabled. The listening end-point is active immediately.

NOTE
It is essential for you to restart the database if you manually configure the listener with IIOP end-points.

For example, to register a listener on the ORAMASTERDB host on end-point port number 2243, issue the following command:

```
regep -pres oracle.aurora.server.SGiopServer -host oramasterdb -port 2243
```

If you statically configure a listener, you need to configure separate ports as listening end-points for both TTC and IIOP connections. The default listener that is configured by the Oracle JVM is configured for both TTC and IIOP listening end-points. You can configure each listener to listen on a well-known port number, and the client communicates with the listener using this port number. To configure the listener manually, you must modify the listener's DESCRIPTION parameter within the **listener.ora** file with a GIOP listening address. The following example configures a GIOP presentation for non-SSL TCP/IP with port number 2481. You use port 2481 for non-SSL and port 2482 for SSL.

For GIOP, the PROTOCOL_STACK parameter is added to the DESCRIPTION when configuring an IIOP connection to support-server:

```
listener=
  (description_list=
    (description=
      (address=(protocol=tcp)(host=support.oramasters.com)(port=2481))
      (protocol_stack=(presentation=giop)(session=raw))))
```

This identifies a presentation of GIOP for IIOP clients. The GIOP supports oracle.server.SGiop.Server using TCP/IP. This also indicates that the session should be in RAW format. The preceding configuration enables the listener to listen at port 2481 for GIOP.

Once the listener configuration is completed, we have to restart the listener. During the listener startup time, the following information will be displayed on the console:

```
(DESCRIPTION=(ADDRESS=(PROTOCOL=TCP)(HOST=support.oramasters.com)
(PORT=2481))(PROTOCOL_STACK=(PRESENTATION=GIOP)(SESSION=RAW)))
```

After configuration, the client directs its request to a URL that includes the host and port that identifies the listener, and either the SID or database service name. The following shows the syntax for this request:

```
sess_iiop://<hostname>:<portnumber>/<SID | service_name>
```

Based on the configuration shown in the **listener.ora** file above, your URL would contain the following values:

```
sess_iiop://support.oramasters.com:2481/oracle
```

Chapter Questions

1. **Which command can you use with the listener control utility to invoke the listener?**

   A. ACTIVATE

   B. STARTUP

   C. INVOKE

   D. START

2. **Assume that there are three listeners configured in the listener.ora file for a particular database server. In order to start all the three listeners, which listener address attribute specified in the listener.ora file should differ between the three listeners?**

   A. GLOBAL_HOME

   B. ORACLE_HOME

   C. PORT

   D. HOSTNAME

3. **You are configuring the listener on your server. Which listener.ora parameter contains the information needed to detect session requests from different client types?**

   A. ADDRESS_LIST

   B. SID_NAME

   C. LISTENER

   D. SERVICE_LIST

4. **In a shared server environment, where does the listener redirect the connection request?**

   A. Net Manager

   B. Shared Server

   C. Agent

   D. Dispatcher

5. **When do you need to specify the database information in the SID_LIST parameter in the listener.ora file, which is commonly referred to as the static service configuration?**

   A. When you want to use Recovery Manager

   B. When you want to use shared server

   C. When you want to use the Oracle Enterprise Manager

   D. When you want to use multiple listeners

6. **Which of the following file should be configured for dynamic service registration?**

   A. LISTENER.ORA

   B. SQLNET.ORA

   C. INIT.ORA

   D. TNSNAMES.ORA

7. **Which of the following processes registers service information with its local listener?**

   A. SMON

   B. PMON

   C. DISPATCHER

   D. CMON

8. **Which of the following display modes cannot be configured through the listener control utility's SET DISPLAYMODE command?**

   A. NORMAL

   B. COMPAT

   C. RAW

   D. VERBOSE

   E. GUI

9. **Setting which parameter will not enable you to configure the listener while it is running?**

   A. ADMIN_RESTRICTIONS_listener_name=on

   B. ADMIN_RESTRICTIONS_listener_name=off

    C. SAVE_CONFIG_ON_STOP_listener_name=true

    D. SAVE_CONFIG_ON_STOP_listener_name=false

    E. LOGGING_listener_name=on

    F. LOGGING_listener_name=off

10. **For connections to IIOP clients, the presentation parameter for the PROTOCOL_STACK in the listener.ora file should be set to which one of the following?**

    A. GIOP

    B. RAW

    C. IIOP

    D. TCP

Answers to Chapter Questions

I. D. START

Explanation To invoke the listener using the listener control utility, you must execute the START command accompanied by the name of the listener you want to start. If no listener is specified Oracle starts the default listener which is specified in the listener.ora.

2. C. PORT

Explanation The three address attributes specified in the ADDRESS_LIST parameter in the listener.ora file are PROTOCOL, HOST and PORT. The host name and the network protocol remain similar, but the port must differ as the client can access a database through a specific listener by including the appropriate port number in the net service name in the client-side tnsnames.ora file.

3. A. ADDRESS_LIST

Explanation The listener listens to those incoming connection requests based on the addresses listed in the ADDRESS_LIST. Each address defined in the ADDRESS_LIST parameter represents different ways by which a listener receives and processes a connection.

4. D. Dispatcher

Explanation In a shared server configuration, the listener redirects a connection request to the dispatcher.

5. C. When you want to use Oracle Enterprise Manager

Explanation Static service configuration is required whenever you want to use the Oracle Enterprise Manager. Dynamic service registration eliminates the need for static configuration of the supported services.

6. C. INIT.ORA

Explanation Dynamic service registration is configured in the database initialization file. Please note that it does not require any configuration in the listener.ora file. However, listener configuration must be synchronized with the information in the database initialization file.

7. B.   PMON

Explanation   The PMON process registers the service information with its local listener on the default local address (TCP/IP and port 1521). As long as the listener configuration is synchronized with the database configuration, PMON can register service information with a non-default local listener or a remote listener on another node.

8. E.   GUI

Explanation   The SET DISPLAYMODE command enables you to configure the output display for the commands that are used at the listener control utility. The options that can be used with this command are NORMAL, COMPAT, RAW, and VERBOSE.

9. A.   ADMIN_RESTRICTIONS_*listener_name*=on

Explanation   The ADMIN_RESTRICTIONS_*listener_name* parameter is a security feature. If the parameter is set to ON, it enables you to restrict runtime administration of the listener. The feature is useful if you are not using a password-protected listener. It does not allow you to configure the listener when it is running until you explicitly set it to OFF and reload the listener.

10. A.   GIOP

Explanation   To configure for IIOP, you must set the presentation=GIOP in the protocol_stack as shown below:

```
(protocol_stack=
   (presentation=giop)
   (session=raw))
```

CHAPTER
4

Basic Oracle Net Services
Client-Side Configuration

n this chapter you will learn about the various naming methods supported by Oracle Net and the advantages and disadvantages associated with each method. We will explain the steps involved in configuring the host naming and local naming methods. We will also explain how to create a net service name using the Oracle Net Manager. Later in this chapter we explain the utilities available to troubleshoot the Oracle Net environment and discuss how to resolve common Oracle Net errors messages. This chapter includes the following topics:

- Naming methods
- Configuring the host naming method
- Configuring the local naming method
- Configuring net service names
- Perform simple connection troubleshooting

In the Oracle network, the services run on the server, and the clients get connected to the service using a connect identifier. The connect identifier can be a net service name or the actual name of the service. The client uses a naming method to resolve the connect identifier to a connect descriptor. The connect descriptor gives the network route to the service, including the listener location and the service name or SID name. Using the connect descriptor, the client requests the listener for a connection. The following example shows a typical connect descriptor:

```
support=
 (DESCRIPTION=
  (ADDRESS=(PROTOCOL=tcp)(HOST=support-server)(PORT=1521))
  (CONNECT_DATA=
     (SERVICE_NAME=support.oramasters.com)))
```

In the previous example, the ADDRESS section contains the listener protocol address, and the CONNECT_DATA section contains the destination service information. In this example, the destination service is a database service named *support.oramasters.com*.

Naming Methods

Oracle Net supports several naming methods like *local naming, directory naming, Oracle names, host naming,* and *external naming.* These naming methods are explained in the following section:

Local Naming

In the local naming method, the client uses the **tnsnames.ora** file to map the service name into the connect descriptor. This local naming method is useful for simple distributed networks with few services.

Directory Naming Method

The directory naming method uses a centralized LDAP-compliant directory like the Oracle Internet directory, Microsoft active directory, and Novell directory services. This directory service helps map the connect identifiers to the connect descriptors and provides centralized administration of database services and net service names. This method simplifies the administration of service names.

The database services are configured during installation by using the Oracle database configuration assistant. The net service names are created using the Oracle Net Manager. You can use the Oracle Net Manager to modify the Oracle Net properties of a database service and the net service name entries. The clients configured to access the directory can use these entries to connect to the database.

Oracle Names

The Oracle names server stores names and addresses of all the services on a network. Oracle names provide centralized setup and administration of the naming service. Oracle names, in a network, provide network address and database link information of the servers available to all nodes. The service name is mapped to the database server network address. The client's requests are sent to the Oracle names server, which resolves the net services names into the network address. The client substitutes the address in place of the service names and contacts the server. To use an Oracle names server, both the client and the Oracle names server must be configured. The centralized configuration changes will simplify the administration tasks.

Centralized naming services offer increased efficiency, server location transparency, simplified administration, and eliminates redundancy.

NOTE
The Oracle names method will not be supported in future releases.

Host Naming

The host naming method is used to identify a global database name via an existing name resolution method, such as domain name system (DNS), network information service (NIS), or a centrally-maintained set of /etc/hosts file. This method enables users to connect to an Oracle server by using a hostname alias. The hostnames are mapped to a connect descriptor service using the name resolution method. The advantage of using this feature is that no client configuration is required.

NOTE
This method is only suitable for simple TCP/IP environments.

External Naming

The external naming method uses third-party naming services like network information service (NIS) and cell directory services (CDS). The external naming method resolves a net service name stored in a non-Oracle naming service to a network address.

Choosing an Oracle Naming Method

The naming method that you select for your network will depend upon the environment and the first name resolution method you want to configure. The advantages and disadvantages of the previously explained naming methods are described in Table 4-1.

Configuring the Host Naming Method

The host naming method is preferred for simple networks but not for large and complex networks. This method eliminates the need for service name lookup. For large and complex networks, selecting another naming method is recommended.

The host naming method is available for TCP/IP network environments only. The clients use the server's global database name in the connect string to connect to the database. The global database name is equivalent to a hostname or an alias in an existing name resolution service. The TCP/IP and Oracle Net protocol adapter should be installed on both the client and the server.

Configuring the host naming method involves two steps:

1. Configure the hostname as the first naming method.

2. Set up the environment.

Before configuring the server side, the global database name must be registered with the listener. This registration depends on the release of the database. For Oracle8*i* or Oracle9*i*, the information about the database is automatically registered with the listener and includes the global database name. For earlier releases of

Naming Method	Advantages	Disadvantages
Local naming	This method is very simple and easy to understand and implement.	Centralized control is not present, and changes in the environment need to be made for each client.
Host naming	Useful for simple network environment with small number of clients. Simple to set up. Client configuration is not needed.	This is suitable only for TCP/IP networks. You cannot use multiple listeners and support for all Oracle Net features is not available.
Oracle names	Central administration. Simple client configuration.	Additional resources are needed to configure and administer names servers.
Directory naming	Central administration. Simple client configuration.	The services are needed to configure and administer directory servers.
External naming	Uses the existing name resolution services. It provides for centralized administration.	Complex to configure and manage. Not widely used.

TABLE 4-1. *Naming Methods Comparison*

Oracle, you will need to configure the listener to register the database information by editing the **listener.ora** file manually.

Configuring HOSTNAME as the First Naming Method

Once the listener has the database information, you can configure the hostname as the first naming method to resolve the connect identifiers. To configure host naming as the first method, you must set the NAMES.DIRECTORY_PATH parameter in the **sqlnet.ora** file. This parameter specifies the order of naming methods Oracle Net will use to resolve connect identifiers to connect descriptors.

To specify host naming as the first naming method, you follow the following steps:

1. Start Oracle Net Manager.

2. In the navigator pane, expand Local/Profile.

3. From the list in the right pane, select Naming.

4. In the Methods window, choose HOSTNAME from the Available Methods list, and then choose the right-arrow button.

5. Select HOSTNAME in the Selected Methods list, and then use the Promote button to move the selection to the top of the list. Figure 4-1 shows that the HOSTNAME method is promoted over the TNSNAMES and ONAMES methods.

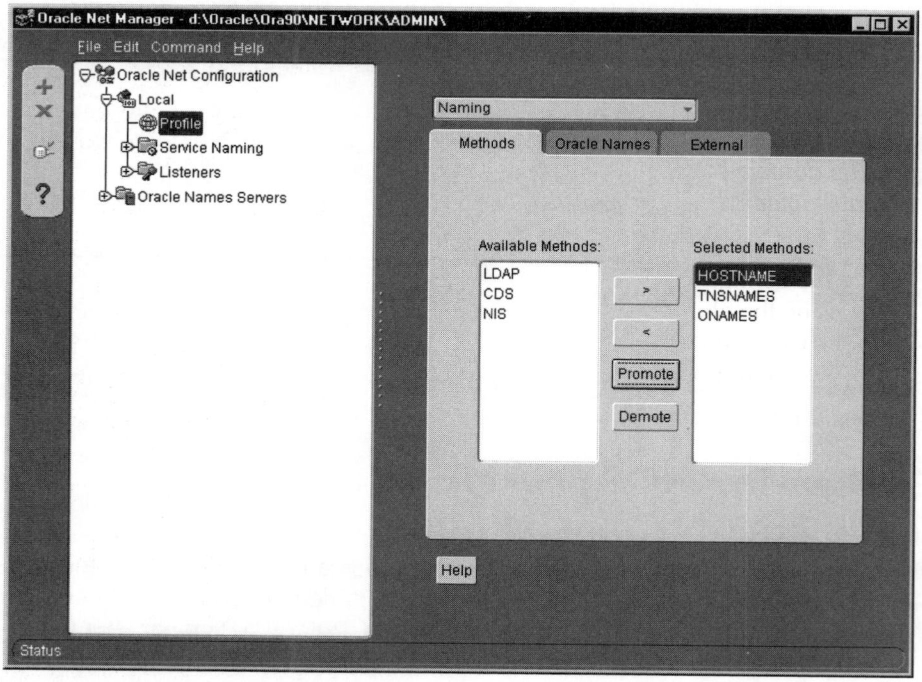

FIGURE 4-1. *Host naming method configuration*

6. Choose File | Save Network Configuration.

7. The NAMES.DIRECTORY_PATH parameter is updated in the **sqlnet.ora** file, listing hostname first as shown in the following code:

```
NAMES.DIRECTORY_PATH=(hostname, tnsnames, onames)
```

Setting Up the HostName Resolution Environment

When using the host naming method, the global database name must be resolved through an IP address translation mechanism, such as a centrally maintained TCP/IP host file, /etc/hosts file, DNS, or NIS.

For example, if a database with a global database name of support.oramasters.com exists on a computer named support-server, the entry in the /etc/hosts file would look like:

```
#IP address of server      host name      alias
208.59.199.25              support-server  support.oramasters.com
```

NOTE
The domain section of the global database name must match the network domain.

Once the configuration has been completed, clients can connect to the database using the alias. Note that at the server side, the listener must be running on default port 1521. In the previous example, a client can use support.oramasters.com in the connect string as shown in the following code:

```
CONNECT username/password@support.oramasters.com
```

NOTE
If the client and server exist in the same domain, for example in oramasters.com, then the client needs to enter only support in the connect string.

Configuring the Local Naming Method

The local naming method uses the **tnsnames.ora** file to map the net service names to the connect descriptor. The **tnsnames.ora** file contains the net service names entries. The following example shows a **tnsnames.ora** file's basic syntax for a net service name mapped to a connect descriptor:

```
support=
(DESCRIPTION=
   (ADDRESS= (PROTOCOL=tcp) (HOST=sukpport-server) (PORT=1521))
   (ADDRESS=(PROTOCOL=tcp) (HOST=support-server) (PORT=1521)
   (CONNECT_DATA=
      (SERVICE_NAME=support.oramasters.com)))
```

In the previous example, the net service name *support* is mapped to the connect descriptor contained in the DESCRIPTION. The DESCRIPTION contains the protocol address and the connect data string that identifies the destination database service.

The local naming method can be configured either during or after installation. Both these configurations are explained in the following section:

Configuring Local Naming Method During Installation

The Oracle Net Configuration Assistant will help us to configure net service names for clients. After the software installation, the Oracle universal installer launches the Oracle Net configuration assistant. For a minimal installation of Oracle, the Oracle Net configuration assistant will prompt you to configure the net service names in the **tnsnames.ora** file to connect to an Oracle database service. During the custom installation of Oracle, the Oracle Net configuration assistant will prompt you for the naming methods. You will have to choose the local naming method to configure the **tnsnames.ora** file.

Configuring Local Naming Method After Installation

You can add the net service names to the **tnsnames.ora** file at any time after the completion of the Oracle software installation. To configure the local naming method, you need to configure the net service names and also set the TNSNAMES as the first naming method to resolve the service names. You can configure the net service names by either using the Oracle Net Manager or the Oracle configuration assistant.

Configuring Local Naming Method
Using the Oracle Net Configuration Assistant

To configure the net service names in the **tnsnames.ora** file using the Oracle Net configuration assistant, you must complete the following steps:

1. Start the Oracle Net configuration assistant. The welcome page appears.

2. Select Local Net Service Name Configuration, and then click Next. You will see the Net Service Name Configuration page. Figure 4-2 displays the various options that can be configured for the net service names.

3. Select Add, and then click Next.

4. Choose an option based on the destination service. If the destination service is an Oracle9*i* or Oracle8*i* database, then choose Oracle8*i* or later database or service. If destination service is an Oracle8 database, then choose Oracle8 release 8.0 database or service. Click Next.

5. Enter the destination service name or the SID. Click Next.

6. Select the protocol type, and click Next.

7. Enter the Hostname and Port Number for the TCP/IP environment.

When the testing page appears and you choose Test, Oracle Net connects to the database server by using the connect descriptor information. Therefore, the database and the listener must be running for a successful test. During testing, a connection test dialog box appears, providing status and test results. A successful test results in the following message:

```
The connection test was successful
```

If the test was not successful, then check if the database and the listener are running before testing. You can also select the Change Login option to change the user name and password and test again.

Configuring TNSNAMES as the First Naming Method

You need to modify the NAMES.DIRECTORY_PATH parameter in the **sqlnet.ora** file to configure local naming as the first method. This parameter specifies the order of the naming methods Oracle Net uses to resolve connect identifiers to connect descriptors. You can use the Oracle Net Manager and configure local naming as the first method as shown in the following steps:

1. Start the Oracle Net Manager.

2. In the Navigator pane, expand Local | Profile.

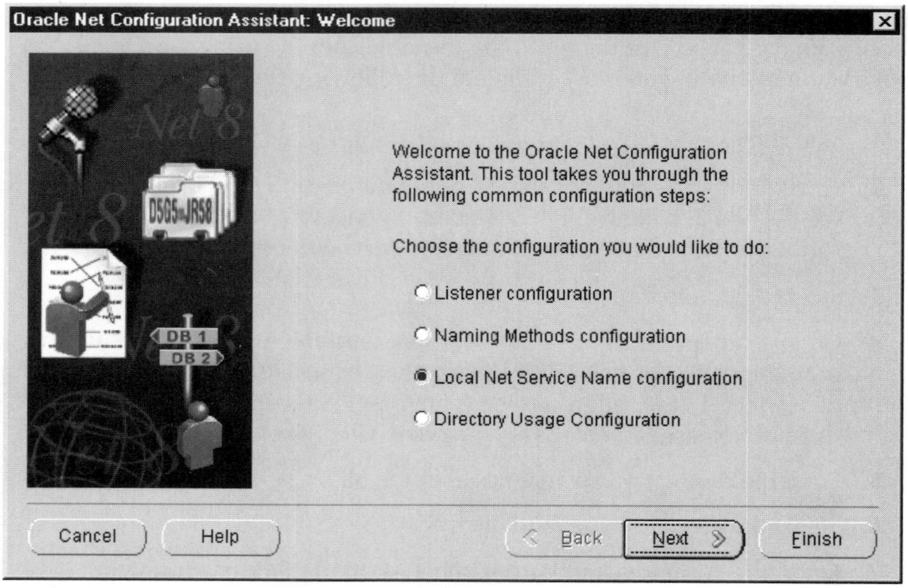

FIGURE 4-2. *Local naming method configuration*

3. From the list in the right pane, select Naming.

4. Select the Methods tab.

5. From the Available Methods list, select TNSNAMES, and then choose the right-arrow button.

6. In the Selected Methods list, select TNSNAMES, and then use the Promote button to move the selection to the top of the list. Figure 4-3 shows that the TNSNAMES method is promoted over the ONAMES and HOSTNAME methods.

7. Select File | Save Network Configuration.

Once the configuration is saved, then the **sqlnet.ora** file gets updated with the NAMES.DIRECTORY_PATH parameter as follows:

```
NAMES.DIRECTORY_PATH=(tnsnames, onames, hostname)
```

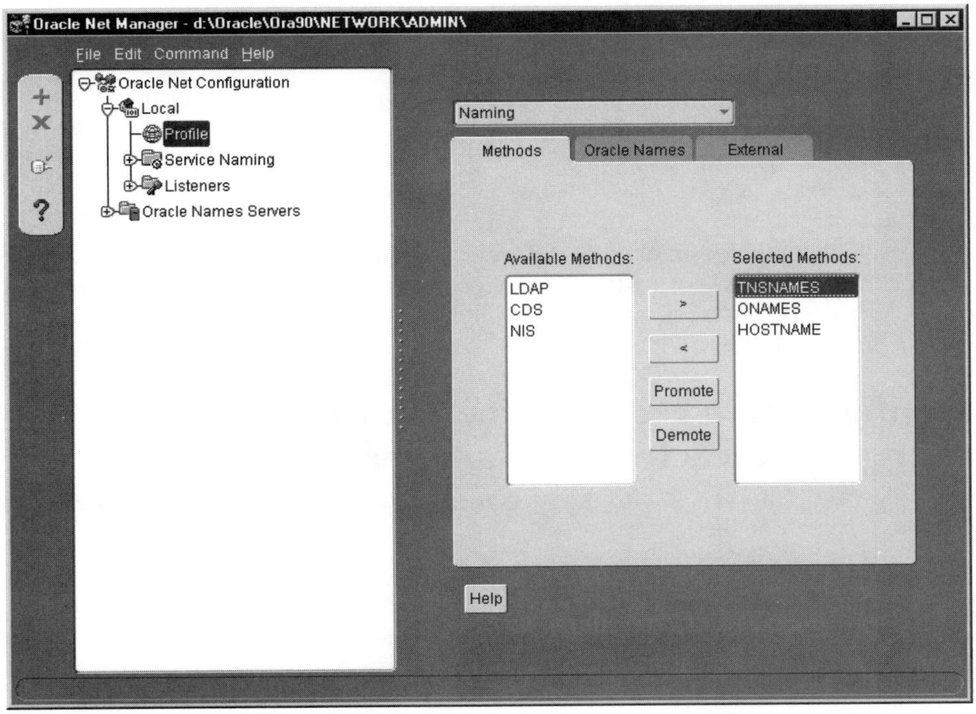

FIGURE 4-3. *Configuring the TNSNAMES as the first naming method*

We can maintain the same configuration files on other clients to ensure consistency. To achieve this, we need to copy the **sqlnet.ora** and **tnsnames.ora** files to the same location on the other clients.

Configuring Net Service Names

The *net service name* is a name that represents the Oracle database service name. The net service name resolves to the connect descriptor, that is, the network address of the database and the name of the database service. Assume that a net service name support is configured at the client side as shown in the following code:

```
support=
(DESCRIPTION=
    (ADDRESS=(PROTOCOL=tcp) (HOST=support-server) (PORT=1521))
```

```
(CONNECT_DATA=
   (SERVICE_NAME=support.oramasters.com)))
```

The previous configuration enables the client to connect to the database using the following SQL*Plus command:

```
SQL> CONNECT username/password@support.
```

Oracle recommends creating a net service name for each service. Users can connect to the database using the net service name instead of the database service name. To create a net service name, use either the Oracle Net Manager or the Oracle Names Control utility.

Configuring a Net Service Name Using the Oracle Net Manager

The following example explains the procedure for creating a Net service name using the Oracle Net Manager:

1. Start the Oracle Net Manager.

2. In the navigator pane, expand Oracle Names Servers.

3. Select an Oracle names server.

4. From the list in the right pane, select Manage Data.

5. Choose the Net Service Names tab.

6. Choose Add.

7. Enter the net service name in the Net Service Name field.

NOTE
*You can qualify the net service name with the client's domain. The net service name is automatically domain-qualified if the **sqlnet.ora** file parameter NAMES.DEFAULT_DOMAIN is set.*

8. Select a protocol from the pick list that the listener is configured to listen on.

9. Enter the appropriate protocol information for the selected protocol in the fields provided.

NOTE
*Additional addresses can be created by choosing
the plus (+) button at the bottom of the Address tab.*

10. Enter a destination service. If the destination service is an Oracle9*i* or
Oracle8*i* database, then enter the service name in the Service Name field. If
destination service is prior to Oracle8*i*, then choose Oracle8 Release 8.0
Compatible Identification, and enter its SID in the SID field.

NOTE
*If you want to configure advanced
CONNECT_DATA options besides the destination
service, choose Advanced.*

11. Click the Execute button.

12. Select File | Save Network Configuration to save your configuration
changes.

Figure 4-4 shows the configuration options that must be specified for adding a
new net service name.

Performing Simple Connection Troubleshooting

Oracle provides a variety of tools to help you test the Oracle names server, listener,
and Connection Manager. Once the Oracle Net configuration is over, you should
make a connection to the database and test that each component is working.

Before you start troubleshooting the Oracle Net environment, you should verify
whether the problem is with the network or with the database. You should also
check if the problem is specific to a single computer or to the whole network. If you
can't make a connection between the server and the client, you should first look at
testing the network connectivity. You should use the PING command to test at the
OS level. You should also ensure that the client and the server are using the same
protocol and that the Oracle network protocol adapter is installed on both the client
and the server.

At the server side, you should connect to the server and check that the listener
and the database are running properly to handle the client's request. You can use the
lsnrctl utility to check the status of the listener and also ensure that it is listening for
that particular database. You need to use the **lsnrctl** utility's SERVICES command to
check if the listener is refusing any connections. You can check the availability of the

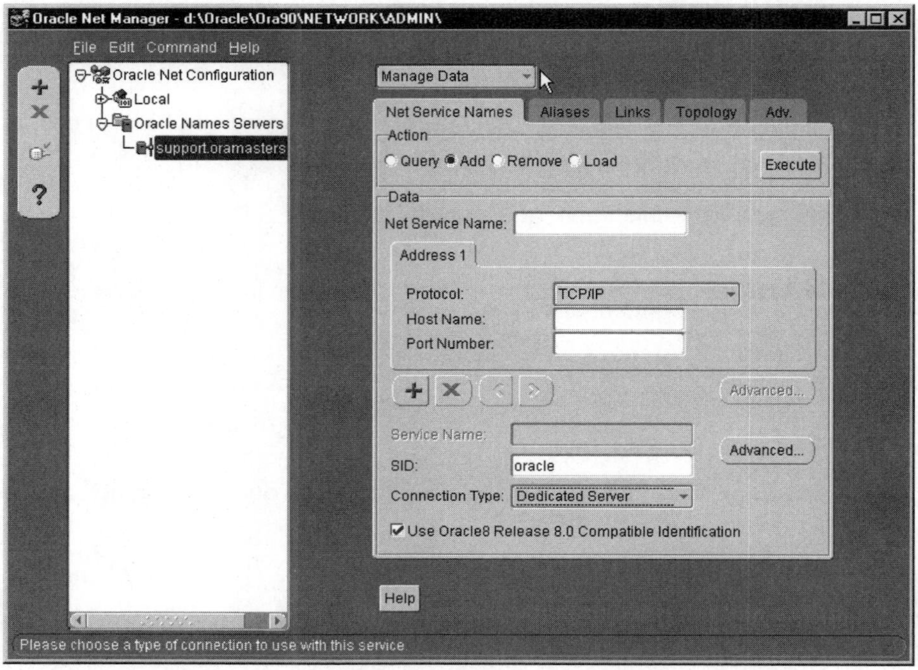

FIGURE 4-4. *Adding the net service names*

database service by connecting directly to the database using a SQL*Plus command as shown in the following code:

```
SQL> CONNECT scott/tiger
```

You can enable the logging and tracing features to get additional information. The log and trace files provide useful information about the workings of the various Oracle Net components. You can enable logging and tracing at the client, middle tier, and at the database server. To enable logging and tracing at the server side, you must configure the **listener.ora** file. If you are using the Connection Manager, you will need to configure the **cman.ora** file. The **sqlnet.ora** file can be configured to enable logging and tracing for all levels.

Troubleshooting Tools

Oracle Net provides the following utilities to help evaluate and test network connectivity:

- TNSPING
- TRCROUTE
- Oracle Net Manager

TNSPING Utility

The **tnsping** utility helps you to determine whether a service, such as an Oracle database, an Oracle Names server, or any other Oracle service on the Oracle Net network, can be reached. If the service can be connected successfully, then the utility returns the estimated time for a roundtrip connection in milliseconds. If the connection fails, then it will display an error message. To check the connectivity of a service using the **tnsping** utility, you do not require a user name and password. You can use this utility to detect network errors without the overhead of the database.

The syntax for using the **tnsping** utility is shown in the following code:

```
tnsping net_service_name [count]
```

where, *net service name* must exist in **tnsnames.ora** file or the name service in use, such as NIS and DCE's CDS. The *count* parameter is optional and specifies how many times the program should attempt to reach the server.

NOTE
*The **tnsping** utility does not test for the connectivity with the database instance; it only checks for the connectivity with the listener.*

TRCROUTE Utility

The *trace route* utility (TRCROUTE) gives the path or route from the client to the server. If **trcroute** utility encounters a problem, it returns an error stack to the client instead of a single error. These additional error messages make troubleshooting easier. The **trcroute** utility collects the TNS addresses of every node along the destination. If any error occurs, it will be displayed on the client screen.

The syntax for using the **trcroute** utility is shown in the following code:

```
trcroute net_service_name
```

Oracle Net Manager

You can use the Oracle Net Manager to verify connectivity for a client computer. The steps to do this is shown in the following list:

1. Start Oracle Net Manager.

2. In the navigator pane, expand Directory or Local | Service Naming.

3. Select the net service name or the database service for testing. Figure 4-5 shows the selected net service name and its corresponding details.

4. Choose Command | Test Net Service from the menu.

NOTE
Testing assumes that the database and listener are running.

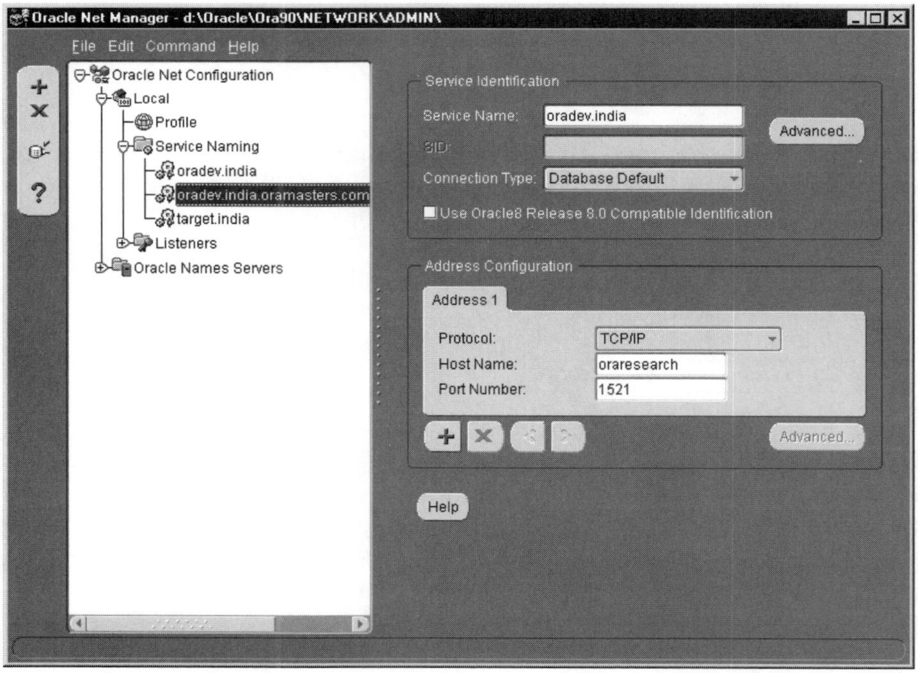

FIGURE 4-5. *Selecting the net service name*

During testing, a Connection Test dialog box appears, providing status and test results. Figure 4-6 shows that the test for the net service name has been successful.

5. If the test fails, you must check whether the listener is running or not. Try using a different user name in the Connection Test dialog box.

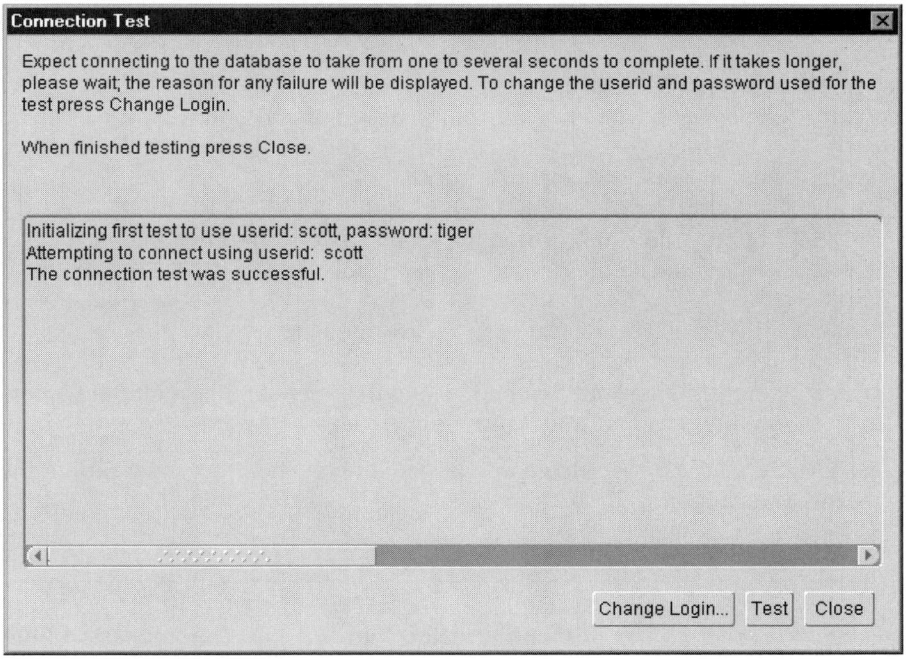

FIGURE 4-6. *Testing the net service*

Troubleshooting Network Problems

Oracle Net Services provide methods for understanding and resolving network problems using log and trace files. These files keep track of the interaction between network components. Evaluating this information will help you to diagnose and troubleshoot the problems. The errors may originate from various sources because of a variety of reasons.

Troubleshooting Network Problems Using Log and Trace Files

The logging and tracing features provided by Oracle helps in obtaining detailed history of the operations performed by the Oracle Net components. When these features are enabled, the errors will help in diagnosing and resolving network problems. The listener log also includes the client connection requests and the control commands information.

To enable logging and tracing options for various network components, you need to configure certain files. Table 4-2 provides a listing of the network components and the files that need to be configured for logging and tracing.

Common Network Errors

Listed in the following section are some of the most common network errors and their corresponding messages. The actions that are required to resolve these errors are also explained in the following section:

ORA-12154: TNS: Could not Resolve Service Name   This error occurs when Oracle Net could not locate the net service name specified in the **tnsnames.ora** configuration file.

To resolve this error, you must do the following steps:

1. Verify the **tnsnames.ora** file, and ensure that there are no multiple copies of the **tnsnames.ora** and **sqlnet.ora** files present.

2. Ensure that the net service name is matching the connect descriptor in the **tnsnames.ora** file.

Network Component	Configuration File for Logging	Configuration File for Tracing
Client	**sqlnet.ora**	**sqlnet.ora**
Database server	**sqlnet.ora**	**sqlnet.ora**
Listener	**listener.ora**	**listener.ora**
Oracle names server	**names.ora**	**names.ora**
Oracle connection manager	**cman.ora**	**cman.ora**

TABLE 4-2.   *Logging and Tracing Configuration Files*

3. If you are using domain names, then there should be an entry NAMES.DEFAULT_DOMAIN in the **sqlnet.ora** file; otherwise, you should specify the domain name in the connect string. If you are not using domain names, then you will need to disable or delete this entry.

4. If you are connecting from a login dialog box, verify that you are not placing an @ symbol before your net service name.

ORA-12198: TNS: Could not Find Path to Destination   This error occurs when the client cannot find the desired database.
   To resolve this error, you must perform the following steps:

1. Verify the net service name ADDRESS parameter in the connect descriptor and check the location of the **tnsnames.ora** file.

2. Ensure that the listener on the remote node is running. If not, start the listener.

3. If you are connecting from a login box, verify that you are not placing an @ symbol before your net service name.

ORA-12203: TNS: Unable to Connect to Destination   This error is a generic error that often shields secondary errors.
   To resolve this error, you must perform the following steps:

1. Check your latest **sqlnet.log** file for secondary ORA messages.

2. Ensure that your net service name is correct in the **tnsnames.ora** file and the address of the net service name is also valid.

3. Verify that your **tnsnames.ora** file is located in the right place.

4. Make sure that the server side **listener.ora** file and the client side **tnsnames.ora** file points to the same name or to the names that are translated to the same IP address using name resolution.

5. Check if the listener is running. If it is not running, start the listener.

6. By using the underlying network protocol, verify that the protocols are running properly. For example, for TCP/IP, try to ping the remote host.

7. Check that you have installed the appropriate Oracle protocol.

ORA-12224: TNS: No Listener   This error occurs when the client request could not be handled because the listener is not running.

To resolve this error, you must check that the specified address and the address in the listener are the same. You should also check for any version incompatibility problem.

ORA-12533:TNS: Illegal ADDRESS Parameters   This error occurs when the protocol specific parameters in the ADDRESS section of the designated connect descriptor are incorrect.

To resolve this error, change the protocol address and check the connectivity.

ORA-12545:TNS: Name Lookup Failure   This error would occur when the remote node's listener cannot be contacted.

To resolve this error, you must perform the following steps:

1. Verify that the ADDRESS in the **tnsnames.ora** file and the **listener.ora** file is correct.

2. Check the listener status using the **lsnrctl** utility's STATUS command as shown in the following code:

   ```
   LSNRCTL> STATUS [listener name]
   ```

3. If the listener is not active, then start it as shown in the following code:

   ```
   LSNRCTL> START [listener name]
   ```

ORA-12560:TNS: Protocol Adapter Error   This error would occur when the listener was unable to start a process connecting the user to the database server.

To gather more information on this error, you should follow the following steps:

1. Turn on tracing and start the listener.

2. Check the contents of the trace file to resolve the problem.

Chapter Questions

1. **Which one of the following methods uses the Domain Names Service (DNS) to resolve the connect descriptor?**

   A. Host naming

   B. Names server

   C. Centralized naming

   D. Local naming

   E. Oracle names

2. **Which one of the following naming methods requires you to modify the tnsnames.ora file?**

   A. Centralized naming

   B. Oracle names

   C. Local naming

   D. Host naming

3. **Which one of the following must the user explicitly specify while establishing a connection using the CONNECT command of the SQL*Plus utility in local naming method?**

   A. Service address

   B. Connect descriptor

   C. Net Service name

   D. Port

   E. Host address

4. **What is the initial step you must perform when configuring local naming using the Oracle Net configuration assistant?**

   A. You must choose the appropriate network protocol.

   B. You must choose the local naming method.

   C. You must specify the hostname and the port number.

   D. You must specify the Net service name.

5. **Which one of the following components of the tnsnames.ora file describes the location of a network listener and the system identifier for the database?**

   A. Connect descriptor

   B. Address

   C. Protocol

   D. Port

6. **Which one of the following connection methods and configuration files requires you to specify the parameter GLOBAL_DBNAME?**

   A. Local naming and **tnsnames.ora**

   B. Local naming and **sqlnet.ora**

   C. Local naming and **listener.ora**

   D. Host naming and **tnsnames.ora**

   E. Oracle Names and **tnsnames.ora**

7. **Which of the following client side configuration files need to be modified when configuring the local naming method?**

   A. **tnsnames.ora** and **sqlnet.ora**

   B. **services.ora** and **sqlnet.ota**

   C. **tnsnames.ora** and **listener.ora**

   D. **tnsnames.ora**, **sqlnet.ora**, and **listener.ora**

8. **Which one of the following files includes the parameter NAMES.DIRECTORY_PATH(hostname)?**

   A. **listener.ora**

   B. **tnsnames.ora**

   C. **cman.ora**

   D. **sqlnet.ora**

9. **What is the cause of the following Oracle error?**
ORA-12154: TNS: Could not Resolve Service Name

   A. The existing location has duplicate copies of the **tnsnames.ora** or **sqlnet.ora** files.

   B. The remote server listener is not started.

   C. The user you are trying to connect is not a valid database user.

   D. The service name ADDRESS parameter in the connect descriptor of your **sqlnet.ora** file is not correct.

10. **Connection Manager features cannot be used with which of the following naming method?**

   A. Oracle names

   B. Local naming

   C. Host naming

   D. Names server

Chapter Answers

1. A. Host naming

Explanation The Domain Name Services (DNS) IP address translation mechanism is used by the host naming connection method to resolve the hostname. Host naming can also use NIS or a centrally maintained TCP/IP host file.

2. C. Local naming

Explanation The **tnsnames.ora** file, which is at the client's side, comprises of the addresses a user needs to connect to a particular listener on a particular node using a specified database. Local naming requires a local **tnsnames.ora** file on the client.

3. C. Net service name

Explanation The user only needs the Net service name to establish a session with the database.

4. B. You must choose local naming method.

Explanation You must choose the local naming method using Net Configuration Assistant to specify the service name, the protocol, the hostname, and the port number.

5. A. Connect descriptor

Explanation The connect descriptor gives the network route to the service including the listener location and the service name or SID name. The connect descriptor enables the client to request the listener for a network session.

6. C. Local naming and **listener.ora**

Explanation The GLOBAL_DBNAME parameter in the **listener.ora** file represents the global database name (hostname). The value of this parameter must exactly match the connect string entered by the user.

7. A. **tnsnames.ora** and **sqlnet.ora**

Explanation In the local naming method you must configure the **tnsnames.ora** and **sqlnet.ora** files at the client end.

8. D. **sqlnet.ora**

Explanation   You can set the parameter NAMES.DIRECTORY_PATH to HOSTNAME if host naming method is used to resolve the Net services. This parameter must be specified in the **sqlnet.ora** file.

9. A.   The existing location has duplicate copies of the **tnsnames.ora** or **sqlnet.ora** files.

Explanation   Oracle can return the client with the mentioned error message if Oracle is unable to find the Net service name in the **tnsnames.ora** file or if there are duplicate copies of the **tnsnames.ora** or **sqlnet.ora** files.

10. C.   Host naming

Explanation   Connection Manager features are not supported with the host naming method. Host naming is used in a two-tier environment whereas Connection Manager works with the three-tier environment.

CHAPTER
5

Usage and Configuration of the Oracle Shared Server

n this chapter, you will learn the concepts and importance of using and configuring the Oracle shared server. You will learn about the various components and the architecture of the shared server. We will also explain the process of configuring the Oracle shared sever. Later in this chapter, we describe the important dynamic performance views related to the shared sever configuration. This chapter includes the following topics:

- Identifying the components of the Oracle shared server

- Oracle shared server architecture

- Configuring the Oracle shared server

- Shared server related dictionary views

Identifying the Components of the Oracle Shared Server

The shared server architecture eliminates the need for a dedicated server process. In a shared server environment, the dispatcher process enables many user processes to share a few server processes. This increases the number of users that can be supported. The shared server is a very effective method for maintaining multiple connections, especially in an OLTP environment, where the chances of the user process staying idle is higher. In the shared server architecture, a small number of shared servers can perform the same amount of processing as several dedicated servers. Using the shared server architecture reduces the number of processes that the O/S has to manage, thus reducing the system overhead.

Shared server architecture does not prevent dedicated server connections from being established because the Oracle internal tasks, like starting and shutting down the database, require the use of dedicated connections. Also, most batch-driven processes work better with dedicated connections.

The various processes that are involved as part of the Oracle shared server architecture are

- The listener process, which is primarily part of the Oracle Net. This process is responsible for connecting the user processes to the dispatcher or the dedicated server processes.

- One or more dispatcher processes.

- One or more shared server processes.

NOTE
To use shared servers, a user process must connect through Oracle Net services or SQL*Net version 2, even if the process runs on the same machine as the Oracle instance.

Oracle Shared Server Architecture

In the shared server environment during instance startup, the PMON process registers the location and load of the dispatchers with the listener, enabling the listener to forward requests to the dispatcher. Figure 5-1 gives the architecture of the Oracle shared server.

For each network protocol that the database clients use, at least one dispatcher process must be configured and started. When the user process request arrives, the listener examines the request and determines whether the user process can use a shared server process. If so, the listener returns the address of the dispatcher process that is currently handling the least number of requests. Then the user process connects to the dispatcher process directly. If the user process requests a dedicated server, the listener creates a dedicated server process and establishes a dedicated server connection.

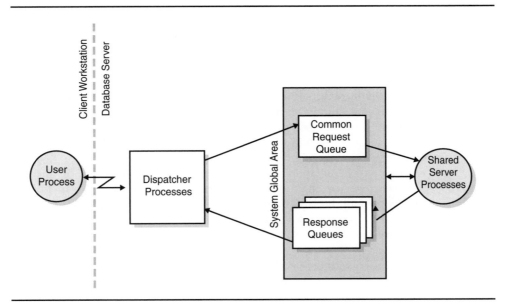

FIGURE 5-1. *Shared server architecture*

The dispatcher is the process to which the client process initially connects. The dispatcher process then directs multiple client requests to a common queue. Each dispatcher can handle multiple client connections concurrently. The connection between the client process (user process) and the dispatcher is permanent.

Each client connection is bound to a virtual circuit. A *virtual circuit* is a piece of shared memory used by the dispatcher for client database connection requests and responses. The virtual circuit will be placed in a common queue called the *request queue* by the dispatcher when the request arrives. The request queue is common to all dispatcher processes of an instance, and it resides in the system global area (SGA). The idle shared server processes pick up the virtual circuit from the common request queue on a first-in-first-out (FIFO) basis and make all necessary calls to the database to complete that request.

NOTE
All dispatchers share one common request queue.

When the server process completes the request, it places the response on the calling dispatcher's *response queue*. Each dispatcher has its own response queue in the SGA. The dispatcher then returns the completed request to the appropriate user process. This approach enables a small pool of server processes to serve a large number of clients. All the user processes targeting the shared servers must be connected through Oracle Net services.

NOTE
Users are connected to the same dispatcher for the duration of a session.

You can create multiple dispatcher processes for a single database instance. You should start with an optimal number of dispatcher processes initially and then add or remove dispatcher processes as required.

The information that constitutes the SGA and the program global area (PGA) is different in a shared server when compared to a dedicated server.

In dedicated server architecture, the SGA contains only the shared pool, and the PGA contains the stack space, the user session data, and the cursor state. The text and the parsed forms of all the SQL statements are stored in the SGA. The cursor state that contains run-time memory values for the SQL statement are in the PGA along with user session data. The PGA also contains local variables, which are part of the stack space.

In the shared server architecture, the SGA contains the shared pool, the cursor state, and the user session data. The PGA in the shared server architecture contains the stack space.

Configuring the Oracle Shared Server

In the following sections, we explain the server side and client side configuration in the shared server environment.

Server Configuration

In order to handle client requests in a shared server environment, the dispatchers must be registered with the listener during the database startup. This means that the listener must be active before the instance starts. You can specify the initialization parameters in the parameter file, which are required to configure the shared server environment.

The following database initialization parameters enable you to configure the database to operate in the shared server mode.

DISPATCHERS

You must set the DISPATCHERS parameter in the initialization parameter file, as shown in the following code, to enable a shared server:

```
DISPATCHERS="(attribute = value)"
```

The attributes can be specified in single or double quotes. The attribute names and their corresponding values are not case sensitive. One of the attributes, listed in Table 5-1, must be specified using the DISPATCHERS parameter.

Attribute	Description
ADDRESS (ADD or ADDR)	You can specify the network protocol address of the endpoint on which the dispatchers listens.
DESCRIPTION (DES or DESC)	You can specify the network description of the endpoint on which the dispatchers listens. This attribute includes the network protocol address. An example would be (DESCRIPTION= (ADDRESS= . . .)).
PROTOCOL (PRO or PROT)	You can specify the network protocol as shown in the following for which the dispatcher would generate a listening endpoint. An example would be (PROTOCOL=tcp).

TABLE 5-1. *Description of Attributes for the Dispatcher*

NOTE
You will need to specify one and only one of the attributes mentioned in Table 5-1 to configure dispatchers in a shared server environment.

The following attributes are optional and can be included with the DISPATCHERS parameter.

CONNECTIONS (CON or CONN)   The CONNECTIONS attribute enables you to specify the maximum number of network connections that must be enabled for every dispatcher. The default value for this attribute is 1024.

DISPATCHERS (DIS or DISP)   The DISPATCHERS attribute enables you to specify the initial number of dispatchers that must be started. The default value is 1.

LISTENER (LIS or LIST)   The LISTENER attribute enables you to specify an alias name for a listener or multiple listeners to which the PMON process registers dispatcher information. You must set the alias to a name that is resolved through the specified naming method. This attribute must be configured if the following conditions are met:

- When the local listener is configured to use the non-default TCP/IP port address of 1521

- When the listener is running on other than the local host

The listener alias is to be resolved through the specified naming method. For example, if the local naming method is used and you specify *support-listener* as the listener alias name, then the **tnsnames.ora** file must contain the following entry, shown in bold:

```
Support-listener =
  (DESCRIPTION =
    (ADDRESS=(PROTOCOL=tcp)(HOST=support-server)(PORT=1521))
```

NOTE
The LISTENER attribute overrides the REMOTE_LISTENER and the LOCAL_LISTENER initialization parameters.

MULTIPLEX (MUL or MULT) The MULTIPLEX attribute must be specified to enable the Connection Manager (CMAN) session multiplexing feature. If this parameter is set either to 1 or ON or YES or TRUE or BOTH, then the session multiplexing feature is enabled for both incoming and outgoing requests.

If this parameter is set to either 0 or OFF or NO or FALSE, then the session multiplexing is disabled for both incoming and outgoing requests. However, if this parameter is set to value OUT, then the session multiplexing is only enabled for outgoing network sessions.

POOL (POO) If the POOL attribute is specified, then the connection pooling is enabled for both incoming and outgoing idle network sessions. To enable connection pooling for an incoming idle connection, you must set the attribute to IN. To enable connection pooling for an outgoing network idle connection, you must set the attribute to OUT. You can also set a timeout for the incoming and outgoing network connection. To set the timeout values, you must specify the numeric value along with the IN and OUT parameters such as IN=20 and OUT=20. If the numeric value of a specified timeout is 0 or 1, then the default value of 10 ticks is used.

If the attribute is set to the value of ON, YES, TRUE, or BOTH, then connection pooling is set for both incoming and outgoing idle network connections. If the attribute is set to the value of NO, OFF, or FALSE, then connection pooling is disabled for both incoming and outgoing network connections.

SERVICE (SER or SERV) The SERVICE attribute specifies the service name or the multiple service names that the dispatchers register with the listeners. If you do not specify a value for this parameter, then the service name specified with the SERVICE_NAMES parameter is used.

SESSIONS (SES or SESS) The SESSIONS attribute enables you to specify the maximum number of network sessions that can be enabled for each dispatcher. Most operating systems (O/S) default to 16KB.

TICKS (TIC or TICK) A tick is the time taken for a message to be sent and to be processed, from a client to the database server or vice versa. This attribute specifies the length of a network tick in seconds. The value set is multiplied with the POOL timeout value to get the total connection pool timeout. The value for this attribute is platform and version-specific. For example, on Solaris using Oracle 9.0.1, the default is five seconds.

MAX_DISPATCHERS
The MAX_DISPATCHERS parameter enables you to specify the maximum number of dispatcher processes that can run concurrently. You can also start more dispatcher

processes as needed, but the number must not exceed the value specified using this parameter.

SHARED_SERVERS

The SHARED_SERVERS parameter specifies the number of shared server processes created at the Oracle instance startup. The number of initial shared server processes for a database system depends on the number of users concurrently connecting to database and the amount of resources required for each user. We recommend that you initially configure around ten shared server processes. Oracle automatically creates the additional shared server processes depending upon client requests. The number of shared server processes cannot exceed the value specified by the MAX_SHARED_SERVERS parameter.

MAX_SHARED_SERVERS

The MAX_SHARED_SERVERS parameter specifies the maximum number of shared server processes that can run concurrently. This parameter must be set to an appropriate value so that it meets the requirement during highest activity. The number of shared server processes that can be created ranges between the values of the initialization parameters SHARED_SERVERS and MAX_SHARED_SERVERS. To know the details of the maximum number of shared server processes started, query the view V$SHARED_SERVER_MONITOR. As queuing of requests should be minimized, this parameter should be set to a high value.

CIRCUITS

The CIRCUITS parameter specifies the total number of virtual circuits that are available for inbound and outbound network sessions.

SHARED_SERVER_SESSIONS

The SHARED_SERVER_SESSIONS parameter specifies the total number of shared server user sessions enabled. You must use this parameter to allow users to establish dedicated server connections.

LARGE_POOL_SIZE

The LARGE_POOL_SIZE parameter specifies the size in bytes of the large pool allocation heap. The session memory for all shared server connections is allocated in the shared pool. You can configure the large pool area instead of using shared pool for shared server connections by using this parameter. Configuring this parameter prevents the user global area (UGA) from causing contention in the shared pool area of the SGA. The large pool stores UGA information, such as the session-state, variables, PL/SQL, and the sort area of the sessions that are connected to a shared server. The large pool must be sized appropriately by obtaining statistics from the dynamic performance view V$SYSSTAT.

Configuring the Shared Server Processes

In the shared server environment, the shared server processes are responsible to service client requests. The SHARED_SERVERS initialization parameter specifies the number of shared server processes that can be started during the instance startup. Based on client requests, Oracle dynamically balances the load across the shared server processes. Oracle automatically spawns a shared server process if no process is available for a client connection request. The shared server processes will be spawned until the number reaches the value specified by the initialization parameter MAX_SHARED_SERVERS.

The MAX_SHARED_SERVERS parameter is a static parameter. The value for this parameter cannot be altered dynamically and requires that you restart the database instance to affect the changes. In contrast, the value for the parameters DISPATCHERS and SHARED_SERVERS can be set using the ALTER SYSTEM command. On execution of this statement, Oracle terminates all the idle shared server processes. If the shared server processes become idle and the shared server processes are more than the minimum limit defined, then Oracle will terminate these idle processes. If you dynamically set the SHARED_SERVERS parameter to the value 0, the shared server is temporarily disabled. The following command dynamically sets the shared server processes:

```
SQL> ALTER SYSTEM SET SHARED_SERVERS = 2;
```

NOTE
You must possess the ALTER SYSTEM privilege to change the parameters DISPATCHER and SHARED_SERVERS.

You can allocate a dispatcher to exclusively accept clients requesting for a specific service. This feature enables you to allocate more resources for mission critical requests. In the following example, we show you how to configure two dispatchers in the initialization parameter file:

```
SERVICE_NAMES=sales.Oramasters.com
INSTANCE_NAME=sales
DISPATCHERS="(PROTOCOL=tcp)"
DISPATCHERS="(PROTOCOL=tcp)(SERVICE=support.oramasters.com)"
```

In the previous example, the first dispatcher services clients requesting the service sales.oramasters.com. The other dispatcher services only clients requesting support.oramasters.com.

Configuring Dispatchers in the Shared Server Environment

The DISPATCHERS parameter controls the number of dispatchers that can be started at the instance startup, but you must ensure that these entries specified in the initialization parameter file are adjacent to each other.

The initial number of dispatchers, which can be configured for an instance, varies from one O/S to another. To estimate the number of dispatchers, you must be aware of the O/S limitation for the possible connections that can be established with each process. The desired performance from the database and the number of connections required for each network protocol should be considered. The instance must be able to provide as many connections as there are concurrent users on the database system.

During instance startup, you can calculate the initial number of dispatchers to create using the following formula:

$$\text{Initial number Of Dispatchers} = \frac{\text{Maximum number of concurrent sessions}}{\text{Connections for each dispatcher}}$$

Note that the number of dispatchers would be the highest whole number.

You can force the IP address and port number used for the dispatchers. The settings, as shown in the following code, specify the IP address of the host system on which the five dispatchers listen:

```
DISPATCHERS="(ADDRESS=(PROTOCOL=tcp)(HOST= 208.59.199.25))
(DISPATCHERS=5)"
```

NOTE
Oracle Net dynamically selects the TCP/IP port for the dispatcher.

You can also force the exact location of the dispatcher to listen using the PORT attribute. An example is shown in the following code:

```
DISPATCHERS="(ADDRESS=(PROTOCOL=tcp)
(HOST=208.59.199.25)(PORT=5000))(DISPATCHERS=5)"
DISPATCHERS="(ADDRESS=(PROTOCOL=tcp)
(HOST=208.59.199.25)(PORT=5001))(DISPATCHERS=5)"
```

Connection Pooling Connection pooling is a resource utilization feature that can be used to maximize the utilization of the resources by minimizing the number of physical network connections to the shared server. The dispatcher shares a set of its connections with multiple client processes. This feature is highly beneficial in environments where the dispatchers have a very high idle or search time. Whenever the system load increases and dispatcher throughput is maximized, instead of adding more dispatchers, you can consider enabling the connection pooling feature to support more users.

Without connection pooling, when the maximum number of sessions is reached for a dispatcher, the new client request must wait until an existing session is disconnected. When the connection pooling feature is enabled, the incoming session request must wait only until any one of the existing sessions becomes idle. When the session becomes idle, Oracle will temporarily disconnect the idle session and enable the new session to use that connection. When the idle session wants to perform some tasks, it will reconnect whenever a session becomes idle.

You can configure connection pooling by setting the DISPATCHERS parameter in the **init.ora** file with the POOL attribute. Here's an example:

```
DISPATCHERS = "(PROTOCOL=TCP)(POOL=ON)(TICK=1)"
```

In the previous statement, the optional attribute POOL enables the Oracle Net connection-pooling feature. The attribute TICK is set to one second.

Multiplexing While using CMAN to handle the client processes, you can enable the multiplexing feature to maintain connections from multiple users to individual dispatchers. A single connection is established from the CMAN process to a dispatcher. CMAN uses the shared connections to handle the communication from the users to the dispatcher. This feature maximizes the usage of the user to dispatcher connections, and it is also useful for multiplexing the database link connections between the dispatchers. You can enable the multiplexing feature as shown in the following code:

```
DISPATCHERS="(PROTOCOL=TCP)(MULTIPLEX=ON)"
```

Client Configuration

You can configure a particular client to always use a dispatcher in the shared server environment. To enable this you must set the attribute SERVER=SHARED in the CONNECT_DATA portion of the connect descriptor, as shown in the following code:

```
Support=
(DESCRIPTION=
  (ADDRESS=(PROTOCOL=tcp)(HOST=support-server)(PORT=1521))
  (CONNECT_DATA=
    (SERVICE_NAME=support.oramasters.com)
    (server=shared)))
```

NOTE
In the previous situation, if the dispatcher is not available at the server side, then the client connection request is rejected.

In the shared server environment, you can configure the client to use a dedicated server process instead of a shared server process. This can be done using one of two methods as described in the following steps:

1. You can specify SERVER=DEDICATED in the CONNECT_DATA section as shown in the following code:

```
support=
(DESCRIPTION=
  (ADDRESS=(PROTOCOL=tcp)(HOST=support-server)(PORT=1521))
  (CONNECT_DATA=
    (SERVICE_NAME=support.oramasters.com)
    (SERVER=dedicated)))
```

NOTE
SRVR is also acceptable as an alternative to the SERVER parameter.

2. In the client profile, which is the **sqlnet.ora** file, we can configure the parameter USE_DEDICATED_SERVER=ON. This adds or overwrites the SERVER=DEDICATED to the CONNECT_DATA section of the connect descriptor the client uses.

Shared Server Related Dictionary Views

When you configure the shared server, you should monitor several parameters to determine the best settings for your environment. You can check the shared server configuration using the **listener control** utility's SERVICES command for the listener process. To obtain information about the shared server configuration and to monitor the shared server, you should be familiar with the following data dictionary views.

V$DISPATCHER

You can use the V$DISPATCHER view to list information about the dispatcher processes associated with the instance. The information includes the shared server process name, network address, status, various usage statistics, and index number. A sample select statement on this view is shown in the following code:

```
SQL> SELECT NAME, NETWORK FROM V$DISPATCHER;

NAME    NETWORK
------- -------------------------------------------------------------
D000    (ADDRESS=(PROTOCOL=tcp)(HOST=ormtest.india.oramasters.com)(P
        ORT=1227))

D001    (DESCRIPTION=(ADDRESS=(PROTOCOL=tcp)(HOST=ormtest.india.oram
        asters.com)(PORT=1229))(PRESENTATION=oracle.aurora.server.Gi
        opServer

D002    (DESCRIPTION=(ADDRESS=(PROTOCOL=tcp)(HOST=ormtest.india.oram
        asters.com)(PORT=1230))(PRESENTATION=oracle.aurora.server.SG
        iopServe
```

The dispatchers are identified by unique names. For example, if you want to shut down the dispatcher d001, you should run the following SQL statement:

```
ALTER SYSTEM SHUTDOWN IMMEDIATE 'D001';
```

V$DISPATCHER_RATE

You can use the V$DISPATCHER_RATE view to list the rate statistics for the dispatcher processes. It gives the current, average, and maximum dispatcher statistics for several categories. The columns displaying the current statistics are prefixed with CUR_; the columns displaying the average statistics are prefixed with AVG_; and the columns displaying the maximum statistics since collection began are prefixed with MAX_. You can review the dispatcher performance by comparing the current values with the maximum values obtained from the V$DISPATCHER_RATE view. For example, if the current and average values are significantly below the maximum recorded, then you should consider reducing the dispatchers.

V$QUEUE

The V$QUEUE contains information on the shared server message queues in the instance. It gives the process, the wait time, and total wait time in the queue. Steadily increasing wait times in the *requests* queue indicate contention for shared servers. You should monitor the V$QUEUE, V$DISPATCHER, and V$DISPATCHER_RATE views if reports indicate that the load on the dispatcher processes is high. If so, you can add additional dispatcher processes to route user requests. If the load is very low, then you can improve system performance by reducing the number of dispatchers. Note that you can add new dispatchers using the ALTER SYTEM statement.

V$SHARED_SERVER

You can use the V$SHARED_SERVER view to list information on the shared server processes. For example, you can determine how many shared servers are currently running by issuing the following query:

```
SQL> select count(*)"Current shared server process" from v$shared_server
where status!='quit';
Current shared server process
--------------------------------------
                   6
```

V$CIRCUIT

You can use the V$CIRCUIT view to list information about virtual circuits. If there is a problem with specific process in the database, you can use the V$CIRCUIT view to get the information for a specific user. The SADDR column of the V$CIRCUIT view provides the session address.

V$SHARED_SERVER_MONITOR

You can use the V$SHARED_SERVER_MONITOR view to tune the shared server. This view displays information of the highest number of virtual circuits in use, shared server sessions in use, the total number of shared servers started and stopped, and the highest number of servers running at one time since the instance started.

V$SGA

You can use the V$SGA view to obtain information regarding the SGA. It specifies the SGA fixed size, variable size, database buffers, and redo buffers values in bytes.

V$SGASTAT

You can use the V$SGASTAT view to obtain detailed statistical information on the SGA including the shared pool, large pool, and Java pool.

V$SHARED_POOL_RESERVED

You can use the V$SHARED_POOL_RESERVED view to list statistics to help tune the reserved pool and the space within the shared pool.

Chapter Questions

1. **Which configuration is best suited for an OLTP environment, where users applications experience a considerable amount of idle time?**

   A. Dedicated server

   B. Shared server

   C. Two-task architecture

   D. None of the above

2. **Which of the following files can be used to configure connection pooling in the shared server environment?**

   A. init.ora

   B. sqlnet.ora

   C. tnsnames.ora

   D. services.ora

   E. listener.ora

3. **The maximum number of concurrent sessions for your server is estimated to be 200, and the connections per dispatcher are ten. What initial number of dispatchers would you start?**

   A. 10

   B. 20

   C. 50

   D. 200

   E. 2,000

4. **Consider that the number of sessions connected to a dispatcher is currently less than what the dispatcher has been configured for. If a client connection request arrives with connection pooling enabled, how would the request be handled?**

   A. The session request is immediately handled.

   B. The session request is not immediately handled.

   C. The session request would wait for the dispatcher to temporarily disconnect an idle connection and then redirect it.

   D. The session request waits for the dispatcher to permanently disconnect an idle connection and then establish a connection for the session.

5. **What does the following SQL statement indicate?**

   ```
   SQL> ALTER SYSTEM SET DISPATCHERS='(PROTOCOL=TCP)(DISPATCHERS=10)';
   ```

   A. The current number of dispatchers now is ten, and the protocol is TCP.

   B. The maximum number of the dispatchers that can be running at any time is ten, and the protocol is TCP.

   C. The protocol of all the dispatchers in now TCP, and the minimum number of dispatchers that can be running at any time is now ten.

   D. The default protocol for all the existing dispatchers plus any dispatcher added in the future is TCP, and the maximum number of dispatchers that can be running at any time is now ten.

6. **Consider that a dispatcher has reached its maximum load. If a connection request were received, how would the session request be handled with connection pooling enabled in the shared server environment?**

   A. A new connection is spawned as the request arrives.

   B. An existing idle connection is redirected for the request.

   C. The session must wait and then resend the request.

   D. The session waits for the dispatcher to temporarily disconnect an idle connection and then establishes a new session.

   E. The session waits for the dispatcher to temporarily disconnect an idle connection and then establishes a connection for the session.

7. **You need to start more dispatcher processes. Which one of the following limitations must you consider? (Choose two.)**

   A. The number of dispatchers cannot exceed the value specified by the DISPATCHERS parameter.

   B. The database must be shutdown prior to adding or removing dispatchers.

   C. The number of dispatchers cannot exceed the value of MAX_DISPTAHCERS.

   D. Each dispatcher to be started must be associated with a separate service.

   E. The protocols of the newly started dispatcher must be defined in the **init.ora** file.

8. **Which of the following parameters must be specified to define the number of dispatchers that need to be started?**

   A. MAX_DISPATCHERS

   B. DISPATCHERS

   C. MIN_DISPATCHERS

   D. SHARED_SERVERS

9. **Which of the following listener control commands would you use to validate that the dispatcher is registered with the listener?**

   A. SERVICES

   B. LISTENER

   C. DISPATCHER

   D. CONNECTION

10. **If the LISTENER attribute in the initialization file is configured, then which of the following files should have the corresponding entry?**

    A. init.ora

    B. listener.ora

    C. tnsnames.ora

    D. service.ora

Chapter Answers

1. B.   Shared Server

Explanation   It is beneficial to configure the database in shared server mode for an OLTP environment. In a shared server environment, a client can either use a dispatcher to establish a connection with a shared server or can prefer to establish a dedicated server connection.

2. A.   **init.ora**

Explanation   The DISPATCHERS parameter in the **init.ora** file is used to configure connection pooling in shared server environment.

3. B.   20

Explanation   The formula used to estimate the initial number of dispatchers is

$$\text{Initial number of dispatchers} = \frac{\text{Maximum number of concurrent users}}{\text{Connections per dispatcher}}$$

4. A.   The session request is immediately handled.

Explanation   When a connection request is received, it is handled immediately if the maximum number of sessions for a dispatcher is less than configured. If not, the session waits for the dispatcher to temporarily disconnect an idle connection and then establishes a connection for the session.

5. A.   The starting number of dispatchers now is ten, and the protocol is TCP.

Explanation   The PROTOCOL attribute specifies which protocol is to be used by a dispatcher (in this case, TCP/IP). The DISPATCHERS attribute specifies the initial number of dispatchers started.

6. E.   The session waits for the dispatcher to temporarily disconnect an idle connection and then establishes a connection for the session.

Explanation   When a connection request is received, it is handled immediately if the maximum number of sessions for a dispatcher is less than configured. If not, the session waits for the dispatcher to temporarily disconnect an idle connection and then establishes a connection for the session.

7. C and E.   The number of dispatchers cannot exceed the value of MAX_DISPTAHCERS, and the protocols of the newly started dispatcher must be defined in the **init.ora** file.

Explanation   If the **init.ora** file starts dispatchers for a particular protocol(s), you cannot start dispatchers for a different protocol(s) later unless you change the init.ora file and restart the database. New dispatchers may be started if their total number does not exceed the value specified by the MAX_DISPATCHERS parameter.

   8. B.   DISPATCHERS

Explanation   To specify the number of dispatchers that must be initially started during the database startup, you must set the DISPATCHERS parameter in the initialization parameter file.

   9. A.   Services

Explanation   The listener control command SERVICES verifies that the dispatcher has registered with the listener or not.

   10. C.   **tnsnames.ora**

Explanation   The **tnsnames.ora** file is used to resolve the listener address specified in the initialization file.

PART

II

Backup and Recovery

CHAPTER
6

Backup and Recovery
Overview

BAs who prepare for the OCP examination are often confused about learning backup and recovery procedures with the *Recovery Manager* (RMAN) tool provided by Oracle. Note that RMAN is just a tool that is provided by Oracle for you to use while backing up a database or restoring and recovering a database. However, it is you, the DBA, that has to design a backup strategy based on the business rules at your site. Similarly, should the system experience a failure, it is you who should know what is the quickest way to recover the database.

Here's a simple example. Let's say you want to take insurance on your car. You need to know what kind of insurance you want, what deductibles you want to pay, what kind of coverage you need, and so on. However, when you insure your car, you go to an insurance agent who gets the job done for you. In this example, the insurance agent is RMAN that performs the kind of backup you need or the recovery operation that you want. Although you can also directly work with the insurance company, it is beneficial for you to go with an insurance agent who understands the inner workings and complexity of the insurance sector. Similarly, user-managed backups and recovery are possible if you don't want to use RMAN.

NOTE
Using RMAN for backup and recovery procedures is also called server-managed backup and recovery, as opposed to user-managed backup and recovery.

Although backup and recovery are very crucial subjects, similar to your car insurance, these are possibly the easiest subjects to master and get ahead in the OCP examination. If you understand the basic concepts of backup and recovery, and how to use RMAN to obtain results, you can gain points quickly in the examination.

In this part of the book, we have a number of chapters that closely follow the blueprint of the OCP DBA Fundamentals II. We start with the concepts of instance and media recovery structures and show you how you can take backups using user-managed mode as well as using RMAN. Similarly, we discuss with examples how to perform a complete recovery versus an incomplete one. We provide in-depth details on the maintenance of RMAN as well as the new features of Oracle9*i* that relate to backup and recovery. By the end of this part, you should be fairly familiar with the backup and recovery procedures of Oracle.

In this chapter, we will give you an overview of Oracle's backup and recovery procedures, which include

- Classification of failures
- Basics of database backup, restoration, and recovery

- Backup and recovery strategies
- Disaster recovery plan
- Oracle's high-availability features

The terms *backup* and *recovery* unveil the most important responsibilities of a database administrator. They are the most crucial aspects of database administration that you need to understand before operating the database, just as the most important part of driving your car is to insure it. Consider a situation in which a database is inoperable due to a crash with no possible way to recover it. This would have a devastating affect on the business, which could lead to loss of data, loss of revenue, and, needless to point out, loss of customers and maybe even losing the business. Performing regular backups and recovering the database during failures are key aspects of database administration. Not only should you worry about "What is the quickest way to recover?" but you should also think "How can crashes be prevented?" This proactive thinking differentiates a good DBA from an exceptional DBA. Organizations operating a single database or multiple databases storing terabytes or even petabytes of data have a common goal: *the need to backup business-critical data and protect themselves from disasters by developing a sound and tested backup and recovery plan.*

One of the fundamental rules of relational databases is that committed transactions must survive failures. This is known as *transaction durability.* Oracle is designed to support the Atomicity, Consistency, Isolation, and Durability (ACID) properties. The ACID properties and their definitions are as follows:

- **Atomicity**   During recovery, applying the complete transaction or not applying the transaction. Oracle can never apply part of a transaction.
- **Consistency**   Viewing and maintaining a consistent state.
- **Isolation**   Private view of the database state.
- **Durability**   Surviving failures for transaction durability.

NOTE
Oracle manages the recovery of data without any user intervention while performing instance *or* crash *recovery. This is internally managed by applying appropriate redo and undo information. This makes it highly impossible to lose data during instance failure, thereby supporting the last property of the ACID properties.*

Classification of Failures

A *failure* can be defined as an incapability of a system to perform a required function within specified limits. A database system has a possibility of crashing due to system or hardware failure, resulting in downtime. The different types of failures are discussed in this section.

Statement Failure

A *statement failure* is defined as the incapability of Oracle to execute a *Structured Query Language* (SQL) operation. The failures pertaining to the statement are dealt by the Oracle server, which responds with an appropriate error to the user. Some of the causes of statement failures are listed here:

- A logical error in the front-end application, such as selecting a table that doesn't exist or Oracle Forms timing out.

- An invalid value entered by the user through a record, where the value fails to fulfill the integrity constraints or does not match the specified datatype.

- A user tries to create or update an object on a specified tablespace where he/she lacks storage space.

- A DBA tries to shut down a database without connecting as SYSDBA. A very simple error, yet one I think every DBA would do at least once in his DBA life.

NOTE
During a statement failure, the statement will be rolled back, but the transaction remains consistent and intact.

Process Failure

A *process failure* is due to the abnormal termination of a process. If the failure occurs with the user process, it disconnects a user from operating on the database, though other sessions connected to the database continue to operate. The most likely cause of process failure could be one of the following:

- The user performed an abnormal disconnection of the session by abruptly closing the window without gracefully logging out.

- The user session abnormally terminated, because the DBA decided to shut the database using the abort option.

■ A software bug; for example, the user program raised an address exception termination of the session since the application was not designed to encounter that exception.

Oracle handles these types of failures by using a background process called PMON. PMON identifies the terminated session and resets the status of the active transaction table, releases locks, and removes the process ID from the list of active processes. In general, a process failure usually has a lesser impact on the database as it pertains to a single user. However, if the process happens to be a background process of Oracle, the impact may be severe as you have to shut down and start up the database again.

Instance Failure

Instance failure occurs when an Oracle instance (SGA and the background processes) is unable to function normally due to a problem. Instance failure may occur due to problems like hardware failures, such as a power outage, or a software problem, such as an O/S crash. During an instance failure, Oracle fails to update the database files since there is no link between the Oracle instance and the physical structure (database files). Instance failure will also occur when one of the background processes such as LGWR, CKPT, or DBW*n* dies. The background processes will cause the instance to terminate if they detect write errors on the disk.

Human Error

Human error, a leading cause of failures and data corruption, includes errors by an operator, user, database administrator, or system administrator. Human errors are something that can be eliminated by proper training procedures for DBAs and users. These errors can be very trivial or have a catastrophic impact on your business. For example, an accidental operation performed by a user such as *delete table rows* or *drop table*, where the data lost is vital for future database operations, could have a catastrophic impact on the business. In such situations, an incomplete recovery would be an option in order to recover your database. Oracle supports various point-in-time recovery (PITR) operations to overcome human errors.

Media Failure

A *media failure* is when a hardware failure occurs and the whole or a part of the physical structure of the database is inaccessible to perform read or write operations. An example would be a physical device failure. When media failure occurs, usually media recovery is required. Media recovery may require the archived log files and online redo log files.

Network Failure

When the database system is based on client-server technology, to access the database a user must establish a session through the network. The network could either be a Local Area Network (LAN) or a Wide Area Network (WAN). Network failures such as aborted phone connections and network communication lapses can hinder the routine operations of a database system. In the client-server era, these failures usually occurred in an intranet environment. With the extensive use of the Internet, a generic network failure can occur anywhere on the Internet. A typical example would be an undelivered email due to the nonavailability of a Domain Name Server (DNS). With Oracle adapting the Internet, you need to reevaluate your single point of failures carefully. For example, if you use iSQL using a Virtual Private Network (VPN) on the Internet to monitor your customer's database remotely, you need to design your backup strategy carefully to overcome network failures.

Basics of Database Backup, Restoration, and Recovery

In this section, you will learn the basic concepts related to backup, restoration, and recovery of the database. Various types of recovery options are also briefly discussed.

What Is a Backup?

A *backup* is a representative copy of data. Backups are divided into two categories: *physical backups* and *logical backups*. Physical backups are copies of the physical database files. These physical copies include important parts of a database structure, such as the control file, the redo logs, and the data files.

Logical backups store data pertaining to the database objects. They are often used to export data between databases or to reorganize data. The backups performed, either physical or logical, are redundant images of the data that are useful to safeguard against unexpected outages such as software failure, hardware failure, human errors, and environmental disasters by providing a procedure to restore the original data and recover in a certain time.

What Is Restore? backed up dataples

A *restore* operation will bring the backed-up data files back on to the disk. You will usually do a restore operation if you need to recover a database. In the user-managed recovery mode, you need to manually restore the data files and the archived redo logs by using Operating System (OS) copy commands. If you use RMAN, it will automatically restore the required database files for you. Restoration of a consistent backup is vital for the successful recovery of a database. For example, when you take a hot backup, the backed-up data files, along with the archived redo log files that were created between the BEGIN BACKUP and END BACKUP commands, provide a consistent backup.

What Is Recovery? ~redo logs applied To restored datafiles

Recovery is the process of reading the redo records from the redo logs and applying them to the restored data files. The redo logs contain redo records, which are changes or modifications done to the database. During recovery, Oracle recognizes the redo logs generated after the physical backup of the database is taken and then performs recovery. The internal operation of recovery involves two discrete Oracle operations:

- Rolling the restored data files forward by applying the redo records from the redo logs.

- Rolling back any uncommitted transactions and restoring the database to its original state. Oracle reads the rollback segments to determine which transactions need to be recovered (rolled back). Therefore, this operation is also called *transaction recovery*.

How Does Recovery Operation Work?

In all possible recovery operations, Oracle sequentially applies the redo records from the redo log files to the Oracle data blocks. The information pertaining to the system change number (SCN) stored in the datafile headers is verified by Oracle from the control file to ascertain whether recovery is required. Recovery, as described earlier, involves two discrete steps to be performed: rolling forward by applying the redo records to the appropriate data blocks and rolling back any uncommitted transactions. Oracle initially determines the changes to be applied to the required blocks and then performs the change. The recovery is done through the SGA.

The following example shows how an uncommitted transaction is rolled back during transaction recovery (the rollback phase). Let us consider that a user issued an UPDATE statement. This starts a transaction and a transaction ID is given by Oracle to this transaction internally. The UPDATE statement is parsed and executed. To perform this operation, the old image is registered in the *server-managed undo* segments and the new image is recorded in the *data segment.* These updates initially take place in the memory structure, the db block buffers. Assume that the server crashes due to a power failure before the changes could be saved to the disk. The transaction stays uncommitted since the user has neither explicitly specified a commit nor instigated an implicit commit.

When the power is restored and the database instance starts again, as part of crash recovery, Oracle rolls forward by applying the redo records to the data blocks from the redo log files. But it then rolls back the transaction since the rollback segment stores the information about this transaction as uncommitted. This leads to restoration of the old value in the data block. In short, all changes to all segments are done in the db buffer cache, and they may or may not be written to the data files later depending on whether the transaction commits or not before failure.

What Are the Types of Recovery?

used Rman fixed automatically by oracle

Oracle recovery can be one of the three basic types: *block recovery*, *thread* (crash recovery) *recovery*, or *media recovery*. Block recovery is an internal mechanism of Oracle and

Ora-01578 blk corruption

doesn't need the DBA's intervention. Thread recovery is done by Oracle as part of crash recovery or instance recovery. Instance recovery performed by the Oracle server is only possible when the database is operating on multiple instances (Real Application Clusters, previously known as the Oracle Parallel Server) where one instance discovers the failure of another instance and recovers it. If you have a single instance, then thread recovery is done as part of crash recovery when you start the instance. Although instance recovery is automatically handled by Oracle without any DBA intervention, crash recovery is done in response to the DBA's STARTUP OPEN command. Media recovery, on the other hand, requires the DBA to issue an Oracle-specific recovery command to perform either a complete database recovery or an incomplete database recovery.

What Are the Various Recovery Options?

The recovery option you choose depends on the type of failure. Oracle provides you with various options for recovering the database. The very first question you need to ask yourself is, "Can I completely recover the database or do I need to do an incomplete recovery?" If you have all the appropriate data files from the backup and all the archived redo log files, it is possible for you to perform a complete recovery. With a complete recovery, you can either recover a specific data file, tablespace, or the entire database. Typically, you need to do an incomplete recovery if you don't have one or more redo log files, which will result in loss of data. If you need to perform an incomplete recovery of the database, you have several options. They are described in this section.

NOTE
Many DBAs think that incomplete recovery means recovering only part of the database. Please note that complete recovery means no loss of data, whereas incomplete recovery means loss of data, which should be a deliberate decision on the part of the DBA.

Point-in-Time Recovery

Point-in-time recovery (PITR) performs a recovery on the database until a specified time. It is widely used to overcome human errors and physical corruptions. Here's an example:

```
SQL> RECOVER DATABASE UNTIL TIME '2001-06-15:13:55:00';
```

Note that in this example, the database would be recovered until 1:55 P.M. on the 15th of June 2001.

Tablespace Point-in-Time Recovery — *data inconsistency*

Tablespace point-in-time recovery (TSPITR) performs a recovery of one or more tablespaces until a specified point in time that is different from the rest of the database. TSPITR can be used to subdue errors relating to tablespace corruptions. TSPITR with Oracle's Transportable-Tablespace feature can be used to restore a lost tablespace. You need to understand the ramifications of using this method as you may induce data inconsistency at an application level. *recover tbs until time '2001-06-15:13:55:00';*

Cancel-Based Recovery *; incomplete recovery*

This is the most commonly used incomplete recovery option. Issue the CANCEL command to terminate a recovery session after applying a limited number of redo log files. After a database crash, if the online redo log files are inaccessible or one of them is corrupted, and you want to recover up to the end of the last good log file, cancel-based recovery is necessary. Here's an example:

```
SQL> RECOVER DATABASE UNTIL CANCEL;
```

Note that in this example, the database is recovered until the last consistent available log file.

Change-Based Recovery

Oracle recovers the database until the specified System Change Number (SCN) through change-based recovery. This is not a normal procedure for recovering the database unless the user identifies the appropriate SCN that the Oracle server has generated internally. This method is usually performed on distributed databases and when one of the databases needs recovery. This option is used to recover the database to a transaction-consistent state. For example,

```
SQL> RECOVER DATABASE UNTIL CHANGE 129782;
```

Note that in this example, all SCNs up to 129781 will be applied.

Note: After incomplete recovery, must use resetlogs

Incomplete recovery needs the database to be opened with the RESETLOGS option, and the database would be thereafter referred to as the *new incarnation*. Opening the database with the RESETLOGS option tells Oracle to discard the redo before the RESETLOGS point. This prevents the Oracle server from applying the redo before RESETLOGS in future recovery operations. Since the existing backups are no longer usable for recovery after the RESETLOGS point, you should make a whole database backup immediately after the resetlog operation.

Recovery from Human Errors Using LogMiner

Oracle provides the *flashback query* feature and the LogMiner utility to recover data from human errors. You can use these features to recover data that has been accidentally deleted or has been overwritten through frequent updates. Refer to the LogMiner Utility section at the end of this chapter for more details.

Int Q: what is your bkup & recovery strategy

Backup and Recovery Strategies

One of the first steps involved in the creation of a database is the planning of the backup and recovery strategy, which would help the DBA protect the database against potential failures. The database administrator needs to develop the strategies involved in maintaining the database availability and protect it against any data loss. Some of the main considerations include the recovery time, log file sizes, and backup procedures among other issues.

The strategy you develop needs approval from the higher cadre of the management. You would normally be responsible for any ramifications derived from an improper strategy. You should ask yourself the following questions before planning a backup and recovery strategy:

- *mission critical* (1) Is it a 24 × 7 × 365 mission-critical database system, where availability is highly valued? If not a 24 × 7 × 365 shop, what is the mission-critical period (example, 9 to 7 only on weekdays)?

- *revenue loss* (2) What would be the revenue loss for the company due to non-availability of the database during a specific time period?

- *management understand* (3) Does the management understand the significance of regularly performing backups and proactively preparing recovery procedures? If not, how do I educate them?

- *system resources* (4) What system resources are required to plan a backup and recovery strategy at my site, which includes a test database?

These details set the standards for a thorough analysis of the business, operations, and technical requisites needed to derive the backup and recovery strategy. In this section, we discuss the business, operational, and technical considerations while designing a backup strategy.

Basic Principles

The best approach to defining a strategy is to anticipate database crashes by planning and taking proactive measures. Though defining a backup and recovery strategy involves an extensive amount of research to figure out various intricacies, the basic principles follow these simple steps as an approach to the larger picture:

1. Multiplexing the control files.

2. Multiplexing the online redo log files.

3. Operating the database in ARCHIVELOG mode and defining multiple destinations for the archiver to generate duplicate copies of the same redo log files.

4. Performing frequent backups of the physical database files and storing them at remote locations. Storing the files at remote locations is a precautionary step against natural calamities, thereby reducing the effort and time involved in reconstructing the database.

5. Taking logical backups of specific vital tables of the database.

6. Exploring the possibilities of setting up a disaster recovery site.

Business Considerations

Database downtime can have a tremendous impact on your organization's business. The nonavailability of the database can lead to loss of revenue, loss of productivity, and lost opportunities. Depending on the business rules, you should evaluate the consequences of any loss due to downtime on the business and take proactive measures in making decisions to minimize downtime or data loss. Following are two of the most important business considerations:

Mean Time to Recover (MTTR)

The average time taken to fully recover a database from a failure is termed as the *Mean Time to Recover* (MTTR). The MTTR depends on the following factors:

- Time to detect the outage

- Time to decide upon a course of action as a remedy

- Time to perform the course of action

- Time to verify the course of action and notify the end-users of the successful completion of recovery

Some systems have MTTR, which can be measured in scant seconds and at some instances even zero, meaning that they have redundant components that take over the available secondary component when the primary encounters failure. Other alternatives may take minutes, hours, or even days to completely recover databases depending on the recovery strategy. If you provide online services to your customers on the Internet or if you are an Application Service Provider, keeping your Web site and Web applications up and running is very crucial. In this case, you need to carefully determine the MTTR, as the requirement could be a few minutes. On the other hand, if you have an analytical data mart, you might have the luxury of having an MTTR, which could be a few hours. The backup and recovery strategy developed should ensure that the database is unavailable during any failures for the least amount of time.

Mean Time Between Failures (MTBF)

The average time a system functions between two consecutive outages is termed as the *Mean Time Between Failures* (MTBF). Proper hardware protection by implementing Redundant Arrays of Inexpensive Disks (RAID) is very popular today for building fault tolerance and improving data availability, thereby reducing the mean time between failures.

NOTE
Various levels of RAID (RAID 0 to RAID 7) are available and they can be implemented in different ways (software or hardware). You can configure your disks to one or a combination of the RAID levels to best suit your requirements for availability and performance.

As MTTR decreases and MTBF increases, the database reaches the availability figure closer to 100 percent. The more complex a system is, the more vulnerable it is to failure. Figure 6-1 gives a pictorial representation of MTTR and MTBF of a database. The availability of the database system can be calculated as follows:

```
Availability = MTBF / (MTBF + MTTR)
```

Operational Considerations

You need to figure out operationally which is the best way for you to back up your system. As previously discussed, Oracle provides two main options: physical backups and logical backups. When you copy the physical data files of the database, it is a physical backup. You can use RMAN to do this or you can use the

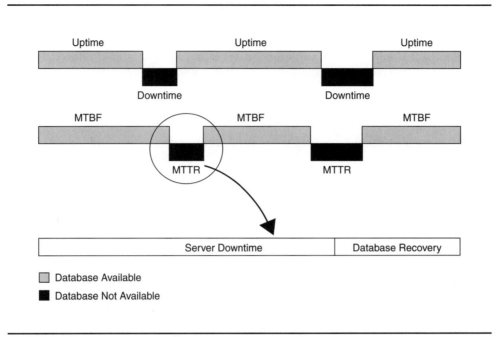

FIGURE 6-1.   *MTTR and MTBF of a database*

user-managed mode and copy it yourself at the OS level. To take a logical backup, you need to use Oracle's export utility. The export utility uses SQL for taking a backup of your data.

Although it has its own advantages (such as not propagating physical corruptions), logical backups are usually slower than physical backups and should be used to copy specific, important tables of the database. Although the export utility should be part of your backup strategy, it is a poor backup strategy to do logical backups alone without any physical backups. Some DBAs with small databases use export as their primary means of backup because it is easy to do online. It is very important to note that logical backups, unlike physical backups, cannot be used to recover data during media failure.

NOTE
The export utility must not be used as a substitute for performing physical database backups.

Recovery Manager (RMAN) Backups

As discussed earlier, Oracle RMAN is an automated backup and recovery utility. Oracle recommends using RMAN to perform physical backups of the database. RMAN supports command-line interfaces as well as graphical user interfaces (GUIs) using the Oracle Enterprise Manager (OEM). Using RMAN has numerous benefits, such as the following:

- Automated backup, restore, and recovery operations.

- It enables backup and restoration of the entire database or individual structures, such as control files, data files, tablespaces, or archive log files.

- Backup and recovery can be performed while the database is open or closed.

- Support for two types of backups: image copies or backup sets.

- Intelligent archive log management for both backup and recovery.

- Detection of corrupt blocks and block media recovery.

- *Tablespace-point-in-time recovery* (TSPITR) support.

- Omission of empty blocks during backup for optimization.

- No extra redo is generated during online backups.

Some of the advanced features like block media recovery, backup optimization, and restore optimization can only be implemented through RMAN. Oracle recommends the use of RMAN over user-managed backup and recovery procedures.

Operating System (OS) Level Backups

You can back up the database at the OS level using OS-specific commands. However, you need to manually document the backup information such as the type of backup, date, frequency, and so on. Some DBAs prefer to use this method when they have only two or fewer small databases.

Oracle Export Utility

The export utility supports logical backups by writing data from the database to OS files in an Oracle-specific format. These files can only be interpreted using the Oracle import utility, which can be used later to import the data into a different database depending upon the requirement. If you are managing a big database (in the range of gigabytes), it is not practical to take a full database export. The export utility is very useful for user-level or table-level exports.

Again, the method you choose to back up your database depends on your business rules. For example, if your database is operating 24 × 7, you cannot execute offline backup (cold backup) procedures using the OS command. You have to take a hot backup either at the OS level or using RMAN. A proper configuration is essential to support such operational requisites.

Technical Considerations

As a DBA, you need to consider the technical implications while planning a backup strategy. Available resources such as disk space, tape drives, and other technical considerations need to be evaluated.

Database Physical Image Copies

A *physical image copy* of the database is needed to perform any recovery operation. The physical database structure is comprised of the control files, the redo log files, the data files, and the archive log files. The physical image copies of the database files consume a significant amount of storage space. The DBA has to be equipped with sufficient resources to perform physical backups.

Database Logical Copies

The *logical copies* involve the extraction of the object definitions and the table data from an Oracle database. These copies are stored in proprietary binary format and can be accessed only by the import utility. The logical export dump files do not consume as many resources as a physical copy of the database does. However, the time to take logical copies will be more than physical backups. The logical exports should not be used to substitute for physical backups. Although this is true for almost everyone, again it depends on your business and the database you have. For example, if you have a 10MB database that contains vital information and a 10GB database, it makes sense to take a full database export of the 10MB database at a regular frequency while taking a table-level backup of certain tables with the 10GB database. Logical backups also help you in reorganizing the data within your database to enhance performance.

Significance of Testing the Backup and Recovery Strategy

Testing backups is equally important when compared with taking backups. Most DBAs tend to neglect and often do not involve themselves in the planning and testing of the backups. You should make sure that the backups performed by you *actually* work. It is always preferable to practice backup and recovery techniques in a test environment before implementing them on the production database. This would avoid any mishap on the production server, which could result in major losses.

Testing your backups regularly could also help you test the completeness of the developed strategies. Regularly performing recoveries in the test environment using the backups taken from the production databases would ensure your awareness of any corruptions in the backups or the archived log files, which would hinder the actual recovery operation in a production environment. If one or more data blocks are corrupted in the database files and if a backup were performed on the database, the corrupted blocks would propagate to the backups, rendering them unusable. Oracle's RMAN utility can detect the corrupted blocks while performing backup operations. This would prepare you in advance to ensure that the corrupted blocks do not hinder the recovery at the production site.

The RMAN utility also enables you to repair the corrupt blocks using its BLOCKRECOVER command. This is an Oracle9*i*-specific feature. Regular testing of the backups and simulating the recovery scenarios would also ensure that you stay familiar and updated with the recovery procedures.

The logical database backups also need to be tested. The DBA should test these backups by performing imports into test databases. An ideal test plan consists of various elements that need to be incorporated in it. Proper documentation of test scenarios with detailed step-by-step illustrations of the recovery process and the time involved to restore and perform either a complete or incomplete recovery needs to be recorded. You also need to record the time required to recover the entire database for access to users (MTTR). Only after completely testing the backup and recovery plan should you implement it on a production database.

To set up the test environment, additional resources are needed, which would involve management to intervene. You should schedule regular testing to perform recovery on the database with the simulation of the most likely occurring failures and disasters in the production environment. Some of the suggested recovery operations that you will have to test for are listed here:

- Try recovering the table, which has been dropped from the user account by performing an incomplete recovery.

- Simulate a disk failure and perform a complete recovery of the database by recovering all the files from the crashed disk.

- Recover the complete database from a system failure.

- Simulate a block corruption in a database file and try recovering the datafile without any data loss. If you have a huge database, you could take sample data and simulate a test database before performing recovery.

Disaster Recovery Plan

There are many issues concerning disaster recovery that must be taken into consideration for any computer system. A clear understanding of the disasters, which can occur on the production environment, holds the key to a complete and successful design of a backup and recovery strategy. First and foremost, the impact of losing data needs to be determined. The amount of effort and time involved to reenter the lost data is to be evaluated. Next, the maximum amount of downtime (for a given failure) that the business can withstand without major impact needs to be determined. A goal needs to be set for availability, such as 98 or 99.5 percent. Finally, the loss of business and revenues due to the database unavailability has to be clearly determined. Oracle provides many high-availability features to overcome loss concerning disasters. They are discussed in the following section.

Oracle's High-Availability Features

It has become a compulsion for a DBA in today's industry to maintain high availability for the database. The DBA needs to configure systems to prevent, detect, and repair any possible outages in a timely manner. With increasing functionality and complexity in Oracle9*i*, you need to clearly understand the various high-availability options that Oracle provides you. In case of an outage, you need to be aware of all the tools and procedures to perform recovery with minimum MTTR.

Distributed Systems and Replication

A distributed database environment enables users to access and perform operations on multiple databases. The databases are usually maintained on different systems that may be in different physical locations. Every database server in the distributed environment is controlled by the local Relational Database Management System (RDBMS). In the distributed environment, each server cooperates to maintain the consistency of the global database. The distributed databases hold the key to database replication. The distributed database stores a single copy of the data. In a distributed database environment, the applications use distributed transactions to modify data at the local database server as well as at the remote database server. Figure 6-2 show the distributed RDBMS architecture.

The primary goal of replication is to improve the performance and maintain high availability of the database. In other words, replicated data enables individual clients to maintain a local copy of it, which would improve the access rate. Moreover, in the event of a disaster at one of the sites, the data will not be lost since the replicas would have the same image. Oracle provides additional features like adding additional columns and sites to the grouped objects in the replicated environment while the users are accessing and updating data, which reduces the need for any planned downtime. Figure 6-3 shows a hybrid replication environment.

Real Application Clusters (RACs)

Real Application Clusters (RACs) are primarily a single-site, high-availability solution from Oracle. They truly explore the fact that the redundancy is provided by clustering to deliver availability with n-1 node failures in an n-node cluster

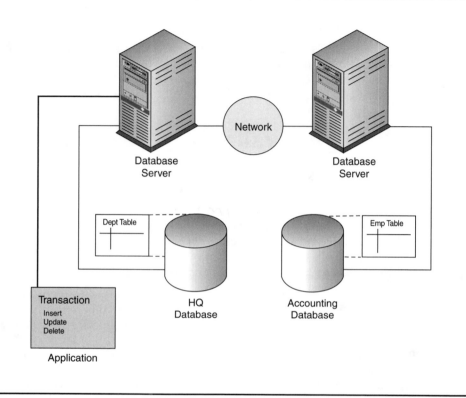

FIGURE 6-2. *Distributed DBMS architecture*

environment. All the users connected to the cluster will have access to all the data as long as there is at least one available node in the cluster. It ensures very high levels of availability for mission-critical applications.

In a RAC environment, Oracle operates on two or more systems that comprise a cluster. All users in this environment have access to a single shared database. If one of the node fails, one of the surviving nodes performs recovery of the failed instance. The failures of one of the systems do not affect users connected to other instances of the surviving nodes in the cluster. Users that are part of the failed instance can failover to the surviving nodes' part of the cluster. Since all the server nodes are active during normal operations, the system resources are managed well and larger loads can be sustained by the database. Additional servers can always be added later to the cluster to improve performance and availability.

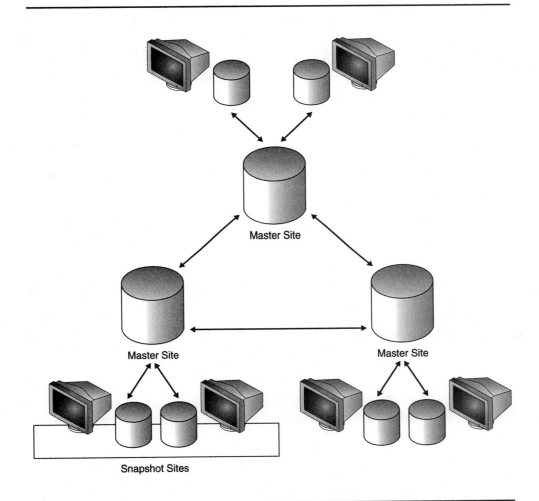

FIGURE 6-3. *Hybrid replication (combination of Multi-Master site and Snapshot site replication)*

NOTE
RACs were known as the Oracle Parallel Server in Oracle8i.

③ Transparent Application Failover

Oracle9*i* with *transparent application failover* (TAF) provides an application with the capability to automatically reestablish sessions for the users after a system has crashed in an RAC environment. Oracle's *fast-start fault recovery* in tandem with clustering also enables the Oracle server to instantly recover from system node failures, thereby minimizing any impact on the users. But a failure, however short, can disrupt the user activities. After a failure, the users may need to reconnect and start the operations again, as the uncommitted data would be lost. But by using TAF, the user may not need to manually reconnect after an instance crash, as the server automatically takes over from the point when the failure occurred. The queries, which were in progress at the time the failure occurred, get transparently restarted. The data display would resume from the point when the failure occurred.

④ Oracle Data Guard (mission critical system)

Oracle Data Guard is a tool built on the Oracle *standby database* technology. Data Guard can be configured to maintain one or more copies of the data at remote sites dispersed across various geographical locations. This data is synchronized with the primary database. Oracle Net is used to connect the primary and standby databases. Whenever the primary database records change, the physical standby databases are sent log information and these are updated at the standby sites automatically. If there is any failure at the primary database site, the standby site is instantly activated and ready for the user to access. A brief description of Oracle Standby Database is given in the following section.

Oracle Standby Database

The Oracle *Standby database* provides an alternate database server to be maintained as a backup at a remote location. The transfer of the archive logs from the primary database to the standby database occurs automatically if the primary database is configured with the remote archiving destination parameter. The standby database automatically applies the logs and is synchronized with the primary database server. The standby database eliminates any time involved in restoring from the backup, since the logs from the primary database are continuously applied at the secondary. The system and network boot times stay about the same, as the standby must be reconfigured to become the primary site during disasters. Some data loss does occur since the online redo logs might be lost during extreme disasters, but Oracle9*i*'s *data guard* (standby database) implementation can be configured to guarantee no data loss. Figure 6-4 shows the standby database architecture.

LogMiner Utility

Any updating done to the database is reflected internally by means of undo and redo, which get registered in the Oracle redo log files. LogMiner generates

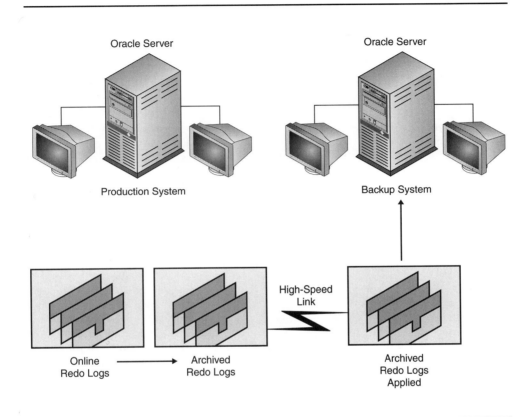

FIGURE 6-4.   *Oracle Standby database*

SQL_REDO as well as SQL_UNDO with primary key information to help the DBA undo the changes. The Oracle9*i* LogMiner feature is an integral part of the Oracle9*i* database and provides the DBA with the ability to audit user operations and recover data if lost due to accidental operations. *(advantages (gminer)*

The online data dictionary can be extracted into the redo log stream, which enables off-line analysis and provides a snapshot of the data dictionary that matches the database objects in logs created at that time. When mining the redo log files, the DBA can access the data dictionary for SQL reconstruction. This reconstructed SQL enables the DBA to reverse the effect of the earlier transaction. The functionality of the Oracle LogMiner can either be used by executing the Oracle PL/SQL packages through the command-line interface or through the LogMiner GUI viewer tool. The data in the mined logs can be displayed either based on the data values or on the committed transactions. The support to track DDL statements was introduced in Oracle9*i*.

Chapter Questions

1. **What is the business justification for a DBA in reducing the MTTR for his or her production database?**

    A. Decrease the number of database failures.

    ⌐**B.** Decrease the downtime cost.

    C. Increase the downtime cost.

    D. Increase the number of database failures.

2. **A user accessing the EMPLOYEE table accidentally deleted all the rows. Which type of failure just occurred?**

    A. Statement failure

    B. Process failure

    C. Media failure

    ✗**D.** Human error

    E. Instance failure

3. **What is the best Oracle technology available today to implement database high availability against disasters, which would not result in any data loss?**

    A. Standby database

    B. Database replication

    C. Real Application Clusters

    D. Oracle Data Guard

4. **What is the significance in simulating the test scenarios and testing the recovery strategy?**

    A. Management should be aware that the DBA is working.

    B. To decrease the Mean Time to Recover (MTTR).

    C. The DBA can ask for more resources.

    D. To decrease the Mean Time Between Failures (MTBF).

5. **User John was in the process of inserting data into the EMPLOYEE table when he encountered the following error message:**

```
SQL> INSERT INTO EMPLOYEE(NAME) VALUES('BACKUPANDRECOVERY');
INSERT INTO EMPLOYEE(NAME) VALUES('BACKUPANDRECOVERY');
*
ERROR at line 1:
ORA-01536: space quota exceeded for tablespace 'USERS'
```

What type of failure did user John encounter?

   A. Statement failure

   B. Process failure

   C. Media failure

   D. Human error

   E. Instance failure

6. **As a DBA, which of the following methods can you use to make a backup of your table?**

   A. Recovery Manager (RMAN) utility

   B. Import utility

   C. Export utility

   D. O/S backup command

7. **One of your users has accidentally deleted a record from a production table in the database. What is the fastest recovery method available to you to recover the data?**

   A. Point-in-time (PITR) recovery on the database

   B. LogMiner utility

   C. Tablespace point-in-time recovery (TSPITR)

   D. Cancel-based recovery

8. **Which of the following statements is incorrect regarding RMAN?**

   A. It detects corrupt blocks.

   B. It performs only offline database backups.

   C. It omits empty blocks during backups.

   D. It performs tablespace point-in-time recovery (TSPITR).

Answers to Chapter Questions

1. B.   Decrease the downtime cost.

Explanation   The DBA must ensure that the *mean time to recover* (MTTR) should not have a major impact on the business. The DBA must decrease the downtime cost by reducing the MTTR.

2. D.   Human error

Explanation   Some of the common human (user) errors include deleting of rows from tables accidentally, dropping tables/objects, or committing data by mistake. The way to minimize on these kinds of failures is to properly train the database user. A statement failure occurs when the Oracle server fails to execute the user's SQL statement. Recovery for a statement failure is handled by Oracle and does not require the DBA's intervention.

3. B.   Database replication

Explanation   The best technology available today for maintaining high availability against disasters is *data replication* in the distributed environment. Oracle's advanced replication feature enables the DBA to maintain redundant copies of data at various geographical locations. The standby database enables the DBA to maintain a secondary database at a remote location. However, you could lose one of the online log files due to a crash, thereby losing data. Oracle Real Application Clusters (RACs) enable the DBA to maintain multiple instances in a clustered environment; however, they are vulnerable to an environmental failure such as an earthquake. The Oracle Data Guard tool is based on the standby database technology.

4. B.   To decrease the Mean Time to Recover (MTTR).

Explanation   MTTR can be decreased with testing the recovery strategy. By simulating a failure, you can test to see how long it takes to recover your database. The Mean Time Between Failures (MTBF) can be reduced by having redundant resources such as RAID technology. The backup and recovery strategy must be thoroughly tested before it can be implemented at the production database.

5. A.   Statement failure

Explanation   A statement failure occurs when the Oracle server fails to execute the user's SQL statement. A statement failure is handled by Oracle and an appropriate feedback is displayed. In this case, John's request would be rolled back and the data would not be entered into the EMPLOYEE table since John doesn't have enough space in the corresponding tablespace.

6. C.   Export utility

Explanation   You can take a backup of your table using the export utility, which is a logical backup. You can take physical backups of the database or tablespaces using either RMAN or the OS level commands. The import utility is used for recovering the tables, not for taking backups.

7. B.   LogMiner utility

Explanation   Oracle's LogMiner utility can be used to undo transactions by mining the redo log files. This is the fastest way possible to recover the deleted record without any database downtime. You can also use point-in-time recovery to get the data back, but it will take much longer and is quite complicated.

8. B.   Performs only offline database backups.

Explanation   Oracle's Recovery Manager (RMAN) utility can be used to perform both online and offline database backups. You can take an offline backup with RMAN while the database is in the mount state.

CHAPTER
7

Instance and Media
Recovery Structures

o safeguard your data against potential failures and to effectively recover the database, you will need to have an in-depth knowledge of the various Oracle structures related to backup and recovery.

In this chapter, you will learn about Oracle's memory structures, background process, and datafiles. We will also discuss the importance of checkpoints during instance recovery and the use of fast-start checkpoints and parallel recovery to tune the recovery process. This chapter includes the following topics:

- Oracle memory structures
- Oracle background processes
- Oracle database files
- Importance of checkpoints during instance recovery

The Oracle server has two main components: the Oracle *instance* and the Oracle *database*. Whenever a database is started, Oracle initially allocates a memory area known as the system global area (SGA) and starts the background processes. This combination of the SGA and the background processes is referred to as the *Oracle server instance*.

An Oracle database is a collection of data. The database has separate logical and physical structures. Because of these separate structures, the physical storage can be managed without affecting the access to the logical storage structures. Figure 7-1 shows the Oracle9*i* architecture.

Oracle Memory Structures

The Oracle memory area is broadly divided into two areas: the System Global Area (SGA) and the Program Global Area (PGA). These two memory areas are described in the following sections.

System Global Area

The SGA is dynamic shared memory area that can be used to perform read-write operations. It manages the data and the control information related to the Oracle instance. Multiple database users can access the SGA concurrently since it is sharable; therefore, the SGA is sometimes referred to as the *shared global area*.

Since the SGA is read-write, all the users connected to a multiple-process database instance can read information contained within an Oracle instance's SGA, and several processes can write to the SGA for modifying existing data.

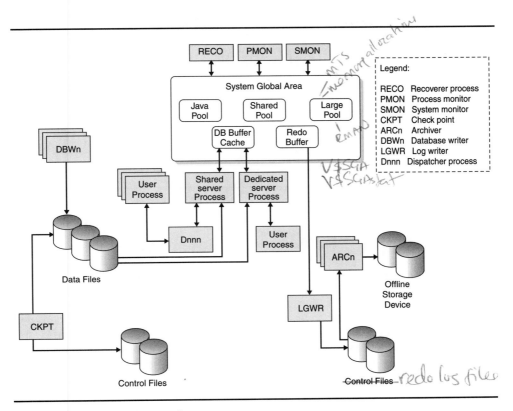

FIGURE 7-1. *Oracle9i* Architecture

The SGA contains various smaller structures including the database buffer cache, redo log buffers, shared pool, and the large pool (optional). Figure 7-2 shows the SGA.

Oracle provides dynamic data dictionary views to obtain information on the various components of the SGA. The views V$SGA and V$SGASTAT are described next.

The V$SGA dynamic performance view displays information related to individual memory structures that constitute the SGA. The NAME column displays the SGA component. The VALUE column displays the memory occupied by different cache components like fixed size, variable size, database buffers, and the redo buffers. A select statement will typically display the following information:

```
SQL> SELECT name, value FROM v$sga;
NAME                        VALUE
--------------------    ----------
```

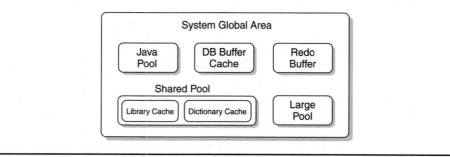

FIGURE 7-2. *SGA*

```
Fixed Size              282556
Variable Size          92274688
Database Buffers       20971520
Redo Buffers             532480
```

The V$SGASTAT dynamic performance view displays detailed information on the SGA. It displays the NAME, BYTES, and POOL columns. The NAME column displays the components and the POOL column displays their designated POOL. The memory size in bytes for each component can be viewed in the BYTES column. A partial output is shown below:

```
SQL> SELECT pool, name, bytes FROM v$sgastat;
POOL           NAME                         BYTES
-----------    -------------------------    -----------
               fixed_sga                      282556
               db_block_buffers             20971520
               log_buffer                     524288
shared pool    1M buffer                     1049088
shared pool    Checkpoint queue               141152
shared pool    DML lock                       100408
shared pool    FileIdentificatonBlock         323292
shared pool    FileOpenBlock                  695504
```

Database Buffer Cache

Oracle maintains copies of the most recently used database blocks in the *database buffer cache,* which is an integral part of the SGA. Oracle stores data in the buffer cache to improve performance by reducing disk I/O. The buffer cache contains both modified and unmodified blocks. The modified blocks or *dirty blocks* are the blocks that have been updated but not yet flushed back to disk. The *database writer* (DBW*n*) background process is responsible for writing dirty blocks to disk.

The buffers in the cache are divided in two lists: the *write list* and the *least recently used* (LRU) list. The write list contains dirty buffers that have been modified but have not yet been written to disk. The LRU list contains *free buffers, pinned buffers,* and *dirty buffers* that have not yet been moved to the write list. On a user request for data, the corresponding server process first searches for the data in the database buffer cache. If the data exists in the cache, it is read directly from the memory. If the data is not found in the cache, a copy of the data is transferred from the datafile to the buffer cache. In the following sections, we discuss the individual components of the buffer cache in detail.

LRU and Write Lists   The initial buffers (head) of the LRU list contains the *most recently used* (MRU) buffers. When an Oracle process accesses a buffer, the buffer is moved to the MRU end of the LRU list. The tail end of the LRU contains the buffers that have not been referenced recently and thereby can be reused. Therefore, the foreground processes begin to search for the free buffers starting at the tail of the LRU list. Buffers on the LRU list can have one of three statuses: free, pinned, or dirty.

Free buffers are the unused buffers that are available to store blocks fetched from the disk. Free buffers are neither dirty nor pinned. Pinned buffers are those that are currently being accessed by the users. The pinned buffers are further categorized as *pinned clean* or *pinned dirty*. Dirty buffers are modified buffers whose contents are not synchronized with their corresponding image on the disk. Dirty buffers are different from pinned dirty buffers in that pinned dirty buffers have users currently accessing them so they cannot be written to disk. (Any pinned buffers, whether pinned clean or pinned dirty cannot be written to disk as they are currently locked by a process for write.) On the other hand, the dirty buffers are freed buffers and can move to the write list and subsequently to disk. When an Oracle process accesses a buffer, the process moves the buffer to the MRU end of the LRU list. But if there is a full table scan, it reads the blocks and puts them on the LRU end (instead of the MRU end) of the LRU list. If you want blocks of the table to be placed at the MRU end of the list during a full table scan, use the CACHE clause while creating or altering a table. The write list contains the dirty buffers that are eligible for disk write by DBW*n*. The write list is also called the *dirty list*. DBW*n* writes buffers to disk when it is signaled to do so.

Multiple Buffer Pools   The database buffer cache can be configured with separate buffer pools depending upon the object's data blocks *age-out* requirement. You should know whether the data pertaining to an object must be available in the buffer cache for reuse or whether it must be made available for new data. You can achieve this by appropriately configuring the buffer pools as KEEP, RECYCLE, or DEFAULT. To retain the object's data blocks in memory, define KEEP using the initialization parameter DB_KEEP_CACHE_SIZE. To eliminate data blocks from the memory the moment they are no longer needed, define RECYCLE using the initialization parameter DB_RECYCLE_CACHE_SIZE. The DEFAULT option is enabled if none of the other pools are configured.

Database Buffer Cache Block Sizes   Oracle9*i* supports multiple block sizes in a single database. For compatibility, Oracle with multiple block sizes also supports varied block buffer sizes. You must specify the standard block size that is applicable to the SYSTEM tablespace by setting the initialization parameter DB_BLOCK_SIZE. The buffer cache for the standard block size can be defined by setting the initialization parameter DB_CACHE_SIZE in bytes. Multiple block sizes can be set for different tablespaces within the database. You can use the multiple block size feature to place objects in tablespaces of appropriate block sizes. In decision (DSS) support systems where full table scans (FTSs) are unavoidable, you should create them in a tablespace with a large block size. In contrast, for tables used by OLTP applications, you should create them in a tablespace with a smaller block size. This maximizes the I/O performance. We give an example of setting multiple block sizes next.

NOTE
*The multiple block size feature introduced in Oracle9*i *will enable you to transport tablespaces from your OLTP systems to your data warehouse with different block sizes more easily.*

You can obtain the block size and the buffer size from the V$BUFFER_POOL view. In the example that follows, the standard block size is 2KB, which would apply to the SYSTEM tablespace. If you now try to create a tablespace using a non-standard block size, it would fail with the ORA-29339 error since the nonstandard block sized buffers are not allocated in the buffer cache. To successfully create this tablespace, you need to first allocate the buffers by using the dynamic parameter DB_nK_CACHE_SIZE as shown:

```
SQL> SELECT name, block_size, resize_state, current_size, buffers FROM
v$buffer_pool;
NAME                 BLOCK_SIZE RESIZE_STA CURRENT_SIZE    BUFFERS
-------------------- ---------- ---------- ------------ ----------
DEFAULT                   2048 STATIC               12       5676

SQL> CREATE TABLESPACE oramatest1 DATAFILE
```

```
'd:\oracle\oradata\target\oramatest01.dbf' SIZE 1m BLOCKSIZE 16k;
CREATE TABLESPACE oramatest1 DATAFILE
'd:\oracle\oradata\target\oramatest01.dbf' SIZE 1m BLOCKSIZE 16k
*
ERROR at line 1:
ORA-29339: tablespace block size 16384 does not match configured block
sizes

SQL> ALTER SYSTEM SET db_16k_cache_size=12m;
System altered.

SQL> SELECT name, block_size, resize_state, current_size, buffers FROM
v$buffer_pool;
NAME                   BLOCK_SIZE RESIZE_STA CURRENT_SIZE    BUFFERS
-------------------- ---------- ---------- ------------ ----------
DEFAULT                      2048 STATIC              12       5676
DEFAULT                     16384 STATIC              12        759

SQL> CREATE TABLESPACE oramatest1 DATAFILE
'd:\oracle\oradata\target\oramatest01.dbf' SIZE 1m BLOCKSIZE 16k;
Tablespace created.
```

NOTE
In earlier versions of Oracle (prior to Oracle9i), the size of the database buffer had to be equal to the size of the database block (that is, the value defined by the initialization parameter DB_BLOCK_SIZE).

You cannot use the DB_nK_CACHE_SIZE parameter to modify the buffer cache configured with the standard block size. The KEEP and RECYCLE buffer pools are only available for the standard block size. Nonstandard block size caches have the DEFAULT pool.

The view V$BUFFER_POOL displays information on the various buffer pool components. The important columns and a brief description of these columns are shown in Table 7-1.

The view V$BUFFER_POOL_STATISTICS displays statistical data for all the available buffer pools. The important columns and a brief description of these columns are shown in Table 7-2.

Redo Log Buffers

The *redo log buffer* is a circular buffer in the SGA. It stores redo record entries. In brief, it is a log of all the changes performed on any data block of the database. Redo records contain the information of any changes made to the database either

COLUMN NAME	COLUMN DESCRIPTION
NAME	Displays the buffer pool names.
BLOCK_SIZE	Displays the blocks size for the buffers in the associated pools.
RESET_STATE	Displays the current state of the resize operation. The values in this column are STATIC, ALLOCATING, ACTIVATING, and SHRINKING.
CURRENT_SIZE	Displays the current size of the subcaches in megabytes.
BUFFERS	Displays the currently allocated buffers.

TABLE 7-1.   *V$BUFFER_POOL*

using DML or DDL operations such as INSERT, UPDATE, DELETE, CREATE, ALTER, DROP, and others pertaining to user object. Redo is also generated for any internal modification done by Oracle to the data dictionary. If a change is made to the undo segment, the redo generated is called the *redo for the undo.* The *log writer* (LGWR) background process is responsible for writing the redo log buffers to the active online redo log files on disk. The initialization parameter LOG_BUFFER determines the size in bytes of the redo log buffer in the SGA. The default size for this parameter in Oracle9*i* is 512KB or 128KB multiplied by the value of CPU_COUNT— whichever is higher.

NOTE
The DDL statements that make structural changes to the database are not logged in the redo buffers. For example, the CREATE TABLESPACE statement will not be logged into the redo log buffers. The structural changes are, however, written to the control file and the alert log file that resides in the destination and are defined by the initialization parameter BACKGROUND_DUMP_DESTINATION.

The Shared Pool
The shared pool area is mainly categorized into two parts: the *library cache* and the *dictionary cache.* The initialization parameter SHARED_POOL_SIZE determines the total size of the shared pool area.

COLUMN NAME	COLUMN DESCRIPTION
NAME	Displays the names of the various buffer pools.
SET_MSIZE	Displays the maximum *set* size for a buffer pool. The sets are related to the number of LRU latch sets.
CNUM_WRITE	Displays the number of buffers on the write list that need to be written to the disk by DBW*n*.
CNUM_SET	Displays the number of buffers in the set.
BUF_GOT	Displays the number of buffers that are got by the set.
FREE_BUFFER_WAIT	Displays the free buffer wait statistic.
WRITE_COMPLETE_WAIT	Displays the write complete wait statistic.
BUFFER_BUSY_WAIT	Displays the wait statistic for the busy buffers.
DB_BLOCK_CHANGE	Displays the statistics for the database blocks that have changed.
DB_BLOCK_GETS	Displays the database blocks gets statistic.
CONSISTENT_GETS	Displays the consistent gets statistic.
PHYSICAL_READS	Displays the physical reads statistic.
PHYSICAL_WRITES	Displays the physical writes statistic.

TABLE 7-2.   *V$BUFFER_POOL_STATISTICS*

Library Cache   The *library cache* contains shared SQL and shared PL/SQL areas when the database is configured as a dedicated server. In addition to the shared SQL and PL/SQL, the library cache contains a private SQL area when Oracle is configured as a shared server. The shared SQL area stores the parse tree and the execution plan for any SQL statement. This shared area is accessible to all users. When different users execute the same SQL statement, the information related to this statement is stored in the shared SQL area and will be repeatedly reused. However, if a session is connected through a shared server process, it uses the private SQL area of the SGA. The private SQL area consists of the *persistent area* and the *runtime area*. The persistent area contains information on the bind variables and is released only after a cursor is closed. The runtime area is freed as soon as the execution of a statement is terminated.

The view V$LIBRARYCACHE displays detailed statistics on the library cache. The important columns and a brief description of these columns are shown in Table 7-3.

Data Dictionary Cache   The data dictionary is one of the most important parts of an SGA. It stores tables that primarily hold user account data, datafile names, segment names, extent locations, table descriptions, privileges, roles, and so forth. The *data dictionary cache* is often accessed by Oracle to validate user access rights and to verify the state of the schema objects. This information is vital for parsing the SQL statements. The data dictionary cache helps speed up the parsing of the SQL statements. The data dictionary tables are initially read and the data that is returned after processing is updated in the data dictionary cache. Since the data dictionary cache stores data as rows and not as buffers, it is also referred to as the *row cache*.

The view V$ROWCACHE displays statistics pertaining to the data dictionary cache. Each row contains statistics for one data dictionary cache item. The important columns and a brief description of these columns are shown in Table 7-4.

The Large Pool

The large pool is an optional memory area. It is used as a storage space by the Recovery Manager (RMAN) utility during database backup and recovery operations. This significantly improves RMAN's performance when RMAN is configured to use multiple I/O slaves. Oracle uses multiple I/O slaves only when the initialization parameter BACKUP_TAPE_IO_SLAVES is set to TRUE. The memory occupied by the large pool is set by the initialization parameter LARGE_POOL_SIZE. The parameter LARGE_POOL_SIZE is set to 0 by default. This means that it must be configured explicitly whenever required. Unlike the shared pool, the large pool does not have a LRU list and the memory allocated in the large pool for a session is released as soon the session is terminated.

COLUMN NAME	COLUMN DESCRIPTION
NAMESPACE	Displays the objects from various classes (SQL area, trigger, and so on).
PINS	Displays the object requests of the namespace.
RELOADS	Displays the number of times an object stored in the library cache had to be reloaded into memory since part of the object was flushed out.

TABLE 7-3.   *V$LIBRARYCACHE*

COLUMN NAME	COLUMN DESCRIPTION
PARAMETER	Displays the name of the cache.
Count	Displays the number of entries allocated to the cache.
GETS	Displays the total number.
GETMISSES	Displays the number of requests resulting in dictionary cache misses.

TABLE 7-4. *V$ROWCACHE*

The parameter DBWR_IO_SLAVES specifies the number of I/O server processes used by the DBW*n* process. The I/O server processes are generally used to simulate asynchronous I/O on platforms that do not support asynchronous I/O. The I/O server processes are also useful in database environments with very large I/O throughput. If you set the parameter DBWR_IO_SLAVES to a nonzero value, the number of I/O server processes is set to 4. The number of I/O server processes used by RMAN is therefore set to 4. This is possible only when asynchronous I/O is disabled. The large pool can also be used in a shared server environment to store part of the data of the *user global area* (UGA). A shared server will use this large pool whenever a session starts. A fixed UGA is allocated in the shared pool and the rest of the memory is utilized from the large pool.

NOTE
It is recommended to use multiple database writers over database write I/O slaves.

The dynamic performance view V$SGASTAT displays information pertaining to the SGA. The columns POOL, NAME, and BYTES give the details of free memory and session heap for the large pool memory area.

Dynamic SGA

Beginning with Oracle9*i*, Oracle enables you to dynamically change the SGA configuration while the database is open. You can change the sizes of the db buffer cache, the shared pool, and the large pool without closing the instance.

The dynamic SGA feature also enables Oracle to use the virtual memory. Oracle starts an instance and allows the SGA components to grow dynamically as per your requirements. The only criterion for the growth of the SGA is that the combined sizes of all the memory structures that are part of the SGA must not exceed the value defined by the initialization parameter SGA_MAX_SIZE.

The initial size of the SGA depends on many initialization parameters, some of which are described next:

- **DB_CACHE_SIZE**   This parameter defines the total size of the buffer cache in bytes based on the standard block size defined using the initialization parameter DB_BLOCK_SIZE.

- **DB_*n*K_CACHE_SIZE**   This parameter must be defined if memory relating to a non-standard block size is to be registered in the buffer cache. If multiple block sizes are being used for the database, the value of *n* must be equal to one of the listed: 2^1, 2^2, 2^3, 2^4, or 2^5.

- **LOG_BUFFER**   Defines the number of bytes to be allocated for the redo log buffer.

- **SHARED_POOL_SIZE**   Defines the size in bytes that is to be dedicated to the shared pool components: library cache, data dictionary cache, an so forth.

- **LARGE_POOL_SIZE**   Defines the size in bytes of the large pool; the default value is 0.

- **SGA_MAX_SIZE**   This parameter defines the maximum size of the SGA for the life span of the instance.

Program Global Area

The *program global area* (PGA) resides in the memory and contains data and control information for a server process. This area is not sharable and is allocated only when a server process in a dedicated server environment starts. Access to the PGA is exclusively given to that server process. Data is updated in the PGA based on the Oracle code that is being executed by the server process. The PGA primarily holds information related to the private SQL area and the sessions. The private SQL area stores the bind information and the runtime memory structure for a SQL statement. The private SQL area is accessible only to the user who issues a SQL statement. The location of a private SQL areas depend on the type of connection established for a session. Session memory allocated in the PGA stores the session's variables.

NOTE
Information that is maintained by the PGA in a dedicated server environment is stored in the shared pool or the large pool, as configured.

Oracle allocates a large amount of memory for operations such as sorting, hash-joins, bitmap merge, and bitmap create statements. The memory area where these operations are performed is known as *work areas*. Work areas constitute a large amount of memory allocated for the runtime memory structure of private SQL areas. The total size of the PGA can be set using the initialization parameter PGA_AGGREGATE_TARGET.

The dynamic performance view V$PGASTAT displays instance level statistics of PGA usage. A partial output is shown here:

```
SQL> SELECT name, value FROM v$pgastat;
NAME                                                              VALUE
------------------------------------------------------------  ----------
aggregate PGA auto target                                              0
global memory bound                                                   0
total expected memory                                                 0
total PGA inuse                                                  5872640
total PGA allocated                                             6288384
maximum PGA allocated                                           6288384
```

Oracle Background Processes

Oracle *background processes* are created to support multi-process, multi-user environments for an instance. There are numerous background processes that Oracle starts, some of them being mandatory for an instance to startup and perform basic operations. These mandatory processes are SMON, PMON, DBW*n*, LGWR, and CKPT. The optional processes can be started dynamically after the instance is started. The optional background processes are ARC*n*, RECO, D*nnn*, LCK*n*, LNSV, BSP*n*, MRP0, LSP0, CJQ0, EMN0, QMN*n*, DMON, RSM0, NSV0, RLAP, LMS*n*, LMON, LMD0, and LMS*n*.

System Monitor Process

The *system monitor process* (SMON) is an important background process. It is responsible for performing instance recovery after an instance failure. It also cleans up the temporary segments that are no longer useful. SMON coalesces the contiguous free extents allocated in a dictionary-managed tablespace.

Process Monitor Process

The *process monitor process* (PMON) is primarily responsible for performing process recovery after a user process failure. It cleans the cache thereby releasing the resources occupied by the failed process. In a shared server environment it checks for failed dispatcher and server process, and if any, it restarts them.

NOTE
If any user process fails, PMON rolls back the uncommitted transactions associated with that process.

Database Writer Process

The database writer (DBW*n*) background process is responsible for writing the modified or dirty buffers from the write list in the database buffer cache to disk. Depending on the requirement, multiple DBW*n* processes can be invoked. Using multiple DBW*n* processes increases the rate at which data is transferred to disk. This results in performance increase for large databases. Using multiple DBW*n* processes is not useful on single processor systems. Multiple DBW*n* processes can be configured using the initialization parameter DB_WRITER_PROCESSES. The DBW*n* process writes dirty buffers to disk if it encounters any of the following conditions:

- If a server process does not find a clean reusable buffer (free buffer) after performing a scan of a certain number of buffers (known as the threshold), it signals the DBW*n* to write the dirty buffers to the disk. (DBW*n* writes the dirty buffers to disk asynchronously.)

- Whenever a DBW*n* timeout occurs. The DBWn timeout value is three seconds. Every time a timeout occurs, it traverses through the database buffer headers to find any dirty blocks.

- Whenever a checkpoint occurs. A checkpoint forces all the dirty buffers to be written to disk. Oracle guarantees that all changes done to the database up to the checkpoint are guaranteed to be on disk.

Log Writer Process

The *log writer process* (LGWR) is responsible for writing data from the redo log buffers to the redo log files. The redo log buffer is a circular buffer that can be reused as soon as the LGWR writes all the redo entries to the files. The server processes overwrites the data with new redo entries. LGWR writes the redo entries to the log files whenever it encounters any of the following conditions:

- Whenever a COMMIT statement occurs; that is, when a user has completed the transaction

- Whenever a timeout of three seconds occurs

- Whenever the redo log buffer is one-third full

- Whenever the DBWn process signals the LGWR to perform a write operation

As part of the Oracle architecture, before the DBW*n* process can write dirty buffers to the disk, the redo generated by the transaction has to be written to the log file by LGWR first. This ensures recovery during a database failure because the redo record contains every change made to the database, committed or uncommitted. So when LGWR activates, it writes all the redo records from the log buffer to the log file.

Fast Commit

If a transaction is committed, the LGWR process copies the corresponding redo entries of the transaction from the redo log buffers to disk (log files) immediately. The corresponding changes to the data blocks are deferred until it is more efficient to write them. This is called a *fast commit* mechanism.

Group Commit

Oracle has come up with the concept of *group commit* to minimize disk I/O and maximize performance of the LGWR. If requests to commit continue at a high rate, then every write (by the LGWR) from the redo log buffer can contain multiple commit records. This is known as group commit.

Checkpoint Process

A *checkpoint* is a synchronization process of the buffer cache with the data files. The *checkpoint process* (CKPT) is responsible for updating all data file headers and the control file, whenever a checkpoint occurs. Simultaneously, the checkpoint process signals the LGWR and DBWR to write the redo entries and dirty buffer to disk respectively. The CKPT process writes the checkpoint SCN value to all the data file headers that are involved in a checkpoint. In the absence of CKPT process, the LGWR process has to perform the above job. By updating the file headers with the checkpoint SCN information, Oracle guarantees that the changes made to the database up to the last checkpoint are on disk. For example, if a database has a checkpoint SCN value of 3000, that means all changes made to that database before 3000 are guaranteed to be on disk.

Archiver Process

The *archiver process* (ARC*n*) is responsible for copying the online redo log files to a pre-configured destination, whenever a log switch occurs and the checkpoint is finished ARC*n* processes can be started only if the database is operating in ARCHIVELOG mode, and automatic archiving is enabled. An Oracle instance can have up to 10 ARC*n* processes (ARC0 to ARC9). The LGWR process starts a new ARC*n* process whenever the current number of ARC*n* processes is insufficient to handle the workload.

Recoverer Process

The *recoverer process* (RECO) is responsible for resolving failures that occur in distributed transactions. The RECO process of a node automatically establishes a connection to other databases, usually after a connection failure and recovers any in-doubt transactions. It removes entries pertaining to pending transactions from the pending transaction table (PENDING_TRANS$) after the in-doubt transactions are recovered.

Server Process

The server process is responsible for handling requests from the user process. It is primarily responsible for communicating with the user process and interacting with Oracle to carry out the request. User process requests in a shared server environment are assigned to an idle server process by the dispatcher. In a dedicated server environment, each user process has a corresponding server process that accepts the requests and processes the data. Each time a client session is established, a new server process is started. A dedicated server process remains associated to the user process for the remainder of the connection.

User Process

The *user process* is responsible for maintaining and executing the software code of an application program. The user process also manages the communication with the server processes.

Note   The V$BGPROCESS view displays detailed information pertaining to the background process and the errors it encounters. The column PADDR displays the address of the process state object. The NAME and DESCRIPTION display the name and description of the processes.

The select statement for the V$BGPROCESS view is shown with the WHERE clause included to display only the active processes:

```
SQL> SELECT paddr, name, description FROM v$bgprocess WHERE paddr NOT IN
('00');
PADDR      NAME        DESCRIPTION
---  ----------  ------------------------------------------------------------
----
7AD90C3C PMON        process cleanup
7AD90F90 DBW0        db writer process 0
7AD912E4 LGWR        Redo etc.
7AD91638 CKPT        checkpoint
7AD9198C SMON        System Monitor Process
```

Note   The V$PROCESS view displays some important columns to identify the active processes for the database, their process id, the operating system process id, the current username associated with the process, and the terminal. The columns pertaining to this view are PID, SPID, USERNAME, and TERMINAL.

Oracle Database Files

The physical database structure of any Oracle database mainly consists of datafiles that are operating system files. We discuss these files next.

Control Files

The *control file* is a binary file that records the physical structure of the database and other related information. The information in the control file is accessed whenever the instance is started and the database is mounted. The control file is used as a reference to identify various other database files. When the physical structure of the database is modified, the control file is updated to reflect this change. The control file contains important information pertaining to the database, such as the

- Database name
- Timestamp of database creation
- Names and locations of associated datafiles and online redo log files
- Tablespace information
- Datafile offline ranges
- Log history
- Archived log information
- Backup set and backup piece information
- Backup datafile and redo log information
- Datafile copy information
- Current log sequence number
- Checkpoint information

The control file also records information pertaining to checkpoints that is crucial for database recovery. When the database is mounted, Oracle opens the control file. The control file must be available for writing by the Oracle database server whenever the database is open.

Multiplexing the Control File

The control file can and should be multiplexed. This enables us to maintain multiple copies of the same file at different destinations (disks). If one of the control files is lost due to failure, the other copies can still be used. The control files should ideally reside on different disks, mounted under different controllers. The following describes the behavior of multiplexed control files:

■ Oracle writes to all the control files listed in the initialization parameter CONTROL_FILES in the init.ora file.

■ If any of the control files become unavailable during database operation, the instance becomes inoperable and will be aborted.

If you don't multiplex the control files and your current control file is lost, you can still recover by creating a new control file using the CREATE CONTROLFILE command. However, you need to have all the data files and log files in tact in order to create a new control file. Oracle strongly recommends that you multiplex your control files and keep a minimum of three copies. Figure 7-3 shows multiplexing the control file.

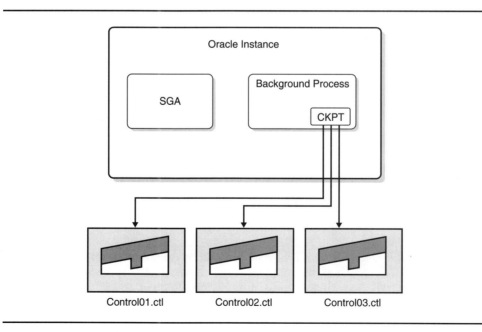

FIGURE 7-3. *Multiplexing the control file*

How to multiplex the controfiles

You can multiplex the control files using the following procedure:

1. Close the database. You can even use the ABORT option, however, this method is generally not advised as Oracle needs to do crash recovery on next startup.

2. Make a copy of the control file to the desired destination.

3. Update the init.ora initialization parameter CONTROL_FILES, appending the new path of the file.

4. Open the database for user operation.

The dynamic performance view V$CONTROLFILE displays the names and the status of the control files through the columns NAME and STATUS, as shown in the following example:

```
SQL> SELECT name, status FROM v$controlfile;
NAME                                        STATUS
------------------------------------------- -------
D:\ORACLE\ORADATA\TARGET\CONTROL01.CTL
E:\ORACLE\ORADATA\TARGET\CONTROL02.CTL
F:\ORACLE\ORADATA\TARGET\CONTROL03.CTL
```

Redo Log Files

The most important files needed to perform successful recovery operations are the online redo log files. An Oracle database must have a minimum of two redo log groups with a minimum of one redo log file (*member*) in each group. While the number of groups you create (two or more) depends on your transaction activity and business rules, Oracle recommends a minimum of two members for each group. The redo log group records all changes or redo made to the database, including both committed and uncommitted changes. Redo is written to the log groups through the redo log buffers of the SGA. The background process LGWR writes the redo sequentially from the redo log buffers to the current online redo log group. Every time a group gets filled, Oracle switches and starts writing redo to a new group and assigns a new *log sequence number* to the new group. The filled online redo log group is available for reuse at a later time depending on the mode of the database. If you are running in NOARCHIVELOG mode, the filled online log group is available right after a checkpoint is done. If you are running in ARCHIVELOG mode (recommended by Oracle) then the filled online log group has to be archived (either by ARC*n* process or manually) before the log group can be reused by LGWR.

Current, Active, and Inactive Online Redo Log Files

At any point of time, the LGWR process actively writes to only one of the online redo log groups. This group of files is termed *current*. The online redo log files that are required for crash recovery are termed *active*. The online redo log files that are not required for crash recovery are termed *inactive*.

Log Switches and Log Sequence Numbers

When the LGWR process has filled the current log files, Oracle triggers a *log switch*. The LGWR now starts to write to the next set of online redo log group. The log switch can be triggered explicitly regardless of whether the group is filled or not, by issuing the following command:

```
SQL> ALTER SYSTEM SWITCH LOGFILE;
```

Whenever there is a physical corruption, the redo log group must be cleared explicitly. To clear a redo log group, issue the following command:

```
SQL> ALTER DATABASE CLEAR LOGFILE GROUP 3;
```

If the corrupt redo log file has not yet been archived, then issue the following command:

```
SQL> ALTER DATABASE CLEAR UNARCHIVED LOGFILE GROUP 3;
```

The ramifications of clearing the online redo log have to be considered before issuing these commands. If you clear the log file that is required by a previous backup for recovery, you will be unable to recover the data. Oracle writes a message in the alert log describing the backups from which you cannot recover. Also, if any tablespace were taken offline without a checkpoint occurring using the OFFLINE IMMEDIATE option, then Oracle would return with the ORA-00393 error. Oracle does not allow you to clear the unarchived redo log file with the above commands unless you explicitly specify the UNRECOVERABLE DATAFILE option with the command.

Note that you will never be able to recover the tablespace to make it online since the redo required to perform recovery has been cleared. The command you will need to use in such situations is as follows:

```
SQL> ALTER DATABASE CLEAR UNARCHIVED LOGFILE GROUP 2 UNRECOVERABLE
DATAFILE;
```

NOTE
If you clear an unarchived online log group, the log group can't be used for recovery. Therefore, you will need to take a complete backup of the database. Be very careful before you use this command as a full database backup may take a long time and is not a trivial task.

(Duplex)

Multiplexing the Online Redo Log File

Not recommended to have many *recommended # of redologs is 2*

Oracle enables you to create multiple copies of the online redo log files. This is important for safeguarding the online redo log files against damage and protecting Oracle from a single point of failure. During normal operation, the LGWR process concurrently writes similar redo information from the redo log buffers to all members of the redo log group. For example, if you create three members in a log group, redo is written by the LGWR to all the three members of the redo log group. When setting up multiple copies of online redo log files, it is recommended to place members of a group on different disks mounted under different controllers. Figure 7-4 shows multiplexing of redo log files.

To add a new redo log group execute the following command:

```
SQL> ALTER DATABASE ADD LOGFILE GROUP 3 ('c:\oradata\orcl\redo3a.log',
'd:\oradata\orcl\redo3a.log') SIZE 1M;
```

It is advisable to specify the entire file path as shown above, because default locations or use of environment variables can cause confusion. The SIZE of the files in the group has to be specified either in bytes, kilobytes, or megabytes.

To add new members to the online groups, execute the following command:

```
SQL> ALTER DATABASE ADD LOGFILE MEMBER 'c:\oradata\orcl\redo3a.log' TO
GROUP 3;
```

The group number must be an existing redo log group. The group number can be viewed from the view V$LOGFILE.

The maximum number of log groups cannot exceed MAXLOGFILES and the maximum log members for a group cannot exceed MAXLOGMEMBERS. Both these parameters are specified while creating the database. The value of MAXLOGMEMBERS and MAXLOGFILES can be reset either while recreating the database or by recreating the control file.

To recreate control file

To recreate the control file you must take a trace of the file. The trace file created will have the CREATE CONTROL file command. You can issue the following command to take a trace:

```
SQL>ALTER DATABASE BACKUP CONTROLFILE TO TRACE;
```

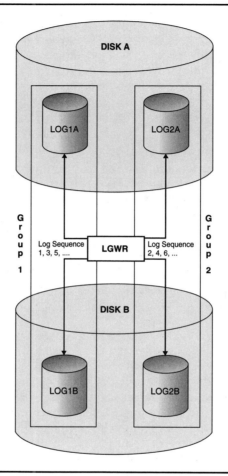

FIGURE 7-4. *Multiplexing of redo log file*

NOTE
For more information about backing up the control file to trace, refer to the section "User-Managed Backups" in Chapter 10.

The trace file would be located in the destination specified by the USER_DUMP_DEST initialization parameter. The file uses the naming convention ORA<pid>.TRC, where pid is the operating system process identifier. You can obtain the pid from the SPID column of the V$PROCESS dynamic performance view. To re-create the control file, modify the trace with the new setting (such as a new value for MAXLOGFILES) and execute it with the database in the NOMOUNT state.

The view V$LOG displays detailed information of the log groups and their status. A brief description of the columns of V$LOG view is given in Table 7-5.

COLUMN NAME	COLUMN DESCRIPTION
GROUP#	Displays the log group number.
THREAD#	Displays the associated log thread number; displays different values if the database is running multiple instances.
SEQUENCE#	Displays the sequence number generated for the log after the last log switch triggered.
BYTES	Displays the size of the log files of an associated log group.
MEMBERS	Displays the number of members in the group.
ARCHIVED	Displays the current status of archiving for the log group; the value could be either YES or NO.
STATUS	Displays the status of the log; the status of the log is either UNUSED, CURRENT, ACTIVE, INACTIVE, CLEARING, or CLEARING_CURRENT.

TABLE 7-5. *V$LOG*

A select statement for the columns described in Table 7-5 follows:

```
SQL> SELECT group#, thread#, sequence#, bytes, members, archived, status
FROM v$log;
GROUP#     THREAD#   SEQUENCE#      BYTES MEMBERS ARC STATUS
------ ---------- ---------- ---------- ------- --- ----------
     1          1        640    1048576       1 NO  INACTIVE
     2          1        641    1048576       1 NO  CURRENT
     3          1        639    1048576       1 NO  INACTIVE
```

The dynamic performance view V$LOGFILE displays the details of individual files in a log group. The MEMBER column displays the name and path of the log file. The STATUS column displays the current status of the files: INVALID (file is inaccessible), STALE (file contents are incomplete), DELETED (file is no longer used), or blank (currently accessed).

Whenever a new member is added to an existing redo log group, it is initially marked as INVALID until all the members (including the new member) in that group are in sync as per the contents. This only happens when there is a log switch and this group is made current. Similarly if the content of the redo log group is incomplete, Oracle displays its status as STALE immediately after restarting the database.

A select statement for the V$LOGFILE view is as follows:

```
SQL> SELECT group#, status, type, member FROM v$logfile;
GROUP# STATUS      TYPE    MEMBER
------ ----------  ------- ------------------------------------
     1             ONLINE  D:\ORACLE\ORADATA\TARGET\REDO01.LOG
     2             ONLINE  D:\ORACLE\ORADATA\TARGET\REDO02.LOG
     3 STALE       ONLINE  D:\ORACLE\ORADATA\TARGET\REDO03.LOG
     2 INVALID     ONLINE  D:\ORACLE\ORADATA\TARGET\REDO01A.LOG
```

The dynamic performance view V$LOG_HISTORY displays the log history information from the control file. The most useful columns are THREAD#, SEQUENCE#, FIRST_TIME, and FIRST_CHANGE#.

A partial output of the SELECT statement for the V$LOG_HISTORY view is shown next:

```
SQL> SELECT thread#, sequence#, first_time, first_change# FROM
v$log_history;
   THREAD#  SEQUENCE# FIRST_TIM FIRST_CHANGE#
---------- ---------- --------- -------------
         1          1 19-SEP-01             1
         1          2 19-SEP-01           261
         1          3 19-SEP-01           767
```

Datafiles

Datafiles are physical files of the operating system that store data pertaining to the logical structures in the database. They are associated with logical structures known as *tablespaces*. You can create a datafile by either attaching it to an existing tablespace or when creating a new tablespace. The datafiles occupy physical disk space to store data and the overhead required for the file header. The first tablespace in any database is always the SYSTEM tablespace; Oracle automatically allocates the first datafiles of any database to the SYSTEM tablespace during the creation of the database. At least one datafile is essential for the database to operate. Oracle stores the data dictionary information in the SYSTEM tablespaces datafile. The destinations of all the datafiles are registered in the control file. Oracle recommends that you create separate tablespaces for different applications or users. For example, it is not recommended that you use the SYSTEM tablespace for storing your user data. Instead you should create a USERS tablespace to store user data.

When starting an Oracle instance, the DB_FILES initialization parameter indicates the amount of SGA space to be reserved for the data file information, thus setting the maximum number of data files that can be created for the instance. This limit applies for the life of the instance. The maximum value for the DB_FILES parameter cannot be greater than the value set for MAXDATAFILES. You can modify the existing MAXDATAFILES parameter by recreating the database or recreating the control file.

The view V$DATAFILE displays detailed information pertaining to the datafiles associated with the database. The important columns and a brief description of these columns are shown in Table 7-6.

A partial output of the SELECT statement for the V$DATAFILE view is as follows:

```
SQL> SELECT file#, name, status, enabled, block_size FROM v$datafile;
FILE# NAME                                       STATUS  ENABLED     BLOCK_SIZE
----- ------------------------------------------ ------- ----------- ----------
    1 D:\ORACLE\ORADATA\TARGET\SYSTEM01.DBF      SYSTEM  READ WRITE        2048
    2 D:\ORACLE\ORADATA\TARGET\UNDOTBS01.DBF     ONLINE  READ WRITE        2048
    3 D:\ORACLE\ORADATA\TARGET\INDX01.DBF        ONLINE  READ WRITE        2048
```

Archived Redo Log Files

Oracle archives the online redo log files to one or more offline destinations, known collectively as the *archived redo logs,* or more simply *archive logs.* The archived redo log files are important to perform media recovery operations.

The archived redo logs are also useful for maintaining the *standby database* for a primary database server. These files are transferred to the remote standby destination and applied to the database, thereby recovering it and synchronizing it with the primary database.

COLUMN NAME	COLUMN DESCRIPTION
NAME	Displays the name of the datafile.
FILE#	Displays the file identification number.
STATUS	Displays the current status of the file. The status could either be OFFLINE, ONLINE, SYSTEM, RECOVER, or SYSOFF.
ENABLED	Displays if the current state is DISABLED, READ ONLY, or READ WRITE.
CHECKPOINT_CHANGE#	Displays the SCN of the last occurred checkpoint.
CHECKPOINT_TIME	Displays the time stamp of the last occurred checkpoint.
OFFLINE_CHANGE#	Displays the change number that is updated only when the datafile or the corresponding tablespace is brought online from an offline state.
BLOCK_SIZE	Displays the file block size.
PLUGGED_IN	Displays a value of 1 if a tablespace associated with the file has been plugged-in to the database and has not yet been made read/write; 0 if not. The tablespace can be plugged-in using the *transportable-tablespace* feature.

TABLE 7-6.   *V$DATAFILE*

Importance of Checkpoints During Instance Recovery

A checkpoint's primary task is to write the dirty buffers from buffer cache to disk. The dirty buffers could either hold committed data or uncommitted data. Whenever a checkpoint occurs, the background process LGWR signals the DBW*n* process to write the dirty buffers to the datafiles on the disk. Oracle first writes the redo generated by a transaction to the log files before writing the dirty buffers to the data files on disk. The CKPT process updates the datafile headers and the control file. For example, if the SCN value is 456 when a checkpoint occurs, that means Oracle guarantees that all changes (SCNs) before 456 will be on disk. Checkpoints, at the database or data file level, occur automatically when the database encounters the following conditions:

- When a log switch occurs
- When configured through the database initialization parameters LOG_CHECKPOINT_INTERVAL and LOG_CHECKPOINT_TIMEOUT
- When an online database backup begins
- When a tablespace is taken offline NORMAL
- When the ALTER SYSTEM CHECKPOINT command is issued
- When the database is closed gracefully

Until a checkpoint completes, all redo log files written since the last checkpoint are needed in case database recovery is needed to open the database. Checkpoints expedite instance recovery because at every checkpoint all changed data is written to disk. Once data resides in the datafiles, redo log entries before the last checkpoint are not needed during the roll forward phase of crash recovery.

The initialization parameters that influence checkpoints in a database, are listed below:

- The initialization parameter LOG_CHECKPOINT_INTERVAL causes a checkpoint to be triggered when the specified number of O/S blocks are written to the redo log files. This insures that no more than a fixed number of redo blocks will have to be read during crash recovery. To disable this parameter, set the value to zero.

- The initialization parameter LOG_CHECKPOINT_TIMEOUT causes a checkpoint to occur after the specified time interval (in seconds) since the last checkpoint. This is again to insure that less redo is read during crash recovery. To disable this parameter, set the value to zero.

- The initialization parameter LOG_CHECKPOINTS_TO_ALERT records the timestamp in the alert log file regarding the checkpoints. This is useful when analyzing the exact time interval for each checkpoint.

NOTE
The LOG_CHECKPOINT_INTERVAL must be set to the number of O/S blocks. If set to a low value it would cause more checkpoints to occur and degrade the performance. Checkpoint is automatically invoked when LGWR switches a log.

Fast-start Checkpoints

The *fast-start* checkpoint enables DBW*n* to write dirty buffers out more aggressively. The earliest buffers dirtied are written to the disk first thereby advancing the position of the checkpoint in the redo log.

The initialization parameter FAST_START_IO_TARGET specifies the number of I/Os that should be needed during crash or instance recovery. Smaller values for this parameter result in faster recovery times. This improvement in recovery performance is achieved at the expense of additional writes needed during normal processing due to additional checkpoints. This parameter has been deprecated in favor of the FAST_START_MTTR_TARGET parameter.

NOTE
Oracle recommends that you use FAST_START_MTTR_TARGET instead of FAST_START_IO_TARGET, since the later is retained for backward compatibility only.

The initialization parameter FAST_START_MTTR_TARGET enables you to specify the amount of time (in seconds) the database should take to perform crash recovery of a single instance. This value is internally converted to a set of parameters that modify the operation of Oracle in such a way that recovery time is as close to this estimate as possible. You must disable the initialization parameters FAST_START_IO_TARGET, LOG_CHECKPOINT_INTERVAL, and LOG_CHECKPOINT_TIMEOUT parameters when using FAST_START_MTTR_TARGET. Setting these parameters to active values obstructs the normal functioning of FAST_START_MTTR_TARGET, thereby resulting in unpredictable results.

The dynamic performance view V$INSTANCE_RECOVERY monitors the mechanisms available to users to limit recovery I/O. This view can be used to calculate the influence of the parameters on the database checkpoints.

Parallel Recovery

You can enable *parallel recovery* to tune the cache recovery phase. During thread or media recovery, the redo log is read, and redo blocks that are to be applied are parsed out. These blocks are subsequently distributed evenly to all recovery processes to be read into the buffer cache. Crash and instance recovery of datafiles on different disk drives are good candidates for parallel recovery.

To enable the parallel recovery, the initialization parameter RECOVERY_PARALLELISM needs to be set with the number of concurrent recovery processes for instance or crash recovery. To use parallel processing, the value must be greater than 1 and must not exceed the value of the PARALLEL_MAX_SERVERS initialization parameter.

Transaction Recovery

[handwritten annotations: roll forward / rollback or transaction recovery]

As we discussed in earlier chapters, Oracle does recovery in two phases. While the first phase is called roll forward phase, the second phase is called rollback phase or transaction recovery. During transaction recovery, Oracle rolls back uncommitted transactions by reading the headers of all the rollback segments in the database. Oracle9*i* uses two advanced features—*fast-start on-demand* rollback and *fast-start parallel* rollback—to increase the efficiency during the recovery phase.

Using the fast-start on-demand rollback feature, Oracle automatically enables new transactions to begin immediately after the cache recovery phase (roll forward phase) of recovery completes. If a user attempts to access a row that is locked by a dead transaction, Oracle rolls back only those changes necessary to complete the transaction. In other words, transaction recovery is done on demand. Consequently, new transactions do not have to wait until all parts of a long transaction are rolled back. Oracle does this automatically, and you don't need to set any parameters or issue any statements to use this feature.

The fast-start parallel rollback feature allows you to specify the number of processes to speed up transaction recovery. The initialization parameter to control the number of processes involved in transaction recovery is FAST_START_PARALLEL_ROLLBACK. It can be set to HIGH, LOW, or FALSE. HIGH indicates that the number of recovery server processes cannot exceed four times the value of the CPU_COUNT parameter. LOW specifies that the number of recovery server processes cannot exceed twice the value of the CPU_COUNT parameter. Setting the value to FALSE disables this feature.

The dynamic performance view V$FAST_START_TRANSACTIONS provides information about the progress of the transactions that Oracle is recovering. The relevant columns for this view are STATE, UNDOBLOCKDONE, UNDOBLOCKSTOTAL, and CPUTIME. The STATE column indicates whether the transaction is RECOVERING, RECOVERED, or TO BE RECOVERED. The CPUTIME indicates the CPU time consumed by the transaction.

The dynamic performance view V$FAST_START_SERVERS provides information about all the recovery slaves (processes) performing parallel transaction recovery. The relevant columns for this view are STATE, UNDOBLOCKSDONE, and PID. The STATE column displays the state of the server—either IDLE or RECOVERING. The UNDOBLOCKSDONE indicates the percentage of the assigned work done so far. The PID is the process id.

Chapter Questions

1. **Which background process is responsible for writing the dirty buffers from the write list to the data files during a checkpoint?**

   A. CKPT

   B. SMON

   C. LGWR

   D. DBW*n*

   E. ARC*n*

2. **Which process is responsible for archiving the online redo log files when the database is operating in NOARCHIVELOG mode and the automatic archiving feature is enabled?**

   A. SMON

   B. CKPT

   C. ARC*n*

   D. RECO

   E. None of the above

3. **What are the consequences of not initializing the LARGE_POOL_SIZE parameter?**

   A. Oracle creates a large pool with the default size.

   B. Recovery Manager utility cannot be used.

   C. Oracle does not create the large pool area by default.

   D. The database can only be mounted.

4. **What is the maximum database block size supported for the Oracle9*i* database?**

   A. 16KB

   B. 32KB

   C. 64KB

   D. 128KB

5. **Where does Oracle maintain the bind and runtime information related to the SQL statement for a database user in a dedicated server environment?**

   A. Program Global Area

   B. Data dictionary Cache

   C. Library Cache

   D. Database Buffer Cache

   E. Redo Log buffers

6. **Where does Oracle store the checkpoint information for the database?**

   A. Data file and control file

   B. Log file and control file

   C. Control file and parameter file

   D. Log file and data file

7. **When does Oracle not require the online redo log files of a given log group to perform instance or crash recovery operations?**

   A. When the status of the redo log file is ACTIVE

   B. When the status of the redo log file is INACTIVE

   C. When the status of the redo log file is CURRENT

   D. When the status of the redo log file is STALE

8. **The database is operating in NOARCHIVELOG mode. The LGWR process has filled up the online redo log group and is about to switch to the next group. What is the crucial factor that would prohibit the LGWR process from continuing to write to the new group?**

   A. The next online redo log file has not been archived.

   B. The next online redo log file is unavailable since it is offline.

   C. The ARC*n* is slow in archiving data.

   D. The next online redo log file is unavailable for reuse until the checkpoint is complete.

9. **If you want to control the down time of the database for a given instance failure, which parameter should you set?**

   A. Set the RECOVERY_PARALLELISM init.ora parameter.

   B. Set the FAST_START_PARALLEL_ROLLBACK init.ora parameter.

   C. Set the FAST_START_IO_TARGET init.ora parameter.

   D. Set the FAST_START_MTTR_TARGET init.ora parameter.

10. **To enable the parallel recovery feature the initialization parameter RECOVERY_PARALLELISM must be set to a value?**

    A. Greater than 1

    B. Greater than 1 and must not exceed PARALLEL_MAX_SERVERS

    C. Greater than PARALLEL_MAX_SERVERS

    D. None of the above

11. **While adding a log member to the online redo log group, you encountered the following error:**

    ```
    SQL> ALTER DATABASE ADD LOGFILE MEMBER
    'c:\oracle\oradata\orcl\redo1d.log' TO GROUP 1;
    ALTER DATABASE ADD LOGFILE MEMBER
    'c:\oracle\oradata\orcl\redo1d.log' TO GROUP 1
    *
    ERROR at line 1:
    ORA-00357: too many members specified for log file, the maximum is 3
    ```

    What is the most appropriate solution?

    A. Add more log groups.

    B. Recreate the database with a higher value for the parameter MAXLOGMEMBERS.

    C. Recreate the control file with a higher value for the parameter MAXLOGMEMBERS.

    D. Add the MAXLOGMEMBERS parameter in the init.ora file.

Answers to Chapter Questions

1. D. DBW*n*

Explanation   The background process DBW*n* writes all the data from the write list that is part of the buffer cache, to the data files. Whenever a checkpoint is triggered, the LGWR and DBW*n* processes start writing the data from their corresponding buffers to the physical files and the CKPT process updates the checkpoint SCN values in the datafile headers and the control file.

2. E. None of the above

Explanation   This is a trick question. When you are running the database in NOARCHIVELOG mode, Oracle doesn't archive the redo log files even if you have automatic archiving turned on. You should not get confused between the mode of the database (ARCHIVELOG or NOARCHIVELOG) and the type of archiving that is enabled (automatic or manual). The type of archiving is only relevant if the database is running in ARCHIVELOG mode.

3. C. Oracle does not create the large pool area by default.

Explanation   The large pool memory structure is not automatically created in the SGA unless the parameter LARGE_POOL_SIZE is set. Oracle creates the large pool only when the LARGE_POOL_SIZE initialization parameter is set to a nonzero value. The large pool is used by RMAN to buffer I/O during backup and restore operations when the BACKUP_TAPE_IO_SLAVES parameter is set to TRUE.

4. B. 32KB

Explanation   The maximum block size supported for the Oracle9*i* database is 32KB. In Oracle9*i*, you can have multiple block sizes for different tablespaces. This is a new feature that was not available in Oracle8*i*. The block size can be specified while creating a tablespace using the CREATE TABLESPACE command. Before creating a tablespace with a nondefault block size, you should reserve the buffer space by dynamically initializing the DB_*n*K_CACHE_SIZE parameter with the appropriate block size.

5. A. Program Global Area

Explanation   In a dedicated server environment, Oracle maintains the bind and runtime information related to the SQL in the Program Global Area (PGA).

6. A.   Data file and control file

Explanation   Oracle maintains the checkpoint SCN information pertaining to the database in the data file headers and in the control file for each data file.

7. B.   When the status of the redo log file is INACTIVE

Explanation   When an online redo log file is in the INACTIVE state, it is not required for instance or crash recovery and the LGWR process tends to overwrite these files. During media recovery, Oracle takes the redo information from the archived log files. The status of the log groups in a database can be viewed from the dynamic performance view V$LOG.

8. D.   The next online redo log file is unavailable for reuse until the checkpoint is complete.

Explanation   You should read this question carefully. Note that the database is in NOARCHIVELOG mode. This makes answers A and C invalid. Whenever a log switch occurs, the switched file is unavailable for reuse until a checkpoint occurs, where the DBW*n* background process writes all the dirty buffers from the database buffer cache to the data files and the CKPT process updates the data file header and the control file with the new checkpoint SCN information.

9. Set the FAST_START_MTTR_TARGET init.ora parameter

Explanation   The initialization parameter FAST_START_MTTR_TARGET enables you to specify the amount of time (in seconds) the database should take to perform crash recovery of a single instance. The FAST_START_IO_TARGET parameter introduced in Oracle8*i* has been deprecated in Oracle9*i* in favor of the FAST_START_MTTR_TARGET. Note that in the question we say "down time," hinting that the parameter will specify time. All other parameters either specify number of processes or I/Os.

10. B.   Greater than 1 and must not exceed PARALLEL_MAX_SERVERS

Explanation   To enable the parallel recovery feature, the initialization parameter RECOVERY_PARALLELISM must be set to a value greater than 1 and must not exceed the value of the PARALLEL_MAX_SERVERS initialization parameter.

11. C. Recreate the control file with a higher value for the parameter MAXLOGMEMBERS

Explanation   The MAXLOGMEMBERS parameter should be set to a higher value than the current value that has been set to 3. This parameter cannot be specified in the init.ora file. It has to be set to a higher value by either recreating the control file or the database. While answer B is technically correct, it is not practical to recreate the database. Therefore, you should take a trace of the control file by issuing the following command:

```
SQL> ALTER DATABASE BACKUP CONTROLFILE TO TRACE;
```

The CREATE CONTROLFILE command will be written to the trace file. You can edit the trace file and increase the value of MAXLOGMEMBERS and execute it while the database is in NOMOUNT state.

CHAPTER
8

Configuring the Database Archive Mode

n this chapter, you will learn the modes in which a database can operate and the ramifications of operating the database in a given mode. You will also learn how to configure a database in ARCHIVELOG mode and to perform manual or automatic archiving. We also discuss how to multiplex the archived logs. At the end of this chapter you will find a listing of the important data dictionary views related to archiving. We explain the columns and their values in detail for these V$VIEWS. This chapter includes the following topics:

- Differences between ARCHIVELOG and NOARCHIVELOG mode
- Configuring a database for ARCHIVELOG mode
- Configuring multiple archive processes
- Configuring multiple destinations, including remote destinations
- Useful V$ Views

Differences Between ARCHIVELOG and NOARCHIVELOG Mode

You can operate an Oracle database in either the *ARCHIVELOG mode* or the *NOARCHIVELOG mode*. You should determine which mode your database should run in. Oracle strongly recommends that you run in ARCHIVELOG mode. The default mode of a newly created database is set to NOARCHIVELOG mode unless explicitly specified in the CREATE DATABASE command. Let's discuss the ramifications of running the database in a specific mode.

NOARCHIVELOG Mode   *restore, but no recover. (no redo log's)*

Every change made to the database creates *redo* information and rollback information (often called *undo*). The redo information is used to reapply the changes to the database, should a failure occur. The undo is needed to rollback a specific transaction. The redo is initially recorded in the redo log buffers and later written to the redo log files. The redo log files are used in a *circular* fashion, as shown in Figure 8-1. Whenever an online redo log file is filled, a log switch occurs. At a log switch, the archive process (ARC*n*) wakes up and archives the filled online log file to an archive destination. However, if you run your database in NOARCHIVELOG mode, these log files are not archived but reused by the log writer process, and the information in log files is overwritten. Once the redo logs are overwritten, media recovery cannot be performed using the last full database backup.

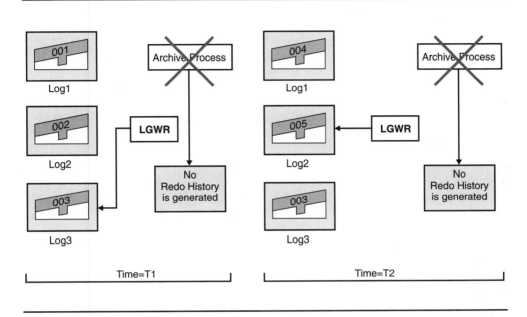

FIGURE 8-1. *NOARCHIVELOG mode*

In NOARCHIVELOG mode, online backups of the database cannot be performed. To implement offline backup procedures, the database needs to be shut down cleanly and made unavailable for the users until the backup completes. You must back up the complete set of database files: the control files, data files, parameter files, and the password files during a full database backup. You don't need to back up the online redo log files if the database has been shut down cleanly. If a database failure occurs and you have to go back to your backup and don't have log files, you can start the database with the RESETLOGS option.

In NOARCHIVELOG mode, recovery cannot be performed since archived redo log files are not available. This means that all changes made to the database since the last backup will be lost. For example, if a datafile is lost, you can only restore the last full database backup. An alternative solution would be to drop the tablespace related to the lost data file. However, in this case, you lose all the data in that specific tablespace. This would work for any tablespace except the *system* tablespace, since it cannot be dropped.

TIP
Oracle strongly recommends that you run your database in ARCHIVELOG mode.

ARCHIVELOG Mode

In ARCHIVELOG mode, the LGWR process writes the contents of the redo log buffer to the redo log files. When the redo log files get filled, Oracle initiates a *log switch*. Oracle generates archive log files every time a log switch occurs. The filled redo log files cannot be reused until the background process ARC*n* copies all its contents to the archive log destination. Figure 8-2 shows the redo history generated in the ARCHIVELOG mode. The DBA can configure one or more destinations for backing up the redo log files. This is called multiplexing of archived redo log files. The files are generally identified with the log sequence number, which the user can define in the INIT*sid*.ora file.

In the ARCHIVELOG mode, you can take an online backup of the database and perform a complete or incomplete recovery of the database. A complete recovery of the database can only be performed if all the archived redo log files are available. You will also need a current control file or a backup control file that has the latest schema of the database. You also need the backup of the database file that needs recovery. Once you restore the backup of the necessary datafiles, you should apply the redo logs from the last backup. While doing a complete recovery of a tablespace

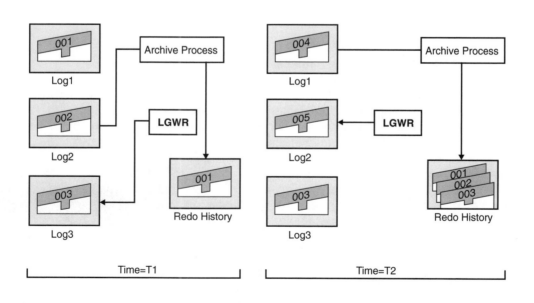

FIGURE 8-2. *ARCHIVELOG mode*

or datafile, you can choose to have the database up and running. However, the tablespace or datafile that you are recovering should be offline. If you perform an incomplete recovery, you can restore the database from a backup and recover to a specific point in time, to the end of the specified archived log file, or to a specific *system change number* (SCN).

When you run your database in ARCHIVELOG mode, you can configure a standby database or use the LogMiner utility to analyze archive log files and get information about the changes done to a database, which can be used to undo a specific user action.

Configuring a Database for ARCHIVELOG Mode

To configure the database to operate in ARCHIVELOG mode, you will need to perform the following steps:

1. Close the database cleanly. Shut it down with *normal*, *transactional*, or *immediate* options. If you shut down the database with the *abort* option, you need to do a crash recovery and shut it down again cleanly using the following command:

```
SQL>SHUTDOWN NORMAL
```

2. Set the initialization parameters related to the database log mode. Also set the following initialization parameters in the INIT*sid*.ora file:

```
LOG_ARCHIVE_START= true
LOG_ARCHIVE_DEST= 'C:\Oracle9i\Oramasters\Arc\dbs\arch'
LOG_ARCHIVE_FORMAT= "T%TS%S.ARC"
```

Note that the parameter LOG_ARCHIVE_START enables automatic archiving. You should not get confused between the mode of the database and the type of archiving you want to use. If you don't enable this parameter, you can still turn on the database to ARCHIVELOG mode, but the database will be in manual ARCHIVELOG mode. If you forget to turn this parameter on in the init.ora file, you can also enable it using the ARCHIVE LOG START command after you open the database. However, this command will be valid only until you shut down the database. Next time when you shut the database down, you need to edit the init.ora file and enable the LOG_ARCHIVE_START parameter.

TIP
If you run your database in ARCHIVELOG mode,
we strongly recommend that you turn on automatic
archiving by setting the LOG_ARCHIVE_START
parameter in your init.ora file.

The LOG_ARCHIVE_DEST parameter tells Oracle where to keep your
archived log files. Similarly, the LOG_ARCHIVE_FORMAT tells Oracle how
to name the archived log files.

3. Mount the database and turn on the ARCHIVELOG mode, as shown here:

```
SQL> STARTUP MOUNT
SQL> ALTER DATABASE ARCHIVELOG;
```

Similarly, to turn off logging for a database, issue the following command in
the mount state:

```
SQL> ALTER DATABASE NOARCHIVELOG;
```

NOTE
The previous commands make an entry in the
control file registering the appropriate log mode,
which is either the ARCHIVELOG mode or the
NOARCHIVELOG mode. This entry is maintained
until the user explicitly changes the log mode.

4. Perform a full database backup. After changing the database log mode from
NOARCHIVELOG to ARCHIVELOG mode, you must perform a full
database backup either using OS-specific commands or using the Recovery
Manager (RMAN). The full database backup would be required to recover
the database during media failures.

5. Periodically transfer the archive log files to an external storage media like
tape and ensure that sufficient free space is available for future archive
storage.

NOTE
It is recommended that you immediately perform a
closed, full database backup after switching the
database into ARCHIVELOG mode. The previous
backups performed when the database was in
NOARCHIVELOG mode would not be useful if you

*need to recover the database for future media
failures. You can do a full hot backup, but you
would stand the risk of losing data until it is
completed.*

Enabling Automatic Archiving

The process of archiving can be automated by setting the following initialization
parameter:

```
LOG_ARCHIVE_START= true
```

You can also enable automatic archiving dynamically by executing one of the
following commands:

```
SQL>ALTER SYSTEM ARCHIVE LOG START TO '<destination>';
```

or

```
SQL>ARCHIVE LOG START
```

For a database operating in ARCHIVELOG mode, if you don't set automatic
archiving, you should manually archive the log files.

Performing Manual Archiving of Logs

To enable manual archiving of the online redo log files, set the initialization
parameter LOG_ARCHIVE_START to FALSE. If your database is running in
ARCHIVELOG mode with automatic archiving turned on, and you want to disable
automatic archiving, use one of the following commands:

```
SQL> ALTER SYSTEM ARCHIVE LOG STOP;
```

or

```
SQL> ARCHIVE LOG STOP
```

During manual archiving, you will need to perform the archiving of redo log
files manually. As a DBA, you will need to keep track of the filled log groups and
then archive them. If all the log groups get filled and they are not archived, the
database will hang. This would occur since the LGWR cannot overwrite the files
with data from the redo log buffers until they are archived.

NOTE
The archive process will not perform the manual archiving requested by the user processes. Instead, the server process corresponding to that user process will perform the manual archiving.

To perform manual archiving, you will need to execute the following command:

```
ALTER SYSTEM ARCHIVE LOG <option>
```

where the <option> can be one of the following:

- **ALL**   Archives all unarchived redo logs excluding the current redo log group.
- **NEXT**   Archives the oldest redo log file that needs to be archived.
- **CHANGE** archives all unarchived redo log files that contain the SCN that is equal to or less than the SCN specified. The column FIRST_CHANGE# of the V$LOG view can be used to obtain the oldest SCN existing in a redo log group.
- **SEQUENCE *integer***   Archives all unarchived redo log files that are older than the specified log sequence number. Note that the redo log file with the sequence number specified in this option will also be archived.
- **LOGFILE *filename***   Archives the specified redo log file.
- **GROUP *integer***   Archives the redo log files for the specified group number. It also archives all the unarchived redo log files that are older than the group specified.
- **CURRENT**   Archives the entire unarchived redo log files, including the current redo log file. A log switch will be triggered immediately.
- **THREAD *integer***   Archives the redo log files that haven't been archived for the specified thread.

If the ARCn process detects a problem, it will take the contents from another member of the same redo log *group*. The ARCn process will never fail if atleast one member of a group is accessible. Though some of the operating systems support direct archiving to tapes, you should generally archive to disk for improved I/O performance. When you back up the archive log files from disk to tape, verify that the files are completely archived.

Configuring Multiple Archive Processes

The Oracle server, depending upon the workload, determines the number of ARC*n* processes required for archiving. To avoid runtime overhead, you can define the initial number of archive processes that will be started during instance startup by using the following initialization parameter:

```
log_archive_max_processes= 3
```

TIP
The maximum number of ARCn processes that can be started is 10. If this parameter is not set, the default process is 1.

To dynamically increase or decrease the number of ARC*n* processes while the database is open, execute the following command:

```
ALTER SYSTEM SET LOG_ARCHIVE_MAX_PROCESSES= 6
```

Each archive process is responsible for archiving to all the specified destinations. A redo log group, which is to be archived, will be assigned to an archive process. If one process is archiving a redo log group, the other archive processes will not archive the same group. Multiplexing the redo log files will help distribute the I/O load since the archive process reads from all the redo log files existing in a group, which are not *invalid*.

Configuring Multiple Destinations, Including Remote Destinations

Archived log files are very important in performing recovery operations for the database. You can configure multiple archive destinations to maintain redundant copies of the archived log files. In this section, you will learn how to specify the file formats and multiple destinations for the archive log files.

Setting Archive Log File Formats

You can set a format for the archive log files using the initialization parameter:

```
LOG_ARCHIVE_FORMAT= "ARCH_FILE_%s_THREAD_%t.arc"
```

The various options available to set the filename format are as follows:

- **%s or %S** Includes the redo log sequence number in the filename.
- **%t or %T** Includes the database instance or thread number in the filename.

The characters in capitals signify that the filename would have a fixed length value to be left padded with zeros. For example, the above-specified format would generate archived log files for log sequence numbers 100 and 101 in thread 1 in the following format:

```
C:\oracle\oradata\orcl\archive\ARCH_FILE_100_THREAD_1.arc
C:\oracle\oradata\orcl\archive\ARCH_FILE_101_THREAD_1.arc
```

Setting Archive Log File Destinations

You can configure multiple archive destinations for a database. If one of the archive log files is unavailable during recovery, the other redundant copy can be used to perform the recovery operation. The combination of LOG_ARCHIVE_DEST and LOG_ARCHIVE_FORMAT will form a valid path and the filename. If the database is operating in ARCHIVELOG mode and no destination is defined in the parameter file, then Oracle generates the archive log files in the default destination, which is operating specific. For example, on a Linux operating system, the default destination for Oracle9*i* is $ORACLE_HOME/dbs/arch.

TIP
Archive log destinations configured using the LOG_ARCHIVE_DEST parameter must point to a valid path or device name. The value must not be set to point to a raw device.

NOTE
Direct archiving to tape devices is only possible on some of the operating systems.

Duplexing Archive Log Files

The initialization parameter to configure a secondary archive log destination is

```
LOG_ARCHIVE_DUPLEX_DEST = <filename or device name>
```

The archive log destinations can also be configured dynamically by executing the command

```
SQL>ALTER SYSTEM SET log_archive_duplex_dest=c:\oracle\oradata\orcl\arch2
```

Figure 8-3 shows how to duplex the archive log files to two separate destinations.

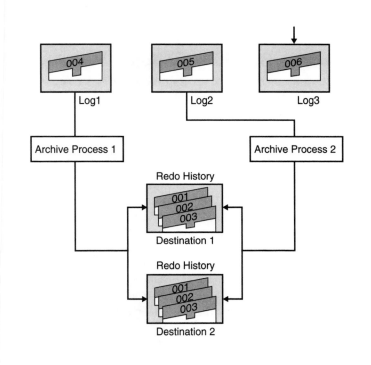

FIGURE 8-3. *Duplexing archive log files*

Limitations of Duplexing the Archive Log Files

You cannot duplex archive log files to a remote destination. Therefore, you cannot automatically archive the log files to a remote standby database. The database cannot have more than two destinations configured for archiving. Though the destinations can be configured dynamically (while the database is open) by issuing the ALTER SYSTEM command, they cannot be altered at the session level. See the

"Multiplexing Archive Log Files" section to see how you can configure Oracle9*i* to send the archived log files to a remote destination.

NOTE
While using the Oracle Enterprise Edition, Oracle recommends the use of the initialization parameter LOG_ARCHIVE_DEST_n instead of LOG_ARCHIVE_DEST as it has been deprecated. The multiplexing of archive log files is only supported in the enterprise edition.

Multiplexing Archive Log Files

Assume that both redundant copies of the archive log files are corrupted. This would result in data loss during recovery operations since the archive log files have to be applied in sequence, and a hole in the redo stream will result in an incomplete recovery. Oracle supports multiplexing the archive log files. Archive log destinations can be configured to maintain a single copy at a maximum of ten destinations. You should use the following parameter to configure multiple archive destinations:

```
LOG_ARCHIVE_DEST_n="LOCATION=<path>|SERVICE=servicename[MANDATORY|OPTIONAL]
[REOPEN=integer]"
```

where *n* ranges from 1 to 10 in the parameter. The LOCATION includes the destination in the form of a specified directory. The directory cannot be an NFS mounted directory. The SERVICE includes the net service name, which is resolved through the TNSNAMES.ORA file. This is generally configured to accumulate archive log files at the standby site. The MANDATORY option enables LGWR to wait until the log file is completely archived before overwriting it. The OPTIONAL option indicates that it is desirable to archive the redo log file to the specified destination before it is overwritten, but this is not mandatory. The REOPEN attribute enables the ARCn process to retry if it fails to archive the log file. The write attempt to archive the same redo log file is made after the duration configured through this attribute. If the attribute is not defined, errors about the OPTIONAL destinations are registered in the alert log file. The errors will be ignored and no further redo log files will be archived to the destination. If errors occur at the MANDATORY destination, the online redo logs will be prevented from being overwritten until archiving resumes successfully at all destinations.

You can dynamically set the parameter either at the system level or at the session level. To set the parameter at the system level, issue one of the following commands:

```
SQL>ALTER SYSTEM SET log_archive_dest_2=
'LOCATION=c:\oracle\oradata\orcl\archive2', MANDATORY,'REOPEN=200'
COMMENT='new archive destination' SCOPE=SPFILE;
```

or

```
SQL>ALTER SYSTEM SET LOG_ARCHIVE_DEST_2=
'LOCATION=c:\oracle\oradata\orcl\archive2 MANDATORY REOPEN=200';
```

To propagate the archive log files to a standby database, you must configure the LOG_ARCHIVE_DEST_n parameter with the SERVICE option, as shown here:

```
Log_archive_dest_2="SERVICE=standby_prod1"
```
When using oracle data Suard.

The value set with SERVICE must be a valid net service name. If the standby database is operating in MANAGED RECOVERY mode, it can be updated simultaneously as and when the archive log files are generated at the primary database site, thus being synchronized with the primary database site. The files are transmitted to the standby site either by the ARCn process or by the server process using Oracle Net with the help of the *Remote File Server* (RFS) process. The creation of files at the standby database is based on the initialization parameters STANDBY_ ARCHIVE_DEST and LOG_ARCHIVE_FORMAT, which must be configured at the standby site. For every ARCn process or every additional remote destination set at the primary site, one RFS process is created. Whenever Oracle applies the archived log files to the standby database, it updates the log history in the control file. To configure an archive log destination using SERVICE, set the initialization parameter:

```
LOG_ARCHIVE_DEST_2= "SERVICE=standby_prod MANDATORY REOPEN=450"
```

> **NOTE**
> *To learn about configuring and managing the standby database server, refer to the Oracle documentation guide, "Oracle9i Data Guard Concepts and Administration."*

Configuring Archive Log Destination States

The initialization parameter that determines whether archiving is to be performed to a configured destination is

```
LOG_ARCHIVE_DEST_STATE_n= ENABLE| DEFER
```

where n ranges from 1 to 10.

This parameter can either be set to one of two values: ENABLE or DEFER. The ENABLE option allows ARCn to archive the log file to the configured destination. The DEFER option stops archiving to the destination until enabled again. For example, if there is insufficient space available to archive to a destination, you can set the parameter to DEFER and reset it back to ENABLE after creating sufficient space. The parameter can also be set dynamically by executing the following command:

```
SQL>ALTER SYSTEM SET LOG_ARCHIVE_DEST_STATE_1= DEFER;
```

Specifying Minimum Destinations to Succeed

The minimum number of destinations that Oracle should successfully archive to before overwriting the online log files can be specified using the following parameter:

```
LOG_ARCHIVE_MIN_SUCCEED_DEST=integer
```

If the duplexing method is used, then the parameter must be initialized to either 1 or 2. If set to 1, it indicates that only LOG_ARCHIVE_DEST is treated as a mandatory destination. If initialized to 2, then both the destinations defined using LOG_ARCHIVE_DEST and LOG_ARCHIVE_DUPLEX_DEST are treated as mandatory destinations. When multiplexing the archive log files, the value can range from 1 to 10.

If LOG_ARCHIVE_MIN_SUCCEED_DEST is set less than the number of destinations in which the mandatory option is chosen, then the value in LOG_ARCHIVE_MIN_SUCCEED_DEST is ignored. If the value set is greater than the specified mandatory destinations, then some of the optional destinations are treated as mandatory.

Setting Trace Parameter

Oracle logs most of the errors related to archiving in the alert log file. Specific errors, which are usually more severe in nature when related to the ARCn process, are recorded into the trace files with detailed descriptions. These trace files are generated in the path defined by the BACKGROUND_DUMP_DEST initialization parameter. To trace errors for the ARCn process, you can use the LOG_ARCHIVE_TRACE parameter with an appropriate value. To enable the tracing feature, you can set the initialization parameter at either the instance level or execute the following commands at the system level:

```
LOG_ARCHIVE_TRACE=20
```

or

```
ALTER SYSTEM SET LOG_ARCHIVE_TRACE=20
```

The value 20 is a combination of trace levels 16 and 4. The trace level 16 will track detailed archive log destination activity. The trace level 4 will track archival operational phase output. The default value set for the LOG_ARCHIVE_TRACE parameter is 0, and at this level, error conditions still generate the appropriate alert and trace entries.

Setting the Source Destination for Fetching Archive Log Files During Recovery

During media recovery, Oracle suggests that the path for archive log files be set, which is based on the configured archive log destination for the database. If the files are available in a different destination, then you must manually configure a new destination, thereby enabling Oracle to treat the new destination as the source for the archive log files. To set a new destination, execute one of the following commands:

```
SET LOGSOURCE path
```

or

```
ALTER SYSTEM ARCHIVE LOG START TO path
```

To view the current database mode and archive information, use the following command. This is a very important command every DBA should remember.

TIP
You should be connected as SYSDBA to run the following command.

```
SQL> ARCHIVE LOG LIST
Database log mode              No Archive Mode
Automatic archival             Enabled
Archive destination            C:\oracle\oradata\ORCL\archive1
Oldest online log sequence     2086
Current log sequence           2089
```

In the previous output, you can see that the database is running in NOARCHIVELOG mode. Though the archive destination is set, and automatic archiving enabled, Oracle will not create any archived log files as the database is in NOARCHIVELOG mode. You can see the log sequence number of the oldest online log group and the current one. There are four log groups in this database.

Useful V$VIEWS

In this section we describe some of the V$VIEWS that provide useful information relating to the mode of the database, archiving, background processes, log groups, and recovery.

V$ARCHIVE_DEST

The V$ARCHIVE_DEST view displays detailed information about the archive log destinations, their values, and statuses. The important columns and a brief description of these columns are shown in Table 8-1.

V$ARCHIVE_PROCESSES

The V$ARCHIVE_PROCESSES view displays detailed information about the ARCn processes currently running. The important columns and a brief description of these columns are shown in Table 8-2.

V$DATABASE

The V$DATABASE view displays the database log mode by retrieving information from the control file of the database. The column LOG_MODE displays the mode in which the database is operating. The value of this column is either ARCHIVELOG or NOARCHIVELOG.

V$INSTANCE

The V$INSTANCE view displays the state of archiving for the current instance. You can also determine if the automatic archiving feature is enabled or disabled from this view. The column ARCHIVER displays the values STOPPED, STARTED, or FAILED. If there is no ARCn process available, the value STOPPED will be displayed. If an ARCn process or processes are currently running, the value displayed will be STARTED. The value FAILED indicates that the ARCn process could not archive a log.

V$LOG

The V$LOG view retrieves log file information from the control files. The information contained in this view is vital to determining the archive state of a group

Column Name	Column Description
DEST_ID	Displays the archive destination number that ranges from 1 to 10.
STATUS	Displays the current status for the destination, which could be any of the following: VALID, INACTIVE, DEFERRED, ERROR, DISABLED, or BAD PARAM.
BINDING	Displays whether a particular destination is either MANDATORY or OPTIONAL.
NAME_SPACE	Displays either SYSTEM or SESSION, depending on the type of command issued during configuration.
TARGET	Displays the value PRIMARY or STANDBY depending on the option specified while specifying the destination through LOCATION or SERVICE.
REOPEN_SECS	Displays the retry time in seconds after a failure has occurred.
DESTINATION	Displays the net service name or the physical location of the archive log file destination.
FAIL_DATE	Displays the date and time at which the last error occurred.
FAIL_SEQUENCE	Displays the log sequence number of the online redo log file when the last error occurred.
ERROR	Displays the error text of the last error.

TABLE 8-1. *V$ARCHIVE_DEST*

and the current status relating to the user activity. Some of the relevant columns and a brief description of these columns are shown in Table 8-3.

V$LOGFILE

The V$LOGFILE view displays detailed information pertaining to redo log groups and the members belonging to these groups. The column GROUP# displays the redo log group number of the redo log member. The column STATUS displays the status of the redo log file, which could be INVALID, STALE, or DELETED. If a file is inaccessible, the status of the member would be INVALID. STALE indicates that the file contents are incomplete. DELETED indicates that the file is no longer used, and if the column STATUS has no value (if the column is blank), it indicates that the file

Column Name	Column Description
PROCESS	Displays the process number, which ranges from 0 to 9.
STATUS	Displays the status of the ARCn processes, that could be any of the following: STOPPED, SCHEDULED, STARTING, ACTIVE, STOPPING, and TERMINATED.
STATE	Displays the current state of the ARCn process. The process could either be BUSY or IDLE.
LOG_SEQUENCE	If the state of an ARCn process is BUSY, then it displays the corresponding log sequence number of the redo log file, which is currently being archived by the process.

TABLE 8-2.   *V$ARCHIVE_PROCESSES*

Column Name	Column Description
GROUP#	Displays the group number.
SEQUENCE#	Displays the sequence number.
ARCHIVED	Displays whether a redo log group is archived or not. The value can be either YES or NO.
STATUS	Displays the status as UNUSED, CURRENT, ACTIVE, CLEARING, CLEARING_CURRENT, or INACTIVE. (Indicates that the online redo log has never been written to so far.)
FIRST_CHANGE#	Displays the lowest SCN, which is present in the log.
FIRST_TIME	Displays the time at which the lowest SCN was generated in the log.

TABLE 8-3.   *V$LOG*

is currently in use. The column MEMBER displays the path and filename for the redo log file.

V$LOG_HISTORY

The V$LOG_HISTORY view displays the lowest and highest SCNs for a redo log file. The column FIRST_CHANGE# displays the lowest SCN and the column NEXT_CHANGE# displays the highest SCN for a log file.

V$ RECOVERY_LOG

The V$RECOVERY_LOG view displays the information related to the archived logs that is required for performing media recovery during failures. The column SEQUENCE# displays the sequence number of the archived log file. The column ARCHIVE_NAME displays the name of the archived file that has been defined using the format string in LOG_ARCHIVE_FORMAT.

V$ARCHIVED_LOG

The V$ARCHIVED_LOG view displays historical ARCHIVELOG file information that is registered in the control file. Some of the relevant columns and a brief description of these columns are shown in Table 8-4.

Column Name	Column Description
THREAD#	Displays the redo log thread number.
SEQUENCE#	Displays the redo log sequence number.
FIRST_CHANGE#	Displays the lowest SCN number for an archived log file.
NEXT_CHANGE#	Displays the first SCN number for the next log file.
COMPLETION_TIME	Displays the time when the ARC*n* process had successfully archived the log file.
FIRST_TIME	Displays the timestamp of the first SCN generated for the log file.
NEXT_TIME	Displays the timestamp of the next change to the log file.

TABLE 8-4.   *V$ARCHIVED_LOG*

The following is the complete list of init.ora parameters in Oracle9*i* that relates to ARCHIVELOG mode.

```
SQL> SHOW PARAMETER log_archive
NAME                                 TYPE         VALUE
------------------------------------ -----------  -------------------------
----
log_archive_dest                     string       C:\target\archives
log_archive_dest_1                   string
log_archive_dest_10                  string
log_archive_dest_2                   string
log_archive_dest_3                   string
log_archive_dest_4                   string
log_archive_dest_5                   string
log_archive_dest_6                   string
log_archive_dest_7                   string
log_archive_dest_8                   string
log_archive_dest_9                   string
log_archive_dest_state_1             string       enable
log_archive_dest_state_10            string       enable
log_archive_dest_state_2             string       enable
log_archive_dest_state_3             string       enable
log_archive_dest_state_4             string       enable
log_archive_dest_state_5             string       enable
log_archive_dest_state_6             string       enable
log_archive_dest_state_7             string       enable
log_archive_dest_state_8             string       enable
log_archive_dest_state_9             string       enable
log_archive_duplex_dest              string
log_archive_format                   string       %s.arc
log_archive_max_processes            integer      1
log_archive_min_succeed_dest         integer      1
log_archive_start                    boolean      TRUE
log_archive_trace                    integer      0
```

Chapter Questions

1. **You are running the database with automatic archiving enabled. You need to determine the oldest online log file sequence number that has been archived. Which of the following commands would you use?**

   A. ARCHIVE LIST

   B. ARCHIVE LOG ALL

   C. LIST ARCHIVE ALL

   D. ARCHIVE LOG LIST

   E. LIST THE ARCHIVES

2. **Your database is operating in ARCHIVELOG mode. At which point will the redo log files be available for reuse?**

   A. After the CKPT process has checkpointed and archiving of the redo log file is complete.

   B. Before the CKPT process has checkpointed and archiving the redo log file is complete.

   C. After the CKPT process has checkpointed and before completion of the redo log file archiving.

   D. Before the CKPT process has checkpointed and before completion of the redo log file archiving.

3. **Bernard is a DBA of a Fortune 500 company. He manages a database that operates in ARCHIVELOG mode. He wants to enable automatic archiving. Which command must he issue?**

   A. ALTER TABLE

   B. ALTER SYSTEM

   C. ALTER DATABASE

   D. ALTER TABLESPACE

   E. ALTER SESSION

4. **Which of the following initialization parameters cannot be declared when the database has the duplex archive destination set in the init.ora file?**

   A. LOG_ARCHIVE_DEST

   B. LOG_ARCHIVE_DEST_n

   C. LOG_ARCHIVE_DUPLEX_DEST

   D. LOG_ARCHIVE_TRACE

5. **Which dynamic performance view can we query to obtain information pertaining to the MANDATORY and OPTIONAL destinations?**

   A. V$ARCHIVE_DEST

   B. V$INSTANCE

   C. V$ARCHIVED_LOG

   D. V$DATABASE

   E. V$ARCHIVE_PROCESSES

6. **Jane is a DBA for an online transaction-processing (OLTP) database. The database has crashed, causing heavy losses to the business and inconvenience to the end-users. The database has been operating in NOARCHIVELOG mode. The last offline full database backup was performed a month ago. Which of the following options are valid?**

   A. Media recovery must be performed.

   B. Media recovery is not essential since the backup still contains current data.

   C. Media recovery must be performed since the backup contains incomplete data.

   D. The database can be opened, but the changes since the last backup will be lost.

7. **Which of the following steps is incorrect in the following sequence of enabling the ARCHIVELOG mode of a database?**

   A. Shut down the database.

   B. Set the appropriate parameters in the init.ora file.

   C. Start the database in NOMOUNT state.

   D. Issue the ALTER DATABASE ARCHIVELOG command.

E. Open the database.

F. Shut down the database.

G. Take a full closed backup.

8. **Manual archiving of the database is the only option when**

   A. The database is in ARCHIVELOG mode and LOG_ARCHIVE_START=true.

   B. The database is in NOARCHIVELOG mode and LOG_ARCHIVE_START=true.

   C. The database is in NOARCHIVELOG mode and LOG_ARCHIVE_START=false.

   D. The database is in ARCHIVELOG mode and LOG_ARCHIVE_START=false.

   E. The database is in ARCHIVELOG mode and MANUAL_ARCHIVING=true.

9. **What is the maximum number of ARCn processes that can be defined using the initialization parameter LOG_ARCHIVE_MAX_PROCESSES?**

   A. 1

   B. 5

   C. 10

   D. 15

   E. Depends on system memory resources

10. **Which initialization parameter defines the default destination for the trace files generated by the ARCn process?**

   A. USER_DUMP_DEST

   B. CORE_DUMP_DEST

   C. BACKGROUND_DUMP_DEST

   D. LOG_ARCHIVE_DEST

Answers to Chapter Questions

1. D.   ARCHIVE LOG LIST

Explanation   The ARCHIVE LOG LIST command can be used to display the information related to the database log mode, automatic archival state, archive log destination, oldest log sequence number, and the current log sequence number. To execute this command, the user should establish a session and connect as SYSDBA.

2. A.   After the CKPT process has checkpointed and archiving of the redo log file is complete.

Explanation   When the database is operating in ARCHIVELOG mode, the redo logs cannot be overwritten until they are archived. When automatic archiving is enabled, the ARCn process archives the oldest unarchived redo log group first. For manual archiving, the ARCHIVE command is issued, a log switch and a checkpoint occur, and the oldest unarchived log group is archived. This group is now available for reuse.

3. B.   ALTER SYSTEM

Explanation   To enable automatic archiving when the database is open, issue this command:

```
SQL>ALTER SYSTEM ARCHIVE LOG START
```

To enable automatic archiving at the start of an instance, set the LOG_ARCHIVE_START initialization parameter to TRUE.

4. B.   LOG_ARCHIVE_DEST_n

Explanation   The initialization parameter LOG_ARCHIVE_DEST_n cannot be configured if the database is configured to use the duplexing method. The initialization parameters for the archived destinations in the duplex environment are as follows:

```
LOG_ARCHIVE_DEST - primary archive log file location
LOG_ARCHIVE_DUPLEX_DEST - secondary archive location for duplexing
LOG_ARCHIVE_TRACE - trace file level
```

5. A.   V$ARCHIVE_DEST

Explanation   The dynamic performance view V$ARCHIVE_DEST displays detailed information about all the archive log destinations, their values, and statuses. The BINDING column displays whether a particular destination is either MANDATORY or OPTIONAL.

6. D.   The database can be opened, but the changes since the last backup will be lost.

Explanation   In NOARCHIVELOG mode, media recovery cannot be performed because the archived redo log files since the previous backup are not available. The only option for Jane is to restore the last full backup made one month ago and open the database.

7. C.   Start the database in NOMOUNT state.

Explanation   The database must be MOUNTED to perform any updates to the control file. The ARCHIVELOG mode is initially set in the control file when you issue the ALTER DATATBASE ARCHIVELOG command. When you open the database in NOMOUNT stage, the background processes and SGA are created, but the controlfile is not open.

8. D.   The database is in ARCHIVELOG mode and LOG_ARCHIVE_START=false.

Explanation   The database must be operating in ARCHIVELOG mode to archive (manually or automatic) the log files. The initialization parameter LOG_ARCHIVE_START, when set to false, requires the DBA to manually perform archiving. Note that MANUAL_ARCHIVING is not a valid initialization parameter. Note that manual archiving is also possible in answer A and may well be needed if LOG_ARCHIVE_MAX_PROCESSES isn't high enough. However, the question says that manual archiving should be the *only* option. Therefore, D is the correct answer.

9. C.   10

Explanation   The maximum number of ARCn processes that can be defined using the initialization parameter LOG_ARCHIVE_MAX_PROCESSES is 10.

10. C.   BACKGROUND_DUMP_DEST

Explanation   The errors pertaining to the ARCn processes are registered in trace files, which are generated in the path defined by the BACKGROUND_DUMP_DEST parameter.

CHAPTER
9

Oracle Recovery
Manager Overview
and Configuration

he *Recovery Manager* (RMAN) utility enables you to perform backup, restore, and recovery operations. RMAN has evolved into a total backup and recovery solution utility since its release with Oracle8 Release 1.

In this chapter, you will learn about the features and components associated with RMAN. We discuss the use of the *recovery catalog* and the *control file* as repositories for RMAN and the advantages of using the recovery catalog. We also discuss RMAN *channels* and explain the architecture of the *media management library*. Finally, we explain how to connect to RMAN without a recovery catalog and describe the various configuration options in the RMAN environment. This chapter includes the following topics:

■ Features of RMAN

■ Components of RMAN

■ RMAN repository

■ RMAN channel allocation

■ Media Management Library Interface

■ Connecting to RMAN without the Recovery Catalog

■ Configuring the RMAN environment

Features of RMAN

RMAN is operated using exclusive command language that is independent of the operating system. It uses the database server sessions to perform backup and recovery operations. This is the primary reason that the backup and recovery operations using RMAN are also referred to as *Server Managed Backup and Recovery*. RMAN can be initiated either using the Oracle Enterprise Manager, a GUI interface, or using the command line interface (CLI). The metadata pertaining to the backup and recovery operations when using RMAN is either maintained in an Oracle schema as the recovery catalog or in the control file of the target database. The target database is the database to which the backup and recovery operations are performed. Figure 9-1 displays the backup and recovery options when using the Oracle Enterprise Manager (OEM) Console.

The features and enhancements made to RMAN in Oracle9*i* (Release 1) increase manageability and greatly expand functionality when compared to user-managed backup and recovery operations. RMAN in the course of time has incorporated numerous features. The following are some of the important features of RMAN:

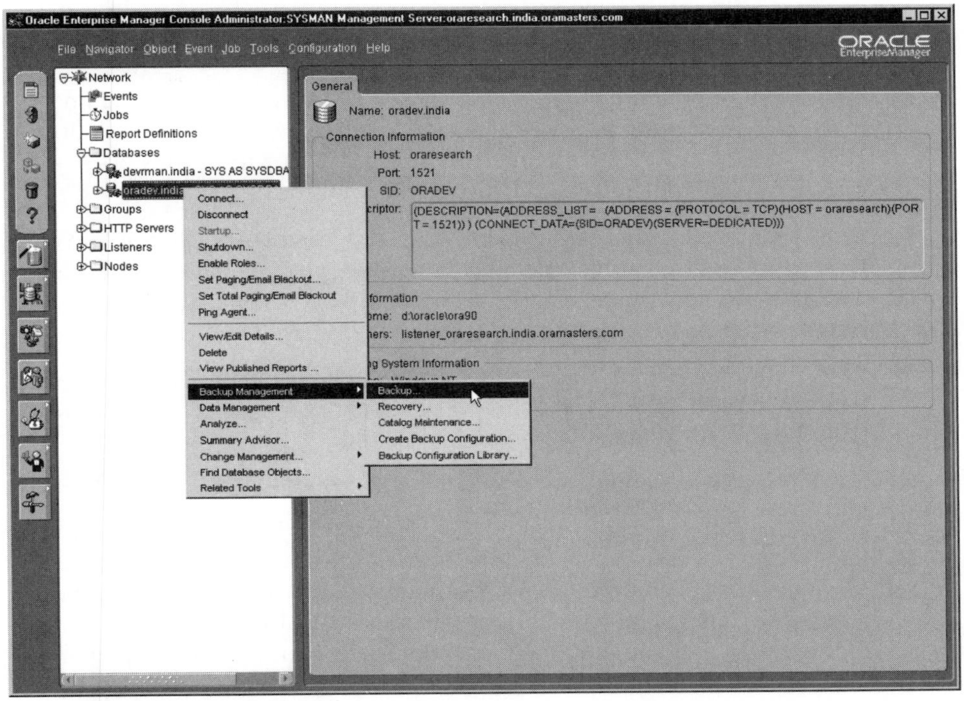

FIGURE 9-1. *OEM Console*

- RMAN enables automation of the backup jobs using two methods:
  - By customizing the RMAN interface and integrating with the scheduler of the operating system to automate backup operations
  - By scheduling backup jobs using the OEM utility (This avoids any user intervention, thereby avoiding human errors while manually performing backup and recovery operations.)
- RMAN can be used proficiently by a DBA to manage centralized backup and recovery procedures that need to be implemented in the enterprise databases environment.

- When using RMAN to perform backup of online tablespaces, it is not required to keep the online tablespaces in backup mode. RMAN does not generate extra redo during online backups.

- You can store pre-configured and compiled RMAN specific backup and recovery scripts, which can be executed any time without recompilation. These scripts are O/S independent and can be ported to various other platforms, which Oracle supports.

- RMAN supports INCREMENTAL backups. It performs a backup of only those data blocks that have changed since the previous backup. If the database is operating in NOARCHIVELOG mode, RMAN still allows you to restore using these incremental backups.

- RMAN detects corrupt blocks and recovers them using the block media recovery (BMR) option. The recovery of the corrupted block is performed with the associated datafile maintained online.

- RMAN has the capability to crosscheck and ensure that backed-up files are intact.

- RMAN enables you to backup only those files, which have not been backed up since a specified time. This is determined based on the user-specified limits. The time can be specified using the NOT BACKED UP SINCE clause of the BACKUP command. If the backup process fails, it can be reinitiated, which will backup only those files that were not backed up by the previous command.

- RMAN enables you to take *backup sets* to tape or disk. During the backup, if RMAN detects a corruption in any of the files that have a redundant copy, it will automatically perform a failover to other copies.

- RMAN skips backups of files that are already backed up, primarily to avoid maintenance of the redundant backup copies (for example, archive logfiles). This is the *backup optimization* feature of RMAN. The FORCE option when used with the BACKUP command enables you to override this feature.

- During the restoration process, RMAN checks the files on the disk and determines whether a restore is necessary and if so, which files need to be restored. If the restoration process fails midway, RMAN restores only those files that were not previously restored successfully. This is the *restore optimization* feature of RMAN. The FORCE option when used with the RESTORE command enables you to override this feature.

- RMAN supports third-party media management software.

- RMAN enables you to generate reports based on the information maintained in the repository. These reports provide vital statistical information pertaining to the files that need backup, the files that have not been backed up in a specified number of days, the files that can be deleted since they are either obsolete or not essential for recovery, and many more. The current settings of RMAN can also be displayed through reports.

■ RMAN enables you to create a duplicate copy of the production database, which can be used as a *standby* database. The standby database can also be backed up using RMAN.

■ During backups, if any of the logfiles are inaccessible due to corruption, RMAN performs archived log failover automatically and considers all logs and log copies listed in the repository as alternative candidates for the backup.

NOTE
RMAN can connect to the following types of databases: target, recovery catalog, and the auxiliary. The auxiliary instance is only used for duplicating a database or to create a standby database with the DUPLICATE command or to perform a tablespace point-in-time recovery.

Components of RMAN

Many components constitute the Recovery Manager environment. While RMAN primarily interacts with the target database, the other important components are the RMAN executable, recovery catalog, channels, auxiliary database, and RMAN packages. In this section, we discuss various components of RMAN.

RMAN Executable

The RMAN executable is installed during Oracle software installation. This file resides in the $ORACLE_HOME/bin on UNIX and %ORACLE_HOME%\bin on Windows NT or Windows 2000. RMAN interprets the user commands and invokes the required server processes to perform related tasks. To invoke the executable, just enter the filename at the command line as shown in Figure 9-2.

Target Database

RMAN performs backup, restore, and recovery operations on a database that is commonly referred to as the *target* database. The target database's control file is used to gather information about the database and to store information pertaining to its operations. The server sessions at the target database are primarily responsible for backup and recovery operations.

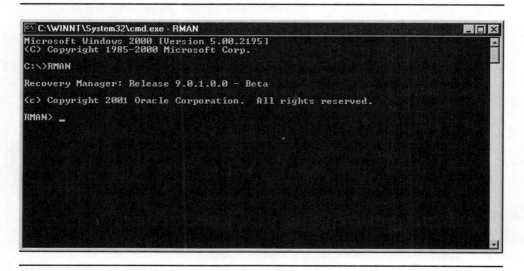

FIGURE 9-2. *Invoking RMAN at the command line*

NOTE
You need the SYSDBA privilege to connect to the target database through RMAN. In UNIX, operating system account holders who are members of the OSDBA group have special database privileges. Members of this group can connect to the database as any user using the SYSDBA privilege. Hence it is important for you to understand the ramifications of including any operating system user in the OSDBA group.

Recovery Catalog Database

The *recovery catalog* database holds the recovery catalog repository. The repository is a collection of objects stored in the RMAN repository owner's schema. The repository is used to maintain the metadata pertaining to operations performed on the target database. While it doesn't have the actual backup files of the database, it maintains the following information about the target database:

- The backup and recovery operations that are performed on the target database
- The backup retention policies
- The pre-configured and compiled backup scripts
- The network files, password files, and parameter files (The PUT command enables you to backup these O/S files. This command would be included in future releases of Oracle9*i*.)
- The image copies
- The backup sets and pieces
- The proxy copies

> **NOTE**
> *A proxy copy is a type of backup in which RMAN turns over control of the data transfer to a media manager that supports this feature, enabling automatic backup and restore operations. RMAN provides a list of files requiring backup or restore to the media manager, which in turn makes all decisions regarding how and when to move the data. The PROXY option of the BACKUP command specifies that a backup should be a proxy copy.*

- The archived redo logs
- The persistent configuration settings
- A recovery catalog can store metadata pertaining to one or more registered target databases.

Processes

RMAN invokes one or more server processes at the target database. These server processes are responsible for performing the backup, restore, and recovery tasks through a PL/SQL interface.

RMAN Channels

A *channel* is the primary means of communication between the Oracle server and the operating system. An RMAN channel represents one stream of data to a device type and corresponds to one server session. RMAN requires at least one channel to perform backup or recovery tasks. A channel establishes a connection between the RMAN executable and the instance of the target database by starting a server session. The server session is responsible for performing RMAN-related operations. One channel communicates with one server session only. If it is essential to communicate to more than one server session, then you must allocate more channels depending on the requirement. We give more details in the "RMAN Channels" section later in this chapter.

Backup Set

A *backup set* is a logical object in an RMAN-specific format that is a result of one complete operation where the individual physical database files constitute the backup set. The backup set is comprised of one or more physical backup pieces. RMAN performs compression on backup sets, which means that datafile blocks that have never been used are not backed up.

Image Copies *includes data empty blocks (not incremental or compressed)*

RMAN enables you to backup database files in the same format they exist in physically on disk. These are called *image copies*. These copies—unlike the backup sets—include the data empty blocks because they are copied byte-for-byte the same as the source, just like an O/S copy. Thus, image copies cannot be incremental or compressed, but they are immediately reusable. These copies can be immediately restored and recovered through O/S commands or by using RMAN.

Auxiliary Database

The *auxiliary* database is a copy of the primary or production database. The advantage of maintaining the auxiliary database is to simulate the production environment when testing the backup and recovery strategies or to create a standby database. The DUPLICATE command can be issued to create the auxiliary database. The auxiliary database is essential for performing tablespace point-in-time recovery using RMAN.

RMAN Packages

RMAN executes packages internally to communicate with the target database and the recovery catalog. RMAN uses the packages DBMS_RCVCAT and DBMS_RCVMAN. These are undocumented packages created when the CREATE CATALOG command is issued. The DBMS_RCVCAT package is responsible for maintaining information in the recovery catalog and the DBMS_RCVMAN is used for querying the recovery catalog or the control file.

The DBMS_BACKUP_RESTORE package is another important package that RMAN uses as an interface with the operating system for creating, restoring, and recovering backups of data files and archive log files. The **dbmsbkrs.sql** and **prvtbkrs.plb** files create this package. Once the operating system receives the information from the packages, the data is stored on a storage device such as a disk.

Media Management Layer (MML) 3rd party tool

The media management layer is based on the media management software. The media management software application is a third-party tool that enables RMAN to perform file backups to storage systems such as tape drives. No direct interaction between the RMAN client and the media management application takes place. The RMAN client is only responsible for establishing a connection with the target database; the media management software manages the backup operations of files to a storage system.

RMAN Repository

The *RMAN repository* is a storage area where RMAN stores the information about the operations that it performs on the target database. It maintains the information in either the recovery catalog or in the control file of the target database as its repository. RMAN can perform most of the backup and recovery operations by using the control file of the target database. However, some RMAN operations require the use of the recovery catalog.

The complete functionality of RMAN cannot be used unless a recovery catalog is used as a repository. The recovery catalog stores the RMAN-specific scripts and operating system files—such as network files, password files, and parameter files—in the recovery catalog. RMAN stands as an interface between the target database and the recovery catalog repository. RMAN obtains information such as the database schema, archived redo logs, backup sets, and datafiles related to the target database through the target database's control file.

Recovery Catalog Repository

Oracle recommends to have a dedicated database to maintain the recovery catalog repository. RMAN determines the procedure to implement backup and recovery tasks based on the information that has been obtained from the target database's control file and stored in the recovery catalog.

It is important for the information in the catalog to be in sync with the target database's control file. Frequent synchronization of the recovery catalog with the target database's control file ensures that the metadata in the catalog is current. Synchronization can either be *full* or *partial*. During a partial synchronization of the catalog, RMAN reads the current control file to update only the changed data, but does not update the schema of the database. During a full synchronization of the catalog, RMAN updates all changed records, including schema records.

RMAN automatically detects when a full or a partial resynchronization is required. It implicitly executes the operation as needed. You can also explicitly force a full resynchronization by issuing the following command:

```
RMAN> RESYNC CATALOG
Starting full resync of recovery catalog
Full resync complete
RMAN>
```

You would select the *resynchronize catalog* option from the *catalog maintenance wizard* as shown in Figure 9-3 to perform a full resynchronization of the recovery catalog.

NOTE
Resynchronization of the catalog must be performed more frequently than the value specified for the parameter CONRTOL_FILE_RECORD_KEEP_TIME.

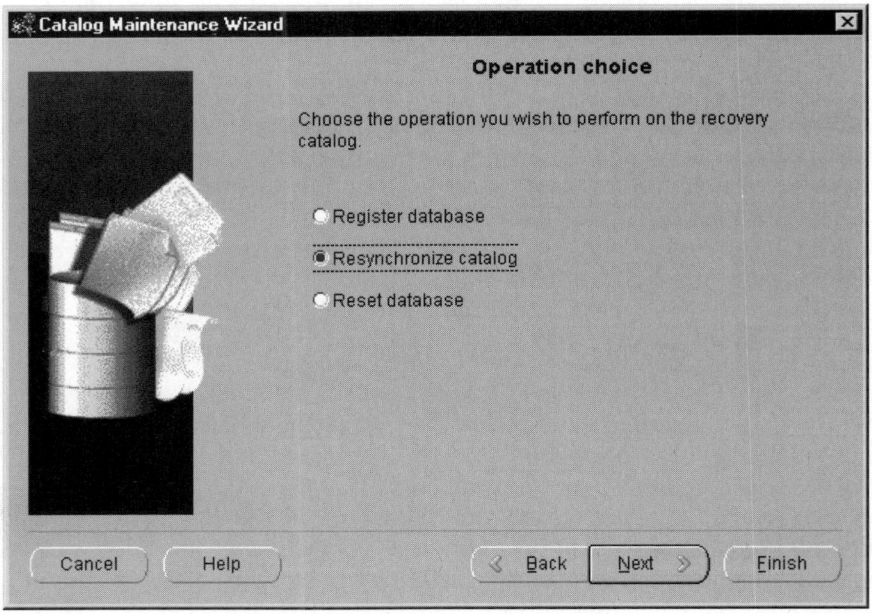

FIGURE 9-3. *Manual resynchronization using the Catalog Maintenance Wizard*

Using the recovery catalog has several advantages; a few of them are listed here:

- Maintains multiple target databases information in a single centralized repository.

- Maintains metadata related to multiple incarnations of a single database, thereby enabling you to restore data from any previous incarnations.

- Stores historical metadata to prepare statistics reports.

- Stores RMAN-specific scripts.

- RMAN decides upon the appropriate files needed for restoring and recovering the database without the users intervention. If a recovery catalog is not used, RMAN requires that the target database's control file be available, since the control file stores information pertaining to the database files.

- Nonavailability of the control file during recovery does not hinder RMAN operations. Pre-configured jobs like automating the tape channel allocation are still available if the target database is operating in the NOMOUNT state.

Using the Control File as a Repository

RMAN can also perform backup and recovery operations using the target database's control file instead of the recovery catalog. It is at times cumbersome to install and administer a separate database for the recovery catalog when the target database is small in size. In such cases the control file can be used as a repository for storing most of the information that would otherwise be stored in the recovery catalog.

The control file is treated as an exclusive source of information for RMAN to perform backup and recovery operations. The amount of information in the control file grows depending upon the frequency of backups, size of the target database, and the implemented retention policy. The control file stores two types of records: circular reuse records and noncircular reuse records.

To view the information kept by the control file for backup and recovery operations, query the V$CONTROFILE_RECORD_SECTION view.

```
SQL> SELECT type,records_used FROM v$controlfile_record_section;
TYPE                    RECORDS_USED
------------------      ------------
DATABASE                         1
CKPT PROGRESS                    0
REDO THREAD                      1
REDO LOG                         4
DATAFILE                         8
FILENAME                        13
```

```
TABLESPACE                9
TEMPORARY FILENAME        1
RMAN CONFIGURATION        2
LOG HISTORY             665
OFFLINE RANGE             5
ARCHIVED LOG             27
BACKUP SET               26
BACKUP PIECE             26
BACKUP DATAFILE          25
BACKUP REDOLOG           56
DATAFILE COPY             2
BACKUP CORRUPTION         0
COPY CORRUPTION           0
DELETED OBJECT            2
PROXY COPY                0
RESERVED4                 0
22 rows selected.
```

Circular Reuse Records

The *circular reuse* records are continuously generated by the database and contain noncritical information. Oracle overwrites these records whenever required. These records are logically arranged in a ring form. If Oracle is unable to find an empty circular reuse record slot, it either increases the size of the control file or overwrites the oldest record so as to accommodate the new record.

The initialization parameter CONTROL_FILE_RECORD_KEEP_TIME specifies the minimum number of days the record must be maintained in the control file before it can be reused. If a low value is specified for this parameter, the records in the control file are overwritten frequently, thereby restricting its growth. The default number of days the records are stored before they are overwritten is seven. The records hold information about the log history, archived redo logs, backups, and offline SCN ranges for datafiles.

Noncircular Reuse Records

The *noncircular reuse records* store critical information like the details of the datafiles, the online redo logs, and the redo threads. This information is indispensable for the proper working of the control file and is not overwritten.

Control File Copies

RMAN sometimes needs to take a temporary backup of the control file. A *snapshot* control file is created any time RMAN needs to view a read-consistent image of the control file. A read-consistent image is required when querying the noncircular reuse records in the control file. Issuing the following command specifies the destination of the snapshot control file:

```
RMAN> CONFIGURE SNAPSHOT CONTROLFILE NAME TO
'c:\oracle\oradata\backup\snapcf_orama.f';
```

Disadvantages of Using the Control File as a Repository

The following features are not available if the control file is used as an RMAN repository:

- RMAN-specific scripts cannot be stored.

- RMAN cannot easily perform restore and recovery operations if all the target database control files are either lost or corrupted.

RMAN Channel Allocation

A *channel* is the primary means of communication between the Oracle server and the operating system. The channels are a requisite for RMAN to execute any command. The channel starts a server session to establish a connection between the RMAN executable and the target database instance as shown in Figure 9-4. RMAN session is solely responsible for communicating with the allocated server sessions (see Figure 9-4).

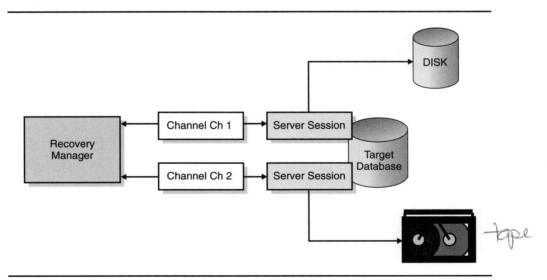

FIGURE 9-4. *RMAN channel allocations*

You can either explicitly allocate a channel in a RUN block or RMAN allocates channels implicitly using AUTOMATIC CHANNEL ALLOCATION. RMAN comes pre-configured with a DISK channel that you can use to create either backup sets or image copies to disk. To automate the channel allocation while backing up to disk or tape, issue the CONFIGURE CHANNEL command.

Every time a script is to be executed using the RUN command, RMAN requires a channel to be allocated either manually or automatically. RMAN determines the device types and allocates necessary channels for maintenance of commands such as RESTORE and DELETE.

The automatic channel allocation feature enables you to configure a set of persistent and automatic channels for all RMAN sessions. The manual channel allocation feature enables you to allocate channels specifically for commands within a RUN block.

You can configure the automatic allocation of channels using the following commands:

```
CONFIGURE DEFAULT DEVICE TYPE
CONFIGURE CHANNEL DEVICE TYPE
CONFIGURE CHANNEL n DEVICE TYPE
CONFIGURE DEVICE TYPE ... PARALLELISM
```

RMAN uses the values defined in the CONFIGURE command for automatic channel allocation. In case you use commands such as BACKUP, RESTORE, and DELETE outside of a RUN block or if you use the commands within a RUN command and don't define any channels, then RMAN automatically allocates channels according to the values defined for the CONFIGURE command. Manual channel allocation in a RUN block overrides the automatic channel allocation settings so that automatic and manual channels cannot be mixed. To override the default settings for automatic channel allocation, use the following command:

```
RMAN> RUN
{
  ALLOCATE CHANNEL chan1 TYPE disk;
  BACKUP DATABASE;
}
```

The pre-allocated channels are used by RMAN to execute the following series of commands:

```
BACKUP DATAFILE 1,2,3;
BACKUP CURRENT CONTROLFILE;
```

If you issue a command such as ALLOCATE or CONFIGURE, then RMAN automatically releases the pre-allocated channels.

Media Management Library Interface

RMAN creates many client connections, or *channels,* between the target database and the backup storage devices. RMAN is able to create backup sets either onto disk or directly onto tape. To use tape storage, RMAN requires a media manager—a software program that loads, labels, and unloads sequential media such as tape for backing up and recovering data. RMAN interacts with the media management software through a layer known as the *media management layer* and it must be linked with the Oracle database kernel. Media management layers are available from members of the Oracle Backup Solutions program through storage vendors such as Legato and Veritas.

The *media management library* (MML) as shown in Figure 9-5 represents a vendor-supplied media management software library that can interface with Oracle. Oracle calls MML software routines to back up and restore datafiles to and from the media, as controlled by the media manager.

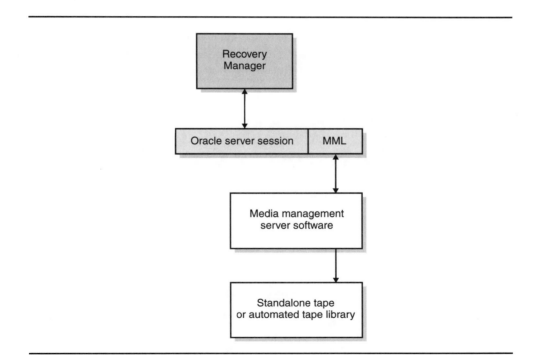

FIGURE 9-5. *Media management library*

RMAN must communicate with a MML to perform backup operations using a media manager. The MML is O/S specific. When you allocate or configure RMAN channels, RMAN first tries to load the library specified for the SBT_LIBRARY parameter of the ALLOCATE CHANNEL or the CONFIGURE CHANNEL commands. If the SBT_LIBRARY parameter is not available, then Oracle loads the default MML. If Oracle is unable to identify the default library, then it tries to load the statically linked library. When Oracle tries to load the default static library, an ORA-19511 error arises. Oracle writes a trace file to the USER_DUMP_DEST directory whenever channel allocation fails.

The following script performs a backup of the database to a tape drive controlled by the media manager.

```
RMAN> RUN
{
  ALLOCATE CHANNEL chan1 TYPE 'sbt_tape';
  BACKUP DATABASE;
}
```

During the execution of this command, RMAN sends a request for performing a backup to the server session. In response, the server session recognizes the channel as a media management device and requests the media manager to upload a tape for performing the write operation.

Connecting to RMAN Without the Recovery Catalog

RMAN uses the target database's control file if the recovery catalog is not accessible to perform the backup and recovery operations. This involves some amount of risk since the metadata pertaining to the operations performed by RMAN are being stored in the control file itself. This makes the control file more vulnerable. On the other hand using the control file saves storage space and the administrative effort involved in maintaining a recovery catalog database.

Connecting to the Target Database Without a Catalog from the Command Line

To establish a connection to the target database without connecting to the recovery catalog from the command line, execute one of the following commands:

```
C:\> rman TARGET /
```

Or

```
C:\> rman TARGET / NOCATALOG
```

Or

```
C:\> rman TARGET SYS/new_pwd@test_alias.org NOCATALOG
```

All of the previous commands establish a connection with the target database. The last command establishes a connection with a remote database user SYS who has the SYSDBA privilege using the net service name test_alias.org. The connection is through Oracle Net.

Connecting to the Target Database Without a Catalog from the RMAN Prompt

To establish a connection to the target database without connecting to the recovery catalog from the RMAN prompt, execute one of the following commands:

```
C:\> rman
RMAN> CONNECT TARGET SYS/new_pwd@test_alias.org
```

Or

```
C:\> rman NOCATALOG
RMAN> CONNECT TARGET SYS/new_pwd@test_alias.org
```

NOTE
If you are not using a recovery catalog for RMAN operations, then it is recommended that you have multiple copies of the control file located on separate disks, preferably mounted under different controllers to protect against media failures. You will also need to keep track of bookkeeping information like what files were backed up, the date they were backed up, and also the names of the backup pieces each file has written to and all the RMAN backup logs. It is also recommended that in such situations you enable the control file AUTOBACKUP feature.

Configuring the RMAN Environment

In this section, we describe how to set up and configure various management tasks in the RMAN environment.

Media Manager

A media manager is third-party software and needs to be integrated with RMAN in order to perform backup and recovery operations. The configuration of RMAN with a media manager depends on the media management product and the platform on which you are running Oracle. For more information, see the "Media Manager" section earlier in this chapter.

Control File Autobackup

RMAN can perform an automatic backup of the control file. RMAN enables you to perform recovery even if the current control file and recovery catalog are lost or inaccessible. Since the autobackup feature uses a standard format, it is quite simple to restore the control file and hence perform recovery. After the control file is restored and mounted, you can use the repository information in the mounted control file to restore the database. The automatic backup of the control file is independent of any other command that is issued manually to back up the control file. If the AUTOBACKUP feature is enabled, RMAN includes the control file implicitly into the backup set as shown:

```
RMAN> BACKUP DATAFILE 3;
Starting backup at 01-OCT-01 using channel ORA_DISK_1
channel ORA_DISK_1: starting full datafile backupset
channel ORA_DISK_1: specifying datafile(s) in backupset
input datafile fno=00003 name=D:\ORACLE\ORADATA\TARGET\INDX01.DBF
channel ORA_DISK_1: starting piece 1 at 01-OCT-01
channel ORA_DISK_1: finished piece 1 at 01-OCT-01
piece handle=D:\ORACLE9I\ORA90\DATABASE\0UD5H09L_1_1 comment=NONE
channel ORA_DISK_1: backup set complete, elapsed time: 00:00:03
Finished backup at 01-OCT-01
Starting Control File Autobackup at 01-OCT-01
piece handle=D:\ORACLE9I\ORA90\DATABASE\C-2842823597-20011001-02
comment=NONE
Finished Control File Autobackup at 01-OCT-01
```

To configure RMAN to perform automatic backup of the control file, execute the following command:

```
RMAN> CONFIGURE CONTROLFILE AUTOBACKUP ON;
```

By default this feature is OFF. RMAN performs the autobackup at the following instances:

- After the completion of any BACKUP or COPY command at the RMAN prompt.

- After every nonconsecutive BACKUP or COPY command within a RUN block.

You can specify a format for the control file backups while enabling the AUTOBACKUP feature as shown:

```
RMAN> CONFIGURE CONTROLFILE AUTOBACKUP FORMAT FOR DEVICE TYPE DISK TO
'c:\backups\%F';
new RMAN configuration parameters:
CONFIGURE CONTROLFILE AUTOBACKUP FORMAT FOR DEVICE TYPE DISK TO
'c:\backups\%F';
new RMAN configuration parameters are successfully stored
starting full resync of recovery catalog
full resync complete
```

Backup Retention Policy

A retention policy determines when RMAN should consider the backups as obsolete. The information of these backups can be either cataloged or stored in the target database's control file. Consider the factors in the following section when you configure the retention policy.

Configuring the Retention Policy for a Recovery Window

The RECOVERY WINDOW enables you to specify the number of days between the current time and the earliest point of recoverability. RMAN ignores any backup or copy as obsolete if it falls within the recovery window.

You can change the retention policy setting by executing the following command:

```
RMAN> CONFIGURE RETENTION POLICY TO RECOVERY WINDOW OF 4 DAYS;
new RMAN configuration parameters:
CONFIGURE RETENTION POLICY TO RECOVERY WINDOW OF 4 DAYS;
new RMAN configuration parameters are successfully stored
starting full resync of recovery catalog
full resync complete
```

RMAN does not automatically delete these backup sets and image copies that are rendered obsolete by the recovery window. You will need to explicitly delete them by executing the command

```
RMAN> DELETE OBSOLETE;
```

Configuring the Retention Policy for Redundancy

The REDUNDANCY parameter of the CONFIGURE RETENTION POLICY command specifies how many backup sets and image copies of each datafile and control file RMAN should keep. In other words, if the number of backup sets and image copies for a specific datafile or control file exceeds the REDUNDANCY setting, then RMAN considers the extra backup sets and image copies as obsolete. You can set the redundancy using the following command:

```
RMAN> CONFIGURE RETENTION POLICY TO REDUNDANCY 2;
old RMAN configuration parameters:
CONFIGURE RETENTION POLICY TO RECOVERY WINDOW OF 4 DAYS;
new RMAN configuration parameters:
CONFIGURE RETENTION POLICY TO REDUNDANCY 2;
new RMAN configuration parameters are successfully stored
starting full resync of recovery catalog
full resync complete
```

NOTE
Observe that the RECOVERY WINDOW configuration is overwritten by the REDUNDANCY parameter of the CONFIGURE RETENTION POLICY command. This implies that only one of these settings will be active at any given point of time.

As you produce more backups, RMAN keeps track of the ones to retain and the ones to discard. Additionally, RMAN retains all archived logs and incremental backups that are needed to recover the nonobsolete backups.

To disable the retention policy, you can execute the following command:

```
RMAN> CONFIGURE RETENTION POLICY TO NONE;
```

This command means that RMAN does not consider any backup or copy as obsolete.

If you need to clear the retention policy (that is, return the retention policy to its default setting), execute the following command:

```
RMAN> CONFIGURE RETENTION POLICY CLEAR;
```

This command returns the retention policy to its default setting, which is REDUNDANCY = 1.

Maximum Size of Backup Sets

Configuring the *maximum set size* for a backup limits the backup set to the specified value, which can be in bytes, kilobytes, megabytes, and so forth. To set the maximum size, execute the following command:

```
RMAN> CONFIGURE MAXSETSIZE TO 75M;
```

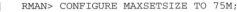

TIP
Remember to set the value for the MAXSETSIZE parameter to a value greater than the largest single file that would be included in the backup set. If this is not done, your backup set creation will fail with the RMAN-06183: datafile or datafilecopy larger than SETSIZE error.

For example, if you have four database files of sizes 100MB, 50MB, 50MB, and 50MB, and you configure the MAXSETSIZE parameter to 75MB, the backup set creation will fail. If you configure the MAXSETSIZE parameter to a value of 120MB, which is greater than the single largest file that needs to be included in the backup set—that is, 100MB— RMAN will include the 100MB file in one backup set and create additional backup sets to include the remaining datafiles. Note that this is one more reason you must test your backup scripts thoroughly before implementing them in a production environment.

Backup Optimization

Run the CONFIGURE command to enable and disable backup optimization. Backup optimization skips the backup of files in certain circumstances if the identical file or an identical version of the file has already been backed up. Note that backup optimization applies only to these commands:

```
BACKUP DATABASE
BACKUP ARCHIVELOG ALL
BACKUP ARCHIVELOG LIKE
BACKUP BACKUPSET ALL
```

You can override optimization at any time by specifying the FORCE option on the BACKUP command. For example, you can run

```
RMAN> BACKUP DATABASE FORCE;
```

or

```
RMAN> BACKUP ARCHIVELOG ALL FORCE;
```

By default, backup optimization is configured to OFF. To enable and disable backup optimization, execute the following commands:

```
RMAN> CONFIGURE BACKUP OPTIMIZATION ON;
RMAN> CONFIGURE BACKUP OPTIMIZATION OFF;
```

To clear the current backup optimization setting and to set it to its default setting (which is OFF), execute this command:

```
RMAN> CONFIGURE BACKUP OPTIMIZATION CLEAR;
```

Number of Backup Copies

RMAN can be configured to store multiple copies of backup pieces. You can specify the number of copies to be created for each backup piece using the following command:

```
RMAN> CONFIGURE DATAFILE BACKUP COPIES FOR DEVICE TYPE sbt TO 3;
```

The CONFIGURE settings apply only to datafiles and archived redo log backups. This feature is known as *duplexing*. By default, the value is 1, meaning one copy for each device type.

Excluding Tablespaces from Whole Database Backups

To exclude tablespaces from a backup being performed using the BACKUP DATABASE command, you can use the CONFIGURE EXCLUDE FOR TABLESPACE feature. The exclusion condition applies to any datafiles that you add to this tablespace in the future. This feature is useful if you need to exempt a tablespace from your regular backup schedule. Common reasons for excluding a tablespace from backing up include

- If a tablespace contains temporary or test data that you do not need to back up

- If you have a read only tablespace that hasn't been modified since the last backup

- A group of tablespaces that are part of a different backup schedule than the regular schedule

You can exclude a particular tablespace from the backup set by issuing the following command:

```
RMAN> CONFIGURE EXCLUDE FOR TABLESPACE users;
tablespace USERS will be excluded from future whole database backups
new RMAN configuration parameters are successfully stored
starting full resync of recovery catalog
full resync complete
```

You can see that the USERS tablespace, which was excluded from the tablespace for future backups, will not be included in the whole database backup set. This is shown in the following code:

```
RMAN> BACKUP DATABASE;
Starting backup at 01-OCT-01
starting full resync of recovery catalog
full resync complete
using channel ORA_DISK_1
file 5 is excluded from whole database backup
channel ORA_DISK_1: starting full datafile backupset
channel ORA_DISK_1: specifying datafile(s) in backupset
input datafile fno=00001 name=D:\ORACLE\ORADATA\TARGET\SYSTEM01.DBF
input datafile fno=00002 name=D:\ORACLE\ORADATA\TARGET\UNDOTBS01.DBF
channel ORA_DISK_1: starting piece 1 at 01-OCT-01
channel ORA_DISK_1: finished piece 1 at 01-OCT-01
piece handle=D:\ORACLE9I\ORA90\DATABASE\17D5H3AS_1_1 comment=NONE
channel ORA_DISK_1: backup set complete, elapsed time: 00:01:56
Finished backup at 01-OCT-01
Starting Control File Autobackup at 01-OCT-01
piece handle=D:\ORACLE9I\ORA90\DATABASE\C-2842823597-20011001-04
comment=NONE
Finished Control File Autobackup at 01-OCT-01
```

NOTE
You cannot exclude the SYSTEM tablespace using the above command when performing a whole database backup. Also note that the temporary tablespace files (tempfiles) will not be included in the backup set. This can also be seen in the above output.

To display the default settings for the RMAN environment, you can use the command SHOW ALL at the RMAN prompt. The output for this command is shown in Figure 9-6.

```
C:\WINNT\System32\cmd.exe - RMAN CATALOG rman/rman TARGET sys/sys@oradev
C:\>RMAN CATALOG rman/rman TARGET sys/sys@oradev

Recovery Manager: Release 9.0.1.0.0 - Beta

(c) Copyright 2001 Oracle Corporation.  All rights reserved.

connected to target database: ORADEV (DBID=1375447924)
connected to recovery catalog database

RMAN> SHOW ALL;

RMAN configuration parameters are:
CONFIGURE RETENTION POLICY TO REDUNDANCY 1; # default
CONFIGURE BACKUP OPTIMIZATION OFF; # default
CONFIGURE DEFAULT DEVICE TYPE TO DISK; # default
CONFIGURE CONTROLFILE AUTOBACKUP OFF; # default
CONFIGURE CONTROLFILE AUTOBACKUP FORMAT FOR DEVICE TYPE DISK TO '%F'; # default
CONFIGURE DEVICE TYPE DISK PARALLELISM 1; # default
CONFIGURE DATAFILE BACKUP COPIES FOR DEVICE TYPE DISK TO 1; # default
CONFIGURE ARCHIVELOG BACKUP COPIES FOR DEVICE TYPE DISK TO 1; # default
CONFIGURE MAXSETSIZE TO UNLIMITED; # default
CONFIGURE SNAPSHOT CONTROLFILE NAME TO 'D:\ORACLE\ORA90\DATABASE\SNCFORADEV.ORA'
; # default

RMAN>
```

FIGURE 9-6. *RMAN default configuration settings*

Environment Variables

RMAN can be configured with globalization support variables NLS_DATE_FORMAT and NLS_LANG. Prior to connecting with RMAN, set the NLS_DATE_FORMAT and NLS_LANG environment variables. These variables determine the date and time format used in RMAN commands such as RESTORE, RECOVER, and REPORT. Examples for setting environment variables is covered in Chapter 15.

Shared Server

RMAN cannot establish a connection with the target database through a shared server dispatcher. It requires a dedicated server process. You can establish a connection through a dedicated server process in the shared server environment by configuring the net service name in the tnsnames.ora file. The SERVER=DEDICATED option must be included in the CONNECT_DATA attribute of the connect string as shown here:

```
ORAMA.INDIA =
  (DESCRIPTION =
    (ADDRESS_LIST =
      (ADDRESS = (PROTOCOL = TCP)(HOST = ormresearch)(PORT = 1521))
    )
    (CONNECT_DATA =
      (SID = oramatest)
      (SERVER = DEDICATED)
    )
  )
```

Chapter Questions

1. **Which of the target database files does RMAN optionally use to store its repository?**

   A. Control file

   B. Logfiles

   C. Datafiles

   D. Parameter file

2. **Where does RMAN store the information related to the backup and recovery operations performed on the target database, if the connection through the RMAN executable is established with the following command?**

   ```
   C:\> rman TARGET /
   ```

   A. Recovery catalog database.

   B. Target database's parameter file.

   C. Recovery catalog's parameter file.

   D. Target database's control file.

   E. It fails to perform any operations since there is no reference of a repository.

3. **After the number of days set by the parameter CONTROL_FILE_RECORD_KEEP_TIME, the information in the control file is overwritten by RMAN. What is this parameter's default value?**

   A. 1 day

   B. 5 days

   C. 7 days

   D. 31 days

4. **Which of the following commands cannot use the functionality associated with the NLS_DATE_FORMAT variable?**

   A. RESTORE

   B. RECOVER

   C. REPORT

   D. BACKUP

5. **Which of the following files are required by RMAN to take a read-consistent image to resynchronize the recovery catalog?**

   A. Snapshot control file (target database)

   B. Autobackup of the control file (target database)

   C. Manual backup of the control file (target database)

   D. Manual backup of the control file (recovery catalog database)

6. **What is the value set as the retention policy after executing the following command?**

   ```
   RMAN> CONFIGURE RETENTION POLICY CLEAR;
   ```

   A. 1

   B. 2

   C. 10

   D. 31

7. **Which type of tablespace would be most suitable for exclusion from a whole database backup by executing the command CONFIGURE EXCLUDE FOR TABLESPACE?**

    A. The USERS tablespace, which is online for 24 × 7 transactions.

    B. The TEMP tablespace containing temporary or test data.

    C. The SYSTEM tablespace of an OLTP database.

    D. The INDX tablespace of an OLTP database containing indexes for the production tables that are updated frequently.

8. **If RMAN identifies a corrupt block while performing a backup of the archive logfiles, what action does it take?**

    A. Ends the backup process

    B. Ignores the blocks

    C. Failover to an existing intact copy

    D. Writes to log

    E. Gives an error

9. **Which of the following commands can be executed to limit the size of the backup set?**

    A. CONFIGURE SETMAXSIZE

    B. CONFIGURE SETMAXPIECESIZE

    C. CONFIGURE MAXSETSIZE

    D. CONFIGURE _MAXSETSIZE

10. **Which of the following databases can be created through RMAN and further used to test backup and recovery operations or perform a tablespace point-in-time recovery?**

    A. Target database

    B. Auxiliary database

    C. Recovery catalog database

    D. Standby database

Answers to Chapter Questions

1. A.   Control file

Explanation   The control file can be used as an optional repository for storing RMAN operations. It is at times cumbersome to install and administer a separate database for the recovery catalog when the target database is small in size. In such cases, the control file can be used as a repository that stores most of the information.

2. D.   Target database's control file

Explanation   RMAN does not obstruct the user from performing any operations on the target database. By default the target database control file is used as a repository.

3. C.   7 days

Explanation   The default value of the initialization parameter CONTROL_FILE_RECORD_KEEP_TIME is seven days. The value set for this parameter determines the number of days the record must be maintained in the target database's control file before it can be reused.

4. D.   BACKUP

Explanation   The NLS_DATE_FORMAT variable can be used to set the appropriate format for specifying the time using RMAN commands such as RESTORE, RECOVER, and REPORT.

5. A.   Snapshot control file (target database)

Explanation   The snapshot control file of the target database is implicitly created by RMAN in the location defined using the command CONFIGURE SNAPSHOT CONTROLFILE. RMAN automatically performs a *resync* of the catalog using the read-consistent image provided by the snapshot control file that is required while querying the noncircular reuse records in the control file.

6. A.   1

Explanation   This command clears any user configured retention policy and returns the retention policy to the default setting, which is REDUNDANCY = 1.

7. B.   The TEMP tablespace containing temporary or test data

Explanation   The TEMP tablespace is appropriate for excluding from a whole database backup, since it contains temporary or test data. The SYSTEM tablespace cannot be excluded from any whole database backup.

8. C.   Failover to an existing intact copy

Explanation   If RMAN discovers a corrupt block during the backup, then RMAN automatically does a failover to an existing intact copy if it exists.

9. C.   CONFIGURE MAXSETSIZE

Explanation   The CONFIGURE MAXSETSIZE command limits the size of the backup sets. The CONFIGURE settings apply to any channel, whether manually or automatically allocated, when the BACKUP command is executed.

10. B.   Auxiliary database

Explanation   The auxiliary database is a copy of the primary or production database. The auxiliary database is essential for performing tablespace point-in-time recovery using RMAN.

CHAPTER
10

User-Managed Backups

n this chapter, you will learn about user-managed backups and an overview of user-managed recovery operations. We will discuss the advantages and disadvantages of using the closed and open database backups and list the steps involved in taking these backups. We will also discuss backup issues related to control files and archive log files. Later in this chapter, we explain the options available to cleanup after a backup failure has occurred and describe the functionality of the dbverify utility. This chapter includes the following topics:

- User-managed backup and recovery
- Closed database backups
- Open database backups
- Backups of read-only tablespaces
- Backups of the control file
- Backups of archived redo logs
- Cleanup operations after failed online backups
- LOGGING and NOLOGGING Options
- dbverify utility

User-Managed Backup and Recovery

Backups are primarily taken to safeguard against unexpected failures resulting in loss of data. If such a failure occurs, data can be re-constructed using a backup. Oracle enables you to perform two types of backups: *logical backups* and *physical backups*. Before performing any type of backups, you should develop a consistent backup and recovery strategy defining your goals clearly. The logical backups hold the logical object definitions and table data. These backups must be taken using the Oracle export utility and are stored in Oracle specific binary format. The physical database backups comprise of the physical database files: control file, log files, data files, and other database files. Physical backups are classified under two major categories: *server-managed* backups and *user-managed* backups.

The server-managed backups are performed using the RMAN utility. RMAN can either be accessed using the command-line interface (CLI) or by using the Oracle Enterprise Manager, a graphical user interface (GUI) tool. In contrast, the user-managed backups do not involve RMAN for performing any type of database backup and recovery operation. The backups of all the database files or selected files are performed using operating system commands. The files that need to be backed up are copied to the desired location, and in the event of a media failure the appropriate files are restored to the original destination and recovered manually using either the SQL*Plus or SQL Worksheet tool.

In this section, we discuss various user-managed backup and recovery options.

Overview of User-Managed Backups

While performing user-managed backups, you can take a whole database backup, a tablespace backup, or a data file backup. We discuss these options in the following sections.

Whole Database Backups

A *whole database backup* is a backup that includes all the physical files of the database. Whole database backups can either be performed in ARCHIVELOG or NOARCHIVELOG mode as discussed in the section "Differences Between ARCHIVELOG and NOARCHIVELOG Mode" of Chapter 8. Prior to taking whole database backups in either of the mentioned modes, be aware of the implications. If the database is operating in NOARCHIVELOG mode, the backups must always be performed when the database is *closed*. This would result in a *consistent* backup. If you perform a whole backup after the database is aborted, ensure that the online redo logs are also backed up. Though this is considered a valid backup, this procedure of performing a closed database backup after SHUTDOWN ABORT is not recommended. When the database is operating in ARCHIVELOG mode, backups can be performed with the database either *opened* or *closed*. If you take a backup when the database is closed cleanly, it will be a consistent backup; however, if you take a backup when the database is open, you have to take the tablespaces into *backup* mode. This backup is inconsistent (or *fuzzy*) but is a valid backup if you have the archived redo log files that were created during the online backup. In other words, while the data files alone are inconsistent, the data files along with the archived redo log files make the backup consistent. Figure 10-1 shows the various options of the user-managed backups available in Oracle9*i*.

Figure 10-1 can also be shown in a table format as shown in Table 10-1.

Tablespace Backups

A *tablespace backup* is a backup taken for a specific tablespace. Your database must be running in ARCHIVELOG mode in order for you to take a tablespace backup. The use and advantages of a tablespace backup are illustrated in the following example.

John is a DBA of a courier company that has a 480GB database. The database has ten tablespaces. The database runs 24 × 7 and the scheduled down time is only once a year. John has to rely on online backups. It takes John about one hour to backup 2GB of data and ten complete days to take a whole database backup. His

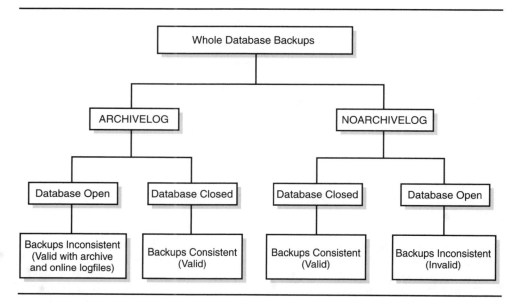

FIGURE 10-1. *Whole database backup options*

Whole Database Backup Methods	Database in ARCHIVELOG Mode	Database in NOARCHIVELOG Mode
Whole database backup with database open.	Inconsistent (or fuzzy) backup. Valid only if backup data files as well as all archived redo creating during the backup is available. Supported by Oracle.	Inconsistent backup. Not valid and unsupported by Oracle.
Whole database backup with database closed gracefully.	Consistent backup. Valid and supported by Oracle.	Consistent backup. Valid and supported by Oracle.

TABLE 10-1. *Whole Database Backup Options*

backup strategy involves backing up one tablespace a day. He uses the following procedure to back up each tablespace:

1. Set tablespace 1 in BEGIN BACKUP mode using ALTER TABLESPACE BEGIN BACKUP command.

2. Backup all the data files that belong to tablespace 1.

3. Set tablespace 1 in END BACKUP mode using ALTER TABLESPACE END BACKUP command.

4. Copy all the archived redo log files generated between step 1 and 3.

Note that in the preceding example, at the end of ten days, John will get a complete backup of this database. *How oft~ does he have to do tei?*

Data File Backups

A data file backup is a backup that involves a specific data file. You can take a data file backup when the database is offline or online. Your database should be in ARCHIVELOG mode for you to take a backup of a data file online. When you add a new data file to a tablespace, it is useful for you to do a data file backup. You need to take the data file offline first, before you can take a backup of the data file at the O/S level. The following example illustrates the use of data file backups.

Tim is a DBA of a Fortune 2000 company. He manages a database with OLTP applications. The database has to be available 24 × 5 Monday through Friday. His backup strategy involves a cold backup every week on Saturday supplemented by a hot backup of selected tablespaces every evening. On Monday morning, Tim realized that he needed to add a data file to the USERS tablespace. While the USERS tablespace is 50GB, the newly added data file is only 1GB. Tim used the following procedure to take a data file backup of the new data file:

1. Issue the ALTER DATABASE DATA FILE <filename> OFFLINE command to take the data file offline.

2. Perform a backup of the data file at the O/S level, for example, a copy command.

3. Issue the ALTER DATABASE DATA FILE <filename> ONLINE command to bring the data file online.

4. Backup the current control file as the structure of the database has changed.

TIP

In the preceding example, if Tim didn't take a backup of the data file and if he lost the file, he could still recover it by using the ALTER DATABASE CREATE DATAFILE command and then by applying the archive log files which are generated from the time the data file was created.

Overview of User-Managed Recovery

While user-managed recovery was common in the past, with RMAN becoming more robust, Oracle recommends that you use system-managed backup and recovery. However, it is a good idea for you to understand different recovery mechanisms and recovery fundamentals. While Chapters 12 and 14 give details of recovery mechanisms, in this section, we discuss the fundamentals of recovery and the basic commands.

Recovery Concepts

We have mentioned earlier that there are two phases in recovering a database: roll forward and roll backward. Roll forward involves sequentially applying the redo records to the corresponding data blocks. Roll back involves rolling back the uncommitted transactions. This phase is also called transaction recovery. Oracle will apply all or none of the changes in an atomic redo transaction. For example, if you insert data into a table but did not commit, Oracle will apply the changes to the table during roll forward and will roll back the data during rollback phase since you did not commit.

Database Recovery

There are three basic recovery options you can use as shown in Table 10-2.

Recovery Option	Database Online	Database Offline
Database Recovery	No	Yes
Tablespace Recovery	Yes	yes
Data file Recovery	Yes (except SYSTEM files and files containing active rollback segments)	Yes

TABLE 10-2. *Recovery Options*

Database recovery is performed when you want to restore all the data files of the database and recover the entire database. If during a media failure, you lose all the data files, this is your only option (unless you have a standby database). While recovering the whole database, you have two options. You can do complete recovery or incomplete recovery. You will not lose any data when you do complete recovery. When you perform incomplete recovery, you will lose data. The only time you should use incomplete recovery is when you cannot perform complete recovery due to a loss of an archived redo log file or an online redo log file. There are special circumstances when you need to do incomplete recovery. For example, if you need to recover an accidentally dropped table, you need to do incomplete recovery on a test instance.

TIP

While doing database recovery, make sure all your data files are online. Offline data files will not be recovered.

The backup can be an offline backup or an online backup. However, you can recover the entire database when the database is offline and the instance is mounted. You should use the RECOVER DATABASE command to recover the entire database.

Tablespace Recovery

If you want to recover only a specific tablespace or a set of tablespaces, you can use the tablespace recovery option. You should use RECOVER TABLESPACE command to recover a tablespace. The biggest advantage of tablespace recovery is that you can recover the tablespace while the remaining database is open and available to users. However, usually, only complete recovery is possible with tablespace recovery. There is a special recovery option called tablespace point-in-time recovery (while using RMAN) that will recover tablespaces to a specific point in time. For more information refer to "Performing RMAN Tablespace Point-in-Time Recovery" section in the Oracle documentation *Oracle9i Recovery Manager User's Guide.*

The prerequisite for using tablespace recovery is that the database should be online and the tablespace being recovered should be offline. Since SYSTEM tablespace can never be taken offline, you can't do tablespace recovery on the SYSTEM tablespace.

Data File Recovery

Data file recovery allows you to recover individual data files. You can use separate terminal sessions to perform parallel recovery of database files thereby speeding up the recovery process. Data file recovery can be performed when the database is offline or online. However, if the database is online, the data file being recovered should be offline. Since SYSTEM data files cannot be taken offline, you can't recover SYSTEM data files using data file recovery when the database is online. You can use the RECOVER DATAFILE command to recover a specific data file.

Closed Database Backups

As discussed earlier, the backup, when performed after the database is shut down cleanly, is termed as *offline* or *cold* or *closed* database backup. The backup of the various database files must be performed using O/S copy commands or an O/S utility. If the database is operating in NOARCHIVELOG mode, then any changes or updates made to the database after the backup was performed are unrecoverable. The recovery would only be as good as the last consistent closed full database backup. If the database is operating in ARCHIVELOG mode, whenever the online redo log files are completely filled, their contents are transferred to the archive log files. During a media failure, if you lose your data files, you need to perform recovery of the database files by restoring the cold backup and issuing the appropriate recovery commands.

TIP
Even if you run the database in NOARCHIVELOG mode, the only time you might recover all committed transactions after a crash, is when the online log files have not been overwritten by LGWR from the time the database was opened.

Advantages

The closed database backup is simple to perform as well as automate. This is a clean and easy way to take a backup. Since the database is closed when you perform the backup, you are guaranteed to have a consistent copy of the database.

Disadvantages

To perform an offline backup, the database must be shut down, which will affect availability. In some businesses, database unavailability could mean loss of revenue. Among other things, the restore time (which affects the mean time to recover a database) depends on the following factors:

- Size of the database
- The rate at which copying of data files are done from tape to disk

NOTE
Whenever the structure of the database is changed
(that is, a new data file is added or a file is renamed
or a tablespace is created or dropped), you should
make a copy of the control file immediately and
also copy any newly added data files.

Performing an Offline Whole Database Backup

The following procedure shows the steps involved in performing a user-managed
consistent whole database backup (see Figure 10-2).

1. Query the dynamic performance views or the data dictionary to identify the
   location of the physical database files—control files, data files, and redo log
   files that constitute the whole database backup. You can query the following
   views:

   ```
   SQL> SELECT name FROM v$controlfile;
   SQL> SELECT name FROM v$datafile;
   SQL> SELECT member FROM v$logfile;
   ```

2. Shut down the database normally using one of the following options:
   IMMEDIATE, TRANSACTIONAL, or NORMAL.

3. Execute the operating system commands to copy the primary database files
   to the backup destination. For example, in Windows NT/2000, you can use
   the following command:

   ```
   C:\>COPY d:\oracle\oradata\target\system01.dbf c:\backups
           1 file(s) copied.
   ```

4. Execute the operating system commands to copy the configuration files,
   initialization parameter file, password file, and other associated database
   files to the backup destination. For example, in Windows NT/2000, you can
   copy the init.ora file using the following command:

   ```
   C:\>COPY d:\oracle\admin\target\pfile\init.ora c:\backups
           1 file(s) copied.
   ```

   Since the init.ora file is static by nature, you can perform a backup of all the
   parameters which have been dynamically altered by querying the
   V$PARAMETER dynamic performance view and spooling the contents into
   a file. Sample code and its partial output follows:

   ```
   SQL> SET HEADING OFF
   SQL> SET FEEDBACK OFF
   SQL> SELECT name||' = '||value FROM v$parameter ORDER BY name;
   O7_DICTIONARY_ACCESSIBILITY = FALSE
   ```

```
audit_trail = NONE
background_dump_dest = d:\Oracle\admin\target\bdump
```

5. Start up the database.

NOTE
Oracle strongly recommends that you do not *back up the online log files whether it's a hot backup or cold backup.*

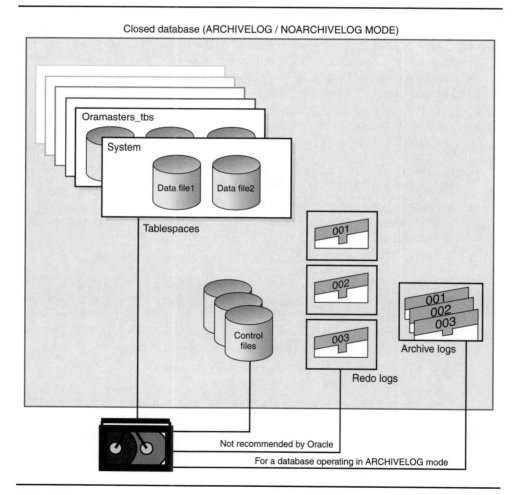

FIGURE 10-2. *Closed database backup*

The preceding note is especially important when you are running the database in ARCHIVELOG mode because, during recovery, if you accidentally overwrite the online log files with the backup online log files, you may end up losing committed transactions. Even while running the database in NOARCHIVELOG mode, you don't need to back up the online log files because, during recovery, you can always restore the data files and control files and start the database with the RESETLOGS option. However, in the real world, some DBAs prefer taking backups of online log files when they run in NOARCHIVELOG mode. This is because it would save them from recreating the log files. Also, during the cold backup, if they shut the database with the ABORT option, they would need the log files for crash recovery. Oracle's answer to this issue is that you should always shut the database down gracefully before taking a cold backup and taking backups of online log files is definitely bad practice.

Open Database Backups

If the database downtime has a drastic impact on your business operations and if it is not feasible to shut down the database and perform an offline backup, Oracle recommends that you perform an *online, open,* or *hot* database backup. To perform an online backup of the database, it is necessary that the database be operating in ARCHIVELOG mode. The online backups would be inconsistent or fuzzy as discussed earlier. However, the backup data files together with the archived redo makes the backup consistent.

While performing online backups, only data files and the current control file need to be backed up. The online redo log files must not be backed up. In fact, online log files should never be copied irrespective of the backup you are taking. Unlike offline backups that back up the entire database, the unit of an online backup is a tablespace, and any or all tablespaces can be backed up as needed. The online backup includes a backup of the data files (for one or more tablespaces), the current control file, and all archived redo log files created during the period of the backup. All archived redo log files generated after the online backup are also required for complete recovery. Though the unit of backup for online backups is a tablespace, all tablespaces need to be backed up eventually, and this is very important. The following example should make this point clear.

Let's assume that you have three tablespaces (T1, T2, and T3) in your database, and you take partial online backups of your database every night. That means you take an online backup of T1 on Monday, T2 on Tuesday, and T3 on Wednesday. You repeat this procedure by taking an online backup of T1 again on Thursday, T2 on Friday, and so on. It means that at the end of every three days (on Wednesday and Saturday, in this example), you will have a complete backup of the database, though not all tablespaces are backed up at the same point in time, as in the case of offline backups. In this example, if a media failure occurs on Friday after the online backups are done and you lose all your database files, you need to restore your entire database from backups. Since you have only two tablespaces (T1 and T2 from Thursday and Friday, respectively) and T3 has not been backed up yet, you need to restore T3 from the Wednesday night's backup. That means you also need to restore all the archived redo log files starting from Wednesday night's backup.

From the preceding example, you can see that recovery using partial backups (data files backed up at different times) begins with the oldest database file being restored. Therefore, you must preserve archived redo log files dating back to the time of the least recently backed up database file. Also, you need to make sure that full database backups are periodically performed to ensure that a backup of all the database files is available.

Advantages

The main advantage of online backups as compared with offline backups is that the database is available for normal user access during the backup, thereby maintaining high availability. Another advantage is that all data files do not have to be backed up at the same time—partial backups can be obtained. Redo logs can be applied to partially backed up tablespaces to perform full database recovery.

Performing an Online Whole Database Backup

The following procedure shows how to do online whole database backups (see Figure 10-3).

1. Query the data dictionary views to identify and locate all the data files associated with a tablespace that need to be backed up. You can do this by executing the following command:

   ```
   SQL> SELECT tablespace_name, file_name FROM dba_data_files;
   ```

2. Execute the SQL command to take the tablespace into backup mode:

   ```
   SQL> ALTER TABLESPACE system BEGIN BACKUP;
   Tablespace altered.
   ```

Note that if you forget to put the tablespace into backup mode or if you accidentally end the backup mode before its completion, then the backup is invalid and is not useful for subsequent recovery operations. You should start the backup from step 2 again. You should not take an online backup of a temporary tablespace as this tablespace is used only for sort operations and is not required during recovery opeations. Therefore, you always need to keep the scripts to create temporary tablespaces. If you ever have to recover from a backup, after recovery, you need to use the scripts to recreate your temporary tablespaces.

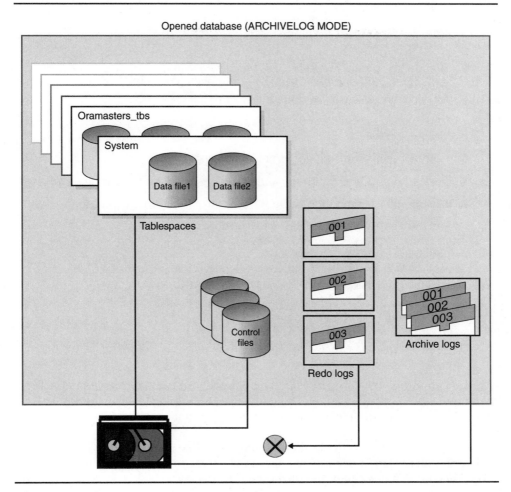

FIGURE 10-3. *Open database backup*

3. Execute the operating system commands to copy the data files pertaining to this online tablespace, to the backup destination.

NOTE
When you put a tablespace in the backup mode, make sure that you copy all the associated data files of that tablespace.

4. Execute the SQL command to take the tablespace out of the backup mode:

```
SQL> ALTER TABLESPACE system END BACKUP;
Tablespace altered.
```

5. Execute the command to archive the current online redo log group. This will archive the redo log file that has the END BACKUP redo record needed for recovery. This can be done by executing the command:

```
SQL> ALTER SYSTEM SWITCH LOGFILE;
System altered.
```

6. Copy all the archived log files generated up to step 5.

7. Repeat steps 2 to 6 for all the tablespaces as per your backup strategy.

8. Execute the command to backup the control file for the database.

```
SQL> ALTER DATABASE BACKUP CONTROLFILE TO
'd:\oracle9i\backup\control.bkp';
Database altered.
```

TIP
*In addition to the preceding command, some DBAs
also issue the ALTER DATABASE BACKUP
CONTROLFILE TO TRACE command.*

You can simultaneously place all the tablespaces in backup mode, and backup the online tablespaces in parallel. The ramifications of doing this should be considered, since it could lead to excessive redo generation if multiple users are updating the tablespaces.

Alternatively, you can perform the backup of online tablespaces by placing the tablespaces in backup mode one at a time. Oracle recommends that you use this serial backup option, since it minimizes the time between the BEGIN BACKUP and END BACKUP statements.

NOTE
*It is recommended that you thoroughly test the
automated scripts required for performing online
backups.*

Backups of Offline Tablespaces and Data Files

Some DBAs with OLTP applications like to take tablespaces offline before they take backups while the database is online. This is to reduce the amount of redo generated during hot backups of tablespaces.

While the database is online, you can perform a backup of either one or more files associated with an offline tablespace. During the backup all the other tablespaces of the database can remain online and available for user access. Assume that a table and its index are located on different tablespaces. If the tablespace associated with the index is taken offline, then the user may encounter errors while issuing DML operations on the table, if the optimizer requires the index to be accessed.

TIP
The SYSTEM tablespace cannot be taken offline to perform a backup while the database is open.

Performing the Backup of an Offline Tablespace

Use the following steps to perform an online backup of an offline tablespace:

1. Query the dictionary view DBA_DATA_FILES, to identify the locations of the files associated with the tablespace to be backed up.

2. Execute the SQL command to take the tablespace offline using the NORMAL option. This ensures that the tablespace can be subsequently brought online without tablespace recovery. For example,

```
SQL> ALTER TABLESPACE oramatest OFFLINE NORMAL;
Tablespace altered.
```

NOTE
If you take a tablespace offline using either the TEMPORARY or IMMEDIATE option, then you cannot bring the tablespace online unless you perform media recovery.

3. Copy the files that are associated with the offline tablespace to the backup destination using O/S commands.

4. Execute the SQL command to bring the tablespace online. Henceforth the tablespace is open and available for user access.

TIP
You must have the MANAGE TABLESPACE or ALTER TABLESPACE system privilege to alter the status of a non-system tablespace to offline or online.

Backups of Read-Only Tablespaces

The primary purpose of read-only tablespaces is to eliminate the need to perform backup and recovery of large, static portions of a database frequently. When a tablespace is in *read-only* mode, write operations are not allowed. Read-only tablespace enables you to drop objects, such as tables and indexes but does not allow you to create or alter the objects. To turn a tablespace into read-only mode, you must execute the following command:

```
SQL> ALTER TABLESPACE oramatest READ ONLY;
Tablespace altered.
```

This command instigates a checkpoint for all the data files belonging to the tablespace and the file headers are frozen with the current SCN number. Hereafter the DBW*n* writes only to those data files that are permitted for read/write operations where normal checkpoints can occur. While performing a backup of a read-only tablespace, you must only use the O/S commands to copy the files to the backup destination. The tablespaces need not be taken into backup mode.

What happens when there is a media failure and one of the tablespaces is a read-only tablespace? Please refer to "Recovery of Read-Only Tablespaces" section of Chapter 12 for more details.

See page 307

TIP
You should take a backup of the control file every time you switch a tablespace from read-only mode to read-write mode, and vice versa.

Backup of the Control File

The control file contains vital information including the structure of the database. The file is opened by Oracle at the database mount stage and is constantly used while performing normal operations. The control file is updated whenever there is a structural change for the database or during checkpoints. Whenever you change the structure of the database (for example, adding a data file), you must perform a backup of the control file. If all the current control files of a database are permanently lost during a media failure, you can create a new control file or use an older control file to recover the database. There are two ways to perform a backup of the control file using SQL commands:

① The first Option is backing up the control file to a binary file. This is the primary method implemented for performing a backup of the control file. The result would be a binary copy of the control file without *tempfile* entries.

```
SQL> ALTER DATABASE BACKUP CONTROLFILE TO 'd:\oracle9i\backup\control.bkp';
Database altered.
```
binary format

② The second option is backing up the control file to a trace file. This option is more appropriate for creating new control files than for backing up the existing control files. You issue the following command to write the control file creation statements to a trace file:

```
SQL> ALTER DATABASE BACKUP CONTROLFILE TO TRACE;
Database altered.
```
txtfile
used to create new control file
can be edited as appropriate
located in the udump

NOTE
Most DBAs use both the options while any kind of backup or structural changes are made to the database.

The TRACE option (the second option) prompts Oracle to write SQL statements, for re-creating the control file, to a trace file. The trace file can be reviewed and modified as appropriate. For example, you can increase the values for MAXDATAFILES. Once you edit this file appropriately, you need to execute the file while the database instance is closed. The trace file would exist in the location defined by the initialization parameter USER_DUMP_DEST on your system.

Backups of Archived Redo Logs

We have learned that when the database is operating in ARCHIVELOG mode, every log switch for the database triggers the ARC*n* process to archive the online redo log file. The availability of space in the archive log destination is essential for the ARC*n* process to create these files. To save disk space in your primary archiving locations, you must back up the archived logs using O/S commands or utilities, either to tape or to an alternative disk location.

Cleanup Operations after Failed Online Backups

Occasionally, the database may encounter an instance failure or the DBA accidentally shuts the database with the ABORT option while performing an online backup. You can categorize these problems mainly into two ways as follows:

- The failure occurred after the completion of the hot backup, but before you can execute the END BACKUP command.
- The failure occurred before you could finish your hot backup.

If it's the first case, technically, the backups are fine. You just need to end the backup mode of the hot backup tablespace. In the second case, the online backups are useless. However, if you are not sure if your backups finished before the crash, it is safe for you to discard the online backups taken during the failure.

When you start the database after the crash, since the checkpoint information in the data file headers (that were involved in the hot back) are frozen, Oracle assumes that the files are restored from a backup and asks you to perform media recovery. In reality, while the content of the data files is current, only the data file headers need to be synchronized. You can use the following command to set the data file header's SCN value to the correct number:

```
SQL> ALTER DATABASE DATAFILE 'd:\oracle\oradata\target\oramatest1.dbf' END BACKUP;
Database altered.
```

If there are multiple data files associated with multiple tablespaces that are in backup mode, Oracle recommends that you issue the following command while the database is still operating in the mount state to universally take the files out of the backup mode:

```
SQL> ALTER DATABASE END BACKUP;
Database altered.
```

The preceding command is new in Oracle9*i* and is useful when you have multiple tablespaces in hot backup mode or a single tablespace with a lot of data files. For example, let's assume that you have five tablespaces in backup mode and each tablespace has ten data files. The database has crashed due to a media failure. During crash recovery, you need to execute the ALTER DATABASE END BACKUP command only once instead of using the ALTER DATABASE DATAFILE END BACKUP command 50 times or the ALTER TABLESPACE END BACKUP command 5 times. In previous releases of Oracle, it was laborious to take each tablespace out of the backup mode individually or to perform media recovery on the database, if the database crashed during an online backup.

>
>
> **NOTE**
> *The ALTER DATABASE DATAFILE END BACKUP command cannot be executed while the database is Open. Oracle gives the ORA-01234 error if you try to execute this command while the database is open.*

An alternative to issuing the ALTER DATABASE END BACKUP command is to perform recovery. This is an alternate way to respond to failed online backups. This method is useful when you are not sure whether a data file is in hot backup mode. In such cases, execute the following command to recover the database:

```
SQL> RECOVER DATABASE;
Media recovery complete.
```

To view information about data files that are currently in backup mode, query the V$BACKUP dynamic performance view. This view displays the file identification number, the current status (that can either be ACTIVE, NOT ACTIVE, OFFLINE, NORMAL, or a description of an error), the SCN, and the time when the backup started.

The dynamic performance view V$DATAFILE_HEADER displays vital information related to data files. It displays information from the data file headers and the control file. This information is important while recovering data files. Some of the important columns in this view are NAME, STATUS, ERROR, RECOVER, FUZZY, RESETLOGS_CHANGE#, RESETLOGS_TIME, BYTES and BLOCKS.

LOGGING and NOLOGGING Options

NOLOGGING is an option provided by Oracle where redo is not generated for specific DML operations on objects. You need to enable this parameter for a table, index, partition, or a tablespace. If you enable NOLOGGING on a tablespace when it is created, specific DML operations like index creation or direct load inserts that are performed on objects that belong to the tablespace will not generate redo.

TIP
Enable the NOLOGGING option on a table just prior to loading table data or when creating an index.

You can set the NOLOGGING option using the following command for a table segment:

```
SQL> ALTER TABLE emp NOLOGGING;
```

dbverify Utility

The dbverify utility is an Oracle-provided external command-line utility that can be used to perform integrity checks on the physical data structures for a database. It enables you to ensure that the backups are valid before they can be restored. It also enables you to diagnose data block corruption in the data files. These checks are limited to *cache-managed blocks,* better known as data blocks. The dbverify utility only works for data files and not for control files and redo log files. The data files can be part of an open database or a backup data file, on a raw partition or on a file system. The dbverify utility has two command-line interfaces that can be invoked by either specifying disk blocks for a single data file or by specifying an entire segment for checking.

To obtain a list of parameters that could be specified with the dbverify utility, you should execute the following command:

```
C:\>dbv help=y
Keyword       Description                       (Default)
-----------------------------------------------------------
FILE          File to Verify                    (NONE)
START         Start Block                       (First Block of File)
END           End Block                         (Last Block of File)
BLOCKSIZE     Logical Block Size                (2048)
LOGFILE       Output Log                        (NONE)
FEEDBACK      Display Progress                  (0)
PARFILE       Parameter File                    (NONE)
USERID        Username/Password                 (NONE)
SEGMENT_ID    Segment ID (tsn.relfile.block)    (NONE)
```

For example, to verify blocks from 100 to 500 for the file system01.dbf using the dbverify utility, you must execute the following command:

```
C:\>dbv FILE=system01.dbf START=100 END=500 BLOCKSIZE=8192
```

PAGES	DESCRIPTION
Examined	Number of blocks in the file.
Processed	Number of blocks that were verified (formatted blocks).
Failing (Data)	Number of blocks that failed the data block checking routine.
Failing (Index)	Number of blocks that failed the index block checking routine.
Marked Corrupt	Number of blocks for which the cache header is invalid, thereby making it impossible for DBVERIFY to identify the block type.
Influx	Number of blocks that are being read and written to at the same time. If the database is open when DBVERIFY is run, DBVERIFY reads blocks multiple times to get a consistent image. But because the database is open, there may be blocks that are being read and written to at the same time (INFLUX). DBVERIFY cannot get a consistent image of pages that are in flux.

TABLE 10-3. *Output description of dbverify*

To understand the output generated by the dbverify utility, a brief description of the pages (blocks) are shown in Table 10-3.

Chapter Questions

1. **What is the significance of the columns change# and time in the V$BACKUP dynamic performance view shown here?**

```
SQL> SELECT file#, status, change#, time FROM v$backup;
    FILE# STATUS                 CHANGE# TIME
--- ------------------ ---------- ---------
        1 NOT ACTIVE                    0
        2 NOT ACTIVE                    0
        3 NOT ACTIVE                    0
        4 NOT ACTIVE                    0
        5 NOT ACTIVE                    0
        6 NOT ACTIVE               246635 23-SEP-01
6 rows selected.
```

   A. They display the SCN and timestamp when the tablespace associated with file 6 was taken out of backup mode.

B. They display the last SCN generated for the data file and the corresponding time.

C. They display the SCN and timestamp when the tablespace associated with file 6 was taken into backup mode.

D. They display the first SCN generated for the data file and the corresponding time.

E. None of the above.

2. **Where does Oracle create the file when the following command is issued?**

```
SQL> ALTER DATABASE BACKUP CONTROLFILE TO TRACE;
```

A. Location defined by the initialization parameter CORE_DUMP_DEST

B. Location defined by the initialization parameter BACKGROUND_DUMP_DEST

C. Location defined by the initialization parameter USER_DUMP_DEST

D. Location defined by the initialization parameter TRACE_DUMP_DEST

E. %ORACLE_HOME%\database

3. **Which of the following shut down options should not be used before performing a consistent whole database backup?**

A. NORMAL

B. TRANSACTIONAL

C. ABORT

D. IMMEDIATE

E. INCONSISTENT

4. **Which data dictionary view displays the error information related to a data file, when an internal read fails on that file?**

A. V$DATAFILE

B. V$DATAFILE_HEADER

C. DBA_DATA_FILES

D. V$DBFILE

E. V$DATAFILE_ERRORS

5. **Read-only tablespace backup is not supported for which of the following tablespaces?**

   A. SYSTEM tablespace

   B. USERS tablespace

   C. Dictionary Managed TEMP tablespace

   D. INDX tablespace

6. **After executing which of the following commands would you deem it most appropriate to back up the control file?**

   A. ALTER SYSTEM CHECKPOINT;

   B. ALTER DATABASE ADD LOGFILE GROUP 4 ('d:\oracle\oradata\target\redo04.log') size 500k;

   C. ALTER SYSTEM SWITCH LOGFILE;

   D. GRANT SYSDBA TO SCOTT;

7. **What privilege must a DBA have to place a tablespace in backup mode?**

   A. CREATE TABLESPACE

   B. DROP TABLESPACE

   C. UNLIMITED TABLESPACE

   D. MANAGE TABLESPACE

8. **You issue the following command to take all the data files out of backup mode. In which state must the database be operating to successfully execute this command?**

   ```
   SQL> ALTER DATABASE END BACKUP;
   Database altered.
   ```

   A. MOUNT

   B. OPEN

   C. CLOSE

   D. NOMOUNT

9. **What is the advantage of using the NOLOGGING option with the table?**

   A. Decreases the systems performance

   B. Increases the redo generation

   C. Eliminates the need for backups

   D. Eliminates redo generation for table direct inserts

10. **What is the significance of using the START option with the dbverify utility?**

   A. It performs integrity checks from the first data file block.

   B. It performs integrity checks from the last data file block.

   C. It performs integrity checks from the block id specified by this option.

   D. It performs integrity checks from the first block of the next extent, which succeeds the specified block id.

Answers to Chapter Questions

1. C.   They display the SCN and timestamp when the tablespace associated with file 6 was taken into backup mode.

Explanation   The V$BACKUP dynamic performance view displays status information about those files that are currently in backup mode. The columns CHANGE# and the TIME displays the SCN and timestamp when the tablespace was placed in the backup mode.

2. C.   Location defined by the initialization parameter USER_DUMP_DEST.

Explanation   The trace file is created in the location defined by the initialization parameter USER_DUMP_DEST. The control file trace can be used to recreate the control file when all the copies of the control files are unavailable.

3. C.   ABORT

Explanation   To perform a consistent whole database backup, you must first shut down the database with one of the following options: NORMAL, TRANSACTIONAL, or IMMEDIATE. The ABORT option shuts the database without finishing the checkpointing on all the data files. You will need to perform recovery after restoration to bring the database into a consistent state.

4. B.   V$DATAFILE_HEADER

Explanation   The V$DATAFILE_HEADER dynamic performance view displays the error information related to data files when an internal read performed by Oracle fails. Apart from this, the view displays the status of the file and whether a file needs media recovery to be performed.

5. A.   SYSTEM tablespace

Explanation   You cannot take the SYSTEM tablespace into read-only mode. An attempt to execute the operation would result in the following error:

```
ORA-01643: SYSTEM TABLESPACE CAN NOT BE MADE READ ONLY
```

It is required that the SYSTEM tablespace be directly taken into backup mode; the excessive redo generated for the SYSTEM tablespace cannot be avoided unlike other tablespaces.

6. B.   ALTER DATABASE ADD LOGFILE GROUP 4
('d:\oracle\oradata\target\redo04.log') size 500k;

Explanation   Most of the ALTER DATABASE statements perform database structural changes. These updates immediately occur in the current control file. Oracle recommendeds that you back up the current control file by issuing the ALTER DATABASE BACKUP CONTROLFILE statement, thereby maintaining a copy the control file contents as a safeguard against failures.

7. D.   MANAGE TABLESPACE

Explanation   The DBA must possess the MANAGE TABLESPACE privilege to take a tablespace into backup mode. The other privilege that would enable you to take the tablespace into backup mode is ALTER TABLESAPCE.

8. A.   MOUNT

Explanation   If the database instance is aborted with the files still in backup mode, you can issue the ALTER DATABASE END BACKUP command with the database mounted. The command takes all the files out of backup mode. To know which files are in backup mode, you can query the V$BACKUP dynamic performance view.

9. D.   Eliminates redo generation for table inserts

Explanation   When data is loaded using a direct load operation with the NOLOGGING option, the inserts are not written in the redo log files. The table should be backed up after the load has been completed. If a failure occurred after the load operation, the inserted data would not be recoverable through crash or media recovery. Data loaded with the NOLOGGING option reduces the processing costs because entries are not recorded in the redo logs. This option is not for regular use in production databases.

10. C.   It performs integrity checks from the block id specified by this option.

Explanation   The START parameter enables the dbverify utility to start performing the integrity checks from the specified block id. For example the following command would start the integrity checks from block id 10:

```
C:\>dbv file=d:\oracle\oradata\target\test8i01.dbf start=10
```

CHAPTER
11

RMAN Backups

n this chapter, you will learn the basic concepts of Recovery Manager (RMAN) and the backup options available. We will explain RMAN's image copy and backup set in detail and describe the process of creating backups using the BACKUP command. We also explain how to back up the control file and the archived redo log files. At the end of this chapter, you will find a listing of the important data dictionary views related to RMAN backups. This chapter includes the following topics:

- RMAN backup concepts
- RMAN image copies
- RMAN backup sets
- Tags for backup sets and image copies
- Backing up the control file
- Backing up the archived redo Log files
- Important V$VIEWS

RMAN Backup Concepts

RMAN performs backup, restore, and recovery operations by spawning numerous Oracle server processes, therefore these backups are termed as *server-managed* backups.

You can use RMAN to perform backups of the following:

- Entire database
- Tablespace
- Data file
- Control file
- Archive log file

NOTE
RMAN will not perform a backup of the online redo log files. Online log files should never be backed up, as you would never require them for recovery.

hot   *cold*

Online and Offline Database Backups   *cold*

You can perform a backup of the database using RMAN when it is closed (offline) or open. To perform a closed database backup, ensure that the target database is not open but mounted. If you use the *recovery catalog*, then the database where the recovery catalog resides must be open. RMAN uses the Oracle server process to generate copies of data files, control files, or archive log files.

> **NOTE**
> *While performing server-managed online backups,*
> *RMAN generates less redo in contrast to the user-*
> *managed online backups that are performed by*
> *issuing the ALTER TABLESPACE . . . BEGIN BACKUP*
> *command.*

Whole Database Backups

A *whole database backup* includes all the target database files—data files and the control file. Whole database backups can either be performed while the database is open or closed. When the database is operating in NOARCHIVELOG mode, only the restore and recovery of the consistent whole database backup is valid. If you run a 24x7 OLTP application, then the only option is for you to take an online backup. You need to run the database in ARCHIVELOG mode in order to take an online backup.

RMAN supports two types of backups: *image copies* and *backup sets*. Both of these RMAN backups are discussed in the following sections.

RMAN Image Copies

When you issue the RMAN COPY command, an Oracle server session creates the image copy. This is similar to using the operating system copy command. RMAN will create image copies of data files, archive log files, and control files. The image copy of the database files and the archive log files can be used to perform recovery operations. While creating the image copy, the Oracle server session performs a validity check on the blocks of the file and records the information related to this copy in the control file.

General Characteristics

An image copy has the following features:

■ The RMAN COPY command creates the image copies only to disk.

■ RMAN ensures that it copies all the blocks (used and unused) pertaining to the data files. While backing up the blocks, Oracle also checks for corrupt blocks. You can disable the Oracle's corrupt block checking feature for enhancing the performance by using the NOCHECKSUM option in the COPY command.

■ The image copy can be included in full or incremental level 0 backups because a file copy will always backup all the blocks.

■ The image copy can only be used with the level 0 incremental backup. RMAN does not support other levels while including the image copy with an incremental backup strategy.

■ The advantage of storing files on disk is that these files can immediately be restored and do not need to be transferred from other media. If the files are already available on the disk but need to be restored to their original destination for recovery, you can direct the control file to point to the image copy using the SWITCH command instead of restoring it. This will update the repository to indicate that the copy has been switched (re-located). The equivalent to RMAN's SWITCH command is the SQL statement ALTER DATABASE RENAME DATAFILE. After issuing this command, you can perform appropriate recovery operations.

■ During media recovery, these RMAN-produced image copies are ready to be restored to their original locations for performing the recovery operations. Restoration of these files can either be done using RMAN or through operating system specific commands. Since the image copies are generated by RMAN and are not stored in RMAN-specific format, they can be manually restored through operating system commands.

■ The image copies are indistinguishable from the copies made using operating system commands. RMAN makes image copies using the Oracle blocks whereas the operating system makes copies using OS blocks.

NOTE
You can use the NOCHECKSUM option while performing an image copy to avoid the data block verification, thereby speeding the copy process.

Performing an Image Copy

To perform an image copy of a data file using the NOCHECKSUM parameter, you must issue the following command:

don't check error in file

```
RMAN> COPY DATAFILE 3 TO 'd:\oracle\backup\DBF_%d_%t' NOCHECKSUM;
Starting copy at 03-OCT-01
using channel ORA_DISK_1
channel ORA_DISK_1: copied datafile 3
output filename=D:\ORACLE\BACKUP\DBF_%D_%T recid=6 stamp=442154950
Finished copy at 03-OCT-01
```

To perform an image copy of the current control file, you must issue the following command:

```
RMAN> COPY CURRENT CONTROLFILE TO 'c:\backups\ctlf.f';
```

To perform an image copy of an archive log file, you must issue the following command:

```
RMAN> COPY ARCHIVELOG 'd:\oracle9i\ora90\rdbms\arc00705.001' TO
'c:\backups\arc705.arc';
```

> **NOTE**
> *When you execute the RESTORE command, RMAN, by default, restores the image copy of a data file or the control file to its original location.*

To create an image copy of data file 5 along with control file and the archive log files, you must issue the following command:

```
RMAN> COPY DATAFILE 5 TO 'c:\backups\df5.f',
2> ARCHIVELOG 'd:\oracle9i\ora90\rdbms\arc00705.001' TO
'c:\backups\arc705.arc',
3> CONTROLFILECOPY 'c:\backups\ctlf.f' TO 'd:\backups\ctl2.f';
```

Cataloging Operating System Copies

The copies of files generated using O/S commands and utilities are similar to RMAN image copies. But these are not recognized by RMAN until you catalog the file copies by executing the RMAN CATALOG command. You can catalog the file copies as shown below:

```
RMAN> CATALOG DATAFILECOPY 'd:\oracle\oradata\target\copyormtest1.dbf';
cataloged datafile copy
datafile copy filename=D:\ORACLE\ORADATA\TARGET\COPYORMTEST1.DBF recid=8
stamp=442156900
```

RMAN Backup Sets

A *backup set* is a logical object in RMAN-specific format. This is a result of one complete operation where one or more individual physical database files constitute the backup set. A backup set includes a complete set of backup pieces that makes up a full or incremental backup of the objects. You can create a backup set by using the BACKUP command.

Backup Pieces

The backup set can be comprised of one or more physical *backup pieces*. The backup piece stores data pertaining to one or more data files, control files, or the archive log files. RMAN, by default, creates a backup set with only one piece.

You can specify a file name for the backup piece by including the FORMAT parameter. RMAN allows you to specify a distinct name for each backup piece by including substitution variables in the FORMAT parameter. If you do not specify the FORMAT parameter, RMAN stores the backup pieces in a platform-specific directory. The destination directory on UNIX is $ORACLE_HOME/dbs and on Windows NT/2000 it is %ORACLE_HOME%\DATABASE. The following example shows how you could include the FORMAT parameter in the BACKUP command:

```
RMAN> BACKUP DATAFILE 3 FORMAT 'd:\oracle\oradata\target\file3_%d_%s_%p';
Starting backup at 03-OCT-01
using channel ORA_DISK_1
channel ORA_DISK_1: starting full datafile backupset
channel ORA_DISK_1: specifying datafile(s) in backupset
input datafile fno=00003 name=D:\ORACLE\ORADATA\TARGET\ORMTEST1.DBF
channel ORA_DISK_1: starting piece 1 at 03-OCT-01
channel ORA_DISK_1: finished piece 1 at 03-OCT-01
piece handle=D:\ORACLE\ORADATA\TARGET\FILE3_TARGET_72_1 comment=NONE
channel ORA_DISK_1: backup set complete, elapsed time: 00:00:04
Finished backup at 03-OCT-01
```

Table 11-1 lists the substitution variables that are available for use in the FORMAT strings to standardize the filenames. The formatting of this information varies by platform.

SUBSTITUTE VARIABLE	SUBSTITUTE VARIABLE DESCRIPTION
%c	Includes the copy number of the backup piece within a set of duplexed backup pieces.
%d	Includes the name of the database in the format string.
%D	Includes the current day of the month from the Gregorian calendar in the format DD.
%F	Specifies the DBID, day, month, year, and sequence in a unique and repeatable generated name.
%M	Includes the month in the Gregorian calendar in format MM.
%n	Includes the database name, padded on the right with x characters to a total length of eight characters.
%p	Includes the piece number within the backup set. This value starts at 1 for each backup set and is incremented by 1 as each backup piece is created.
%s	Includes the backup set number in the format string. This number is a sequential counter in the control file that is incremented for each backup set. The value starts with 1 and is unique for the lifetime of the control file.
%t	Includes the backup set time stamp, which is a four-byte value derived as the number of seconds elapsed since a fixed reference time. The combination of %s and %t can be used to form a unique name for the backup set.
%T	Includes the year, month, and day in the format YYYYMMDD.
%u	Includes an eight-character name constituted by compressed representations of the backup set number and the time the backup set was created.
%U	Includes convenient shorthand for %u_%p_%c that guarantees uniqueness in generated backup filenames. RMAN uses the format %U by default if you do not specify a format.
%Y	Includes the year in the format YYYY.
%%	Includes the '%' character. For example, %%d translates to the string %d.

TABLE 11-1. *FORMAT String Substitute Variables*

NOTE
If you specify PROXY, then the %p variable must be
included in the FORMAT string either explicitly or
implicitly within %U.

RMAN by default creates only one backup piece for a backup set. RMAN enables
you to create more than one backup piece for a backup set by restricting a backup
piece to a specified size. The reason for specifying the maximum piece size for a
device is to restrict the backup piece size to fit in the designated storage media. For
example, if you are backing up to a tape cartridge, you would configure the
MAXPIECESIZE such that it would be accommodated on the tape. To restrict the size
of the backup piece, you must set the MAXPIECESIZE parameter of the CONFIGURE
CHANNEL or ALLOCATE CHANNEL commands. An example of this is as follows:

```
RMAN> CONFIGURE CHANNEL DEVICE TYPE DISK MAXPIECESIZE = 5M;
```

This command restricts the backup piece size to 5MB. The following conditions
determine the number and size of the backup sets created:

- The value specified for BACKUPSPEC clause

- The size and number of input files specified for each BACKUPSPEC clause

- The number of allocated channels

- The value specified through the FILESPERSET parameter (The specified value
limits the number of the files included in a backup set.)

- The value specified through the MAXSETSIZE parameter specified at the
CONFIGURE and BACKUP commands

A backup specification list contains a list of one or more BACKUPSPEC clauses.
A BACKUPSPEC clause minimally contains a list of one or more objects that require
backing up. These objects are BACKUPSET, DATAFILE, DATAFILECOPY,
TABLESPACE, DATABASE, CURRENT CONTROLFILE, and CONTROLFILECOPY.

Backup Set Parameters

The two main backup set parameters that influence the number and size of backup
sets created by RMAN are described in the following sections.

FILESPERSET Parameter

You can specify the maximum number of input files for inclusion in the backup set
by specifying the FILESPERSET parameter. For example, if you set the FILESPERSET

parameter to 5, then RMAN never includes more than 5 files in a backup set. The default value for the FILESPERSET parameter is the lesser of 64 or the total number of the input files divided by the number of channels. For example, if you backup 100 data files by using 10 channels, RMAN sets the value for the parameter as 10.

RMAN balances the workload against the number of allocated channels by creating sufficient backup sets. At times this is not true if there are more channels than files to back up. Assume that RMAN needs to perform a backup of 5 data files when there are 6 channels allocated. This would result in one channel being idle and the value for the FILESPERSET parameter set to 1.

MAXSETSIZE Parameter

You can specify the maximum size for a backup set that a channel can produce by setting the MAXSETSIZE parameter in the CONFIGURE or BACKUP commands. You should use this parameter to configure backup set size so that each set can fit on one tape rather than span multiple tapes. If you don't use this parameter and one tape of a multi-volume backup set fails, then you would lose that data on all the tapes rather than just one. When the files are located on a single disk and do not create an I/O distribution problem, then MAXSETSIZE parameter is easier to use than the FILESPERSET parameter. When you need to manage I/O distribution for backups on multiple disks, the FILESPERSET parameter is more useful.

NOTE
Since FILESPERSET has a default value, the parameters MAXSETSIZE and FILESPERSET take effect when MAXSETSIZE is initialized. RMAN attempts to limit the size in bytes of the backup sets based on the value specified by the MAXSETSIZE parameter, thereby treating FILESPERSET as an upper limit for the number of files to be included in each set.

Rules for Backup Set Creation

The rules in the algorithm for backup set creation are listed as follows:

- Every allocated channel that is active produces a backup set. As a default, each backup set contains a minimum of one backup piece.

- RMAN tries to maintain an equal amount of workload on each of the allocated channels. This ensures that the allocated channels have equal amount of work to do.

- The FILESPERSET parameter of the BACKUP command determines the maximum number of the data files on each backup set.

■ The lower values of the FILESPERSET and MAXOPENFILES parameters limit the number of data files multiplexed in a backup set.

■ The MAXSETSIZE parameter of the CONFIGURE or BACKUP command determines the maximum size of a backup set.

You can create backup sets as either full backups or incremental backups. Both methods of creating backup sets are discussed in the following sections in detail.

Guidelines for Using the BACKUP Command

You must follow the guidelines listed here before executing the BACKUP command:

■ Before executing the BACKUP command, either mount or open the target database. In such situations, RMAN can either perform a consistent or an inconsistent backup.

■ You must use the current control file.

■ If the automatic channel allocation for a device is not pre-configured, then you must allocate a channel manually for each execution of the BACKUP command. RMAN is by default pre-configured with DISK channels.

■ You must provide a unique name for each backup piece. You can specify the substitution variables in the format string. The %p variable can be used here.

■ You must use valid media for backup, however, RMAN can backup files on any device that can store an Oracle data file. If you choose the sbt DEVICE TYPE, then RMAN functions with the media management software. If you choose the device DISK, then RMAN will back up to disks.

■ If you are running in NOARCHIVELOG mode, you can't do normal or incremental backups if the database is open or if the database has not been shutdown gracefully.

Full Backups

A *full backup* is a backup of all the used blocks in the database. In a full backup, RMAN ensures that it takes the backup of all the data blocks in the data files but skips the blocks that are unused. RMAN does not skip any blocks while backing up the control file and the archive log files. Full backups are not considered as part of the incremental strategy as these backups do not affect which blocks are included in subsequent incremental backups.

what it is?

Incremental Backups

RMAN allows you to take *incremental backups*. An incremental backup enables you to backup only those blocks that have changed since the last backup. RMAN enables you to create incremental backups for data files, tablespaces, or the whole database. During media recovery, RMAN prefers to use incremental backups over the available archive log files to recover the database. We will illustrate this with the following example. Figure 11-1 shows the incremental backup strategy of a company. A level 0 backup (which includes all data files, control file, and archived redo) was taken on Sunday. As shown in Figure 11-1, a level 2 backup was taken on Monday, Tuesday, Thursday, and Friday. A level 1 backup was taken on Wednesday. The database crashed on Saturday. There are two ways that RMAN can now recover the database:

■ It can restore the level 0 backup from Sunday and apply all the archived redo logs up to Saturday, when the crash happened.

■ The second option is for RMAN to restore the full backup from Sunday, apply the incremental backup taken on Wednesday. This will make the backup current up to Wednesday. Further, RMAN will apply the Thursday and Friday incremental backups making the restored database current up to Friday. RMAN will then apply all the redo logs generated since the Friday incremental backup.

add in script duplicates
delete

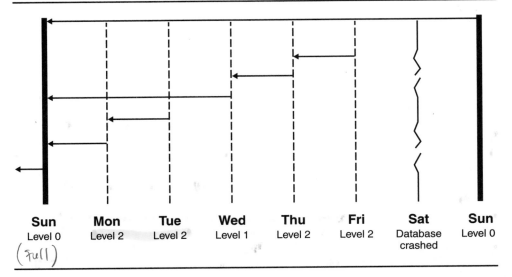

Sun	Mon	Tue	Wed	Thu	Fri	Sat	Sun
Level 0	Level 2	Level 2	Level 1	Level 2	Level 2	Database crashed	Level 0

(full)

FIGURE 11-1. *Example of an incremental backup strategy*

TIP
By default, RMAN always chooses the second option previously described.

NOTE
RMAN includes the control files in the incremental backup set and ensures that the complete control file is backed up.

Benefits

There are several advantages to taking incremental backups. Some of these advantages are listed below:

- Saves considerable amount of storage area, whether disk or tape

- Saves network bandwidth if backups are being performed over the network

- Enables you to recover objects that have been created with the NOLOGGING option (This option is usually enabled for objects while doing a direct load insert, which does not log redo information though changes to data blocks are inevitable. These changes are captured by the incremental backups that can further be used for recovering the data in these objects.)

- A possible substitute for a whole database backup after the database is shutdown normally when the database is operating in NOARCHIVELOG mode (In NOARCHIVELOG mode, taking whole database backups consumes significant amount of time and storage space.)

Multilevel Incremental Backups

You can create multilevel incremental backups through RMAN. Performing incremental backups ensures that all the blocks are not backed up all the time, thereby consuming less storage space and time. The size of the backup files depends on the number of the blocks that are modified and the incremental backup level.

Incremental backup levels are denoted as level 0, level 1, level 2, level 3, and level 4. The level 0 incremental backup is a base for the succeeding incremental backups to be performed. RMAN copies all the blocks that contain data while performing a level 0 backup. There is only one primary difference between full backup and level 0 incremental backup. The full backups cannot be included in the incremental backup strategy and henceforth cannot be used as a base though both contain similar data.

NOTE
*If there is no level 0 backup and you run a level 1
or higher backup, then RMAN automatically
performs a level 0 backup to serve as the base.*

Differential Incremental Backups   In a differential incremental backup, all the blocks that have changed since the most recent backup at level *n* or lower will be backed up. This is the default incremental backup method. For example, in a differential backup at level 3, RMAN determines which backup (that is, level 2 or level 3) has occurred most recently and backs up all blocks modified since that backup was performed. If no level 2 backup is available, RMAN copies all blocks changed since the base level 1 backup and so on. You must execute the following command to perform a base level 0 backup of the database:

```
RMAN> BACKUP INCREMENTAL LEVEL 0 DATABASE;
```

Cumulative Incremental Backups   Oracle provides an option to make cumulative incremental backups at level 1 or greater. In a cumulative level n backup, RMAN backs up all the blocks used since the most recent backup at level n-1 or lower. For example, in a cumulative level 3 backup, RMAN determines which level 2 backup has occurred most recently and copies all blocks changed since that backup was performed. If no level 2 backup is available, RMAN backs up all blocks changed since the level 1 backup and so on. You must execute the following command to perform a level 2 cumulative backup of the database:

```
RMAN> BACKUP INCREMENTAL LEVEL 2 CUMULATIVE DATABASE;
```

The cumulative incremental backups reduce significant amount of work involved in restoration of the files by ensuring that you only need one incremental backup from any particular level. The cumulative incremental backups require more storage space and time than differential backups, since they duplicate the blocks that have already been backed up since the previous backups at the same level.

Tags for Backup Sets and Image Copies

A *tag* is a name given to backup sets and image copies. The tag can be up to 30 characters in length. This makes it easier to identify the backup sets and image copies. Tags do not have to be unique; therefore, you can create one or more copies or backup sets with the similar tag. While executing the RESTORE or CHANGE command, you can specify the appropriate tag instead of using the filenames. You can use the following command to create a backup set containing all the database files by specifying the tag name as shown below:

```
RMAN> BACKUP DATABASE INCLUDE CURRENT CONTROLFILE TAG 'Daily Backup';
```

To view the metadata information and the tag associated to the backup, you must execute the following command:

```
RMAN> LIST BACKUPSET OF DATABASE;
```

Backing Up the Control File

It is important to back up the control file frequently, especially when the control file is used as the RMAN repository. The loss of the control file without any backups could result in total loss of the RMAN metadata. Therefore it is recommended in such situations to create multiple copies of the control file using Oracle's *multiplexing* mechanism or through the use of *disk mirroring.*

NOTE
Oracle recommends that you use the control file multiplexing feature even if you mirror your hardware.

The backup of the control file can be performed with the database either open or closed. RMAN uses the snapshot control file for read consistency. If the AUTOBACKUP feature is enabled, then RMAN automatically backs up the control file after execution of the BACKUP or COPY commands. RMAN generates a file with a distinct name for the AUTOBACKUP command. When the INCLUDE CONTROLFILE command option is used, RMAN will backup the control file as part of the main backup set.

The control file AUTOBACKUP feature, can be enabled by executing the following command:

```
RMAN> CONFIGURE CONTROLFILE AUTOBACKUP ON;
```

If the control file AUTOBACKUP feature is disabled, you can perform a backup of the control file in one of the following ways:

- By issuing the BACKUP CURRENT COTNROLFILE command
- By including the backup of the control file within any backup by specifying the INCLUDE CURRENT CONTROLFILE option in the BACKUP command

- By performing the backup of data file 1 (SYSTEM data file), which automatically includes the control file in the backup

NOTE

A manual backup of the control file is different from the AUTOBACKUP. While performing the manual backup of the control file, the control file backup only contains the metadata related to the backups within the current RMAN session.

The different methods for manually performing control file backups are discussed in the following sections.

Backing Up the Current Control File Only

To perform a backup of the current control file, you must execute the following command at the RMAN prompt:

```
RMAN> BACKUP CURRENT CONTROLFILE;
Starting backup at 24-SEP-01
allocated channel: ORA_DISK_1
channel ORA_DISK_1: sid=9 devtype=DISK
channel ORA_DISK_1: starting full datafile backupset
channel ORA_DISK_1: specifying datafile(s) in backupset
including current controlfile in backupset
channel ORA_DISK_1: starting piece 1 at 24-SEP-01
channel ORA_DISK_1: finished piece 1 at 24-SEP-01
piece handle=D:\ORACLE9I\ORA90\DATABASE\05D4R4E7_1_1 comment=NONE
channel ORA_DISK_1: backup set complete, elapsed time: 00:00:02
Finished backup at 24-SEP-01
```

Including the Current Control File in Another Backup

The current control file can be included in any backup set by specifying the INCLUDE CURRENT CONTROLFILE option in the BACKUP command. For example, to backup the tablespace TOOLS and include the current control file in the backup set, you must execute the following command:

```
RMAN> BACKUP TABLESPACE tools INCLUDE CURRENT CONTROLFILE;
Starting backup at 24-SEP-01
allocated channel: ORA_DISK_1
channel ORA_DISK_1: sid=10 devtype=DISK
channel ORA_DISK_1: starting full datafile backupset
```

```
channel ORA_DISK_1: specifying datafile(s) in backupset
input datafile fno=00004 name=D:\ORACLE\ORADATA\TARGET\TOOLS01.DBF
including current controlfile in backupset
channel ORA_DISK_1: starting piece 1 at 24-SEP-01
channel ORA_DISK_1: finished piece 1 at 24-SEP-01
piece handle=D:\ORACLE9I\ORA90\DATABASE\04D4R33J_1_1 comment=NONE
channel ORA_DISK_1: backup set complete, elapsed time: 00:00:04
Finished backup at 24-SEP-01
```

NOTE
*RMAN creates two control file backups if the
AUTOBACKUP feature is enabled. One is a due to
the command explicitly issued by you and the other
is automatically performed as a result of the
AUTOBACKUP feature.*

To obtain the details related to the backups of the control file, you must execute
the following command:

```
RMAN> LIST BACKUP OF CONTROLFILE;
```

Backing Up the Archive Redo Log files

You can use RMAN to perform backups of the archive log files by using the BACKUP
ARCHIVELOG command and specifying desired filtering options. RMAN enables
you to clear the disk space occupied by the archive log files while performing the
backup of these files to tape. You can do this by either specifying the DELETE INPUT
option or DELETE ALL INPUT option with the BACKUP command. RMAN deletes
the archive log files as soon as it completes the backup. If the DELETE ALL INPUT
option is specified, RMAN deletes the log files from all enabled archiving
destinations after backing up each specified log sequence number. In contrast, if you
specify the DELETE INPUT option, RMAN only deletes the files in the specific disk
that it backed up. For example, you must issue the following command to back up
all the archive log files and delete all the input:

```
RMAN> BACKUP ARCHIVELOG ALL DELETE ALL INPUT;
```

NOTE
*You must understand that if a database has multiple
archive destinations configured, RMAN does not
include redundant copies of the same log sequence*

> *number into a backup set. The BACKUP*
> *ARCHIVELOG ALL command backs up exactly one*
> *copy of each distinct log sequence number. In the*
> *preceding output observe that RMAN searches for*
> *the archive logs through various destinations.*

RMAN also allows you to perform a backup of a range of archive log files based on time, SCN, or log sequence number. In the preceding command, RMAN backed up all the archive log files since there was no option specified. You must execute the following command to back up all the archived log files created more than five and less than ten days ago:

```
RMAN> BACKUP ARCHIVELOG FROM TIME 'SYSDATE-10' UNTIL TIME 'SYSDATE-5';
```

NOTE
The UNTIL TIME option specified in the preceding
command restricts RMAN to automatically switch
out of the current online redo log and archive it.

Similarly, you must execute the following command to back up all the archived log files created between the sequence numbers 9100 and 9111:

```
RMAN> BACKUP ARCHIVELOG FROM SEQUENCE 9100 UNTIL SEQUENCE 9111;
```

The following command must be executed to back up all the archived log files created between the SCN numbers 596000 and 597148:

```
RMAN> BACKUP ARCHIVELOG FROM SCN 596000 UNTIL SCN 597148;
```

You can also back up archive log files along with other objects. You can do this by including the PLUS ARCHIVELOG option with the BACKUP command. This enables RMAN to perform a backup of all the archive log files along with the other objects.

The following series of events occurs when you execute the BACKUP command with the PLUS ARCHIVELOG option:

1. RMAN executes the ALTER SYSTEM ARCHIVE LOG CURRENT command. This command archives the current online log file.

2. It then executes the BACKUP ARCHIVELOG ALL command. This command backs up all the archive log files available in the archive log destination.

3. RMAN performs a backup of all the files specified in BACKUP command.

4. Finally, it executes the ALTER SYSTEM ARCHIVE LOG CURRENT command again.

5. RMAN performs a backup of the remaining archived log files that are generated in the course of the backup. This ensures that the data files that are being backed up are recoverable to a consistent state.

NOTE
If the backup optimization feature is enabled, then RMAN skips the archive logs that it has already backed up to the specified device. However, further checking is done to determine whether to skip the file, since both the retention policy feature and the backup duplexing feature influence the internal algorithm that determines whether RMAN has enough backups on the specific drive.

You can override the settings that have been enabled through the CONFIGURE . . . COPIES command by executing the BACKUP . . . COPIES command. An example of this is given in the following:

```
RMAN> BACKUP DEVICE TYPE DISK COPIES 3 ARCHIVELOG ALL;
```

In the preceding command, the number of copies can range from 1 to 4.
To perform the backup of all archive log files along with the tablespace USERS, you must issue the following command:

```
RMAN> BACKUP TABLESPACE users PLUS ARCHIVELOG;
```

Important V$VIEWS

This section includes the list of the dynamic performance views that provide information pertaining to RMAN backups.

The dynamic performance view V$BACKUP_DATAFILE enables you to determine the number of blocks in each data file, which is helpful for creating equal-sized backup sets. You can also obtain the number of corrupt blocks for the data file from this view.

The dynamic performance view V$BACKUP_REDOLOG displays information about archived logs that are stored in a backup set. This information is obtained from the control file. RMAN ensures that it first archives the current redo log and then backs it up. An archive log backup set can contain one or more archived logs.

This dynamic performance view **V$BACKUP_SET** displays the information related to the backup sets from the control file. This view can be accessed to obtain a new entry after every successful backup operation that generates a backup set.

This dynamic performance view **V$BACKUP_PIECE** displays information about backup pieces from the control file. Each backup set consists of one or more backup pieces.

The dynamic performance view **V$BACKUP_CORRUPTION** displays information about corruption in the data file backups that was detected while the backup set was being created. This information is obtained from the control file. The relevant columns in the view are PIECE#, FILE#, BLOCK#, BLOCKS, and MARKED_CORRUPT. If the MARKED_CORRUPT column is set to YES, then it indicates the corruption was detected while performing the backup of the data files.

NOTE
The backup will fail if corruption is detected in the control file or the archived log backups.

The dynamic performance view **V$COPY_CORRUPTION** displays information related to the data file copy corruption. You can query this view to obtain information on the corrupt blocks that were detected when performing an image copy. This information is obtained from the control file. The relevant columns in the view are COPY_RECID, FILE#, BLOCK#, BLOCKS, CORRUPTION_CHANGE#, and MARKED_CORRUPT. The CORRUPTION_CHANGE# displays the change number at which the logical corruption was detected. If this column is set to 0, it indicates that media corruption was detected. If the MARKED_CORRUPT column is set to YES, then it indicates that corruption was detected while performing the image copy of the data files. RMAN will continue the backup process even if it detects corrupt blocks until the number of corruptions reach the maximum allowed number set by the SET MAXCORRUPT command. In the following output, RMAN terminates the backup process when the number of corruptions exceeds 2 as specified by the SET MAXCORRUPT command.

The dynamic performance view **V$SESSION_LONGOPS** displays information related to the status of various operations that run for longer than six seconds on the target database. These operations currently include many backup and recovery functions, statistics gathering, and query execution. It enables you to identify backup operations that consume more time.

Chapter Questions

1. **A whole database backup contains which of the following?**

   A. The data file 1 and control file

   B. All the data files and archive log files

   C. All the data files and the control file

   D. The control file and archive log files

   E. None of the above

2. **You have performed an incremental backup of the database at level 0, level 1, and level 2. Which of the mentioned backups is equivalent to a full backup?**

   A. level 0

   B. level 1

   C. level 2

   D. None of the above

3. **What is the significance of specifying the DELETE INPUT option while performing the backup of archive log files?**

   A. RMAN will delete the archive log files from the first archive destination, LOG_ARCHIVE_DEST_1.

   B. RMAN deletes the archive log files from all enabled archiving destinations after backing up.

   C. RMAN deletes the duplicate archived logs from all active archive destinations except the primary destination.

   D. RMAN deletes any other files from its location that accompany the archive log files as input during the backup operation.

   E. None of the above

4. **Which of the following commands does not create a control file backup?**

   A. BACKUP DATAFILE 1;

   B. BACKUP CURRENT CONTROLFILE;

   C. BACKUP DATAFILE 2 INCLUDE CURRENT CONTROLFILE;

D. COPY DATAFILE 2 TO 'c:\backups\ic_df2.f' INCLUDE CURRENT CONTROLFILE;

5. **Which of the following views must you query to identify any corrupt data file blocks that have been detected during backup set creation?**

   A. V$COPY_CORRUPT

   B. V$COPY_CORRUPTION

   C. V$BACKUP_CORRUPT

   D. V$BACKUP_CORRUPTION

6. **Which view would you query to obtain information about backed up archive log files?**

   A. V$BACKUP

   B. V$BACKUP_REDOLOG

   C. V$BACKUP_ARCHIVELOG

   D. V$BACKUP_DATAFILE

7. **What happens when you execute the following command?**

   ```
   RMAN> BACKUP INCREMENTAL LEVEL 0 CUMULATIVE DATABASE;
   ```

   A. The backup command will fail.

   B. RMAN will perform a level 0 incremental backup.

   C. RMAN will perform a level 1 incremental backup.

   D. RMAN will perform a level 2 incremental backup.

   E. RMAN will perform a level 3 incremental backup.

8. **James is a DBA working for a Fortune 500 company. He has developed and implemented an incremental backup strategy using RMAN. He runs the database in ARCHIVELOG mode. When a media failure occurs, what does RMAN do to recover the data?**

   A. Uses all the incremental backups first before applying any archived redo logs while performing the recovery

   B. Applies only archive log files to perform recovery

   C. Only performs a simple restore of the files

   D. None of the above

9. **Which of the following can be treated as a default value for the parameter FILESPERSET?**

    A. The total number of the input files multiplied by the number of the channels

    B. The total number of the input files divided by the number of the channels

    C. Sum of the total number of input files and the number of channels

    D. Difference of the total number of the input files and the number of the channels

10. **%U is the default substitution variable in a format string during backup set creations. Which of the following set of variables does it represent?**

    A. %u, %p, and %s

    B. %u, %y, and %t

    C. %p, %s, and %t

    D. %u, %p, and %c

Chapter Answers

1. C.   All the data files and control file

Explanation   A whole database backup is comprised of all the target database files—data files and control file. If a backup contains the archive log files, it is called a full backup.

2. A.   level 0

Explanation   RMAN includes all the data file blocks that have been used in a level 0 incremental backup. This is similar to performing a full backup. The only major difference between both is that the level 0 incremental backup can be used as a base for future incremental backups, whereas the full backup cannot be part of the incremental strategy.

3. A.   RMAN will delete the archive log files from the first archive destination, LOG_ARCHIVE_DEST_1.

Explanation   The DELETE INPUT option of the BACKUP command enables you to delete the archive log files from the LOG_ARCHIVE_DEST_1 and leaves the files in the other log archive destinations. You can delete the archive log files from all enabled archiving destinations by performing a backup using the DELETE ALL INPUT option.

    4. D.   COPY DATAFILE 2 TO 'c:\backups\ic_df2.f' INCLUDE CURRENT CONTROLFILE;

Explanation   You can perform a backup of the control file when:

- The BACKUP CURRENT CONTROLFILE command is issued

- Including the backup of the control file within any backup using the INCLUDE CURRENT CONTROLFILE option of the BACKUP command

- Performing the backup of the data file 1 (SYSTEM data file), which automatically includes the control file in the backup

The options A, B, and C enable the user to create a control file backup. The option D fails, as the INCLUDE CURRENT CONTROLFILE option cannot be specified for the COPY command.

    5. D.   V$BACKUP_CORRUPTION

Explanation   The dynamic performance view V$BACKUP_CORRUPTION displays information about corruption in data file backups that was detected while the backup set was being created. The backup will fail if block corruption is detected during the control file or the archived log backups.

    6. B.   V$BACKUP_REDOLOG

Explanation   To obtain information related to backed up archive log files, you must query the dynamic performance view V$BACKUP_REDOLOG. RMAN ensures that it first archives the current redo log and then backs it up. An archive log backup set can contain one or more archived logs.

    7. B.   RMAN will perform a level 0 incremental backup.

Explanation   The RMAN command will not fail, but will perform a level 0 differential incremental backup.

    8. A.   Uses all the incremental backups while performing the recovery

Explanation   RMAN chooses incremental backups over archive log files while performing recovery operations.

9. B.   The total number of the input files divided by the number of the channels

Explanation   In other words, the total number of the input files is divided by the number of the channels.

10. D.   %u, %p, and %c

Explanation   The %U substitution variable specifies a convenient shorthand for %u_%p_%c, which guarantees uniqueness in the generated backup filenames. The first variable %u substitutes an eight-character name constituted by a compressed representations of the backup set number and the time that the backup set was created. The variable %p substitutes the piece number within the backup set and finally the %c variable specifies the copy number of the backup piece within a set of duplexed backup pieces (provided you use duplex backup).

CHAPTER
12

User-Managed
Complete Recovery

n this chapter we discuss various procedures for doing complete recovery of the database in the user-managed mode. Many DBAs are confused between the concepts *complete recovery* and *incomplete recovery*. Complete recovery is only possible when you apply all the redo and there is no loss of data. Please do not get confused between the type of recovery we do versus the type of command we use or how we start the database. For example, you can use the RECOVER DATABASE UNTIL CANCEL command but if you apply all the redo logs, it is still called complete recovery.

In this chapter we provide test cases for performing media recovery while the database is running in ARCHIVELOG and NOARCHIVELOG mode. You should always run your database in ARCHIVELOG mode if you want to protect your database from media failures and loss of data.

This chapter includes the following topics:

- Media recovery

- Performing user-managed complete recovery

- Performing recovery in NOARCHIVELOG mode

- Performing complete recovery in ARCHIVELOG mode

- Restoring data files to different locations

- Relocating and recovering a tablespace using archived redo log files

- Loss of an online inactive redo log group and recovery

- Recovery of read-only tablespaces

Media Recovery

It is important that you review the section "Overview of User-Managed Recovery" of Chapter 10 before you read this chapter. While instance and crash recovery are done by the database automatically, *media recovery* is done in response to a recovery command issued by the DBA. It is used to make backup data files current or to restore changes that were lost when a data file went offline without a checkpoint. For example, if you take a tablespace offline using the IMMEDIATE option, the data files belonging to the tablespace will go offline without a checkpoint being performed by Oracle. Media recovery needs to be applied when you bring them online again. This is done by applying archived log files and online log files.

A restored data file backup always needs media recovery, even if it can be accomplished with the online log files. The same is true of a data file that went offline without a checkpoint. The database cannot be opened if any of the online data files needs media recovery. A data file cannot be brought online while the database is open if it needs media recovery. Depending on the failure and the recovery procedure you want to use, you can recover the database while a portion of the database is open; but if the database is open, the file to be recovered must be offline.

Media Failure

The failure that hinders normal database read and write operations on disk due to physical media problem is known as *media failure*. Quite often, media failure is due to a disk head crash that causes the loss of database files on a disk drive. Media failure can damage one or all types of database files: data files, online redo log files, and control files. The archived redo log files, password files, and parameter files that are stored on the physical media are equally vulnerable.

The database operations on online redo log files or control files after a media failure depend primarily on whether the database files are multiplexed or not. Multiplexing of these files helps secure data by maintaining a duplicate copy of the files in distinct locations. Assume that there is a media failure and one of the redo log members is unavailable. Oracle usually continues to operate without any interruption as long as it can write to at least one member. In contrast, if the log files are not multiplexed, you could lose an unarchived online log file during a media failure. This is a single point of failure for the database. You could even lose committed transactions if you do not multiplex your online log files. Therefore, it is strongly recommended that you run all your production databases with multiplexed redo logs.

In the case of multiplexed control files, damage to any one of the control files would result in an immediate halt of the database activities. Therefore, it is imperative that you protect all your control files by placing them on separate disks mounted under separate controllers.

Complete and Incomplete Media Recovery

The simple definition of *complete recovery* means there will be no loss of data. Irrespective of the recovery commands you use, if you can recover all you data, you have done complete recovery. Oracle enables you to recover the whole database, a tablespace, or a data file during media recovery, depending on the failure. While performing recovery, you must restore one or more database files depending upon the files lost.

To perform a complete recovery on the database, you need to recover files up to the point the crash happened. The following files are required for you to do a complete recovery:

- A valid backup containing all database files or the backup of the damaged data files

- All archive log files since the backup was performed
- The current online redo log files that contain the transactions

NOTE
If you don't have the current control file, you can use a backup control file or create a new control file. Creating a new control file, whenever possible, is the preferred option.

Incomplete recovery means that you will lose data after media recovery is performed. In other words, you do not apply all of the redo records generated after the most recent backup. You usually perform incomplete recovery of the whole database in the following situations:

- Media failure destroys some or all of the online redo logs (which have not been archived) and you do not have multiplexed logs.

- A user error causes data loss; for example, a user inadvertently drops a table.

- You cannot perform complete recovery because an archived redo log is missing.

NOTE
As a DBA, your goal is to always perform complete recovery. If you are multiplexing the logs and the control file and have a proper backup strategy, you should be able to do complete recovery for all media failures. Incomplete recovery should only be your last option.

To perform incomplete media recovery, you must restore all data files from the backups and recover to a specific point in time, prior to the time of the crash and then open the database with the RESETLOGS option when recovery is completed.

Take the example of losing the current control file and a data file. Note that you can use a backup control file and do media recovery on the data file. If you have all the redo logs, you can completely recover the database and open it with the NORESETLOGS option. However, when you use a backup control file, even if you have done complete media recovery, you have to start the database with the RESETLOGS option. This is considered as complete recovery and *not* incomplete recovery, though you need to start the database with the RESETLOGS option. Of course, you need to understand the ramifications of starting the database with the

RESETLOGS option, as you need to take a complete backup of the database after using the RESETLOGS option.

TIP
Complete recovery is possible when you perform complete media recovery without losing a single transaction, irrespective of whether you start the database with RESETLOGS or NORESETLOGS option.

Restrictions of User-Managed Recovery

The following restrictions apply when performing media recovery operations:

- All the recovery sessions must be compatible. For example, you cannot perform complete recovery through one session and incomplete recovery through another.

- Oracle does not enable you to perform media recovery when a user session is established through a shared server process.

- You must have the SYSOPER privilege to perform complete recovery. However, if you need to do incomplete recovery, you must have the SYSDBA privilege.

Performing User-Managed Complete Recovery

Your goal as a DBA is to not lose *any* data during a media failure and to keep the mean time to recover (MTTR) as low as possible. You need to have a proper backup strategy and an excellent recovery testing procedure to meet this goal. When you do complete recovery, you have two options. The first option is to do a complete recovery of the database while the database is open. This is called *online* recovery. The second option is to do recovery when the database is closed (mounted), which is called *offline* recovery. Please refer to Table 12-1 to see the data file or tablespace status while doing online or offline recovery. Again, your goal should be to do online recovery if and when possible since this option will allow users to use a part of the database while you recover the damaged files. For example, if a DBA has 20 tablespaces and the data files that belong to the USER5 tablespace are damaged, it doesn't make sense for you to do offline recovery. Instead, you should do online recovery. You should use the following five-step procedure to do online recovery:

1. Take the damaged data files offline.

2. Open the database. (It is optional to take the damaged tablespace offline.)

3. Restore the data files.

4. Recover the data files.

5. Bring the data files (or tablespace) online.

In this procedure, the optional part of Step 2 should be done only if you want to do tablespace recovery. You should know the ramifications of doing online recovery. If you take a specific tablespace offline, no user can access the data in that tablespace. If you take a specific data file offline, then users can access data in the other data files that belong to the tablespace but if the application tries to access the offline data file, the application will return a error. For example, if you take tablespace INDEX offline, then all users using the USER tablespace can work fine. However, if a table in USER has an index that resides in INDEX, and if your query tries to do an index scan, it will fail. If the damaged file belongs to a SYSTEM data file, you can't do online recovery because the SYSTEM data files can never be taken offline (as required in Step 1). This is because the SYSTEM tablespace contains the data dictionary that is required for all DML and DDL operations.

Oracle enables you to perform media recovery by executing the SQL*Plus RECOVER command. You must appropriately specify one of the following command options with the RECOVER command:

```
RECOVER [AUTOMATIC] DATABASE
RECOVER [AUTOMATIC] TABLESPACE <tablespace number>| <tablespace name>
RECOVER [AUTOMATIC] DATAFILE <datafile number>| <datafile name>
```

NOTE
Oracle also provides the ALTER DATABASE command to perform media recovery operations. Though the ALTER DATABASE command can be used instead of RECOVER DATABASE in the preceding code, it is not recommended. This is because using the ALTER DATABASE command suppresses some important error messages that are displayed on the console while performing recovery.

Table 12-1 shows you various recovery options and the database, tablespace and data file statuses for each kind of recovery.

Recovery Command	Database Status	Data File/Tablespace Status	Comments
RECOVER DATABASE	Database closed (offline recovery)	All data files *must be* online.	Offline data files won't be recovered.
RECOVER TABLESPACE	Database closed (offline recovery)	Tablespace can be online or offline.	Tablespace status is ignored if the database is not open.
RECOVER TABLESPACE	Database open (online recovery)	Tablespace *must be* offline.	Cannot recover online tablespaces.
RECOVER DATAFILE	Database open (online recovery)	Data file *must be* offline.	SYSTEM files can't be recovered since they can't be taken offline.
RECOVER DATAFILE	Database closed (offline recovery)	Data file can be online or offline.	Data file status is ignored if the database is not open.

TABLE 12-1. *Recovery Options*

Performing Recovery in NOARCHIVELOG Mode

One day I received a letter from a DBA who works at a research organization. I would like to share part of its contents with you:

> "I have a production system in NOARCHIVELOG mode and have been fighting with management for eight months to get me some drives in order to implement archive logging to save data in the event of a failure. Last week such a failure occurred, and I was forced to recover the database from the last cold backup, losing a day's worth of work and many thousands of dollars. Only then did management wake up to the fact that data loss is real, and I am on my way to implementing archive logging."

I have heard this time and again from many of DBAs who work for smaller companies but have the requirement to protect their data against media failures.

If the database is operating in NOARCHIVELOG mode, archiving of the online redo logs is disabled. In NOARCHIVELOG mode, if you have a media failure where some or all the data files are damaged, the only option is to restore the most recent whole database backup and open the database. You would then lose all the data entered between the time of the most recent whole database backup, and the media failure. To recover, you need to perform a simple restore of the database from the backup and start up the database. This would result in an incomplete recovery.

Let's look at Test Case 1 to see how to recover from a media failure when you are running in NOARCHIVELOG mode.

Test Case 1: NOARCHIVELOG Mode and Recovery

The purpose of this case study is to show the ramifications of operating the database in NOARCHIVELOG mode. There are some risks involved in operating in this mode, and this case study should make them clear. While we only mention the procedure for restoration here, the actual simulation with code is provided in section "Incomplete Recovery in NOARCHIVELOG Mode" of Chapter 14.

Scenario

John uses an Oracle database to maintain the inventory of his grocery store. Once every week he runs a batch job to insert, update, and delete data in his database. He uses a stand-alone Windows NT machine running Oracle9*i*. John starts the database at 8 A.M. in the morning, shuts it down at 8 P.M., and operates the database all day in NOARCHIVELOG mode. He takes an offline (cold) backup of the database once a week on Sundays by copying all the data files, online log files, and control files to tape.

Problem

On a Wednesday morning, John realized that he had lost a data file that contained all the user data. He tried to start up the database using the STARTUP OPEN command and got the following error:

```
ORA-01157: cannot identify/lock data file 5 - see DBWR trace file
ORA-01110: data file 5: 'D:\ORACLE\ORADATA\TARGET\USER01.DBF'
```

He realized that he had accidentally deleted one of the data files while trying to free up some space on the disk.

Solution

The solution in this case is to restore the complete database from the recent offline backup taken on Sunday and to start up the database.

NOTE
He will lose the data entered on Monday
and Tuesday.

Follow these steps:

1. Take a backup of all the current data files, online log files, and control files. This is a precautionary step, in case your backup data files are bad.

2. Delete all the control files, data files, and online log files.

3. Restore all the control files, data files, and online log files from Sunday's offline backup.

4. Start up the database using the STARTUP OPEN command.

Observation

When the database is operating in NOARCHIVELOG mode, the changes made to the database are not archived to the archive log files. So in this case, after John restores the database, it is current as of Sunday. All the changes he made to the database from Monday through Wednesday are lost and he needs to reenter the data. If the data file that is lost doesn't contain any data (for example, a data file belonging to the TEMPORARY tablespace), you can start the database and rebuild the tablespace.

There is one particular case when you can recover completely after a media failure, even if you are running with NOARHIVELOG mode. Take the case where you have started the database after performing a whole backup of your database. After a short while, a media failure occurred and you lost the data files. However, Oracle has not overwritten the online log files that are needed for media recovery. While this is a unique situation, it is usually the exception and not the norm. However, you can recover the database completely from this situation.

NOTE
If the database is operating in NOARCHIVELOG mode and one of the data files is damaged, you do not have to restore all the Oracle database files, if none of the redo log files has been overwritten since the last backup. This would result in a complete recovery of the database. However, this is extremely rare; instead it is recommended that you operate the database in ARCHIVELOG mode.

Performing Complete Recovery in ARCHIVELOG Mode

When the database is operating in ARCHIVELOG mode, you can perform complete as well as incomplete recovery operations. This entirely depends on the media failure and what files were lost. We will discuss incomplete recovery in detail in Chapter 14. We will discuss complete recovery in this section.

First you need to determine if you want to do online recovery or offline recovery. See Table 12-1 for the various recovery options available.

There are two steps to do media recovery for a database operating in ARCHIVELOG mode. First, you will need to restore the lost data files from backup. Next, you should issue a recovery command (for example, RECOVER DATAFILE) and Oracle will apply the archived redo log files as necessary. If you perform recovery while the database is open, make sure that the data file or tablespace in question is offline before recovering the same. If you don't lose any of the data files but only the current control file, you can simply create a new control file.

You must follow these steps to perform a complete recovery on a tablespace or a data file:

1. Take the appropriate tablespace or data file that needs recovery offline (if the database is open).

2. Restore the data files that you need to recover.

3. Apply the redo by issuing a RECOVER command.

4. Bring the data file or tablespace online.

We discuss the following recovery scenarios next:

- System data file recovery
- Recovery of data files that have no backups available

System Data File Recovery

In this scenario, we simulate a system data file loss and show you how to recover it. To obtain information on the database and the mode it is operating in, the following statements are executed:

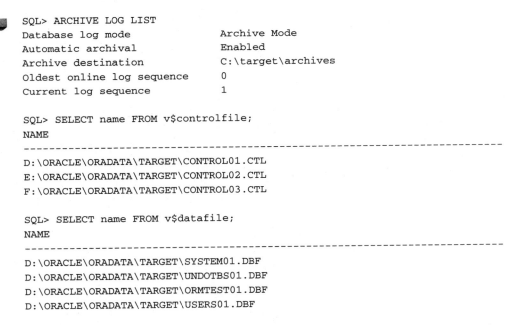

```
SQL> ARCHIVE LOG LIST
Database log mode               Archive Mode
Automatic archival              Enabled
Archive destination             C:\target\archives
Oldest online log sequence      0
Current log sequence            1

SQL> SELECT name FROM v$controlfile;
NAME
--------------------------------------------------------------------------
D:\ORACLE\ORADATA\TARGET\CONTROL01.CTL
E:\ORACLE\ORADATA\TARGET\CONTROL02.CTL
F:\ORACLE\ORADATA\TARGET\CONTROL03.CTL

SQL> SELECT name FROM v$datafile;
NAME
--------------------------------------------------------------------------
D:\ORACLE\ORADATA\TARGET\SYSTEM01.DBF
D:\ORACLE\ORADATA\TARGET\UNDOTBS01.DBF
D:\ORACLE\ORADATA\TARGET\ORMTEST01.DBF
D:\ORACLE\ORADATA\TARGET\USERS01.DBF
```

We have performed a full database backup at this point. Let's add some test data and simulate a crash as follows:

```
SQL> CREATE TABLE systest
  2   (num NUMBER)
  3    TABLESPACE SYSTEM;
Table created.
```

```
SQL> INSERT INTO systest VALUES(1);
1 row created.

SQL> INSERT INTO systest VALUES(2);
1 row created.

SQL> INSERT INTO systest VALUES(3);
1 row created.

SQL> COMMIT;
Commit complete.

SQL> SELECT * FROM systest;
      NUM
----------
        1
        2
        3

SQL> ALTER SYSTEM SWITCH LOGFILE;
System altered.

SQL> ALTER SYSTEM SWITCH LOGFILE;
System altered.
```

We now simulate a crash by shutting down the database and removing the SYSTEM datafile. When the database is started, it fails with an error shown as follows:

```
C:\>SQLPLUS /NOLOG
SQL*Plus: Release 9.0.1.0.0 - Beta on Tue Oct 9 13:04:06 2001
(c) Copyright 2001 Oracle Corporation. All rights reserved.

SQL> CONNECT sys/sys as sysdba
Connected to an idle instance.

SQL> STARTUP open PFILE='d:\oracle\admin\target\pfile\init.ora'
ORACLE instance started.
Total System Global Area    72118004 bytes
Fixed Size                    282356 bytes
Variable Size               54525952 bytes
Database Buffers            16777216 bytes
Redo Buffers                  532480 bytes
Database mounted.
ORA-01157: cannot identify/lock data file 1 - see DBWR trace file
ORA-01110: data file 1: 'D:\ORACLE\ORADATA\TARGET\SYSTEM01.DBF'
```

We now restore and recover the SYSTEM datafile using the RECOVER DATABASE command as follows:

```
C:\>COPY c:\9iBackup\system01.dbf d:\oracle\oradata\target\
        1 file(s) copied.

SQL> RECOVER DATABASE;
Media recovery complete.

SQL> ALTER DATABASE OPEN;
Database altered.

SQL> SELECT * FROM systest;

       NUM
----------
         1
         2
         3
```

Recovery of Data Files—No Backups Available

Oracle enables you to recover data files that have no backups and belong to the nonsystem tablespace. The following conditions must be met for recovering these data files:

- You must have all the archived redo and online log files since the creation of the data files.

- You must have the current or a backup control file, which was created after the data files were created (that is, the control file should recognize the data files).

- If an open database recovery needs to be done, you must take the data files or the associated tablespace, offline.

The procedure to perform recovery of the data files that have no backup follows:

1. If the database is closed, then mount the instance. Otherwise, perform all the operations with the database open.

2. Take the tablespace or data file on the disk(s) that failed offline.

NOTE
If you are doing data file recovery while the database is open, you must use the IMMEDIATE option for bringing tablespace or data files offline. Since Oracle will attempt to perform a checkpoint when you use the NORMAL option, this operation will fail as the data files do not exist.

3. You can regenerate the data files that are lost or damaged by executing the following command:

```
SQL> ALTER DATABASE CREATE DATAFILE
  2 'd:\oracle\oradata\target\ormtest01.dbf'
  3 AS 'c:\oracle\oradata\target\ormtest01.dbf';
```

NOTE
In the preceding code, we are relocating the file to drive C because drive D has crashed.

4. Recover the tablespace or datafile using the RECOVER command.

5. Bring the tablespace or datafiles online using the appropriate statement.

NOTE
You cannot re-create any of the data files associated with the SYSTEM tablespace by using the preceding CREATE DATAFILE clause, since the necessary redo data is not available.

Enabling Automatic Recovery

While executing the RECOVER command, Oracle enables you to specify manually the absolute file names of each archived redo log or the online redo log that must be applied for recovery. If the archived redo log files have default filenames that are specified using the initialization parameters LOG_ARCHIVE_FORMAT with LOG_ARCHIVE_DEST_*n* (where *n* is the highest value for all the enabled local destinations), then you can automate the recovery process using one of the following methods:

- Issue SET AUTORECOVERY ON before executing the RECOVER command.

- Include the AUTOMATIC keyword in the RECOVER command.

- Specify the AUTO option at the recover prompt while executing the RECOVER command.

Restoring Data Files to Different Locations

You can restore the database files to an alternative location if the original location is damaged by a media failure and is inaccessible. In this situation, you can restore the data file to an alternative location using the following procedure:

1. If the database is open, you will need to shut it down.

2. Restore all of the data files, control files, and archived redo log files of the whole database backup. If the hardware problem has not been corrected, then some or all the database files must be restored to alternative locations.

3. Edit the restored parameter file to indicate the new location of the control files if the control files are restored to a new location.

4. Start an instance using the new parameter file and mount the database. (Do not open the database.)

5. If the restored datafile and log file filenames are different, then rename the restored datafiles in the control file. You can do this by using the RENAME command as follows:

   ```
   ALTER DATABASE RENAME FILE <'old path'> TO <'new path'>;
   ```

6. Recover the database if necessary and open the database.

Relocating and Recovering a Tablespace Using Archived Redo Log Files

In this section, we provide a procedure for relocation and recovery of a nonsystem tablespace. To obtain information of the database structure, the following statements are executed:

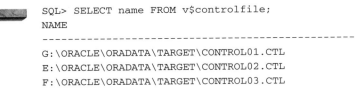

```
SQL> SELECT name FROM v$controlfile;
NAME
--------------------------------------------------
G:\ORACLE\ORADATA\TARGET\CONTROL01.CTL
E:\ORACLE\ORADATA\TARGET\CONTROL02.CTL
F:\ORACLE\ORADATA\TARGET\CONTROL03.CTL
```

```
SQL> SELECT tablespace_name, file_name FROM dba_data_files
  2    ORDER BY tablespace_name;
TABLESPACE_N FILE_NAME
------------ -------------------------------------------
ORMTEST      D:\ORACLE\ORADATA\TARGET\ORMTEST1.DBF
ORMTEST      D:\ORACLE\ORADATA\TARGET\ORMTEST2.DBF
ORMTEST      E:\ORACLE\ORADATA\TARGET\ORMTEST4.DBF
ORMTEST      E:\ORACLE\ORADATA\TARGET\ORMTEST3.DBF
SYSTEM       E:\ORACLE\ORADATA\TARGET\SYSTEM01.DBF
UNDOTBS      E:\ORACLE\ORADATA\TARGET\UNDOTBS01.DBF
USERS        E:\ORACLE\ORADATA\TARGET\USERS01.DBF
7 rows selected.
```

Note that the ORMTEST tablespace has four data files associated with it. While two of its data files are on drive D, the remaining data files are on drive E. We have performed a full database backup at this point. Let's add some test data and simulate a crash of drive D as shown:

```
SQL> CREATE TABLE tbstest
  2    (num NUMBER)
  3    TABLESPACE ormtest;
Table created.

SQL> INSERT INTO tbstest VALUES (1);
1 row created.

SQL> INSERT INTO tbstest VALUES (2);
1 row created.

SQL> INSERT INTO tbstest VALUES (3);
1 row created.

SQL> COMMIT;
Commit complete.

SQL> SELECT * FROM tbstest;
      NUM
----------
        1
        2
        3
```

We simulate a crash here of drive D. Let's startup the database and see what happens:

```
SQL> STARTUP open PFILE='d:\oracle\admin\target\pfile\init.ora'
ORACLE instance started.
```

```
Total System Global Area    72118004 bytes
Fixed Size                    282356 bytes
Variable Size               54525952 bytes
Database Buffers            16777216 bytes
Redo Buffers                  532480 bytes
Database mounted.
ORA-01157: cannot identify/lock data file 3 - see DBWR trace file
ORA-01110: data file 3: 'D:\ORACLE\ORADATA\TARGET\ORMTEST1.DBF'
```

Since the two data files on drive D are lost, let's rename these data files to point to the backup data files from our whole database backup:

```
SQL>  ALTER DATABASE RENAME FILE 'd:\oracle\oradata\target\ormtest1.dbf'
  2          TO 'c:\9ibackup\ormtest1.dbf';
Database altered.

SQL>  ALTER DATABASE RENAME FILE 'd:\oracle\oradata\target\ormtest2.dbf'
  2          TO 'c:\9ibackup\ormtest2.dbf';
Database altered.

SQL> ALTER DATABASE OPEN;
ALTER DATABASE OPEN
*
ERROR at line 1:
ORA-01113: file 3 needs media recovery
ORA-01110: data file 3: 'C:\9IBACKUP\ORMTEST1.DBF'

SQL> ALTER DATABASE DATAFILE 3 OFFLINE;
Database altered.
SQL> ALTER DATABASE DATAFILE 5 OFFLINE;
Database altered
```

Oracle gave an error since the two data files (data files 3 and 5) are from a backup. We need to take the data files offline before we can perform recovery as shown previously. Let's open the database and perform recovery:

```
SQL> ALTER DATABASE OPEN;
Database altered.

SQL> SELECT name, status FROM v$datafile;
NAME                                      STATUS
----------------------------------------  -------
E:\ORACLE\ORADATA\TARGET\SYSTEM01.DBF     SYSTEM
E:\ORACLE\ORADATA\TARGET\UNDOTBS01.DBF    ONLINE
C:\9IBACKUP\ORMTEST1.DBF                  RECOVER
```

```
E:\ORACLE\ORADATA\TARGET\USERS01.DBF        ONLINE
C:\9IBACKUP\ORMTEST2.DBF                     RECOVER
E:\ORACLE\ORADATA\TARGET\ORMTEST3.DBF        ONLINE
E:\ORACLE\ORADATA\TARGET\ORMTEST4.DBF        ONLINE
7 rows selected.

SQL> RECOVER TABLESPACE ormtest;
ORA-00283: recovery session canceled due to errors
ORA-01124: cannot recover data file 7 - file is in use or recovery
ORA-01110: data file 7: 'D:\ORACLE\ORADATA\TARGET\ORMTEST4.DBF'
```

You can see from the error that Oracle will not allow you to do recovery for this tablespace since the tablespace has other data files that are online and in use. We must take the tablespace offline and then perform recovery operations as follows:

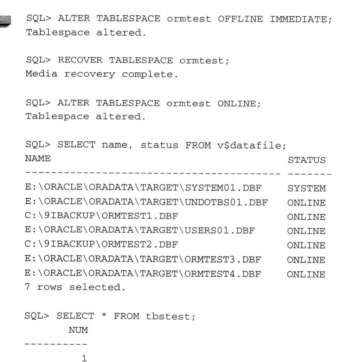

```
SQL> ALTER TABLESPACE ormtest OFFLINE IMMEDIATE;
Tablespace altered.

SQL> RECOVER TABLESPACE ormtest;
Media recovery complete.

SQL> ALTER TABLESPACE ormtest ONLINE;
Tablespace altered.

SQL> SELECT name, status FROM v$datafile;
NAME                                         STATUS
---------------------------------------- -------
E:\ORACLE\ORADATA\TARGET\SYSTEM01.DBF       SYSTEM
E:\ORACLE\ORADATA\TARGET\UNDOTBS01.DBF      ONLINE
C:\9IBACKUP\ORMTEST1.DBF                     ONLINE
E:\ORACLE\ORADATA\TARGET\USERS01.DBF        ONLINE
C:\9IBACKUP\ORMTEST2.DBF                     ONLINE
E:\ORACLE\ORADATA\TARGET\ORMTEST3.DBF        ONLINE
E:\ORACLE\ORADATA\TARGET\ORMTEST4.DBF        ONLINE
7 rows selected.

SQL> SELECT * FROM tbstest;
      NUM
----------
        1
        2
        3
```

Loss of an Online Inactive Redo Log Group and Recovery

The loss of an online log file could happen due to a media failure or a block corruption in the redo log group. Even if you are multiplexing the log files, you need to distribute the members of a given log group properly. Instead, if all the members are on the same drive, you will run the risk of losing the entire redo log group if the drive fails. In such a situation, you can still recover the database with no data loss, provided these two conditions are met:

- Lost redo log group is not the CURRENT redo log being written by LGWR.

- Lost redo log group has already been archived.

If the preceding conditions are met, then this redo log group can be recovered without any data loss.

Recovery of Read-Only Tablespaces

You need to understand the ramifications of recovering read-only tablespaces with the *current* control file as well as a *backup* control file. While recovery with a current control file is simple, recovering the database with a backup control file is tricky and needs attention. We will describe this with the help of an example. Let's consider the following three scenarios as shown in Figure 12-1.

Figure 12-1 gives the three scenarios in which read-only tablespaces are used. In all three scenarios, point A denotes the time when a cold backup of the database is taken. Also, point A shows whether the tablespace in question is in read-only or read-write mode at the time the cold backups are taken. Point B is when the tablespace is changed from read-only mode to read-write mode or vice versa, depending on the scenario. Point C indicates the time when a media failure occurred where all the data files are lost. In all scenarios, we restore all the data files from point A and perform media recovery. We test the three scenarios, first with the current control file and then with a backup control file. Note that if we are using the current control file, this is the control file at point C. If using a backup control file, the asterisk (*) in Figure 12-1 indicates the point when the backup of the control file is taken. Now let's see how we need to perform the six tests for these three scenarios.

As shown in Figure 12-1, scenario 1, the tablespace was in read-only mode at the time of last backup. The tablespace was also in read-only mode when the media failure occurred. We will show how to do recovery for this scenario in Test case 1 using the current control file. In Test case 4 that follows, we will demonstrate recovery for the same scenario using the backup control file. In scenario 2, the

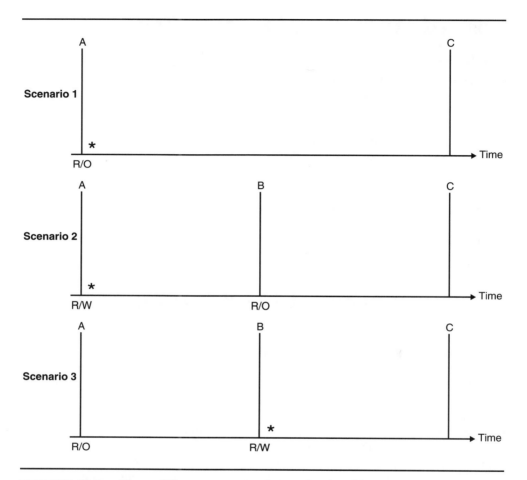

FIGURE 12-1. *Three different scenarios for read-only tablespaces*

tablespace was in read-write mode at the time of last backup. The tablespace was in read-only mode when the media failure occurred. Test case 2 and Test case 5 will show the procedure for recovering the database in this scenario using a current control file and backup control file respectively. Finally in scenario 3, the tablespace was in read-only mode at the time of last backup. The tablespace was in read-write mode when the media failure occurred. Test case 3 and Test case 6 will show the procedure for recovering the database in this scenario using a current control file and backup control file respectively.

Test Case 1

As shown in scenario 1 of Figure 12-1, the tablespace was in read-only mode at the time of last backup. While the media failure occurred, the tablespace was still operating in read-only mode. The steps to recover this tablespace using the current control file follow:

1. Restore the files pertaining to the tablespace to their default location.

2. Mount the database.

3. Recover the database using the RECOVER DATABASE command.

4. Open the database.

Test Case 2

As shown in Figure 12-1, scenario 2, the tablespace was initially in read-write mode at the time of the last backup. When the media failure occurred, the tablespace was operating in read-only mode. The steps to recover this tablespace using the current control file are identical to those shown in Test case 1.

Test Case 3

In scenario 3, the tablespace was in read-only mode at the time of the last backup. When the media failure occurred, the tablespace was operating in read-write mode. The steps to recover this tablespace using the current control file are identical to those shown in Test case 1.

The procedures for recovering the tablespace for the preceding three scenarios using the backup control file are explained in the following sections.

Test Case 4

The tablespace was in read-only mode at the time of last backup (see Figure 12-1). When the media failure occurred, the tablespace was still operating in read-only mode. The steps to recover this tablespace using the backup control file are as follows:

1. Restore the entire database files.

2. Mount the database.

3. Take the read-only data file offline.

4. Execute the following command to recover the database using the backup control file:

```
SQL> RECOVER DATABASE USING BACKUP CONTROLFILE;
```

5. Apply all the archive log files and the available online redo logs needed for recovery and open the database using the RESETLOGS option.

6. Bring the read-only data file online.

Test Case 5

The tablespace was initially in read-write mode at the time of last backup. While the media failure occurred, the tablespace was operating in read-only mode. The steps to recover this tablespace using the backup control file are as follows:

1. Restore the entire database files.

2. Mount the database.

3. Use the backup control file, which was taken between points A and B, so that the control file recognizes the data file in question as a read-write file.

4. Execute the following command to recover the database using the backup control file:

    ```
    SQL> RECOVER DATABASE USING BACKUP CONTROLFILE;
    ```

5. Apply all the archive log files and the available redo logs needed for recovery and open the database using the RESETLOGS option.

NOTE
Oracle does not change the mode of the data file to read-only until the database is opened with RESETLOGS. You can view this by querying the ENABLED column of V$DATAFILE dynamic performance view.

Test Case 6

The tablespace was in read-only mode at the time of the last backup. When the media failure occurred, the tablespace was operating in read-write mode. The steps to recover this tablespace using the backup control file are as follows:

1. Restore the entire database files.

2. Mount the database.

3. Use the backup control file taken between points B and C so that the control file recognizes the data file in question as a read-write file.

4. Execute the following command to recover the database using the backup control file:

```
SQL> RECOVER DATABASE USING BACKUP CONTROLFILE;
```

5. Apply all the archive log files and the available redo logs needed for recovery and open the database using the RESETLOGS option.

Observations

Test cases 1, 2, and 3 show that if you use the current control file, there is little you need to worry about. Oracle takes care of all issues whether you have data files in read-only mode or they are changed between read-only and read-write mode. Note that in Test case 4, the backup control file from point A is used. When you use a backup control file, you have to start up the database with the RESETLOGS option that will write certain information to the data file headers. Since Oracle can't write this (or any) information to read-only files, it won't allow you to recover read-only files. Therefore, you have to take the read-only files offline before recovery when you use the backup control file. Note that the read-only tablespace can be brought online once we open the database with the RESETLOGS option. It is important to note that Oracle does not allow you to read any files from before a RESETLOGS was done, with the exception of read-only tablespaces and any tablespaces that are taken offline with the NORMAL option.

Test case 5 also uses a backup of the control file from point A as denoted by the * in scenario 2 of Figure 12-1. If you use a backup control file after point B in this case, recovery won't work because you have to take the read-only data files offline. This is because the control file from point B will identify the data file as read-only. So, you need to have a backup copy of the control file that recognizes the files as being in read-write mode from point A (or anywhere between points A and B). For the same reason as mentioned in Test case 6, when a backup control file is used, it cannot be from point A but has to be from point B (or anywhere between points B and C). The reason for this is that if you use the backup control file from point A, the control file identifies the data files as being in read-only mode, so you have to take them offline. If the data files are taken offline, the changes made to the data files between points B and C will not be applied as part of recovery.

To summarize the preceding tests, you need to note the following points:

■ If you are using the current control file, crash recovery or media recovery with a read-only data file is no different from a read-write data file. There is nothing special you need to do. Oracle will recognize the files and do the appropriate recovery automatically.

■ If a data file is in read-only mode and doesn't change to read-write during media recovery, the file should be offline during recovery if you are using a backup control file. You should bring the tablespace online after recovery.

■ If you are doing media recovery, and if any data files switch between read-only and read-write modes during recovery, you should use the current control file if available. If you don't have a current control file, then use a backup control file that recognizes the files in read-write mode. If you don't have a backup control file, then create a new control file using the CREATE CONTROLFILE command.

NOTE
From the preceding three points, it should be clear that you should take a backup of the control file every time you switch a tablespace from read-only mode to read-write mode, and vice versa.

Chapter Questions

1. **Which of the following would you use to enable automatic media recovery for a database?**

    A. SET AUTORECOVERY ON

    B. SET RECOVERY ON

    C. SET AUTO ON

    D. You cannot enable automatic media recovery.

2. **What is the outcome of executing the following command when the database is in the mount state?**

    ```
    SQL> ALTER DATABASE RENAME FILE 'C:\ORACLE\ORADATA\ORCL\INDX01.DBF'
    TO 'C:\ORACLE\ORADATA\ORCL\X01.DBF';
    Database altered.
    ```

    A. The database resynchronizes with the catalog.

    B. The Recovery catalog resynchronizes with the database.

    C. The command moves the data file to a specified destination at the operating system.

    D. The command updates the control file with the new location of the data file.

3. **Which view must you query to obtain the log sequence number of an online redo log group?**

   A. V$LOG_HIST

   B. V$LOG

   C. V$LOGFILE

   D. V$DATABASE

4. **Which of the following data files cannot be recovered when the database is open and is operating in ARCHIVELOG mode?**

   A. SYSTEM data file

   B. USER data file

   C. TOOLS data file

   D. TEMP data file

5. **Which of the following operations invalidates all the redo in the online redo log files and requires that you to perform a fresh whole database backup?**

   A. Performing recovery of system data file

   B. Relocating the control file

   C. Opening the database with the RESETLOGS option

   D. While performing recovery of a nonsystem data file using the current control file and online redo log files

6. **Which view must you query to obtain the status (ONLINE or OFFLINE) of the data file? Choose two.**

   A. V$DBFILE

   B. V$DATAFILE

   C. DBA_DATA_FILES

   D. DBA_TEMP_FILES

   E. V$DATAFILE_HEADER

7. **Loss of which of the following types of files does not require you to open the database with the RESETLOGS option? Choose two.**

   A. Archived redo log files needed for recovery

   B. Online redo log group that has not been archived

   C. Data files

   D. Parameter files

8. **Which of the following commands cannot be executed when the database open?**

   A. RECOVER DATABASE

   B. RECOVER TABLESPACE

   C. RECOVER DATAFILE

   D. ALTER DATABASE RECOVER DATAFILE

9. **Your database is operating in NOARCHIVELOG mode and a media failure occurred resulting in a loss of all the data files. What do you require to restore the database to operation?**

   A. Only the backed up data files

   B. A valid closed database backup

   C. Only the backed up data files and the current online redo logs

   D. Only the backed up data files and the archived logs

10. **The following error message was generated when you attempted to open the database:**

```
SQL> ALTER DATABASE OPEN;
ORA-00283:  Recovery session canceled due to errors
ORA-01122:  database file 1 failed verification check
ORA-01110:  data file 1: '/ora1/oraresearch/dbfile/system01.dbf'
ORA-01207:  file is more recent than control file - old control file
```

What is the solution to the preceding problem?

A. You must restore the backup control files and perform recovery.

B. You must restore the backup data file and perform recovery.

C. You must perform a simple restore of the entire database, since recovery cannot be performed.

D. You must re-create the database since the error is pertaining to the system data file.

Chapter Answers

1. A. SET AUTORECOVERY ON

Explanation You can enable automatic media recovery by issuing the SET AUTORECOVERY ON command prior to executing the RECOVER command.

2. D. The command updates the control file with the new location of a data file.

Explanation Whenever a media failure occurs and you lose a disk drive, you need to restore a data file to a new location. To do this you must first physically copy the file to the new location using O/S commands. You must then mount the database instance and issue the preceding command to update the control file with the new location of the data file.

3. B. V$LOG

Explanation You must query the V$LOG dynamic performance view to obtain information related to the log sequence numbers of the online groups. It also displays the STATUS of the log groups.

4. A. SYSTEM data file

Explanation System data files can't be recovered while the database is online. This is because you need to take the data file offline to do online data file recovery. System data files can't be taken offline.

5. C. Opening the database with the RESETLOGS option

Explanation After performing an incomplete recovery of the database or using a backup control file for recovery, you must open the database with the RESETLOGS option. The RESETLOGS operation invalidates all redo in the online logs. If you need to use the backups that were done before the RESETLOGS point, you can recover only up to the RESETLOGS point but can't go through this point. Therefore, using the RESETLOGS option requires you to perform a fresh backup of the database. (There are ways of doing recovery through RESETLOGS that is not recommended by Oracle.)

6. B. and E.   V$DATAFILE and V$DATAFILE_HEADER

Explanation   The V$DATAFILE dynamic performance view displays details of the data files: NAME, STATUS, BLOCKS, BLOCK_SIZE, and PLUGGED_IN. The V$DATAFILE_HEADER dynamic performance view displays mostly similar information to V$DATAFILE. Some of the important details in the V$DATAFILE_HEADER are ERROR, FORMAT, RECOVER, and FUZZY.

7. C. and D.   Data files and Parameter files

Explanation   This is a trick question. Note that loss of an online redo log group which has not been archived, and loss of archived log files will force you to do an incomplete recovery.

8. A.   RECOVER DATABASE

Explanation   The RECOVER DATABASE command can only be executed when the database is in MOUNT state. Note that tablespace or data file recovery is done while the database is online or offline. However, if you recover while the database is online, you need to make sure that the corresponding data files and tablespaces are offline. Database recovery always requires you to keep the database offline (database mounted) while all the data files that you need to recover should be online.

9. B.   A valid closed database backup

Explanation   For a database operating in NOARCHIVELOG mode to restore after media failure, you must possess a valid closed database backup. You can't perform media recovery since archived redo is not available. You can only perform a simple restore of the entire database files—data files, control files, and redo logs. Any data entered since the last full backup is lost.

10. B.   You must restore the backup data file and perform recovery.

Explanation   The ORA-01207 error indicates that the control file change sequence number in the data file is greater than the number in the control file. This error occurs if you have restored only the control file from the backup but not the data file. You must restore the backup data files and perform recovery.

CHAPTER
13

RMAN
Complete Recovery

I n this chapter we provide test cases for performing complete media recovery using Recovery Manager (RMAN), while the database is running in ARCHIVELOG and NOARCHIVELOG modes. We also explain the procedure for restoring the data files to different locations. We explain how to do recovery of a tablespace by using RMAN. Finally, in this chapter we discuss the concepts of block media recovery (BMR). This chapter is identical to Chapter 12, except that we do recovery using RMAN.

This chapter includes the following topics:

- Server-managed media recovery using RMAN

- Performing recovery in NOARCHIVELOG mode

- Performing complete recovery in ARCHIVELOG mode

- Restore data files to different locations using RMAN

- Relocate and recover a tablespace by using archived redo log files

- Block media recovery feature

Server-Managed Media Recovery Using RMAN

We recommend that you read Chapter 12 before reading this chapter. RMAN requires Oracle server sessions to perform recovery operations. This is known as *server-managed recovery*. Unlike *user-managed recovery*, the server-managed recovery operations are managed and implemented with greater ease and also minimize the need for user interaction. RMAN automates most of the operations, thereby minimizing operational errors that might occur while manually performing the operations. It also performs rigorous checks on the database files during backup and recovery operations. This helps keep the DBA informed of any inconsistency in the backup sets or image copies.

Advantages of Performing Media Recovery Using RMAN

There are many advantages to performing restore and recovery operations using RMAN. Listed in the following are some of the advantages of using RMAN for performing recovery operations:

- Improves usability by enabling you to reuse the scripts to perform recovery operations

- Enables you to automate restore and recovery operations
- Intelligent management of the archived redo log files for both backup and recovery
- Detects block corruption during restoration and recovery operations
- Can be used to perform tablespace point-in-time recovery
- Enables you to perform BMR
- Can be configured for restore optimization
- Capable of recovering through unrecoverable (NOLOGGING) operations when using incremental backups

Performing Restoration and Recovery Using RMAN

RMAN performs backup, restore, and recovery operations based on the metadata, which is stored in the repository. While performing recovery, RMAN obtains the information about the available backups from the repository and decides upon the files that are appropriate for restoration and then recovery. Depending upon this information RMAN coordinates with the Oracle server process, which then performs the required operations.

You do not need to maintain detailed historical information of the database file backup or any of the restore and recovery operations at any given point of time because RMAN automatically maintains and manages all this information in the recovery catalog or the target database's control file. RMAN greatly simplifies recovery by identifying the most appropriate backups and archive log files to use during the recovery process. Very complex recovery operations, such as database point-in-time recovery or tablespace point-in-time recovery, are made very simple because the restoration of the required files and the use of the archive log files is intelligently managed by RMAN without any user intervention.

Procedure to Perform Media Recovery Using RMAN

RMAN is intelligently programmed to plan and then perform the recovery operations. During the recovery process, it uses the appropriate incremental backups and archive log files that need to be applied. All this is quite transparent to the DBA. You must restore the required database files using the RESTORE command. Similarly, the recovery operations on the restored files must be performed using the RECOVER command. Listed in the following steps is a generic procedure to perform complete media recovery using RMAN:

1. You must first determine the database files that need recovery.

2. Place the database in the appropriate state to perform recovery, depending upon the database files that are lost during media failure. For example, to recover the SYSTEM data file or a data file associated with the UNDO tablespace containing active transactions, you must MOUNT the database; to recover any non-system data file, you can perform an OPEN database recovery.

3. Perform a restoration of the appropriate files using the RESTORE command.

4. Perform recovery on the restored files using the RECOVER command.

5. Bring the database or data files online for normal user activities. For example, if a data file is taken offline, bring it back online after completing recovery.

Prior to performing restore and recovery operations, you must ensure that the backups are available at their designated location. If the backups are available in the form of image copies, then you can avoid the process of restoring the files. It is recommended that you switch to the copy file when the data files occupy a large amount of space and takes considerable time for restoration. If you use an incremental backup strategy, RMAN automatically chooses the most recent level 0 backup and then applies the incremental backups from there on. To perform a complete recovery, RMAN may also need to apply the archived redo log files.

Performing Recovery in NOARCHIVELOG Mode

Operating the database in NOARCHIVELOG mode does not enable you to recover changes made to the database since the last backup, in case of a media failure. This means that you would lose all the changes made to the database since the last backup. Operating the database in NOARCHIVELOG mode does not enable you to explore the complete functionality of RMAN. However, there are reasons to use RMAN to perform recovery operations in NOARCHIVELOG mode.

While restoring the database files, RMAN uses the repository to obtain the information about the location of the backups and where they need to be restored. You should use the following guidelines to restore the database:

1. The target database must be in the NOMOUNT state to restore all the data files and the control files.

2. All the data files and control files must be restored from the full database backup.

3. You must open the database with the RESETLOGS option as shown in the following code:

```
RMAN> OPEN RESETLOGS DATABASE;
```

You must immediately perform a full database backup using RMAN. RMAN can only restore backups if they are cataloged in the repository.

NOTE
The recovery operation performed in NOARCHIVELOG mode due to media failure would always result in incomplete recovery.

Complete recovery of the database in NOARCHIVELOG mode is usually not possible. In rare cases where one or more data files are lost during media failure and none of the online redo log groups have been overwritten since the last backup, you could perform a complete recovery of the database.

Performing Complete Recovery in ARCHIVELOG Mode

Complete recovery in ARCHIVELOG mode using RMAN is similar to complete recovery in user-managed mode. In this section, we explain how to recover non-SYSTEM data files using RMAN. We explain the procedure to recover the non-SYSTEM data file that contains no active rollback segments in the test case shown in the following code:

```
SQL> SELECT * FROM v$log;
GROUP# THREAD#  SEQUENCE#      BYTES MEMBERS ARC STATUS    FIRST_CHANGE# FIRST_TIM
------ ------- ---------- ---------- ------- --- -------- ------------- ---------
     1       1          7     512000       1 NO  CURRENT        1152397 13-OCT-01
     2       1          5     512000       1 YES INACTIVE       1131951 13-OCT-01
     3       1          6     512000       1 YES INACTIVE       1151959 13-OCT-01

SQL> CREATE TABLE ormtest2(sln number) TABLESPACE users;
Table created.
```

```
SQL> INSERT INTO ormtest2 VALUES(1);
1 row created.

SQL> INSERT INTO ormtest2 VALUES(2);
1 row created.

SQL> INSERT INTO ormtest2 VALUES(3);
1 row created.

SQL> COMMIT;
Commit complete.

SQL> ALTER SYSTEM SWITCH LOGFILE;
System altered.

SQL> SELECT * FROM ormtest2;
       SLN
----------
         1
         2
         3

SQL> SELECT * FROM v$log;
GROUP# THREAD#  SEQUENCE#      BYTES MEMBERS ARC STATUS     FIRST_CHANGE# FIRST_TIM
------ ------- ---------- --------- ------- --- -------- ------------- ---------
     1       1          7    512000       1 YES ACTIVE          1152397 13-OCT-01
     2       1          8    512000       1 NO  CURRENT         1152611 13-OCT-01
     3       1          6    512000       1 YES INACTIVE        1151959 13-OCT-01

SQL> SHUTDOWN IMMEDIATE;
Database closed.
Database dismounted.
ORACLE instance shut down.
```

We have deleted the users01.dbf data file at this point. Let's start the database:

```
SQL> STARTUP PFILE=d:\oracle\admin\target\pfile\init.ora
ORACLE instance started.
Total System Global Area    72118004 bytes
Fixed Size                    282356 bytes
Variable Size               54525952 bytes
Database Buffers            16777216 bytes
Redo Buffers                  532480 bytes
Database mounted.
ORA-01157: cannot identify/lock data file 4 - see DBWR trace file
ORA-01110: data file 4: 'D:\ORACLE\ORADATA\TARGET\USERS01.DBF'
```

The previous error message indicates that the file cannot be accessed. Because the lost data file is a non-SYSTEM data file, we can take the file offline and open the database. Restore and recovery operations using RMAN can be performed after the database is open, as shown in the following code:

```
C:\>RMAN CATALOG rman/rman TARGET sys/sys@target.india
Recovery Manager: Release 9.0.1.0.0
(c) Copyright 2001 Oracle Corporation.  All rights reserved.
connected to target database: TARGET (DBID=2842823597)
connected to recovery catalog database

RMAN> SQL 'ALTER DATABASE DATAFILE 4 OFFLINE';
sql statement: ALTER DATABASE DATAFILE 4 OFFLINE

RMAN> OPEN DATABASE;
database opened

RMAN> RESTORE DATAFILE 4;
Starting restore at 13-OCT-01
configuration for DISK channel 2 is ignored
allocated channel: ORA_DISK_1
channel ORA_DISK_1: sid=13 devtype=DISK
channel ORA_DISK_1: starting datafile backupset restore
channel ORA_DISK_1: specifying datafile(s) to restore from backup set
restoring datafile 00004 to D:\ORACLE\ORADATA\TARGET\USERS01.DBF
channel ORA_DISK_1: restored backup piece 1
piece handle=C:\BACKUPS\4FD6G73V.1 tag=null params=NULL
channel ORA_DISK_1: restore complete
Finished restore at 13-OCT-01

RMAN> RECOVER DATAFILE 4;
Starting recover at 13-OCT-01
using channel ORA_DISK_1
starting media recovery
media recovery complete
Finished recover at 13-OCT-01

RMAN> SQL 'ALTER DATABASE DATAFILE 4 ONLINE';
sql statement: ALTER DATABASE DATAFILE 4 ONLINE

SQL> SELECT * FROM ormtest2;
      SLN
----------
        1
        2
        3
```

Note that we have performed online recovery in the previous test. The current control file and the online logs were used to perform complete recovery.

Restore Data Files to Different Locations Using RMAN

RMAN enables you to restore the data files to a non-default location. Relocating the data files to an alternative location is useful when storage is limited or when you need to reorganize the database to improve performance.

The following test shows the procedure to restore the file to a different location and then perform a data file recovery. You must determine which data file requires to be restored to a non-default location and then mount the database as shown in the following code:

```
SQL> STARTUP MOUNT PFILE=d:\oracle\admin\oemdb\pfile\initoemdb.ora;
```

We connect to the target database and the recovery catalog database using the RMAN executable as shown in the following code:

```
C:\>RMAN CATALOG rman/rman@orama.india TARGET sys/sys@oemdb
```

You must now create a RMAN script that will perform the following actions:

- Setting a new location for the data file users01.dbf. This is essential for updating the control file with the new location of the data file.

- Restoring the data file.

- Recovering the data file. This is required to apply the changes made to the data file from its last backup to the current time.

To perform the previous operations, we execute the script as shown in the following code at the RMAN prompt:

```
RMAN> run{
2> allocate channel c1 type disk;
3> set newname for datafile 8 to 'c:\datafiles\users01.dbf';
4> restore datafile 8;
5> switch datafile 8;
6> recover datafile 'c:\datafiles\users01.dbf';
7> sql' ALTER DATABASE OPEN';
8> }
```

Perform an appropriate backup after verifying that the data file has been restored to the proper location.

Relocate and Recover a Tablespace Using the Archived Redo Log Files

You can recover tablespaces that contain one or more lost or damaged data files. If a data file cannot be accessed due to a media failure, you need to restore the data file to an alternative location. For example, if data files ormtest01.dbf, ormtest02.dbf, and ormtest03.dbf associated with the tablespace ORMTEST are inaccessible due to a disk failure, you must restore these files to an alternative destination or switch to an existing image copy available on a separate disk before you start recovery. You must update the control file with the new location of the data files before performing tablespace recovery.

NOTE
To perform a restoration of the tablespace, ensure that it is initially taken offline.

The following procedure illustrates how to relocate and recover a tablespace:

I. Determine the physical location of the data file from the data dictionary view DBA_DATA_FILES:

```
SQL> SELECT file_id, file_name, bytes FROM dba_data_files WHERE
file_id=8;
    FILE_ID FILE_NAME                               BYTES
---------- ------------------------- ----------
         8 C:\DATAFILES\USERS01.DBF       10485760
```

2. Connect to the target database and the recovery catalog database using the RMAN executable:

```
C:\>RMAN CATALOG rman/rman@orama.india TARGET sys/sys@oemdb
```

3. Prepare an RMAN script, which performs the following actions:

- Take the tablespace offline.
- Relocate the data file to a new location.
- Restore the tablespace from the backups

- Switch the data file to update the control file and recovery catalog.
- Recover the tablespace.

NOTE
RMAN uses the repository (either the target database control file or the recovery catalog) to decide the backups, archive logs, or image copies needed for recovery.

For example to perform the previous operations, execute the following script at the RMAN prompt:

```
RMAN> run{
2> allocate channel c1 type disk;
3> sql 'ALTER TABLESPACE users OFFLINE IMMEDIATE';
4> set newname for datafile 8 to 'd:\oracle\oradata\oemdb\users01.dbf';
5> restore tablespace users;
6> switch datafile 8;
7> recover tablespace users;
8> sql 'ALTER TABLESPACE USERS ONLINE';
9> }
```

4. Verify the location of the data file associated with the USERS tablespace by selecting from the DBA_DATA_FILES view as shown in the following code:

```
SQL> SELECT file_id, file_name, bytes FROM dba_data_files WHERE
file_id=8;
   FILE_ID FILE_NAME                                          BYTES
---------- -------------------------------------------- ----------
         8 D:\ORACLE\ORADATA\OEMDB\USERS01.DBF             10485760
```

Block Media Recovery (BMR)

RMAN enables you to perform BMR in Oracle9i. This feature is a great asset to any DBA who is using RMAN as it reduces the granularity of a recovery unit from a data file to a data block. If a small number of data blocks require media recovery, you can selectively restore and recover damaged blocks rather than performing a recovery on the complete data file. Note that while performing media recovery on an individual block in a data file, you do not need to take the data file offline. RMAN performs the recovery with the file online.

When Oracle detects a block with corruption, it can be either a physical corruption, in which case, the block contents are invalid, or a logical corruption, which means the block header is incorrect, but the block contents may (or may not) be fine. If Oracle cannot resolve the corruption by rereading the block from disk and applying redo records from the current log file to rebuild the block image (known as *block level recovery*), the block is marked as corrupt. Oracle only has one method of marking a block corrupt.

Information on the corrupt blocks can be selected from the views V$BACKUP_CORRUPTION and V$COPY_CORRUPTION. Now with Oracle9i, you can perform block media recovery using the BLOCKRECOVER command on these corrupted blocks, at the RMAN prompt. The command option CORRUPTION LIST enables you to recover all the corrupted blocks listed in the V$BACKUP_CORRUPTION and V$COPY_CORRUPTION views.

Chapter Questions

1. **Ronald is a DBA working for a Fortune 100 company. The test database he administers is operating in NOARCHIVELOG mode. He uses RMAN to back up the database. Due to a media failure, the database has become inoperable. He fixed the hardware problem, but in the process lost all the database files. What state must the target database be operating in to restore all the control files for the database?**

   A. OPEN

   B. MOUNT

   C. NOMOUNT

   D. None of the above

2. **Which of the following statements is not true about RMAN?**

   A. It improves usability by enabling you to reuse the scripts to perform recovery operations.

   B. It detects block corruption while restoration and recovery operations.

   C. It can also be used to perform tablespace point-in-time recovery.

   D. It enables you to perform block media recovery.

   E. It is capable to recover through unrecoverable operations, with only full database backups.

3. **Which of the following commands can you use to restore the whole database backup?**

   A. RESTORE CONTROLFILE DATABASE;

   B. RESTORE WHOLE DATABASE;

   C. RESTORE DATABASE;

   D. RESTORE CONTROLFILE AND DATABASE;

   E. None of the above

4. **RMAN enables you to open the target database when it is already mounted. Which command must you execute at the RMAN prompt to open the database?**

   A. 'SQL ALTER DATABASE OPEN';

   B. SQL ALTER DATABASE 'OPEN';

   C. OPEN DATABASE;

   D. DATABASE OPEN;

5. **When the script shown is executed, it would fail. At which line would the script fail?**

   A. `run{`

   B. `allocate channel c1 type disk;`

   C. `set newname datafile 8 to 'c:\datafiles\users01.dbf';`

   D. `restore datafile 8;`

   E. `switch datafile 8;`

   F. `recover datafile 'c:\datafiles\users01.dbf';}`

6. **Charles is a DBA managing a production database. Due to an environmental outage, one of the disks crashed, resulting in the loss of the most critical data file, system01.dbf. Fortunately, Charles had backups of this system data file as image copies and backup sets on disk. Which of the following options can Charles use to bring back his database online and reduce the MTTR?**

   A. Using the SWITCH command, Charles must relocate the image copy as current and then recover.

   B. Charles must restore the image copy into the data file default location and then perform recovery.

   C. Charles must use RMAN backup sets to restore the file to their default location and then recover.

   D. Charles must execute the RESTORE CONTROLFILE DATABASE command and restore all the database files.

7. What happens when you execute the following command at the RMAN prompt?

```
RMAN> BLOCKRECOVER CORRUPTION LIST
```

   A. Restores and recovers all the corrupted blocks that presently exist in the target database's data files

   B. Restores and recovers all the corrupted blocks that presently exist in the data files where the recovery catalog resides

   C. Restores and recovers all the corrupted blocks that are listed only in the view V$BACKUP_CORRUPTION

   D. Restores and recovers all the corrupted blocks that are listed only in the view V$COPY_CORRUPTION

   E. Restores and recovers all the corrupted blocks that are listed in the views V$COPY_CORRUPTION and V$BACKUP_CORRUPTION

8. To perform an open database tablespace recovery, you must initially execute which of the following commands?

   A. ALTER TABLESPACE users ONLINE;

   B. ALTER TABLESPACE users READ ONLY;

   C. ALTER TABLESPACE users OFFLINE;

   D. ALTER TABLESPACE users READ WRITE;

9. Which text file registers the information pertaining to data block corruptions?

   A. init.ora

   B. spfile.ora

   C. alert.log

   D. log files

10. **Which one of the following statements is incorrect about BMR?**

   A. RMAN does not enable you to recover logical corrupted blocks but only physical corrupted blocks.

   B. To recover the corrupted blocks, you must have a full backups performed through RMAN. Incremental backups are not enabled.

   C. BMR lowers the MTTR because BMR acts only on blocks specified for recovery. RMAN restores and recovers only these corrupt blocks.

   D. BMR increases redo application time and avoids I/O overhead during recovery.

Chapter Answers

1. C.   NOMOUNT

Explanation   The control files must be restored while the target database is in the NOMOUNT state. In the NOMOUNT state, Oracle starts the background processes and creates the SGA. In the MOUNT state, Oracle opens and reads the control files. Therefore, you must ensure that all the control files specified using the CONTROL_FILES parameter in the initialization parameter file must be available prior to the database being MOUNTED.

2. E.   It is capable to recover through unrecoverable operations with only full database backups.

Explanation   RMAN enables you to recover through unrecoverable operations, such as when the NOLOGGING feature is enabled for a segment, but by only using the available incremental backups.

3. A.   RESTORE CONTROLFILE DATABASE;

Explanation   To restore the whole database backup (include the data files and the control files) to their default location, you must issue the following command:

```
RMAN> RESTORE CONTROLFILE DATABASE;
```

You can also restore the control files and the data files using the RESTORE CONTROLFILE and RESTORE DATABASE commands, respectively.

4. C.   OPEN DATABASE

Explanation   RMAN enables you to open the target database using the OPEN DATABASE command. To mount the target database from NOMOUNT state, you must execute the MOUNT DATABASE command. Alternatively, you can also use the ALTER DATABASE MOUNT and ALTER DATABASE OPEN commands.

5. C. `set newname datafile 8 to`
       `'c:\datafiles\users01.dbf';`

Explanation   The keyword FOR is missing in the statement. The statement must be modified and the script reexecuted. The correct syntax for this statement is shown in the following code:

```
SET NEWNAME FOR DATAFILE <fileno> TO '<file location>';
```

6. A.   Using the SWITCH command, Charles must relocate the image copy as current and then recover.

Explanation   The best method to make the database available and keep the MTTR to the least is by using the SWITCH command and relocating the system01.dbf data file. This would save time in actually restoring the data file from backup to their default destination.

7. E.   Restores and recovers all the corrupted blocks that are listed in the views V$COPY_CORRUPTION and V$BACKUP_CORRUPTION.

Explanation   RMAN enables you to perform block media recovery using the BLOCKRECOVER command. The command option CORRUPTION LIST enables you to recover all the corrupted blocks listed in the V$BACKUP_CORRUPTION and V$COPY_CORRUPTION dynamic performance views.

8. C.   ALTER TABLESPACE users OFFLINE;

Explanation   You must ensure that the tablespace is taken OFFLINE prior to performing online recovery operations on a tablespace.

9. C.   alert.log

Explanation   The information pertaining to the corrupt blocks can be obtained from the alert log file, which is located in the path specified through the initialization parameter BACKGROUND_DUMP_DEST in the target database's parameter file.

10. D.   BMR increases redo application time and avoids I/O overhead during recovery.

Explanation   BMR minimizes redo application time and avoids I/O overhead during recovery.

CHAPTER
14

User-Managed Incomplete Recovery

n this chapter, you will learn about user-managed incomplete recovery operations for a database operating in ARCHIVELOG or NOARCHIVELOG modes. We will explain the procedure for performing incomplete recovery using test cases. We also discuss the various possible incomplete recovery operations and the importance of using the RESETLOGS option. Later in this chapter, we discuss the recovery options available when an online redo log is lost and finally explain the parallel media recovery process. At the end of this chapter, we discuss the important V$VIEWS relating to media recovery. This chapter includes the following topics:

- Incomplete recovery
- Identifing the loss of a current online redo log file
- Media recovery in parallel
- Important V$VIEWS

Incomplete Recovery

We have learned that while performing any type of media recovery, Oracle has a roll forward phase and a roll backward phase. Note that changes made to undo data blocks are similar to those made to any other data block, in that any changes made to undo segments also create redo. This is called redo for the undo. In the roll forward phase, we apply all redo while performing complete recovery. While performing an incomplete recovery of a database, you apply only partial redo. Therefore, incomplete recovery always results in data loss. You would normally perform incomplete recovery if one of the following occurs:

- The online redo log group is lost. The loss could be due to hardware failure with this log group not archived.

- A user has accidentally performed an operation that has resulted in loss or corruption of critical data. For example, the user has accidentally dropped an important production table. This requires you to recover the database until the time the table was dropped.

NOTE
In the preceding case, incomplete recovery needs to be done on a test machine and the table is transported to the production database.

■ An archived redo log file needed to perform complete recovery is not available or corrupted.

■ A DBA executed the wrong batch job, logically corrupting the data in the application.

NOTE
In the preceding case, incomplete recovery needs to be done for the production database.

TIP
In all the preceding cases, you need to open the database using the RESETLOGS option after recovery.

Incomplete Recovery in NOARCHIVELOG Mode

In NOARCHIVELOG mode, archiving for the database is disabled and Oracle does not generate archived log files. A database operating in NOARCHIVELOG mode would protect the database from instance failure and not media failure. If a media failure occurs and damages some or all of the data files, then the only option for recovery is usually to restore the most recent whole database backup. You would loose all the changes since the most recent full backup until the time of the media failure.

Follow these steps to restore the most recent whole database backup without the redo log files to the default location:

1. If the database is open, shut it down.

2. If possible, correct the media problem so that the backup database files can be restored to their original locations.

3. Restore the most recent whole database backup using operating system commands. Restore all of the data files and the control files of the whole database backup, not just the damaged files.

4. In order to allow Oracle to reset the online redo logs, you must first perform incomplete recovery. Since there is no recovery involved here, you need to fake recovery by using the RECOVER DATABASE UNTIL CANCEL command.

336 OCP Oracle 9i Database: Fundamentals II Exam Guide

5. Issue the command **RECOVER DATABASE UNTIL CANCEL**. If Oracle gives an error, ignore it. Type **cancel**. We are only using this command so that Oracle will allow us to use the RESETLOGS option. We are not recovering anything here.

6. Open the database using the RESETLOGS option. This option resets the current redo log sequence to 1.

A RESETLOGS operation invalidates all redo in the online logs. Restoring from a whole database backup and then resetting the logs discards all changes to the database made from the time the backup was taken to the time of failure.

Incomplete Recovery in ARCHIVELOG Mode

If your database is operating in ARCHIVELOG mode, you can perform incomplete media recovery only if the following files are available:

■ A valid open or closed database backup. The backup must include all the data files and, optionally, the control file. You can always use the current control file if the schema of the database has not changed.

■ If you have a hot backup, all archived log files generated during the hot backup.

■ All the archived redo log files created from the backup until the time you need to recover.

To perform an incomplete recovery of the database, you must use the following procedure:

1. Initially, perform a full database backup.

2. Before recovery, ensure that the database is shut down prior to restoring all the database files from the backup.

3. Restore all the data files. If the current control file is not available, you should try to create a new control file. If that's not possible, you must restore the backup control file.

4. Mount the database and recover it using one of the following options available with the RECOVER DATABASE command:

```
RECOVER [AUTOMATIC] DATABASE <option>
```

where <option> can be one of the following:

```
UNTIL CANCEL
UNTIL TIME 'YYYY-MM-DD:HH24:MI:SS'
```

NOTE
You cannot alter the time format in the UNTIL TIME option. It is not dependent on NLS settings.

```
UNTIL SCN<integer>
USING BACKUP CONTROLFILE
```

5. Open the database by using the RESETLOGS option.

6. Perform a backup of the entire database.

NOTE
You can also use the ALTER DATABASE RECOVER command instead of the RECOVER DATABASE command.

Let's discuss various incomplete recovery options as previously shown in step 4. You can perform the following types of media recovery operations.

Cancel-Based Recovery

In *cancel-based* recovery, the recovery proceeds by prompting you to specify the absolute path of the files. The recovery operations can be terminated at any point of time by issuing the CANCEL command. Oracle applies recovery from the end of one archived log to the other. You must use this approach to perform an incomplete media recovery if a current redo log group is damaged and is not available to perform recovery. Multiplexing the redo log files can prevent this situation from occurring.

Another reason for using cancel-based recovery is when an archived redo log file needed for recovery is unavailable either due to the loss of the file or corruption. Archiving to multiple destinations or backing up the files more frequently can avoid such errors.

Time-Based Recovery

In *time-based* recovery, Oracle consistently recovers the database to a specific point in time. You must use this option to perform incomplete media recovery if a logical error occurred due to an accidental operation performed by the user (for example, the execution of statements that delete data, drop objects, or the untimely execution of batch jobs). Better implementation of user security and thorough monitoring of activities must prevent the need for this type of recovery.

NOTE
Oracle9i LogMiner utility enables you to track changes by mining the logs and also helps you make decisions to undo the DML operation.

The following test case shows how to recover a table that has been accidentally dropped by a user:

```
SQL> SELECT name FROM v$controlfile;
NAME
----------------------------------------
D:\ORACLE\ORADATA\TARGET\CONTROL01.CTL
D:\ORACLE\ORADATA\TARGET\CONTROL02.CTL
D:\ORACLE\ORADATA\TARGET\CONTROL03.CTL

SQL> SELECT file#, name FROM v$datafile;
     FILE# NAME
---------- ----------------------------------------
         1 D:\ORACLE\ORADATA\TARGET\SYSTEM01.DBF
         2 D:\ORACLE\ORADATA\TARGET\UNDOTBS01.DBF
         3 D:\ORACLE\ORADATA\TARGET\INDX01.DBF
         4 D:\ORACLE\ORADATA\TARGET\TOOLS01.DBF
         5 D:\ORACLE\ORADATA\TARGET\ORMTEST01.DBF

SQL> CONNECT EX_TEST/X@TAR

SQL> SELECT count(*) FROM test1;
  COUNT(*)
----------
         2
```

As previously shown, the test1 table has two rows. We now take a backup of the database by copying all the data files and control files, and connecting to the database.

```
SQL> CONNECT EX_TEST/X@TAR

SQL> INSERT INTO test1 SELECT rownum FROM dict;
1096 rows created.

SQL> INSERT INTO test1 SELECT * FROM test1;
1098 rows created.

SQL> INSERT INTO test1 SELECT * FROM test1;
```

```
2196 rows created.

SQL> COMMIT;
Commit complete.

SQL> SET TIME ON
20:26:45 SQL> SELECT count(*) FROM test1;
  COUNT(*)
----------
      4392

20:26:59 SQL>

20:27:34 SQL> DROP TABLE TEST1;
Table dropped.

20:27:59 SQL> CREATE TABLE TEST2
20:28:08   2   (num NUMBER) TABLESPACE ormtest;
Table created.

20:28:26 SQL> INSERT INTO test2 VALUES(1);
1 row created.

20:28:49 SQL> INSERT INTO test2 VALUES(2);
1 row created.

20:29:00 SQL> INSERT INTO test2 SELECT rownum FROM dict;
1096 rows created.

20:29:17 SQL> COMMIT;
Commit complete.

20:29:20 SQL> SELECT count(*) FROM test2;
  COUNT(*)
----------
      1098

SQL> SELECT count(*) FROM test1;
SELECT count(*) FROM test1
                       *
ERROR at line 1:
ORA-00942: table or view does not exist
```

As you have seen from the preceding code, the table test1 was accidentally dropped at 20 hours, 27 minutes, and 59 seconds. We now restore the control files, data files, required log files, and the **init.ora** file to a test machine. We have edited the **init.ora** file to point to the control files on the test machine. Next we mounted the database and renamed all the data files appropriately. Now let's perform time-based recovery on the test instance as shown here:

```
SQL> STARTUP MOUNT PFILE=c:\oracle\admin\target\pfile\init.ora
ORACLE instance started.
Total System Global Area    84700976 bytes
Fixed Size                    282416 bytes
Variable Size               62914560 bytes
Database Buffers            20971520 bytes
Redo Buffers                  532480 bytes
Database mounted.

SQL> RECOVER DATABASE USING BACKUP CONTROLFILE UNTIL TIME '2001-10-12:20:27:00';
ORA-00279: change 326399 generated at 10/12/2001 20:13:44 needed for thread 1
ORA-00289: suggestion : D:\ORACLE\ORADATA\TARGET\ARCHIVE\4.ARC
ORA-00280: change 326399 for thread 1 is in sequence #4
Specify log: {<RET>=suggested | filename | AUTO | CANCEL}
d:\oracle\oradata\target\redo01.log
Log applied.
Media recovery complete.

SQL> ALTER DATABASE OPEN;
ALTER DATABASE OPEN
*
ERROR at line 1:
ORA-01589: must use RESETLOGS or NORESETLOGS option for database open

SQL> ALTER DATABASE OPEN RESETLOGS;
Database altered.

SQL> CONNECT EX_TEST/X@TEST

SQL> SELECT count(*) FROM TEST1;
  COUNT(*)
----------
      4392

SQL> SELECT count(*) FROM TEST2;
SELECT count(*) FROM TEST2
                     *
ERROR at line 1:
ORA-00942: table or view does not exist
```

We export the table TEST1 using the **export** utility from the test server and then abort the test server instance:

```
SQL> CONNECT sys/sys@TEST as sysdba
Connected.

SQL> SHUTDOWN ABORT
ORACLE instance shut down.
SQL>
```

Note that we have recovered the test database just until the DROP TABLE command was issued. You can see that all the 4392 rows have been recovered. We have taken an export of this table. You need to perform an import of this table into the production database:

```
SQL> CONNECT ex_test/x@tar
Connected.

SQL> SELECT * FROM TAB;
TNAME                           TABTYPE  CLUSTERID
------------------------------  -------  ----------
TEST2                           TABLE
```

We now import the table TEST1 using the **import** utility into the production server and verify the records as shown:

```
SQL> SELECT * FROM TAB;
TNAME                           TABTYPE  CLUSTERID
------------------------------  -------  ----------
TEST1                           TABLE
TEST2                           TABLE

SQL> SELECT count(*) FROM test1;
  COUNT(*)
----------
      4392

SQL> SELECT count(*) FROM test2;
  COUNT(*)
----------
      1098
```

Change-Based Recovery

In *change-based* recovery, the recovery would be terminated after all the committed changes have been applied up to the specified system change number (SCN). You must use this approach to perform recovery if you are in a distributed database environment or if you know until which SCN you want to recover.

NOTE
The cancel-based recovery approach is generally better when compared to change- or time-based recovery because recovery is done until the end of a log file.

Recovery Using Backup Control File

Oracle enables you to recover the database using a backup copy of the control file. The backup control file can be used with all three options of the RECOVER command—CANCEL, TIME, or CHANGE—while doing incomplete recovery. The recovery operations would terminate if the specified option for recovery is completed (for example, recover until the time specified in UNTIL TIME) or if the control file is fully recovered. You need to recover the database using the backup control file if all the control files are lost and cannot be re-created. To avoid this, you must multiplex the control files.

Another reason for using the backup control file is when you need to recover the database having a different structure, unlike the current database structure. For example, the backup schema has a read-write file that is recognized only by the backup control file. Recovering the database with the backup control file could be a bit tricky. The important point is that if you are using the online log files as part of recovery, make sure you apply the correct online log file. Note that the first log group won't necessarily have the oldest online log sequence number. You should look at V$LOG to figure out which log group has the oldest online log sequence number.

Ramifications of Using RESETLOGS Option

The RESETLOGS option is used to open the database after performing an incomplete recovery. To open the database with the RESETLOGS option, all data files must be recovered to the same SCN. If a backup control file is restored, it must also be recovered until the same SCN.

Oracle generates a new RESETLOGS SCN and timestamp every time you successfully open the database using this option. Archived redo logs also have these values stored in their file headers. The RESETLOGS option prevents you from corrupting the data files with old archive log files, because Oracle will not allow you to apply an archived redo log to a data file unless the RESETLOGS SCN and the timestamp match.

The ramifications of resetting the online redo log sequence are as follows:

■ Oracle discards any redo information that was not applied during recovery and ensures that it will never be applied.

■ Oracle reinitializes the control file metadata regarding online redo logs and redo threads.

■ Oracle erases the contents of the online redo logs and creates the online redo log files if they are unavailable.

■ Oracle resets the log sequence number of the current group to 1.

■ You have to take a complete backup of your database after the RESETLOGS point. Oracle doesn't support using the backups taken before a RESETLOGS point and recovering through RESETLOGS. Although there is a procedure to recover through RESETLOGS, Oracle recommends that you take a complete backup of your database.

Before deciding on the use of the RESETLOGS and NORESETLOGS options, you must follow these guidelines:

■ Use the RESETLOGS option after performing an incomplete recovery, which means you didn't recover the redo completely and you have data loss.

■ Use the RESETLOGS option if the backup control file is used to recover the database, regardless of whether you are performing a complete or incomplete recovery.

TIP
The type of recovery command you use doesn't determine whether it's complete or incomplete recovery. For example, you can use the RECOVER DATABASE UNTIL CANCEL command but apply all the logs. This would be complete recovery, not incomplete recovery. In this case, you can start the database with the NORESETLOGS option.

■ While using the archived log files with the standby database, you must avoid using the RESETLOGS option or else you may need to re-create the standby database.

NOTE
*If you do not specify any option after a recovery,
Oracle, by default, uses the NORESETLOGS to open
the database.*

Identifying Loss of a Current Online Redo Log File

If a media failure damages all the members of an online redo log group, you must know which part of the group is affected by the failure. You will need to perform recovery based on the status of the damaged online redo log group. You can avoid this kind of failure if you properly distribute the members of a log group to multiple disk drives mounted under different controllers. Let's look at some of the statuses of the online log groups that can be damaged.

INACTIVE

If the status of the damaged redo log group is INACTIVE, then the recovery scenario is much simpler as this group in not needed to perform crash recovery. Since the log group has been archived, in case of recovery, you can recover completely and not lose data.

ACTIVE

If the status of the damaged redo log group is ACTIVE, the recovery scenario would be critical since this group is needed for crash recovery. You must attempt to issue a checkpoint and clear the log. If this is not possible, then you must restore a backup and perform an incomplete recovery up to the most recent available log.

CURRENT

If the status of the damaged redo log group is CURRENT, the recovery scenario would be more complicated because the LGWR background process is currently using this file to perform write operations. If a LGWR I/O fails, then the instance would crash. If the instance is still running, you must first attempt to clear the log group. If this is not possible, you must restore the entire database backup and perform an incomplete recovery until you have applied the most recent available log. This scenario is discussed in the following section. This is a single point of failure if you don't multiplex your online redo log files or don't distribute your log members properly. The following test illustrates a damaged redo log group that is CURRENT.

In the following test, we examine the online logs. Then we generate data (two rows), switch the log file, and generate more data (two more rows) in the CURRENT online log file:

```
SQL> STARTUP PFILE=c:\oracle\admin\target\pfile\init.ora
ORACLE instance started.
Total System Global Area    84700976 bytes
Fixed Size                    282416 bytes
Variable Size               62914560 bytes
Database Buffers            20971520 bytes
Redo Buffers                  532480 bytes
Database mounted.
Database opened.

SQL> SELECT * FROM v$log;
GROUP# THREAD#  SEQUENCE#     BYTES MEMBERS ARC STATUS      FIRST_CHANGE# FIRST_TIM
------ -------  ----------  -------- ------- --- --------   ------------- ---------
     1       1           5  1048576       1 YES INACTIVE          285293 12-OCT-01
     2       1           6  1048576       1 YES INACTIVE          305465 12-OCT-01
     3       1           7  1048576       1 NO  CURRENT           325646 12-OCT-01

SQL> CREATE TABLE test1
  2  (num NUMBER) TABLESPACE ormtest;
Table created.

SQL> INSERT INTO test1 VALUES(1);
1 row created.

SQL> INSERT INTO test1 VALUES(2);
1 row created.

SQL> COMMIT;
Commit complete.

SQL> ALTER SYSTEM SWITCH LOGFILE;
System altered.

SQL> SELECT * FROM v$log;
GROUP# THREAD#  SEQUENCE#     BYTES MEMBERS ARC STATUS      FIRST_CHANGE# FIRST_TIM
------ -------  ----------  -------- ------- --- --------   ------------- ---------
     1       1           8  1048576       1 NO  CURRENT           326164 12-OCT-01
     2       1           6  1048576       1 YES INACTIVE          305465 12-OCT-01
     3       1           7  1048576       1 YES ACTIVE            325646 12-OCT-01

SQL> INSERT INTO test1 VALUES(3);
```

```
1 row created.

SQL> INSERT INTO test1 VALUES(4);
1 row created.

SQL> COMMIT;
Commit complete.

SQL> SELECT * FROM v$log;
GROUP# THREAD#  SEQUENCE#   BYTES MEMBERS ARC STATUS   FIRST_CHANGE# FIRST_TIM
------ ------- ---------- -------- ------- --- -------- ----------- ---------
     1       1          8  1048576       1 NO  CURRENT       326164 12-OCT-01
     2       1          6  1048576       1 YES INACTIVE      305465 12-OCT-01
     3       1          7  1048576       1 YES ACTIVE        325646 12-OCT-01

SQL> SHUTDOWN ABORT
ORACLE instance shut down.
```

We have deleted all members of log group 1 (log sequence number 8), which is the CURRENT online log group. Let's start the database now and see what happens:

```
SQL>   STARTUP PFILE=c:\oracle\admin\target\pfile\init.ora
ORACLE instance started.
Total System Global Area    84700976 bytes
Fixed Size                    282416 bytes
Variable Size               62914560 bytes
Database Buffers            20971520 bytes
Redo Buffers                  532480 bytes
Database mounted.
ORA-00313: open failed for members of log group 1 of thread 1
ORA-00312: online log 1 thread 1: 'D:\ORACLE\ORADATA\TARGET\REDO01.LOG'
ORA-27041: unable to open file
OSD-04002: unable to open file
O/S-Error: (OS 2) The system cannot find the file specified.

C:\>COPY c:\9iBackup\*.dbf d:\oracle\oradata\target
c:\9iBackup\INDX01.DBF
c:\9iBackup\ORMTEST01.DBF
c:\9iBackup\SYSTEM01.DBF
c:\9iBackup\TEMP01.DBF
c:\9iBackup\TOOLS01.DBF
c:\9iBackup\UNDOTBS01.DBF
        6 file(s) copied.

SQL> ALTER DATABASE OPEN;
```

```
ALTER DATABASE OPEN
*
ERROR at line 1:
ORA-01113: file 1 needs media recovery
ORA-01110: data file 1: 'D:\ORACLE\ORADATA\TARGET\SYSTEM01.DBF'

SQL> RECOVER DATABASE UNTIL CANCEL;
ORA-00279:change 325985 generated at 10/12/2001 18:55:41 needed for thread 1
ORA-00289: suggestion : D:\ORACLE\ORADATA\TARGET\ARCHIVE\7.ARC
ORA-00280: change 325985 for thread 1 is in sequence #7
Specify log: {<RET>=suggested | filename | AUTO | CANCEL}
[Enter]
ORA-00279:change 326164 generated at 10/12/2001 19:15:17 needed for thread 1
ORA-00289: suggestion : D:\ORACLE\ORADATA\TARGET\ARCHIVE\8.ARC
ORA-00280: change 326164 for thread 1 is in sequence #8
ORA-00278: log file 'D:\ORACLE\ORADATA\TARGET\ARCHIVE\7.ARC' no longer needed
for this recovery
Specify log: {<RET>=suggested | filename | AUTO | CANCEL}
CANCEL
Media recovery cancelled.

SQL> ALTER DATABASE OPEN;
ALTER DATABASE OPEN
*
ERROR at line 1:
ORA-01589: must use RESETLOGS or NORESETLOGS option for database open

SQL> ALTER DATABASE OPEN RESETLOGS;
Database altered.

SQL> SELECT * FROM test1;
     NUM
----------
       1
       2
```

As you have seen in the preceding test, since archive log 7 was the last online log file, we had to perform incomplete recovery and start the database with the RESETLOGS option. A SELECT statement shows that only two rows exist in the table test1. The two rows with the values 3 and 4, which were present in the current online redo log (log sequence # 8), are lost.

Recovering When Archived Logs Are in a Non-Default Location

If the archive log files exist in a non-default location (which could happen if you run out of storage space on your default location), the process is no different from the one used with files located in the default location, except for minor changes. While using the RECOVER DATABASE command, Oracle prompts you to supply the archive log file path needed for recovery. You must specify the non-default location of the files that need to be applied as follows.

```
SQL> RECOVER DATABASE UNTIL CANCEL;
ORA-00279:change 325985 generated at 10/12/2001 18:55:41 needed for thread 1
ORA-00289: suggestion : D:\ORACLE\ORADATA\TARGET\ARCHIVE\7.ARC
ORA-00280: change 325985 for thread 1 is in sequence #7
Specify log: {<RET>=suggested | filename | AUTO | CANCEL}
X:\oracle\target\backup\archive\7.arc
```

However, if you have a lot of archived log files to apply in your non-default location, you might want to automate the recovery process so Oracle can automatically apply the log files. Since Oracle only knows your archive log destination through the LOG_ARCHIVE_DEST_*n* parameter, you can override that location by using the SET LOGSOURCE command before issuing the RECOVER command as follows:

```
SQL> SET LOGSOURCE 'c:\oracle\temp\'
SQL> RECOVER AUTOMATIC DATAFILE 'd:\oracle\oradata\target\ormtest01.dbf';
```

NOTE
Overriding the redo log source during recovery operations does not affect the archive redo log destination for online redo logs groups being archived.

Media Recovery in Parallel

In *parallel media* recovery, Oracle uses a division of labor mechanism where it allocates different processes to a different range of data blocks during the roll forward phase. This enables Oracle to speed up the recovery process. For example, if the parallel recovery is performed with PARALLEL 6 and only one data file is to be recovered, then Oracle spawns six processes that read blocks from the data file and applies redo records that are normally done by one process.

Typically, the recovery procedure is I/O-bound on reads to data blocks. Parallelism at the block level may only help recovery performance if it increases total I/Os (for example, by bypassing operating system restrictions on asynchronous I/Os). Systems with efficient asynchronous I/O typical see little improvement from using parallel media recovery.

NOTE
The RECOVER PARALLEL command specifies parallel media recovery. The default is NOPARALLEL option. This command selects a degree of parallelism equal to the number of CPUs available on all participating instances times the value of the PARALLEL_THREADS_PER_CPU initialization parameter. The maximum number of parallel recovery processes cannot exceed the value specified by the parameter PARALLEL_MAX_SERVERS.

To invoke parallel recovery, execute the following command using SQL*Plus:

```
SQL> RECOVER PARALLEL 6;
```

The integer value specifies the number of recovery processes used for media recovery.

NOTE
The initialization parameter RECOVERY_PARALLELISM can be initialized to the number of concurrent recovery processes to be started for instance or crash recovery. This does not affect any media recovery operations.

Important V$VIEWS

In this section we describe some of the important V$VIEWS that provide useful information related to media recovery.

The V$RECOVER_FILE dynamic performance view displays the status of files during media recovery. Some of the relevant columns and a brief description of these columns are shown in Table 14-1.

COLUMN	COLUMN DESCRIPTION
FILE#	Displays the file identification number.
ONLINE_STATUS	Displays the status of the file that is either ONLINE or OFFLINE.
ERROR	Displays OFFLINE NORMAL if you have gracefully taken the file offline. Displays FILE NOT FOUND if the file is not present in the designated destination.
CHANGE#	Displays the SCN where the recovery must start.
TIME	Displays the time of the SCN.

TABLE 14-1. *V$RECOVER_FILE View*

The V$LOG_HISTORY dynamic performance view displays detailed log history information that is obtained from the control file. Some of the relevant columns and a brief description of these columns are shown in Table 14-2.

The V$RECOVERY_LOG dynamic performance view displays information on the archived logs that are needed for media recovery. This view contains useful information used by the Oracle process when performing recovery. When RMAN directs a server process to perform recovery, only RMAN is able to obtain the relevant information from this view. In this case, the view will not display any information to other Oracle users. This view is based on the V$LOG_HISTORY dynamic performance view. Some of the important columns are THREAD#, SEQUENCE#, TIME, and ARCHIVE_NAME.

The V$RECOVERY_STATUS dynamic performance view displays the statistics of the current recovery process. This view contains useful information only for the Oracle process doing the recovery. When RMAN directs a server process to perform recovery, only RMAN is able to obtain relevant information from this view. In such cases, the view would not display any information to the Oracle users. Some of the important columns are RECOVERY_CHECKPOINT, THREAD, SEQUENCE_NEEDED, PREVIOUS_LOG_NAME, PREVIOUS_LOG_STATUS, and REASON.

The V$RECOVERY_FILE_STATUS dynamic performance view displays a record for each data file while issuing a RECOVER statement. This view contains useful information only for the Oracle process doing the recovery. When RMAN directs a server process to perform recovery, only RMAN is able to obtain the relevant information in this view. The view does not display any information to all other Oracle users. Some of the important columns are FILENUM, FILENAME, and STATUS.

COLUMN	COLUMN NAME
THREAD#	Displays the thread number of the archived redo log.
SEQUENCE#	Displays the sequence number of the archived log.
FIRST_CHANGE#	Displays the lowest SCN, which is recorded in the log.
NEXT_CHANGE#	Displays the highest SCN, which is recorded in the log.
RECID	Displays the control file record ID.
STAMP	Displays the control file record stamp.

TABLE 14-2. *V$LOG_HISTORY View*

Chapter Questions

1. **Using the command shown here, what time format must you specify to recover the database until a point-in-time?**

   ```
   SQL> RECOVER DATABASE UNTIL TIME '<time format>';
   ```

   A. YYYY-DD-MM:HH24:SS:MI

   B. YYYY-DD-MM:HH24:MI:SS

   C. YYYY-MM-DD:HH24:MI:SS

   D. YYYY-DD-MM:SS:MI:HH24

2. **Which dynamic performance view displays the information about the files associated with the locally managed temporary tablespace in Oracle9*i*?**

   A. V$DATAFILE

   B. V$TEMPFILE

   C. V$DBFILE

   D. V$DATAFILE_HEADER

3. **Which of the following options cannot be used with the RECOVER DATABASE command while performing user-managed incomplete recovery?**

    A. UNTIL TIME time

    B. UNTIL CANCEL

    C. UNTIL CHANGE scn

    D. UNTIL SEQUENCE seqno

4. **Susan is a DBA managing a development database that is operating in NOARCHIVELOG mode at a Fortune 500 company. She performs regular offline backups of all the database files—data files, control files, and online redo log files. Due to a media failure, if all the database files are lost, what must she do to recover the database to make it available to users?**

    A. Perform a simple restore from the backup and open the database with RESETLOGS option.

    B. Perform a simple restore from the backup and open the database with NORESETLOGS option.

    C. Restore and recover the database using the backup control file.

    D. Restore and recover the database using the current control file.

5. **Jeremy is a DBA managing a production database that is operating in ARCHIVELOG mode at a Fortune 500 company. He performs regular offline backups of all the database files—data files, control files, archived redo log files, and online redo log files. Due to a media failure, he lost a disk that contains all the data files. What files must he restore from backup to recover the database completely?**

    A. Restore all data files, archived redo logs, online redo logs, and the backup control file

    B. Restore all data files, archived redo logs, and online redo logs

    C. Restore all data files and archived redo logs

    D. Restore only the data files

6. **What is the consequence of opening the database with the RESETLOGS option?**

   A. Oracle discards any redo information that will be generated after the RESETLOGS operation.

   B. Oracle reinitializes the control file's data about online redo logs and redo threads.

   C. Oracle re-creates the online redo log files by deleting the ones that already exist.

   D. Oracle resets the log sequence number of the current group to 0.

7. **All the members that belong to a current online redo log group are unavailable. Which one of the following is the best incomplete recovery option?**

   A. Time-based recovery using the current control file

   B. Cancel-based recovery using the current control file

   C. Change-based recovery using the backup control file

   D. None of the above

8. **You are not able to perform any operations on the database since it is hanging. You suspect that a redo log file is lost. Which dynamic performance view would you query to obtain information about the redo log group whose status is CURRENT?**

   A. V$LOGFILE

   B. V$LOG_HISTORY

   C. V$LOG

   D. V$RECOVERY_LOG

9. **Which view must you query to obtain statistics of the current recovery process?**

   A. V$RECOVERY_STATUS

   B. V$RECOVERY_LOG

   C. V$RECOVER_FILE

   D. V$DATAFILE_HEADER

10. **Which type of recovery is not affected by specifying the initialization parameter RECOVERY_PARALLELISM?**

    A. Instance recovery

    B. Crash recovery

    C. Media recovery

    D. None of the above

11. **Which command must be used to re-create a data file if there are no backups available, but all the archived redo log files are available since the data file was created?**

    A. ALTER DATABASE CREATE DATAFILE

    B. CREATE TABLESPACE . . . DATAFILE

    C. ALTER TABLESPACE . . . ADD DATAFILE

    D. CREATE DATAFILE

Chapter Answers

1. C. YYYY-MM-DD:HH24:MI:SS

Explanation While performing point-in-time recovery of the database, you must specify time in the format YYYY-MM-DD:HH24:MI:SS. For example, if recovery needs to be performed until October 12, 2001 at 8:26:00 P.M., you must execute the following command:

```
SQL> RECOVER DATABASE USING BACKUP CONTROLFILE UNTIL TIME '2001-10-
12:20:26:00';
```

2. B. V$TEMPFILE

Explanation To obtain detailed information about the data files associated with the temporary tablespace, you must query the V$TEMPFILE or DBA_TEMP_FILES views in Oracle9*i*. Some of the important columns in the V$TEMPFILE dynamic performance view are NAME, FILE#, TS#, STATUS, ENABLED, and BYTES.

3. D. UNTIL SEQUENCE seqno

Explanation While performing user-managed incomplete recovery, you must use one of the following commands:

```
RECOVER DATABASE UNTIL CANCEL;
RECOVER DATABASE UNTIL CHANGE scn;
RECOVER DATABASE UNTIL TIME time;
```

The RECOVER DATABASE UNTIL SEQUENCE seqno can only be used while performing server-managed incomplete recovery through RMAN.

4. B.   Perform a simple restore from the backup and open the database with the NORESETLOGS option.

Explanation   If the database is operating in NOARCHIVELOG mode, then Susan cannot perform recovery of the database. The only option is to perform a simple restore of all the database files (in this case the control files, data files, and online redo log files). Since the online redo log files for the database are also backed up, she may open the database with the NORESETLOGS option. (Note that Oracle recommends that you don't backup online log files, especially if you are running the database in ARCHIVELOG mode.)

5. C.   Restore all the data files and archived redo logs

Explanation   Since the database is operating in ARCHIVELOG mode, Jeremy can perform complete recovery of the database. Note that although only the data files have been lost, the current control file and the online log groups are intact. You should never restore the online log files from the backup as it would overwrite the current online log files on disk making it impossible for you to do complete recovery. (Oracle strongly recommends not to backup online log files for this exact reason.) Therefore answers A and B are wrong since they are restoring online log files. D is incorrect since you need all the archived redo logs to do complete recovery. Note that Jeremy is copying all the online log files as part of the offline backup strategy, which is not recommended.

6. B.   Oracle reinitializes the control file data about online redo logs and redo threads.

Explanation   Whenever you open the database with the RESETLOGS option, Oracle reinitializes the control file data regarding the online redo logs and redo threads. Apart from this, it also ensures the following:

- Oracle discards any redo information that was not applied during recovery and ensures that it will never be applied.

- Oracle erases the contents of the online redo logs and creates the online redo log files if they are unavailable.

- Oracle resets the log sequence number of the current group to 1.

7. B.   Cancel-based recovery using the current control file

Explanation   Cancel-based recovery enables you to apply recovery until the end of a log file. Since this is the case here, this is the best option. To do time-based recovery, you need to know the time of the last SCN of the last existing online log file. Similarly, you need to have the first SCN value of the lost online log file. Although you can get this information from V$LOG_HISTORY view (meaning you can see this view while the database is mounted since its stored in the control file), the cancel-based recovery will be the easiest.

8. C.   V$LOG

Explanation   The dynamic performance view V$LOG displays the SEQUENCE# and the STATUS of the online redo log groups. To obtain detailed information about the members belonging to a redo log group, query the V$LOGFILE view.

9. A.   V$RECOVERY_STATUS

Explanation   The V$RECOVERY_STATUS dynamic performance view displays the statistics of the current recovery process. This view contains useful information only for the Oracle process doing the recovery. The important columns in this view are RECOVERY_CHECKPOINT, SEQUENCE_NEEDED, TIME_NEEDED, PREVIOUS_LOG_NAME, PREVIOUS_LOG_STATUS, and REASON.

10. C.   Media recovery

Explanation   The initialization RECOVERY_PARALLELISM parameter can be initialized to the number of concurrent recovery processes to be started for instance or crash recovery. This does not affect any media recovery operations.

11. A.   ALTER DATABASE CREATE DATAFILE

Explanation   You must execute the following command to re-create the data file if no backups exist:

```
SQL> ALTER DATABASE CREATE DATAFILE <file name>;
```

After creating the data file, you must perform recovery on the data file.

CHAPTER
15

RMAN
Incomplete Recovery

n this chapter, you will learn about incomplete recovery operations using RMAN. You must read Chapter 14 before reading this chapter. In this chapter, we explain the procedure for performing an incomplete database recovery using RMAN with the UNTIL TIME and UNTIL SEQUENCE commands. We also explain the concepts of RMAN's restore optimization feature. This chapter includes the following topics:

- Incomplete recovery using RMAN
- Perform incomplete database recovery using UNTIL TIME
- Perform incomplete database recovery using UNTIL SEQUENCE
- Restore optimization

Incomplete Recovery Using RMAN

Incomplete database recovery operations using RMAN is similar to that of user-managed incomplete recovery operations. You can perform incomplete media recovery by specifying time, log sequence number, or the SCN value.

After completion of the incomplete recovery session, you must open the database with the RESETLOGS option. The RESETLOGS option updates the existing online redo logs with a new timestamp and SCN or re-creates the redo log files if they are missing and then registers the timestamp and SCN. This eliminates the possibility of data file corruption by the application due to obsolete archived redo logs.

The recovery of all the data files must be performed prior to opening the database with the RESETLOGS option. Oracle prevents you from resetting the logs if a data file is offline.

NOTE

Once you open the database with RESETLOGS option, any data files that need recovery from the previous redo can't be recovered. The only exception is the files that were taken offline with the NORMAL option and read-only files since they don't require any redo to be applied.

You can perform database point-in-time recovery (DBPITR) by one of the following methods:

- Specifying the SET UNTIL statement before executing the RESTORE and RECOVER commands in a RUN block

■ Specifying the UNTIL clause with the RESTORE and RECOVER commands
individually

NOTE
*Using the SET UNTIL statement to perform DBPITR
is less complicated because it sets the desired time
for any subsequent RESTORE, SWITCH, and
RECOVER commands in the same RUN block.*

You must understand that if the SET UNTIL statement is specified after the
RESTORE and prior to executing a RECOVER command, you may not be able to
recover the database to the point in time required because the restored files may
already have a timestamp more recent than the specified time. You must ensure that
the SET UNTIL statement is specified prior to the RESTORE command.

To open the database, you must specify the OPEN RESETLOGS DATABASE
command at the RMAN prompt. The OPEN RESETLOGS DATABASE command
directs RMAN to create a new database incarnation record in the recovery catalog.
This incarnation record indicates that the target database has a new incarnation—
that is, the database has reset its online redo logs. RMAN associates all subsequent
backups and log archiving done by the target database with the new database
incarnation. You cannot use the backups of the database made before the
RESETLOGS was performed because these backups are associated with the old
database incarnation. Therefore, it is essential that you take a full database backup
after resetting the online redo log sequence.

Procedure to Perform an Incomplete Database Recovery

To perform an incomplete database recovery, you must use the following steps:

1. Ensure that the database is closed.

2. Connect to the target database and optionally to the recovery catalog
database.

3. Mount the target database, using the following command:

    ```
    RMAN> STARTUP MOUNT PFILE=d:\oracle\admin\target\pfile\init.ora
    ```

4. Determine the time, SCN, or log sequence that must be specified in the
recovery command.

5. Prepare an RMAN script that performs the following actions in the RUN block:

    A. Configure channels if automatic channels for the device are not configured.

    B. Set the environment variables NLS_LANG and NLS_DATE_FORMAT for the Oracle session.

    C. Either set the recovery time, SCN, or log sequence number to perform an incomplete database recovery.

NOTE
While specifying the appropriate time at which the recovery must end, you must use the date format specified in the NLS_LANG and NLS_DATE_FORMAT environment variables.

    D. You must specify the RESTORE and RECOVER commands with appropriate objects to be restored and recovered.

6. Execute the script. After completion of the recovery operation, open the database with the RESETLOGS option using the following command:

```
RMAN> OPEN RESETLOGS DATABASE;
```

7. It is recommended that you perform an immediate whole database backup prior to making it available for user operations. You can do this as follows:

    A. Close the database and re-mount it.

```
RMAN> SHUTDOWN IMMEDIATE
RMAN> STARTUP MOUNT PFILE=d:\oracle\admin\target\pfile\init.ora
```

    B. Perform an immediate backup of the database by executing the following command:

```
RMAN> BACKUP DATABASE INCLUDE CURRENT CONTROLFILE;
```

    C. Open the database as follows:

```
RMAN> OPEN DATABASE;
```

Perform an Incomplete Database Recovery Using UNTIL TIME

Follow the steps given in the following code to recover the database until a specified point in time. In the following test we show you the procedure to recover a table called TEST1, which was accidentally dropped by a user.

First, let's simulate the loss of a table as in the following manner:

```
SQL> SELECT count(rowid) FROM test1;
COUNT(ROWID)
------------
      308571

SQL> SET TIME ON
15:19:28 SQL>

15:20:53 SQL> DROP TABLE test1;
Table dropped.

SQL> SHUTDOWN IMMEDIATE;
Database closed.
Database dismounted.
ORACLE instance shut down.
```

Note that the table has been dropped at 15 hours, 20 minutes, and 53 seconds. In the real world, you need to restore and recover the database on a test machine before you extract the table using the export utility. Now let's connect to the target database and to the recovery catalog and mount the target database as follows:

```
C:\>RMAN CATALOG rman/rman TARGET sys/sys@target.india
Recovery Manager: Release 9.0.1.0.0
(c) Copyright 2001 Oracle Corporation.  All rights reserved.
connected to target database (not started)
connected to recovery catalog database

RMAN> STARTUP MOUNT PFILE=d:\oracle\admin\target\pfile\init.ora
Oracle instance started
database mounted
Total System Global Area       72118004 bytes
Fixed Size                       282356 bytes
Variable Size                  54525952 bytes
Database Buffers               16777216 bytes
Redo Buffers                     532480 bytes
```

Now let's execute an RMAN script to perform database restore and recovery until a specified time: 15:20:00. We then open the database with the RESETLOGS option as follows:

```
RMAN> RUN
2> {
3>     sql "ALTER SESSION SET NLS_DATE_FORMAT=''DD-MON-YYYY HH24:MI:SS''";
4>     SET UNTIL TIME '12-OCT-2001 15:20:00';
5>     RESTORE DATABASE;
6>     RECOVER DATABASE;
7> }

sql statement: ALTER SESSION SET NLS_DATE_FORMAT=''DD-MON-YYYY HH24:MI:SS''
executing command: SET until clause
Starting restore at 12-OCT-01
configuration for DISK channel 2 is ignored
allocated channel: ORA_DISK_1
channel ORA_DISK_1: sid=10 devtype=DISK
skipping datafile 3; already restored to file
D:\ORACLE\ORADATA\TARGET\ORMTEST.DBF
skipping datafile 4; already restored to file
D:\ORACLE\ORADATA\TARGET\USERS01.DBF
channel ORA_DISK_1: starting datafile backupset restore
channel ORA_DISK_1: specifying datafile(s) to restore from backup set
restoring datafile 00001 to D:\ORACLE\ORADATA\TARGET\SYSTEM01.DBF
restoring datafile 00002 to D:\ORACLE\ORADATA\TARGET\UNDOTBS01.DBF
channel ORA_DISK_1: restored backup piece 1
piece handle=C:\BACKUPS\40D6DG66.1 tag=null params=NULL
channel ORA_DISK_1: restore complete
Finished restore at 12-OCT-01
Starting recover at 12-OCT-01
using channel ORA_DISK_1
starting media recovery
media recovery complete
Finished recover at 12-OCT-01

RMAN> OPEN RESETLOGS DATABASE;
database opened
database registered in recovery catalog
starting full resync of recovery catalog
full resync complete
```

We now connect to the target database and verify the existence of the table
TEST1 as shown in the following code:

```
SQL> SELECT TABLE_NAME FROM USER_TABLES;
TABLE_NAME
------------------------------
TEST1

SQL> SELECT count(rowid) FROM test1;
COUNT(ROWID)
------------
      308571
```

After recovering this table on a test instance, you should export this table and
import it into the production database. This step is not shown here.

Perform Incomplete Database Recovery Using UNTIL SEQUENCE

In the following test we show you how to perform an incomplete database recovery
using the UNTIL SEQUENCE option of the RECOVER DATABASE command.

Let's obtain the information about the online redo logs and the CURRENT group
by querying the data dictionary. Then let's add test data and switch the CURRENT
log group, as shown here:

```
SQL> SELECT * FROM v$log;
```

GROUP#	THREAD#	SEQUENCE#	BYTES	MEMBERS	ARC	STATUS	FIRST_CHANGE#
1	1	1	512000	1	YES	INACTIVE	1130803
2	1	2	512000	1	YES	INACTIVE	1131002
3	1	3	512000	1	NO	CURRENT	1131009

```
SQL> CREATE TABLE test2 (slno NUMBER);
Table created.

SQL> INSERT INTO test2 VALUES(1);
1 row created.

SQL> INSERT INTO test2 VALUES(2);
1 row created.

SQL> INSERT INTO test2 VALUES(3);
1 row created.
```

```
SQL> COMMIT;
Commit complete.

SQL> ALTER SYSTEM SWITCH LOGFILE;
System altered.

SQL> SELECT * FROM v$log;
GROUP# THREAD# SEQUENCE#    BYTES MEMBERS ARC STATUS    FIRST_CHANGE#
------ ------- --------- ------- ------- --- ---------- -------------
     1       1         4  512000       1 NO  CURRENT          1131033
     2       1         2  512000       1 YES INACTIVE         1131002
     3       1         3  512000       1 YES ACTIVE           1131009
```

Note that the CURRENT log group's log sequence number is 4, and the initial test data is part of the redo log group having log sequence number 3. We now append more test data to the table and later simulate a crash of the online CURRENT redo log group with the sequence number 4.

```
SQL> INSERT INTO test2 VALUES(4);
1 row created.

SQL> INSERT INTO test2 VALUES(5);
1 row created.

SQL> INSERT INTO test2 VALUES(6);
1 row created.

SQL> COMMIT;
Commit complete.

SQL> SHUTDOWN ABORT
ORACLE instance shut down.
```

We now delete the redo log group, which is CURRENT (log sequence number 4), and connect to the target database and the recovery catalog database using RMAN and perform restore and recovery operations as shown in the following code:

```
C:\>RMAN CATALOG rman/rman TARGET sys/sys@target.india
Recovery Manager: Release 9.0.1.0.0
(c) Copyright 2001 Oracle Corporation.  All rights reserved.
connected to target database (not started)
connected to recovery catalog database

RMAN> STARTUP MOUNT PFILE=d:\oracle\admin\target\pfile\init.ora
```

```
Oracle instance started
database mounted
Total System Global Area      72118004 bytes
Fixed Size                      282356 bytes
Variable Size                 54525952 bytes
Database Buffers              16777216 bytes
Redo Buffers                    532480 bytes

RMAN> RESTORE DATABASE;
Starting restore at 13-OCT-01
configuration for DISK channel 2 is ignored
allocated channel: ORA_DISK_1
channel ORA_DISK_1: sid=10 devtype=DISK
channel ORA_DISK_1: starting datafile backupset restore
channel ORA_DISK_1: specifying datafile(s) to restore from backup set
restoring datafile 00001 to D:\ORACLE\ORADATA\TARGET\SYSTEM01.DBF
restoring datafile 00002 to D:\ORACLE\ORADATA\TARGET\UNDOTBS01.DBF
restoring datafile 00003 to D:\ORACLE\ORADATA\TARGET\ORMTEST.DBF
restoring datafile 00004 to D:\ORACLE\ORADATA\TARGET\USERS01.DBF
channel ORA_DISK_1: restored backup piece 1
piece handle=C:\BACKUPS\49D6FJ89.1 tag=null params=NULL
channel ORA_DISK_1: restore complete
Finished restore at 13-OCT-01

RMAN> RECOVER DATABASE UNTIL SEQUENCE 4 THREAD 1;
Starting recover at 13-OCT-01
using channel ORA_DISK_1
starting media recovery
archive log thread 1 sequence 2 is already on disk as file
C:\TARGET\ARCHIVES\2.ARC
archive log thread 1 sequence 3 is already on disk as file
D:\BACKUPS\ARCHIVES\3.ARC
archive log filename=C:\TARGET\ARCHIVES\2.ARC thread=1 sequence=2
archive log filename=D:\BACKUPS\ARCHIVES\3.ARC thread=1 sequence=3
media recovery complete
Finished recover at 13-OCT-01

RMAN> OPEN RESETLOGS DATABASE;
database opened
database registered in recovery catalog
starting full resync of recovery catalog
full resync complete

SQL> SELECT * FROM test2;
     SLNO
----------
```

```
1
2
3
```

The test data, which was part of the online CURRENT redo log group, has not been recovered because we have lost the entire set of files of that group. In real life you can avoid this problem if you multiplex the log files by distributing members on different drives mounted under different controllers.

Restore Optimization

The restore optimization feature using RMAN is introduced in Oracle9*i* to optimize the restore operation for already restored data files. If the file that needs to be restored already exists in its default location and its header contains the correct information, then RMAN does not proceed with the restoration of the file. In prior releases, RMAN always restored the requested files. You still have control over the restoration process if you wish to override this feature of RMAN. To do this you must use the FORCE option of the RESTORE command.

RMAN optimization is useful when the restore process is abruptly terminated (for example, due to a power outage), resulting in an incomplete restore of the database files. When you restore the database files again, RMAN will not restore all the files but only those that have not yet been restored or those not correctly restored.

NOTE
The restore optimization technique only checks the data file headers while performing a restore. It does not verify individual data blocks for corruption.

Chapter Questions

1. **Which of the following commands must you execute at the RMAN prompt to open the database after an incomplete recovery?**

   A. ALTER DATABASE OPEN;

   B. OPEN NORESETLOGS DATABASE;

   C. DATABASE RESETLOGS OPEN;

   D. OPEN DATABASE RESETLOGS;

   E. OPEN RESETLOGS DATABASE;

2. **Whenever the database is opened with the RESETLOGS option, what action does Oracle perform?**

   A. It updates the online redo logs with a new timestamp and SCN.

   B. It updates the online redo logs with the next value of the last SCN before the recovery.

   C. It identifies the missing log files and applies them to the database.

   D. It ignores the size of the last online redo logs and sets the new size to the log files.

3. **To perform a database point-in-time recovery (DBPITR) using RMAN, after database restoration, you must ensure that the database is in which of the following states?**

   A. OPEN

   B. MOUNTED

   C. NOMOUNT

   D. CLOSE

4. **The following script is used to perform a DBPITR using RMAN. Examine the script carefully and find which line of the following script results in an error?**

   A. RUN{

   B. sql "ALTER SESSION SET NLS_DATE_FORMAT="DD-MON-YYYY HH24:MI:SS'"";

   C. SET UNTIL TIME '12-10-2001 15:20:00';

   D. RESTORE DATABASE;

   E. RECOVER DATABASE;}

5. **Which of the following dynamic performance view would you query to identify the online CURRENT redo log group?**

   A. V$LOG

   B. V$LOGHIST

   C. V$LOGFILE

   D. V$LOG_HISTORY

6. **Which of the following commands would you use in RMAN to perform a recovery of the database until a specified log sequence number?**

   A. RECOVER DATABASE UNTIL SEQUENCE <seqno>;

   B. RECOVER UNTIL SEQUENCE <seqno>;

   C. RECOVER DATABASE UNTIL SEQUENCE <seqno> THREAD <threadno>;

   D. RECOVER UNTIL SEQUENCE <seqno> THREAD <threadno>;

7. **A power outage had an online transaction processing (OLTP) database system down for a day. While opening the database you encountered the following error:**

   ```
   ERROR:
   ORA-01034: ORACLE not available
   ORA-27101: shared memory realm does not exist
   ```

   Which of the following commands would you use at the RMAN prompt for connecting to the target database?

   A. RECOVER DATABASE;

   B. RESTORE DATABASE;

   C. SET UNTIL TIME <time>;

   D. STARTUP PFILE=<pfilename>;

8. **Which of the following statements is true about restore optimization?**

   A. RMAN checks the entire data file and the header during restoration.

   B. RMAN checks the entire data file and the header for corruptions during restoration.

   C. RMAN checks the data file headers during restoration.

   D. RMAN checks all the database files except the data files for corruptions during restoration.

9. **What happens when the following statement is executed while performing an incomplete recovery until a specified log sequence using RMAN?**

   ```
   RMAN> RECOVER DATABASE UNTIL SEQUENCE 2911 THREAD 1;
   ```

   A. RMAN fails to execute the statement due to incorrect syntax.

   B. RMAN performs an incomplete database recovery until the sequence number 2910.

    C. RMAN performs an incomplete database recovery until the sequence number 2911.

    D. RMAN uses the sum of the thread number and the sequence number and performs incomplete recovery until the log sequence number 2912.

  10. **Which command option must you use to override restore optimization used in RMAN?**

    A. IMMEDIATE

    B. FORCE

    C. OVERRIDE

    D. CANCEL

    E. None of the above

Chapter Answers

  I. E. OPEN RESETLOGS DATABASE;

Explanation   After performing an incomplete recovery, you must open the database by executing the OPEN RESETLOGS DATABASE command at the RMAN prompt.

  2. A. It updates the online redo logs with a new timestamp and SCN.

Explanation   Whenever you open the database with the RESETLOGS option after an incomplete recovery, Oracle updates the online redo logs with a new timestamp and SCN. It also resets the log sequence number to 1.

  3. B. MOUNTED

Explanation   After restoring the entire database, you must MOUNT the database to perform an incomplete recovery using RMAN. To mount the database using RMAN, you must execute the following command:

```
RMAN> STARTUP MOUNT
```

Or if the database is already in the NOMOUNT state, then you must execute the following command:

```
RMAN> MOUNT DATABASE
```

4. C. SET UNTIL TIME '12-10-2001 15:20:00';

Explanation There is a mismatch in the format string and the value specified. You must ensure that the date value specified in the SET UNTIL TIME option matches the format string defined by NLS_DATE_FORMAT. The correct format for the script shown in the question would be SET UNTIL TIME '12-OCT-2001 15:20:00';

5. A. V$LOG

Explanation You must query the V$LOG dynamic performance view to obtain information about the online CURRENT redo log group. The relevant columns of the view are GROUP#, THREAD#, SEQUENCE#, and STATUS.

6. C. RECOVER DATABASE UNTIL SEQUENCE *<seqno>* THREAD *<threadno>*;

Explanation To recover the database until a specified sequence number, you must specify the sequence number as well as the thread number. Specify thread number as 1 if it is a single instance database. This command is used while using RMAN only.

7. D. STARTUP PFILE=*<pfilename>*;

Explanation You must start up the database using the OPEN priority. If the database fails to open, then you must take an appropriate action based on the error that you encounter.

8. C. RMAN checks the data file headers during restoration.

Explanation The restore optimization feature using RMAN was introduced in Oracle9*i*. While restoring the files, RMAN checks the data file headers. It does not verify individual data blocks for corruption.

9. B. RMAN performs an incomplete database recovery until the sequence number 2910.

Explanation This command performs recovery of the database until log sequence 2910.

10. B. FORCE

Explanation To override restore optimization, you must use the FORCE option with the RESTORE command.

CHAPTER
16

RMAN Maintenance

n this chapter, you will learn the various commands available to maintain the RMAN repository. We will discuss the purpose of the CROSSCHECK command and explain the procedure to perform cross checking of backup pieces and image copies. We will also explain the process of changing the availability status of the backup sets and image copies and how to make them exempt from the retention policy. Later in this chapter, we explain how to catalog backups made with operating system (O/S) commands. This chapter includes the following topics:

- RMAN crosscheck

- Performing crosscheck of backup sets and image copies

- Updating the repository when backups have been deleted

- Changing the availability status of backup sets and image copies

- Making a backup set or an image copy exempt from the retention policy

- Cataloging backups made with the O/S commands

RMAN Crosscheck

RMAN enables you to crosscheck the availability of the backup sets by verifying the information stored in its repository with the backup sets that are physically available in the designated storage medium. This feature is helpful in identifying the backup sets or image copies that are either corrupted or have been accidentally deleted from the disk or tapes in the media management library. The CROSSCHECK command in RMAN enables you to detect missing files or files that are unusable due to corruption.

NOTE
RMAN performs a thorough crosscheck on only those files that are registered in its repository (recovery catalog or target database's control file).

Regular usage of the CROSSCHECK command against backup sets and image copies keeps you informed about their status and enables you to take pro-active measures. If an image copy or a backup piece is either unreadable or physically unavailable during the execution of the CROSSCHECK command, then RMAN marks the image copy or the backup piece as EXPIRED in the RMAN repository. You can obtain the status of these files by using the LIST command with the appropriate option. Note that if the missing or corrupted image copy or backup piece were replaced with a copy, which is in good condition, then RMAN would modify the status of the piece to AVAILABLE in the repository.

For example, consider that an image copy was deleted physically using an O/S command because it was not required. If you use the CROSSCHECK command, RMAN does not automatically delete the information pertaining to this image copy from the repository because it is physically not available, but only marks it as EXPIRED. You will need to explicitly issue the DELETE EXPIRED command to delete all the backup sets and image copies that are expired from the repository. If for some reason the file still exists on the media, then RMAN issues the following error and aborts the delete operation:

```
RMAN-00571: ==========================================================
RMAN-00569: =============== ERROR MESSAGE STACK FOLLOWS ===============
RMAN-00571: ==========================================================
RMAN-00579: the following error occurred at 10/22/2001 18:03:01
RMAN-03006: non-retryable error occurred during execution of command: delete
RMAN-12004: unhandled exception during command execution on channel ORA_DISK_1
RMAN-20502: DELETE EXPIRED cannot delete objects that exist - run CROSSCHECK
```

Performing a Crosscheck of Backup Sets and Image Copies

You can crosscheck the backup pieces or image copies by executing the CROSSCHECK command. CROSSCHECK determines whether or not the header of a backup piece is valid.

NOTE
If the backup pieces are stored on tapes, then this command only validates their existence.

To crosscheck backup pieces, you must follow the procedure given in the following steps:

1. Issue the LIST BACKUP command, as shown in the following code, to identify the desired backup pieces, backup sets, or proxy copies, which you need to crosscheck.

```
RMAN> LIST BACKUP;

List of Backup Sets
===================
BS Key  Type LV Size       Device Type Elapsed Time Completion Time
------- ---- -- ---------- ----------- ------------ ---------------
14416   Full    64K           DISK       00:00:01     29-OCT-01
        BP Key: 14417   Status: AVAILABLE   Tag: MONDAY_BACKUP
        Piece Name: D:\ORACLE\ORA90\DATABASE\0ND7QK90_1_1
  List of Datafiles in backup set 14416
  File LV Type Ckp SCN    Ckp Time  Name
  ---- -- ---- ---------- --------- ----
  4       Full 158996     29-OCT-01
D:\ORACLE\ORADATA\DEVRMAN\TOOLS01.DBF


BS Key  Device Type Elapsed Time Completion Time
------- ----------- ------------ ---------------
14423   DISK          00:00:01     29-OCT-01
        BP Key: 14424   Status: AVAILABLE   Tag:
        Piece Name: D:\ORACLE\ORA90\DATABASE\0OD7QK95_1_1

  List of Archived Logs in backup set 14423
  Thrd Seq     Low SCN    Low Time   Next SCN   Next Time
  ---- ------- ---------- --------- ---------- ---------
  1    6536    158993     29-OCT-01 158999     29-OCT-01

BS Key  Type LV Size       Device Type Elapsed Time Completion Time
------- ---- -- ---------- ----------- ------------ ---------------
14427   Full    1M            DISK       00:00:01     29-OCT-01
        BP Key: 14428   Status: AVAILABLE   Tag:
        Piece Name: D:\ORACLE\ORA90\DATABASE\0QD7QKC2_1_1
  List of Datafiles in backup set 14427
  File LV Type Ckp SCN    Ckp Time  Name
  ---- -- ---- ---------- --------- ----
  5       Full 159003     29-OCT-01
D:\ORACLE\ORADATA\DEVRMAN\USERS01.DBF
```

2. Allocate one or more channels of type MAINTENANCE explicitly, if automatic channels are not already configured as shown in the following code:

```
RMAN> ALLOCATE CHANNEL FOR MAINTENANCE DEVICE TYPE DISK;

released channel: ORA_DISK_1
allocated channel: ORA_MAINT_DISK_1
channel ORA_MAINT_DISK_1: sid=8 devtype=DISK
```

3. You can either specify the backup set or a backup piece for verification using the CROSSCHECK command. In the example given in the following code, we crosscheck the backup sets 14416 and 14423 that are registered in the repository.

```
RMAN> CROSSCHECK BACKUPSET 14416,14423;

crosschecked backup piece: found to be 'AVAILABLE'
backup piece handle=D:\ORACLE\ORA90\DATABASE\0ND7QK90_1_1 recid=18
stamp=444420384
crosschecked backup piece: found to be 'AVAILABLE'
backup piece handle=D:\ORACLE\ORA90\DATABASE\0OD7QK95_1_1 recid=19
stamp=444420390

RMAN> CROSSCHECK BACKUPPIECE TAG='monday_backup';

crosschecked backup piece: found to be 'AVAILABLE'
backup piece handle=D:\ORACLE\ORA90\DATABASE\0ND7QK90_1_1 recid=18
stamp=444420384
```

NOTE
*The keys 14416 and 14423 correspond to the backup sets that contain the **TOOLS01.dbf** file and the archive log file with sequence number 6536, respectively. These key numbers can be obtained by issuing the LIST BACKUP command as shown in step 1.*

4. You should release the channels, if they are manually allocated, using the command given in the following code:

```
RMAN> RELEASE CHANNEL;
released channel: ORA_MAINT_DISK_1
```

To crosscheck image copies, you must follow the procedure given in the following steps:

1. Issue the LIST COPY command, as shown in the following code, to view detailed information of all the image copies:

```
RMAN> LIST COPY;

List of Datafile Copies
Key       File S Completion Time Ckp SCN    Ckp Time        Name
-------   ---- - --------------- ---------- --------------- ----
14433     4    A 29-OCT-01       159008     29-OCT-01       C:\BACKUPS\DF4.DBF
14431     5    A 29-OCT-01       159006     29-OCT-01       C:\BACKUPS\DF5.DBF
14370     5    A 26-OCT-01       158029     26-OCT-01       C:\BACKUPS\DF5.F

List of Controlfile Copies
Key       S Completion Time Ckp SCN    Ckp Time        Name
-------   - --------------- ---------- --------------- ----
14435     A 29-OCT-01       159008     29-OCT-01       C:\BACKUPS\CNTRLFILE.F
14369     A 26-OCT-01       158014     26-OCT-01       C:\BACKUPS\CTL.F

List of Archived Log Copies
Key       Thrd Seq     S Low Time   Name
-------   ---- ------- - --------- ----
14303     1    6516    A 24-OCT-01 D:\ORACLE\ORA90\RDBMS\ARC06516.001
14304     1    6517    A 24-OCT-01 D:\ORACLE\ORA90\RDBMS\ARC06517.001
14305     1    6518    A 24-OCT-01 D:\ORACLE\ORA90\RDBMS\ARC06518.001
14306     1    6519    A 24-OCT-01 D:\ORACLE\ORA90\RDBMS\ARC06519.001
```

2. Allocate one or more channels of type MAINTENANCE explicitly, if automatic channels are not already configured as shown in the following code:

```
RMAN> ALLOCATE CHANNEL FOR MAINTENANCE DEVICE TYPE DISK;
allocated channel: ORA_MAINT_DISK_1
channel ORA_MAINT_DISK_1: sid=14 devtype=DISK
```

3. You should verify whether or not the image copies exist. For example, we crosscheck the existence of control file copy CTL.F and the data file copies with keys 14370 and 14433 using the following commands:

```
RMAN> CROSSCHECK CONTROLFILECOPY 'C:\BACKUPS\CTL.F';

validation succeeded for controlfile copy
controlfile copy filename=C:\BACKUPS\CTL.F recid=1 stamp=444147040

RMAN> CROSSCHECK DATAFILECOPY 14370,14433;

validation succeeded for datafile copy
datafile copy filename=C:\BACKUPS\DF5.F recid=2 stamp=444147658
validation succeeded for datafile copy
datafile copy filename=C:\BACKUPS\DF4.DBF recid=4 stamp=444420572
```

4. You should release the channels if they are manually allocated using the command given in the following code:

```
RMAN> RELEASE CHANNEL;
released channel: ORA_MAINT_DISK_1
```

NOTE
If the backup set or image copy is no longer available, RMAN marks it as EXPIRED. If the backup set or image copy was marked EXPIRED and is now available, then RMAN marks it as AVAILABLE.

Updating the Repository When Backups Have Been Deleted

The RMAN repository maintains the information pertaining to each backup set or image copy created using RMAN. These files are stored at the O/S with the location registered in the repository. During media failure, RMAN uses the appropriate files to restore and perform recovery by acquiring the information from the repository. In case any of these files are physically deleted using O/S commands, you must delete the corresponding information registered in the repository. When you use a command to delete a backup set or image copy, RMAN performs the following actions:

1. The physical file from the O/S is removed.

2. The backup set or image copy records are updated in the control file to the status DELETED.

3. If the recovery catalog is used as the repository, the backup set or image copy records are removed from the catalog tables.

When you use the CROSSCHECK command, RMAN makes necessary updates to the repository. RMAN marks the records, which are maintained in the repository, as EXPIRED. You can then issue the DELETE EXPIRED command to remove the expired records from an existing catalog. This would result in updating the control file records status to DELETED. You can also execute the DELETE command specifying the files you have already removed from the O/S. This is shown in the following code. Let's delete the physical files at the O/S level and issue the following command:

```
RMAN> DELETE DATAFILECOPY 14370;

released channel: ORA_DISK_1
allocated channel: ORA_DISK_1
channel ORA_DISK_1: sid=8 devtype=DISK

List of Datafile Copies
Key      File S Completion Time Ckp SCN     Ckp Time          Name
-------  ---- - --------------- ----------  ---------------   ----
14370    5    A 26-OCT-01       158029      26-OCT-01         C:\BACKUPS\DF5.F
Do you really want to delete the above objects (enter YES or NO)? YES
deleted datafile copy
datafile copy filename=C:\BACKUPS\DF5.F recid=2 stamp=444147658
```

NOTE
If the files exist at the OS level and you issue the DELETE command, then RMAN deletes the record as well as the corresponding O/S files.

Alternatively, you can also run the CHANGE . . . UNCATALOG command, which removes the records of the specified backup sets and image copies from the catalog and updates the control file records status as DELETED. For example, to delete a control file image copy you must issue the following command at the RMAN prompt:

```
RMAN> CHANGE CONTROLFILECOPY 'C:\BACKUPS\CTL.F' UNCATALOG;
uncataloged controlfile copy
controlfile copy filename=C:\BACKUPS\CTL.F recid=1 stamp=444147040
```

To UNCATALOG the backup sets that contain the TOOLS01.dbf file and the archive log file with sequence number 6536, you must issue the following command:

```
RMAN>CHANGE BACKUPSET 14416,14423 UNCATALOG;
```

The values 14416 and 14423 are keys of the backup sets that contain the TOOLS01.dbf and the archive log file with sequence number 6536. These backup set keys can be obtained by issuing the LIST BACKUP command as shown in the previous section.

If you create a full database backup set using the target database's control file as the repository, then you can query the dynamic performance view V$BACKUP_SET to obtain information on the backup sets from the target database's control file. If you use the recovery catalog, information on the backup sets can be obtained from the catalog view RC_BACKUP_SET.

Because the V$ views residing at the target database and the catalog tables differ in the way they store information, this affects how RMAN handles repository records. RMAN only updates the status of the files to DELETED in the target database's control file when you explicitly issue the DELETE command. On the other hand, it deletes the record from the recovery catalog. This is because the data in the control file is stored in an internal data structure in the circular reuse sections, unlike the records that are maintained in the recovery catalog tables, which can be immediately deleted.

Changing the Availability Status of Backup Sets and Image Copies

To update the status of a backup set or image copy as AVAILABLE or UNAVAILABLE, you must use the CHANGE . . . AVAILABLE | UNAVAILABLE command at the RMAN prompt. RMAN would then update the repository to reflect the respective backup files as either available or unavailable.

The primary use of changing the status of the backup sets or image copies is when the disk drive where the files reside is either being upgraded or replaced. These files can be temporarily marked as unavailable during the maintenance period. The moment maintenance is completed, you can alter the status to reflect the availability of these files. You can then execute the CROSSCHECK command to perform a thorough verification of their availability.

NOTE
During Media recovery, RMAN always ignores the backup sets and image copies whose status is UNAVAILABLE and restores those that are marked AVAILABLE.

To change the status of backup sets or image copies from AVAILABLE to UNAVAILABLE, you must follow the steps given in the following procedure:

I. To obtain the present status and related information about the backup sets and image copies, you must execute the LIST BACKUP and LIST COPY commands. For example, to view information pertaining to image copies created using RMAN, execute the following command:

```
RMAN> LIST COPY;

List of Datafile Copies
Key       File S Completion Time Ckp SCN    Ckp Time        Name
-------   ---- - --------------- ---------- --------------- ----
14433     4    A 29-OCT-01       159008     29-OCT-01       C:\BACKUPS\DF4.DBF
14431     5    A 29-OCT-01       159006     29-OCT-01       C:\BACKUPS\DF5.DBF

List of Controlfile Copies
Key       S Completion Time Ckp SCN    Ckp Time        Name
-------   - --------------- ---------- --------------- ----
14435     A 29-OCT-01       159008     29-OCT-01       C:\BACKUPS\CNTRLFILE.F

List of Archived Log Copies
Key       Thrd Seq     S Low Time  Name
-------   ---- ------- - --------- ----
14303     1    6516    A 24-OCT-01 D:\ORACLE\ORA90\RDBMS\ARC06516.001
14304     1    6517    A 24-OCT-01 D:\ORACLE\ORA90\RDBMS\ARC06517.001
14305     1    6518    A 24-OCT-01 D:\ORACLE\ORA90\RDBMS\ARC06518.001
14306     1    6519    A 24-OCT-01 D:\ORACLE\ORA90\RDBMS\ARC06519.001
14307     1    6520    A 24-OCT-01 D:\ORACLE\ORA90\RDBMS\ARC06520.001
14308     1    6521    A 25-OCT-01 D:\ORACLE\ORA90\RDBMS\ARC06521.001
```

2. Execute the CHANGE . . . UNAVAILABLE command to mark a backup set or an image copy as UNAVAILABLE. For example, to change the availability status of the image copies of data files and archive log files, execute the following commands:

```
RMAN> CHANGE DATAFILECOPY 'C:\BACKUPS\DF4.DBF' UNAVAILABLE;

changed datafile copy unavailable
datafile copy filename=C:\BACKUPS\DF4.DBF recid=4 stamp=444420572

RMAN> CHANGE COPY OF ARCHIVELOG SEQUENCE BETWEEN 6516 AND 6519 UNAVAILABLE;

changed archive log unavailable
archive log filename=D:\ORACLE\ORA90\RDBMS\ARC06516.001 recid=1 stamp=443967293
changed archive log unavailable
archive log filename=D:\ORACLE\ORA90\RDBMS\ARC06517.001 recid=2 stamp=443968476
```

```
changed archive log unavailable
archive log filename=D:\ORACLE\ORA90\RDBMS\ARC06518.001 recid=3 stamp=443968519
changed archive log unavailable
archive log filename=D:\ORACLE\ORA90\RDBMS\ARC06519.001 recid=4 stamp=443989723
```

To change the availability status of the backup sets, execute the following commands:

```
RMAN> CHANGE BACKUPSET 14427 UNAVAILABLE;
```

```
RMAN> CHANGE BACKUP OF CONTROLFILE UNAVAILABLE;
```

To change the status of a backup set or image copies from UNAVAILABLE to AVAILABLE, you must follow the steps given in the following procedure:

1. To determine the availability status of RMAN backup sets and image copies, issue the LIST BACKUP and LIST COPY commands, respectively. For example, to view status pertaining to image copies created using RMAN, execute the following command:

```
RMAN> LIST COPY;

List of Datafile Copies
Key       File S Completion Time Ckp SCN    Ckp Time        Name
-------   ---- - --------------- ---------- --------------- ----
14433     4    U 29-OCT-01       159008     29-OCT-01       C:\BACKUPS\DF4.DBF
14431     5    A 29-OCT-01       159006     29-OCT-01       C:\BACKUPS\DF5.DBF


List of Controlfile Copies
Key       S Completion Time Ckp SCN    Ckp Time        Name
-------   - --------------- ---------- --------------- ----
14435     A 29-OCT-01       159008     29-OCT-01       C:\BACKUPS\CNTRLFILE.F


List of Archived Log Copies
Key       Thrd Seq     S Low Time  Name
-------   ---- ------- - --------- ----
14303     1    6516    U 24-OCT-01 D:\ORACLE\ORA90\RDBMS\ARC06516.001
14304     1    6517    U 24-OCT-01 D:\ORACLE\ORA90\RDBMS\ARC06517.001
14305     1    6518    U 24-OCT-01 D:\ORACLE\ORA90\RDBMS\ARC06518.001
14306     1    6519    U 24-OCT-01 D:\ORACLE\ORA90\RDBMS\ARC06519.001
14307     1    6520    A 24-OCT-01 D:\ORACLE\ORA90\RDBMS\ARC06520.001
14308     1    6521    A 25-OCT-01 D:\ORACLE\ORA90\RDBMS\ARC06521.001
```

2. Allocate one or more maintenance channels if automatic channels are not already configured.

3. After an unavailable backup set or image copy is reinstated, you must issue the following command to mark the files as AVAILABLE in the repository:

```
RMAN> CHANGE DATAFILECOPY 'C:\BACKUPS\DF4.DBF' AVAILABLE;
```

```
released channel: ORA_DISK_1
allocated channel: ORA_DISK_1
channel ORA_DISK_1: sid=8 devtype=DISK
changed datafile copy available
datafile copy filename=C:\BACKUPS\DF4.DBF recid=4 stamp=444420572
```

To make backup sets AVAILABLE, you must issue the following command:

```
RMAN> CHANGE BACKUPSET 14423 AVAILABLE;
```

Making a Backup Set or an Image Copy Exempt from the Retention Policy

The backup sets or image copies can be created exempting them from the retention policy. RMAN's BACKUP . . . KEEP command enables you to exempt a backup set or an image copy from the retention policy when used with the FOREVER or UNTIL options. It overrides any configured retention policy and forces RMAN to keep the specified backup set for a longer period of time than specified by the existing retention policy. RMAN treats these backup sets or image copies as valid and restores them even if the time duration for these files has exceeded the retention policy. These kinds of backups are termed as *long-term backups*.

NOTE
The KEEP FOREVER clause of the BACKUP command requires you to have a recovery catalog as the repository instead of a control file.

You can specify the LOGS option to save archived log files for recovery and the NOLOGS option when you do not want to save the archived log files. You can issue the CHANGE command to alter the KEEP status if you decide against maintaining a long-term backup. The options available with the BACKUP . . . KEEP command are also available with the CHANGE . . . KEEP command. You can issue the following command to keep a backup forever, exempting it from the retention policy:

```
RMAN> CHANGE BACKUPSET 14427 KEEP FOREVER LOGS;

using channel ORA_DISK_1
keep attributes for the backup are changed
backup will never be obsolete
archived logs required to recover from this backup will expire when this backup expires
backup set key=14427 recid=20 stamp=444420483
```

For a backup to work in accordance with the retention policy, you must issue the command, shown in the following code, using the NOKEEP option. In the following example, the backup set would be marked obsolete by the retention policy, as it has exceeded the duration specified by the retention policy:

```
RMAN> CHANGE BACKUPSET 14427 NOKEEP;

using channel ORA_DISK_1
keep attributes for the backup are deleted
backup set key=14427 recid=20 stamp=444420483
```

You can also specify a time duration for which a backup set or an image copy must be maintained in the repository without being in compliance with the retention policy. The following example makes a data file copy exempt from the retention policy for 60 days:

```
RMAN> CHANGE DATAFILECOPY 'C:\BACKUPS\DF5.DBF' KEEP UNTIL TIME 'SYSDATE+60' LOGS;

released channel: ORA_DISK_1
allocated channel: ORA_DISK_1
channel ORA_DISK_1: sid=8 devtype=DISK
keep attributes for the datafile/controlfile copy are changed
copy will be obsolete on date 28-DEC-01
archived logs required to recover from this copy will expire when this copy expires
datafile copy filename=C:\BACKUPS\DF5.DBF recid=3 stamp=444420550
```

Cataloging Backups Made with the Operating System Commands

Image copies of database files and archived redo logs created using RMAN are no different from those that are created using O/S commands. The files created using RMAN are registered in the repository, which would later be used by RMAN to perform restore and recover operations. In contrast, the image copies created using O/S commands must be manually restored and recovered. You can, however, register these files with the repository by using the CATALOG command.

It is always advantageous to catalog the image copies of files that are created using O/S commands (for example, files created using hot backup) because you can then use RMAN for restore and recovery operations. Without cataloging, you need to perform these operations manually. To catalog files, you must ensure that the following conditions are met:

- The files are accessible on disk.

- The files are complete image copies of single files.

- The image copies are of data files, control files, or archived redo log files.

In the following example, we explain the procedure to catalog an image copy that was manually created using the O/S COPY command. We first take a tablespace into backup mode to copy the file associated with the tablespace at the O/S. This is shown in the following code:

```
SQL> ALTER TABLESPACE ormtest BEGIN BACKUP;
Tablespace altered.

C:\>COPY d:\oracle\oradata\target\ormtest01.dbf c:\backups\ormtest01_bup.dbf
        1 file(s) copied.

SQL> ALTER TABLESPACE ormtest END BACKUP;
Tablespace altered.
```

We now establish a connection to the target database and to the repository. Now let's execute the following command at the RMAN prompt:

```
RMAN> CATALOG DATAFILECOPY 'c:\backups\ormtest01_bup.dbf';

cataloged datafile copy
datafile copy filename=C:\BACKUPS\ORMTEST01_BUP.DBF recid=4 stamp=443553858
```

Chapter Questions

1. **What is the status of a backup piece in the repository if a CROSSCHECK command is issued after physically deleting the backup piece?**

    A. EXPIRED

    B. INVALID

    C. UNAVAILABLE

    D. OBSOLETE

2. **During the cleaning up process of your recovery catalog, you found several backup sets and image copies with the status EXPIRED. Which command must you issue at the RMAN prompt to remove the information pertaining to these nonexistent files?**

    A. DELETE EXPIRED

    B. REMOVE EXPIRED

    C. RELOCATE EXPIRED

    D. CLEANUP EXPIRED

3. **What action does RMAN take, when you issue the CROSSCHECK command at the RMAN prompt with the backup sets available on disk?**

    A. Checks all the blocks of the backup files for corruptions

    B. Determines whether the header of the backup piece is valid

    C. Only confirms whether or not the backup file exists

    D. Prepares a list of all the backup files

4. **Which of the following statements is incorrect regarding the CHANGE . . . UNCATALOG command of RMAN?**

    A. It removes the catalog records for the specified backup sets and image copies from the recovery catalog.

    B. It updates the status of the specified backup sets and image copies in the target database's control file to DELETED.

    C. It deletes the specified backup sets or image copies at the O/S.

    D. It does not delete any files from the O/S.

5. **Where can you obtain information about full database backup sets created using RMAN, if the control file was used as the repository?**

    A. V$BACKUPSET

    B. RC_DATABASE

    C. V$BACKUP_SET

    D. RC_BACKUP_SET

6. **Which of the following is not a valid RMAN command?**

    A. CHANGE . . . AVAILABLE

    B. CHANGE . . . UNCATALOG

    C. CHANGE . . . UNAVAILABLE

    D. CHANGE . . . EXPIRE

7. **Yash is maintaining an OLTP database. He performs a backup of the database using RMAN. He wants to perform maintenance tasks for the disk where the backups of archived redo log files starting from the sequence number 35 to 75 reside. Which of the following commands must Yash execute to make these files temporarily unavailable for RMAN?**

    A. CHANGE COPY OF ARCHIVELOG SEQUENCE FROM 35 TO 75 UNAVAILABLE;

    B. CHANGE COPY OF ARCHIVELOG SEQUENCE BETWEEN 35 AND 75 UNAVAILABLE;

    C. REMOVE COPY OF ARCHIVELOG SEQUENCE FROM 35 TO 75;

    D. MARK COPY OF ARCHIVELOG SEQUENCE FROM 35 TO 75 UNAVAILABLE;

8. **The KEEP FOREVER clause of the BACKUP or CHANGE command requires that:**

    A. The target database's control file be used as the repository

    B. The recovery catalog be used as a repository

    C. A media management software be used

    D. The control files be multiplexed

9. **Which CHANGE command options can you use to exempt a backup set or an image copy from the configured retention policy? (Choose two.)**

    A. KEEP FOREVER

    B. EXEMPT

    C. KEEP UNTIL

    D. NOKEEP

    E. EXCLUDE

10. **Which of the following files cannot be cataloged using the CATALOG command?**

    A. Data files

    B. Control files

    C. Archived log files

    D. Files storing RMAN scripts

Chapter Answers

1. A.   EXPIRED

Explanation   If a backup piece is inaccessible while executing the CROSSCHECK command, RMAN marks the backup piece as EXPIRED in the repository. You can view the status of a backup piece by executing the LIST command. If the backup piece is made available at the O/S, then you can issue the CROSSCHECK command to modify the status of the backup piece to AVAILABLE.

2. A.   DELETE EXPIRED

Explanation   You must issue the DELETE EXPIRED command to delete all the expired backup sets and image copies. RMAN removes the records pertaining to the nonexistent files from the repository. If, for some reason, the file still exists on the media, then RMAN issues the following error:

```
RMAN-20502: DELETE EXPIRED cannot delete objects that exist - run CROSSCHECK
```

3. B.   Determines whether the header of the backup piece is valid.

Explanation   The CROSSCHECK feature of RMAN checks the status of a backup set or image copy that is either available on disk or tape. If the backup set or image copy is on disk, then the CROSSCHECK command determines whether or not the header of the backup piece is valid. If the backup is on tape, then it simply checks for the existence of the backups.

4. C.   It deletes the specified backup sets or image copies at the O/S.

Explanation   The CHANGE . . . UNCATALOG command removes only the records for the specified backup sets and image copies from the recovery catalog. If the repository is the control file, then it marks the records status as DELETED. This command does not delete the files from their physical location.

5. C.   V$BACKUP_SET

Explanation   You can obtain the information pertaining to full database backup sets created using RMAN from the V$BACKUP_SET dynamic performance view that is present in the target database. This view reflects the information stored in the target database's control file. If you use a recovery catalog, then you can also see the records in the RC_BACKUP_SET catalog view.

6. D.   CHANGE . . . EXPIRE

Explanation   You can execute the CHANGE . . . AVAILABLE command to change the status of the backup sets and image copies from UNAVAILABLE to AVAILABLE. You can execute the CHANGE . . . UNCATALOG command to remove the record pertaining to the backup sets and image copies from the recovery catalog. This will modify the status to DELETED in the target database's control file.

You can execute the CHANGE . . . UNAVAILABLE command to change the status of the backup sets and image copies from AVAILABLE to UNAVAILABLE. This would enable you to perform the necessary maintenance tasks.

CHANGE . . . EXPIRE is not a valid RMAN command.

7. B.   CHANGE COPY OF ARCHIVELOG SEQUENCE BETWEEN 35 AND 75 UNAVAILABLE;

Explanation   RMAN enables you to change the status of the files temporarily from AVAILABLE to UNAVAILABLE using the CHANGE . . . UNAVAILABLE command. This command can also be used for specifying a range of archived redo log backups.

8. B.   The recovery catalog is used as a repository.

Explanation   You must use the recovery catalog as the repository to use KEEP FOREVER clause with the BACKUP or CHANGE command.

9. A and C.   KEEP FOREVER and KEEP UNTIL

Explanation   The KEEP UNTIL option enables you to specify a time period for which the backup set or image copy must be treated as valid and not obsolete. The KEEP FOREVER option enables you to store the information about the backup set and image copies until you explicitly specify the NOKEEP option with the CHANGE command.

10. D.   Files storing RMAN scripts

Explanation   RMAN enables you to catalog the image copies of database files that are backed up using O/S commands. You can catalog control files, data files, and archived redo log files.

CHAPTER
17

Recovery Catalog
Creation and Maintenance

n this chapter, you will learn the advantages of using the recovery catalog as the repository for RMAN and the process of creating a recovery catalog. We will explain the process of registering, resynchronizing, and resetting the target database with the recovery catalog. We will also explain with examples the usefulness of the LIST and REPORT commands. Later in this chapter, we explain how to create, store, and run scripts when using the recovery catalog. At the end of this chapter, you will find a listing of the important recovery catalog views. This chapter includes the following topics:

- Contents of the recovery catalog
- Recovery catalog creation
- Use RMAN to register, resynchronize, and reset a database
- Query the recovery catalog to generate reports and lists
- Create, store, and run scripts
- Methods of backing up and recovering the recovery catalog
- Important recovery catalog views

Contents of the Recovery Catalog

The *recovery catalog* is the most important component of RMAN. A repository is required to maintain the information regarding the operations performed when using RMAN. The repository can either be a recovery catalog or the target database's control file.

NOTE
It is recommended that you use the recovery catalog as a repository to utilize the full functionality of RMAN.

The information about RMAN operations stored in the recovery catalog includes

- Backup pieces and backup sets of data files and archived redo log files
- Image copies of data files
- Image copies of archived redo logs
- Details of the tablespaces and data files that reside on the target database

- RMAN stored scripts
- Persistent RMAN configuration settings

Recovery Catalog Considerations

It is recommended that you use a recovery catalog when managing multiple databases. A separate database for the recovery catalog is also recommended. However, if you have multiple databases and want to create the recovery catalog in one of the existing databases, you need to be aware of the ramifications. A media failure affecting the database where the recovery catalog resides would mean that you not only risk loosing the application data, but you also risk loosing the RMAN data.

Following are considerations while creating and managing the recovery catalog:

- If you have just one database and you are using RMAN, you could use the target database's control file as the repository. However, you must safeguard the current control file by multiplexing it to different locations.

- If you have multiple databases and want to use RMAN, you must follow the following guidelines:

    - If you want to store the recovery catalog in one of the existing databases, select the database that is smallest in size to keep the recovery catalog.

    - If all your databases are large, create a new database to hold the recovery catalog.

    - Include cross backups of the recovery catalog database.

    - Take an operating system (O/S) backup of the recovery catalog (offline or online).

    - Run all databases in ARCHIVELOG mode and maintain multiple backup copies of archived redo log sets.

NOTE
Ensure that the recovery catalog database and target databases do not reside on the same disks; if they do and you lose one database, you will lose the others.

Recovery Catalog Creation

The steps involved in creating the recovery catalog are divided into two phases. In the first phase, you need to configure the RMAN database. After you have either created a new catalog database or found an existing database to host the catalog, you must allocate appropriate disk space for the recovery catalog tablespace and other supporting tablespaces. Table 17-1 lists the typical recovery catalog space requirements for one year. These are rough guidelines, and you need to determine the space depending on your business rules and backup strategy.

Tablespace	Space Requirement (in Megabytes)
SYSTEM	90
TEMP	5
Rollback or UNDO	5
Recovery catalog	15

TABLE 17-1. *Typical Recovery Catalog Space Requirements*

NOTE
It is recommended that you have a minimum of three online log groups for the database and a minimum of two members in each group.

After sizing the SYSTEM, UNDO, and TEMP tablespaces to meet your requirement, you need to create the recovery catalog tablespace to store the catalog schema, as shown in the following code:

```
SQL> CREATE TABLESPACE rcvcat DATAFILE 'd:\oracle\oradata\support\rcvcat01.dbf' SIZE 40M
  2   EXTENT MANAGEMENT LOCAL
  3   SEGMENT SPACE MANAGEMENT AUTO;
Tablespace created.
```

You must create a separate user who would own the catalog schema. This user must be granted the RECOVERY_CATALOG_OWNER role, which provides the privileges to maintain and query the recovery catalog schema as shown in the following code. You can also grant the user other roles like CONNECT and RESOURCE.

```
SQL> CREATE USER rman IDENTIFIED BY rman
  2   DEFAULT TABLESPACE rcvcat
  3   TEMPORARY TABLESPACE temp
  4   QUOTA UNLIMITED ON rcvcat;
User created.

SQL> GRANT RECOVERY_CATALOG_OWNER TO rman;
Grant succeeded.
```

After you complete the previous steps, you are ready to create a recovery catalog. You must initially run the RMAN executable and establish a connection with the RMAN user where the catalog needs to be created as shown in the following code:

```
C:\>RMAN CATALOG rman/rman
Recovery Manager: Release 9.0.1.0.0 - Beta
(c) Copyright 2001 Oracle Corporation.  All rights reserved.
connected to recovery catalog database
recovery catalog is not installed
```

You must now issue the CREATE CATALOG command at the RMAN prompt to create the necessary objects by specifying the recovery catalog tablespace name as shown in the following code:

```
RMAN> CREATE CATALOG TABLESPACE 'RCVCAT';
recovery catalog created
```

NOTE
The name of the tablespace must be enclosed within single quotes without any white spaces. The tablespace name is case sensitive. If you specify the tablespace name in lowercase, you will get the following error message:

```
RMAN> CREATE CATALOG TABLESPACE 'rcvcat';
error occurred in source file: krmk.pc, line: 6746
text of failing SQL statement: î_?_
ORACLE error from recovery catalog database: ORA-00959: tablespace 'rcvcat'
does not exist
RMAN-00571: ===========================================================
RMAN-00569: =============== ERROR MESSAGE STACK FOLLOWS ===============
RMAN-00571: ===========================================================
RMAN-00579: the following error occurred at 10/23/2001 11:51:21
RMAN-06433: error installing recovery catalog
```

Use RMAN to Register, Resynchronize, and Reset a Database

The following sections explain the process of registering, resynchronizing, and resetting the target database with the recovery catalog.

Registering a Database

You must first connect to the recovery catalog and to the target database and then register as shown in the following code:

```
C:\>RMAN CATALOG rman/rman TARGET sys/sys@target.india
Recovery Manager: Release 9.0.1.0.0 - Beta
(c) Copyright 2001 Oracle Corporation.  All rights reserved.
connected to target database: TARGET (DBID=2842823597)
connected to recovery catalog database

RMAN> REGISTER DATABASE;
database registered in recovery catalog
starting full resync of recovery catalog
full resync complete
```

After you execute the previous command, RMAN identifies the database with a unique database identifier (dbid) and then creates rows in the repository that store information about the target database. RMAN then performs a full resynchronization with the recovery catalog in which it transfers all pertinent data about the target database from the control file and saves it in the recovery catalog.

NOTE
Because RMAN identifies a database by dbid and not by name, you can't register two databases cloned from the same database.

To test whether or not RMAN has successfully registered the target database, you can execute any command that queries the details of the target database from the recovery catalog. As an example, we execute the REPORT SCHEMA command, which displays the target database structure from the recovery catalog repository:

```
RMAN> REPORT SCHEMA;
Report of database schema
File K-bytes    Tablespace    RB segs Datafile Name
---- ----------  ------------- ------- -------------------
1       225280 SYSTEM          YES      D:\ORACLE\ORADATA\TARGET\SYSTEM01.DBF
2       128000 UNDOTBS         YES
D:\ORACLE\ORADATA\TARGET\UNDOTBS01.DBF
3         5120 INDX_TS         NO       D:\ORACLE\ORADATA\TARGET\INDX01.DBF
6          100 USERS           NO       D:\ORACLE\ORADATA\TARGET\USERS.DBF
```

You would encounter the following error if any command were executed against the target database that is not registered with the recovery catalog:

```
RMAN> BACKUP DATABASE;
Starting backup at 23-OCT-01
RMAN-00571: ===========================================================
RMAN-00569: =============== ERROR MESSAGE STACK FOLLOWS ===============
RMAN-00571: ===========================================================
RMAN-00579: the following error occurred at 10/23/2001 12:50:52
RMAN-03002: failure during compilation of command
RMAN-03013: command type: backup
RMAN-06004: ORACLE error from recovery catalog database:
RMAN-20001: target database not found in recovery catalog
```

The recovery catalog is automatically updated each time a BACKUP, COPY, RESTORE, or SWITCH command is executed using RMAN.

NOTE
Information related to the redo logs switches and archived redo log files is not automatically updated in the recovery catalog. It is recommended that you manually resynchronize the catalog to update this information.

Resynchronization of the Database

Resynchronization with the recovery catalog can be either *full* or *partial*. As part of a partial resynchronization, RMAN reads the target database's control file to update changed information related to new backups, new archived logs, and so on. It is important that you perform a full resynchronization more frequently than the value (in days) specified for the CONTROL_FILE_RECORD_KEEP_TIME initialization parameter.

During full resynchronization, RMAN updates all changed records and resynchronizes the metadata about the target database's logical and physical structure: data files, tablespaces, redo threads, undo segments (while the database is open), and online redo logs.

RMAN performs the following steps while resynchronizing:

1. Creates a snapshot of the target database control file

2. Compares the information about the target database in the recovery catalog with the snapshot

3. Performs an update of any information that is unavailable in the catalog

RMAN performs a partial or full resynchronization automatically when certain RMAN commands like BACKUP, COPY, and DELETE are issued. This avoids the need to manually resynchronize the catalog using the RESYNC CATALOG command. You will need to perform manual resynchronization when

■ The database is operating in ARCHIVELOG mode, and the rate at which archive logs are being generated is high.

NOTE
The changes to the target database must be propagated to the recovery catalog periodically. If a database crashes, resulting in a loss of all files including control files, then RMAN would not be able to use the archived redo logs generated since the last resynchronization, and hence, you would need to perform user-managed recovery to apply all the available archived redo logs.

■ A structural change occurred to the database, for example, adding or dropping of tablespaces, data files, log groups, and log members.

To perform a manual resynchronization, you must execute the following command:

```
RMAN> RESYNC CATALOG;
starting full resync of recovery catalog
full resync complete
```

Resetting a Database

RMAN cannot use the recovery catalog information about a database if the database has been opened with the RESETLOGS option after an incomplete recovery. You must issue the RESET DATABASE command to reflect that the target database has been opened with the RESETLOGS option. RMAN automatically generates a new database incarnation record in the recovery catalog if you execute one of the following commands:

```
RMAN> ALTER DATABASE OPEN RESETLOGS
RMAN> OPEN RESETLOGS DATABASE
```

RMAN updates the recovery catalog with a unique number to distinguish between the present and the previous incarnations. This prevents any archived redo logs or online redo logs from being applied to an incorrect incarnation of the database. RMAN enables you to restore backups, which are from a different incarnation, by undoing the effects of RESETLOGS. You must execute the following command specifying the incarnation key:

```
RMAN> RESET DATABASE TO INCARNATION 181;
```

NOTE
To obtain the information related to database incarnations, you must execute the LIST INCARNATION command.

Maintain the Recovery Catalog by Using RMAN Commands

In certain circumstances, you need to move a database from one recovery catalog to another as part of your modified backup and recovery strategy. You can do this by deregistering a database from one recovery catalog and registering it with the other recovery catalog. RMAN has the provision to deregister a database using the DBMS_RCVCAT package, which is explained in the following section.

Deregistering a Database from the Recovery Catalog Using the DBMS_RCVCAT Package

Once the deregistration process is over, you can no longer use the backup sets that were taken with the recovery catalog for recovering the target database. For deregistering a database, you need to obtain the database details, such as database id number (DB_ID) and database key (DB_KEY), that are stored in the recovery catalog. You can obtain the values for DB_ID and DB_KEY by querying the RC_DATABASE view as shown in the following code:

```
SQL> SELECT * FROM rc_database;

    DB_KEY    DBINC_KEY         DBID NAME     RESETLOGS_CHANGE# RESETLOGS
---------- ---------- ---------- -------- ----------------- ---------
       897        898 2842823597 TARGET             1238199 18-OCT-01
      1057       1058  766397535 DEVRMAN                  1 06-OCT-01
```

After obtaining the values for DB_KEY and DB_ID, you should execute the DBMS_RCVCAT.UNREGISTERDATABASE procedure to deregister the database as shown in the following code. In this example, the DB_KEY and DB_ID values are 1057 and 766397535, respectively:

```
SQL> EXECUTE dbms_rcvcat.unregisterdatabase(1057,766397535);
PL/SQL procedure successfully completed.
```

Query the Recovery Catalog to Generate Reports and Lists

In Oracle9*i*, RMAN provides detailed reporting features. You can use the REPORT or the LIST commands to generate comprehensive reports on backup sets and image copies. In the following section, we discuss these commands in detail.

LIST Command

The LIST command queries the repository and generates a list of all the backup sets and image copies recorded in the RMAN's metadata that are specific to a database. This command generates a list and helps you determine which backup sets or image copies are available. The following information can be obtained from the repository using the LIST command:

- Backup sets or image copies of a specified database, tablespace, data file, archived redo log, or control file

- Expired backup sets or image copies

- Backup sets and image copies restricted by options such as time, path name, device type, tag, or recoverability

- The incarnation of a specified database or all databases registered with the recovery catalog

NOTE
Ensure that you have at least one whole database backup available at any given time. The STATUS column in the LIST command output displays the availability of backup sets and image copies.

Refer to Oracle9*i* Recovery Manager Reference Guide of the Oracle documentation for complete syntax of the LIST and REPORT commands.

To list all the backup sets and the associated backup pieces, you must execute the following command:

```
RMAN> LIST BACKUP;

List of Backup Sets
===================
BS Key  Type LV Size      Device Type Elapsed Time Completion Time
------- ---- -- ---------- ----------- ------------ ---------------
63      Full    2M         DISK        00:00:01     19-OCT-01
        BP Key: 69   Status: AVAILABLE   Tag: FRIDAYCTLBUP
        Piece Name: C:\BACKUPS\0BD6VU47.1
  Controlfile Included: Ckp SCN: 1239583     Ckp time: 19-OCT-01

BS Key  Type LV Size      Device Type Elapsed Time Completion Time
------- ---- -- ---------- ----------- ------------ ---------------
247     Full    231M       DISK        00:00:43     23-OCT-01
        BP Key: 248   Status: AVAILABLE   Tag:
        Piece Name: C:\BACKUPS\0KD7ARSL.1
  Controlfile Included: Ckp SCN: 1327666     Ckp time: 23-OCT-01
  List of Datafiles in backup set 247

  File LV Type Ckp SCN    Ckp Time  Name
  ---- -- ---- ---------- --------- ----
  1       Full 1327667    23-OCT-01 D:\ORACLE\ORADATA\TARGET\SYSTEM01.DBF
  2       Full 1327667    23-OCT-01 D:\ORACLE\ORADATA\TARGET\UNDOTBS01.DBF
  3       Full 1327667    23-OCT-01 D:\ORACLE\ORADATA\TARGET\INDX01.DBF
  6       Full 1327667    23-OCT-01 D:\ORACLE\ORADATA\TARGET\USERS.DBF
```

To list all the image copies, you must execute the following command:

```
RMAN> LIST COPY;
```

To list all the expired backup sets and the associated backup pieces, you must execute the following command:

```
RMAN> LIST EXPIRED BACKUPSET;
```

To list all the expired image copies, you must execute the following command:

```
RMAN> LIST EXPIRED COPY;

List of Datafile Copies
Key     File S Completion Time Ckp SCN   Ckp Time        Name
------- ---- - --------------- --------- --------------- ----
80      6    X 22-OCT-01       1285852   22-OCT-01       D:\ORACLE\ORADATA\TARGET\BACKUP\MYUSER
```

To list the backup of data files for the tablespace USERS that were performed before October 25, 2001, you must execute the following command:

```
RMAN> LIST BACKUP OF TABLESPACE users COMPLETED BEFORE '25-OCT-01';

List of Backup Sets
===================
BS Key  Type LV Size       Device Type Elapsed Time Completion Time
------- ---- -- ---------- ----------- ------------ ---------------
7579    Full 1M            DISK        00:00:37     24-OCT-01
        BP Key: 7580   Status: AVAILABLE   Tag:
        Piece Name: C:\BACKUPS\05D7CPU1_1_1.F
  List of Datafiles in backup set 7579
  File LV Type Ckp SCN   Ckp Time  Name
  ---- -- ---- ---------- --------- ----
  5       Full 156051    24-OCT-01 D:\ORACLE\ORADATA\DEVRMAN\USERS01.DBF
```

To list the database incarnations registered in the database, you must execute the following command:

```
RMAN> LIST INCARNATION OF DATABASE;

List of Database Incarnations
DB Key  Inc Key DB Name  DB ID            CUR Reset SCN  Reset Time
------- ------- -------- ---------------- --- ---------- ----------
1       2       TARGET   2842823597       NO  1238199    18-OCT-01
1       96      TARGET   2842823597       NO  1306977    23-OCT-01
1       181     TARGET   2842823597       NO  1307214    23-OCT-01
1       205     TARGET   2842823597       YES 1327474    23-OCT-01
```

REPORT Command

The REPORT command performs detailed analysis of the information stored in the repository and displays detailed outputs on backup sets or image copies. The output of the REPORT command can also be stored in a message log file. For saving reports in a file, you need to specify the MSGLOG or LOG option while connecting to RMAN from the O/S command prompt.

The REPORT command can be used to obtain the following information:

- Files that need backups

- Files on which unrecoverable operations have been performed

- Backup sets or image copies that are obsolete

- Physical schema of a database at a previous time

- Files that have not been backed up recently

The following example displays details of the objects that need a backup and conform to the retention policy:

```
RMAN> REPORT NEED BACKUP;
RMAN retention policy will be applied to the command
RMAN retention policy is set to redundancy 1
Report of files with less than 1 redundant backups


File #bkps Name
---- ----- -------------------------------------------------------
1     0     D:\ORACLE\ORADATA\DEVRMAN\SYSTEM01.DBF
2     0     D:\ORACLE\ORADATA\DEVRMAN\UNDOTBS01.DBF
3     0     D:\ORACLE\ORADATA\DEVRMAN\INDX01.DBF
4     0     D:\ORACLE\ORADATA\DEVRMAN\TOOLS01.DBF
5     0     D:\ORACLE\ORADATA\DEVRMAN\USERS01.DBF
```

You can specify various parameters with the REPORT NEED BACKUP command. These are defined in the following section.

The REDUNDANCY parameter specifies the minimum number of backup sets or image copies that must exist for a data file to be considered as not in need of a backup. If you do not specify the parameter, REDUNDANCY defaults to 1. The DAYS parameter indicates that recovery must begin by using logs more than the value specified (in days). To override the retention policy, run REPORT NEED BACKUP DAYS. Any files older than the DAYS parameter value need a new backup because their backups require the specified number of DAYS worth of archived logs for recovery (see the following command):

```
RMAN> REPORT NEED BACKUP DAYS=7 DATABASE;
```

To determine which files need an incremental backup, specify the INCREMENTAL parameter. If complete recovery of a data file requires more than the specified number of incremental backups, then RMAN considers it in need of a new backup. For example, execute the following command to use the INCREMENTAL parameter:

```
RMAN> REPORT NEED BACKUP INCREMENTAL = 1 DATABASE;
```

To display all data files that cannot be recovered from existing backups, you must execute the following command:

```
RMAN> REPORT UNRECOVERABLE;
Report of files that need backup due to unrecoverable operations

File Type of Backup Required Name
---- ---------------------- -----------------------------------
1    full                     D:\ORACLE\ORADATA\DEVRMAN\SYSTEM01.DBF
```

In the previous example, the output shows that the data file SYSTEM01.DBF cannot be recovered. You should note that RMAN considers a tablespace or data file unrecoverable only when an unrecoverable operation has been performed against an object residing in the data file since the last backup of the data file was completed.

NOTE
RMAN will not consider the nonexistence of any backup of a data file as unrecoverable.

To list all the backup sets and image copies that are OBSOLETE and can be deleted, you must execute the following command:

```
RMAN> REPORT OBSOLETE;
RMAN retention policy will be applied to the command
RMAN retention policy is set to redundancy 1
Report of obsolete backups and copies
Type             Key   Completion Time   Filename/Handle
---------------- ----- ---------------- --------------------
Backup Set       7579  24-OCT-01
```

```
    Backup Piece    7580    24-OCT-01        C:\BACKUPS\05D7CPU1_1_1.F
Backup Set          7592    24-OCT-01
    Backup Piece    7594    24-OCT-01        D:\ORACLE\ORA90\DATABASE\06D7CQUU_1_1
Backup Set          7593    24-OCT-01
    Backup Piece    7595    24-OCT-01        D:\ORACLE\ORA90\DATABASE\07D7CQUU_1_1
```

To display the physical schema of the database by querying the information from the repository, you must execute the following command:

```
RMAN> REPORT SCHEMA;
Report of database schema

File K-bytes    Tablespace    RB segs Datafile Name
---- ---------- ------------------ ------- -------------------
1      153600   SYSTEM        YES     D:\ORACLE\ORADATA\DEVRMAN\SYSTEM01.DBF
2       87040   UNDOTBS       YES     D:\ORACLE\ORADATA\DEVRMAN\UNDOTBS01.DBF
3        5120   INDX          NO      D:\ORACLE\ORADATA\DEVRMAN\INDX01.DBF
4        5120   TOOLS         NO      D:\ORACLE\ORADATA\DEVRMAN\TOOLS01.DBF
5       10240   USERS         NO      D:\ORACLE\ORADATA\DEVRMAN\USERS01.DBF
```

NOTE
You must use a recovery catalog when issuing a REPORT SCHEMA command with the TIME, SCN, or LOGSEQ options. Otherwise, a recovery catalog is not required for the REPORT command.

Create, Store, and Run Scripts

A *stored script* is a sequence of RMAN commands stored within the recovery catalog repository. It provides a common repository of frequently executed RMAN commands. It is recommended that you maintain the stored scripts that are often used to perform backup operations in the recovery catalog repository. Storing the scripts in the repository requires minimal effort.

To create a new script, you must use the CREATE SCRIPT command at the RMAN prompt. For example, you can execute the following commands to create a new script, which would perform a full backup and include all the archived redo log files:

```
RMAN> CREATE SCRIPT Full_backup
2> {
3> ALLOCATE CHANNEL ch1 TYPE DISK;
4> ALLOCATE CHANNEL ch2 TYPE DISK;
```

```
5> ALLOCATE CHANNEL ch3 TYPE DISK;
6> ALLOCATE CHANNEL ch4 TYPE DISK;
7> BACKUP FULL
8>      TAG weekly_inc_backup
9>      FILESPERSET 6
10>     DATABASE PLUS ARCHIVELOG;
11> }
created script Full_backup
```

You can use the RC_STORED_SCRIPT and RC_STORED_SCRIPT_LINE views of the recovery catalog to view the information about this script, as shown in the following command:

```
SQL> SELECT * FROM rc_stored_script;
DB_KEY DB_NAME  SCRIPT_NAME
------ -------- --------------------------------------------
  7768 DEVRMAN  Full_backup

SQL> SELECT text FROM rc_stored_script_line WHERE db_key=7768
  2  AND script_name='Full_backup';
TEXT
-------------------------------------------------------------
{
ALLOCATE CHANNEL ch1 TYPE DISK;
ALLOCATE CHANNEL ch2 TYPE DISK;
ALLOCATE CHANNEL ch3 TYPE DISK;
ALLOCATE CHANNEL ch4 TYPE DISK;
BACKUP FULL
TAG weekly_inc_backup
FILESPERSET 6
DATABASE PLUS ARCHIVELOG;
}
```

To replace an existing script in the recovery catalog, you must use the REPLACE SCRIPT command. For example, you can execute the following command to replace the existing script Full_Backup with a set of new commands as shown in the following code:

```
RMAN> REPLACE SCRIPT Full_backup
2> {
3>   BACKUP DATABASE INCLUDE CURRENT CONTROLFILE;
4> }
replaced script Full_backup
```

You can then confirm the changes by querying the RC_STORED_SCRIPT_LINE view as shown below:

```
SQL> SELECT text FROM rc_stored_script_line WHERE db_key=7768
  2  AND script_name='Full_backup';
TEXT
------------------------------------------------------------
{
BACKUP DATABASE INCLUDE CURRENT CONTROLFILE;
}
```

NOTE
The stored scripts are specific to the target database that you are connected to. In case you want to run the same script for another target database, you can do so by editing the stored script using DML operations on the RC_STORED_SCRIPT and RC_STORED_SCRIPT_LINE views.

To execute a stored script, you must use the EXECUTE SCRIPT command in a RUN block, as shown in the following code:

```
RMAN> RUN {EXECUTE SCRIPT Full_backup;}
executing script: Full_backup
Starting backup at 24-OCT-01
allocated channel: ORA_DISK_1
channel ORA_DISK_1: sid=12 devtype=DISK
channel ORA_DISK_1: starting full datafile backupset
channel ORA_DISK_1: specifying datafile(s) in backupset
including current controlfile in backupset
input datafile fno=00001 name=D:\ORACLE\ORADATA\DEVRMAN\SYSTEM01.DBF
input datafile fno=00002 name=D:\ORACLE\ORADATA\DEVRMAN\UNDOTBS01.DBF
input datafile fno=00005 name=D:\ORACLE\ORADATA\DEVRMAN\USERS01.DBF
input datafile fno=00003 name=D:\ORACLE\ORADATA\DEVRMAN\INDX01.DBF
input datafile fno=00004 name=D:\ORACLE\ORADATA\DEVRMAN\TOOLS01.DBF
channel ORA_DISK_1: starting piece 1 at 24-OCT-01
channel ORA_DISK_1: finished piece 1 at 24-OCT-01
piece handle=D:\ORACLE\ORA90\DATABASE\0CD7CRJV_1_1 comment=NONE
channel ORA_DISK_1: backup set complete, elapsed time: 00:00:35
Finished backup at 24-OCT-01
```

In order to delete an existing script, you must use the DELETE SCRIPT command and specify the name of the script, as shown in the following code:

```
RMAN> DELETE SCRIPT Full_backup;
deleted script: Full_backup
```

Methods of Backing Up and Recovering the Recovery Catalog

It is almost impossible to perform recovery on the target database if the recovery catalog is inaccessible. Because all information related to backup sets and image copies is maintained by the catalog, it is recommended that you have a sound backup and recovery strategy for the recovery catalog database.

If a backup of the recovery catalog database is not available and the catalog database crashes, then you run the risk of loosing some or all of your RMAN data. To avoid this situation, you must consider building a consistent backup and recovery strategy for the catalog database. You must back up the recovery catalog as frequently as you back up your target database. In addition, *cross backups* should be performed, which will be discussed in the following sections. You must also perform a physical and logical backup of the catalog database. The physical and logical backup options are discussed in detail in the following section.

NOTE
It is recommended that you operate the recovery catalog database in ARCHIVELOG mode.

Physical Backups

The physical backup of the recovery catalog database can be performed using RMAN or O/S commands. The advantage of performing a backup of the catalog database using O/S commands is that you do not need to use RMAN to restore the backups during the course of a media failure.

You can perform a backup of the recovery catalog database using RMAN, but you must start RMAN with the NOCATALOG option so that the backup repository for the recovery catalog is the control file in the catalog database. You must then perform frequent backups of this control file. For example, you can back up the control file using the SQL command shown in the following code:

```
SQL> ALTER DATABASE BACKUP CONTROLFILE TO 'c:\backup\cf.bak' REUSE;
```

NOTE
You must remember to set the CONTROL_FILE_RECORD_KEEP_TIME initialization parameter to a value that is high enough to store an adequate amount of historical backup data.

It is important that you create cross backups of the recovery catalog database. For example, let's assume you have four databases: db1, db2, db3, and db4. You can keep backup information of db1, db2, and db4 in catalog 3 that resides on db3. The backup information of db3 can reside in catalog 4 that resides on db4. This is called cross backups. If you lose both db3 and db4, you can't perform recovery. Therefore, it is good practice to take a physical backup of one of the catalog databases in addition to your regular backup strategy.

Some DBAs create another recovery catalog in a separate database. The main catalog is kept synchronized as normal, while the secondary catalog is synchronized manually by periodically issuing the RESYNC catalog command. Never store a recovery catalog containing the RMAN repository for a database in the same database as your target database.

Logical Backups

You can perform logical database backup using the **export** utility. You can perform a logical backup of the recovery catalog database or the required schema objects by running the export executable. To perform an export of the user who owns the recovery catalog objects, you must execute the following command at the O/S command prompt:

```
C:\>EXP USERID=system/manager@support.india FILE=rmancat.dmp LOG=rmancat.log OWNER=rman CONSISTENT=Y
```

Always ensure that the export is successfully performed without any errors and warnings by viewing the export log file.

Recovering the Recovery Catalog

Recovery operations for the recovery catalog database entirely depend on the backup strategy you implement. We have discussed in the previous section about different types of backups options that you can use. Therefore, the possible recovery operations are based on the backup method used:

- If you have backed up the recovery catalog database using O/S commands, then you must use the O/S commands to restore the backup and perform a user-managed recovery using the **SQL*Plus** utility.

- If you have used RMAN to perform a backup of the catalog database, then you must use relevant restoration and recovery procedures.

- If a logical backup of the recovery catalog schema was performed, then you must use the **import** utility to recover. If the entire database has crashed, you will need to create a new database and a user who would hereafter own the repository. After the creation of the new database, you would need to perform an import from the export dump file into this newly created user by specifying the FROMUSER and TOUSER import parameters. The command to import the recovery catalog is shown in the following code:

```
C:\> IMP USERID=system/manager@new_cat FILE=rmancat.dmp
LOG=rmancatimp.log FROMUSER=rman TOUSER=rcat
```

Re-Creating the Recovery Catalog

If you don't have cross backups and the recovery catalog database has crashed and you are not able to recover the data using normal Oracle recovery mechanisms, then you must re-create the catalog. You have two options for partially re-creating the contents of the old catalog:

- Issue CATALOG commands to recatalog all the archived redo logs, backup control files, and data file copies.

- Use the RESYNC CATALOG FROM CONTROLFILECOPY command to extract information from a backup control file, and rebuild the recovery catalog from it.

You can re-create information about backup sets only by using the RESYNC CATALOG FROM CONTROLFILECOPY command because the CATALOG command does not support recataloging of backup pieces or backup sets. RMAN does not verify that the files being recataloged still exist, so the resynchronization may add records for files that no longer exist. Remove such records by issuing the CHANGE . . . CROSSCHECK or CROSSCHECK BACKUP commands.

Important Recovery Catalog Views

We have described some of the important recovery catalog views in Table 17-2. By querying these recovery catalog views, you can obtain the information about the target database structure, incarnations, synchronization information, backup sets, image copies, and corruptions. You can also view the stored scripts, which are recorded in the recovery catalog.

View Name	Description
RC_DATABASE	This view displays information about the target databases, which are registered in the recovery catalog.
RC_DATABASE_INCARNATION	This view displays the incarnation information about all target databases that are registered with the recovery catalog.
RC_RESYNC	This view displays information about the recovery catalog resynchronizations.
RC_RMAN_CONFIGURATION	This view displays information about RMAN's persistent configuration settings.
RC_STORED_SCRIPT	This view displays information about scripts stored in the recovery catalog.
RC_STORED_SCRIPT_LINE	This view displays the lines of code for each script that is stored in the recovery catalog.
RC_TABLESPACE	This view displays all the tablespaces that exist or existed for a target database and also those tablespaces that belong to databases of previous incarnations.
RC_DATAFILE	This view displays information about all data files registered in the recovery catalog.
RC_REDO_LOG	This view displays information about the online redo log files for all the incarnations of the database since the last catalog resynchronization.
RC_LOG_HISTORY	This view displays the historical data about the online redo logs.
RC_REDO_THREAD	This view displays the data about all redo threads for all incarnations of the database since the last catalog resynchronization.
RC_ARCHIVED_LOG	This view displays historical information about archived and unarchived redo logs.

TABLE 17-2. *Recovery Catalog Views*

View Name	Description
RC_BACKUP_CONTROLFILE	This view displays information related to the backup of the control file.
RC_BACKUP_DATAFILE	This view displays information about the target database data files in backup sets.
RC_BACKUP_REDOLOG	This view displays the information about archived redo logs in backup sets.
RC_BACKUP_SET	This view displays the information about backup sets from all the incarnations of the database.
RC_BACKUP_PIECE	This view displays the information about backup pieces.
RC_CONTROLFILE_COPY	This view displays information regarding control file copies stored on disk.
RC_DATAFILE_COPY	This view lists information about data file copies stored on disk.
RC_BACKUP_CORRUPTION	This view displays the corrupt block ranges that occur in data file backups.
RC_COPY_CORRUPTION	This view displays the corrupt block ranges that occur in data file copies.

TABLE 17-2. *Recovery Catalog Views (continued)*

Chapter Questions

1. **RMAN stores information about the operations performed on the target database in the recovery catalog. Which of the following is not stored in the recovery catalog?**

   Information regarding:

   A. Backup sets of data file and archived redo log files

   B. Backup sets of online redo log files

   C. Image copies of data files

   D. Image copies of archived redo logs

   E. RMAN stored scripts

2. **Which of the following roles provides the privileges to maintain and query the recovery catalog schema?**

   A. EXECUTE_CATALOG_ROLE

   B. CONNECT

   C. RESOURCE

   D. RECOVERY_CATALOG_OWNER

   E. RECOVERY_CATALOG_USER

3. **What action would you perform to overcome the following error?**

   ```
   RMAN-00571: ===============================================================
   RMAN-00569: =============== ERROR MESSAGE STACK FOLLOWS ===============
   RMAN-00571: ===============================================================
   RMAN-00579: the following error occurred at 10/23/2001 12:50:52
   RMAN-03002: failure during compilation of command
   RMAN-03013: command type: backup
   RMAN-06004: ORACLE error from recovery catalog database: RMAN-20001:
   target database not found in recovery catalog
   ```

   A. Create a recovery catalog.

   B. Increase the size of the tablespace that holds the objects pertaining to the catalog.

C. Resynchronize the catalog with the target database.

D. Register the target database.

E. Reset the target database because the recovery catalog does not recognize the database after starting with the RESETLOGS option.

4. **Which one of the following steps is performed by RMAN while resynchronizing the catalog?**

   A. Creates a snapshot of the target database control file

   B. Compares the information about the target database in the recovery catalog with the AUTOBACKUP of the control file

   C. Updates the target database control file with the information that is available in the catalog

   D. Deletes all the data from the recovery catalog and rebuilds it based on any new data present in the control file

5. **Which of the following commands requires you to manually reset the database using the RESET DATABASE command?**

   A. RMAN> BACKUP DATABASE;

   B. RMAN> ALTER DATABASE OPEN RESETLOGS;

   C. RMAN> SQL 'ALTER DATABASE OPEN RESETLOGS';

   D. RMAN> OPEN RESETLOGS DATABASE;

   E. SQL> ALTER DATABASE OPEN NORESETLOGS;

6. **Which of the following commands displays the information about the incarnation of all the databases registered in the recovery catalog?**

   A. LIST COMPLETE INCARNATION

   B. LIST INCARNATION

   C. REPORT INCARNATION

   D. DATABASE INCARNATION

7. **Pam has created a separate database that is operating in ARCHIVELOG mode to store the recovery catalog. She uses RMAN to perform backup and recovery operations for three production databases. She creates image copies of all the catalog database files once a month using O/S commands. If the recovery catalog database crashes, resulting in a loss of data files and the current control file, what must she do to recover the catalog database?**

   A. Restore the earlier backup and perform a user-managed complete recovery.

   B. Restore the earlier backup and perform a server-managed incomplete recovery.

   C. Create a new database and import the logical backups.

   D. Create a new database and change the mode to NOARCHIVELOG mode.

8. **Which is the most appropriate view that you could query to obtain information about the target database's incarnation, which is available in the recovery catalog?**

   A. RC_DATABASE

   B. RC_RESYNC

   C. RC_DATABASE_INCARNATION

   D. RC_RMAN_CONFIGURATION

   E. RC_INCARNATION_DATABASE

9. **Which view must you query to display the code associated with RMAN stored scripts?**

   A. RC_STORED_SCRIPT

   B. RC_STORED_SCRIPT_LINE

   C. RC_SCRIPTS

   D. RC_STORED_LINE_SCRIPT

   E. None of the above

10. **Which command must you execute to extract information from a backup control file to rebuild the recovery catalog?**

    A. RESET DATABASE TO INCARNATION <integer>;

    B. RESYNC CATALOG FROM CONTROLFILECOPY;

    C. RESYNC CATALOG;

    D. RESET DATABASE;

    E. RESYNC CATALOG FROM BACKUP CONTROLFILECOPY;

Chapter Answers

1. B.   Backup of online redo log files

Explanation   RMAN does not back up the online redo logs. RMAN only stores information about the redo log files that are archived.

2. D.   RECOVERY_CATALOG_OWNER

Explanation   The user must be granted the RECOVER_CATALOG_OWNER role to maintain and query the recovery catalog schema.

3. D.   Register the target database.

Explanation   You get this error if the target database is not registered with the catalog. You must register the target database before performing any RMAN operations while using the catalog.

4. A.   Creates a snapshot of the target database's control file

Explanation   RMAN performs the following steps as part of resynchronizing the recovery catalog:

- Creates a snapshot of the target database's control file

- Compares the information about the target database in the recovery catalog with the snapshot

- Performs an update of any information that is unavailable in the catalog

5. C.   RMAN> SQL 'ALTER DATABASE OPEN RESETLOGS';

Explanation   RMAN requires you to execute the RESET DATABASE command whenever you open the database with the RESETLOGS option. RMAN automatically generates a new database incarnation record in the recovery catalog if you execute any of the following RMAN commands:

```
RMAN> ALTER DATABASE OPEN RESETLOGS
```

or

```
RMAN> OPEN RESETLOGS DATABASE
```

Note that if you open the database with the RESETLOGS option using the SQL command (enclosed in the SQL '<command>'), then you must manually reset the database information thereby creating a new incarnation.

6. B.   LIST INCARNATION

Explanation   To view the various incarnations that are registered in the recovery catalog, you must execute the LIST INCARNATION command.

7. A.   Restore the earlier backup and perform a user-managed complete recovery.

Explanation   Pam must perform a user-managed complete recovery by restoring all the data files and control files from the backup. She can recover completely as she has the online log files and the archived redo logs.

8. C.   RC_DATABASE_INCARNATION

Explanation   You must query the recovery catalog view RC_DATABASE_INCARNATION to obtain the incarnation information about all the target databases that are registered with the recovery catalog. RMAN appends a record about the database present incarnation whenever you execute the RESET DATABASE command after opening the database with the RESETLOGS option.

9. B.   RC_STORED_SCRIPT_LINE

Explanation   You must query the recovery catalog view RC_STORED_SCRIPT_LINE to obtain the code associated with the RMAN stored scripts. This view contains one row for each line of the stored script.

10. B. RESYNC CATALOG FROM CONTROLFILECOPY

Explanation The RESYNC CATALOG FROM CONTROLFILECOPY command extracts information from a backup control file and rebuilds the recovery catalog from it. You can re-create information about backup sets only by using this command because the recovery catalog does not support recataloging of backup sets and backup pieces.

CHAPTER
18

Transporting Data
Between Databases

n this chapter, you will learn the concepts and importance of using the **export** and **import** utilities. You will learn the various modes for **export** and **import** and how to invoke the utilities. This chapter includes the following topics:

- Oracle logical backups

- Export concepts and structures

- Import concepts and structures

- List of export and import parameters

- Methods to invoke export and import

- Perform export and import operations

- List guidelines for using export and import

Oracle Logical Backups

We have discussed physical backups in the previous chapters. A *logical backup* is defined as a backup of the logical schema objects. A logical backup copies the data in the database, but does not record the physical location of the data copied.

To perform a logical backup, you must use the **export** utility that is provided with the Oracle server. The **export** utility creates a file in an Oracle-specific binary format to store the data and the metadata pertaining to the various logical objects of the database. The export file in turn can be used by the **import** utility to restore the data back to an Oracle database. The full database backups performed using the **export** utility can be used to supplement physical backups, but it is recommended that you include both types of backups in your backup and recovery strategy.

Advantages of Using the Export and Import Utilities

There are numerous advantages of performing logical backups with the **export** utility. A few of them are given in the following list:

- The **export** utility checks for corrupt data blocks because it uses SQL to scan and copy the data. Unless you fix the corruptions, you can't export the data successfully.

- The export backups provide an extra level of protection against human errors. For example, if a user has accidentally dropped a static table, you can use the **import** utility to restore the table. In case of dynamic tables, you can still import the table data and definition, but any changes made to the table since the last export would be lost.

■ You can use the **export** utility to export part of the table data by specifying the QUERY parameter.

■ The binary dump files generated with the **export** utility are portable across platforms. This helps you transfer data objects between Oracle databases residing on different machines.

■ You can use the **export** utility to reorganize and defragment data.

■ You can use the **export** and **import** utilities to change the partitioning scheme.

■ You can use the **export** and **import** utilities to upgrade to a newer version or release of Oracle.

The disadvantage of performing logical backups using the **export** utility is that it takes more time to export data when compared to performing a physical backup. Another major disadvantage of using the **export** utility is that any changes made to an object after performing an export would not be stored into the export dump file. This means that changes made to the objects since the export was done cannot be recovered because redo cannot be applied to the export dump file.

Export Concepts and Structures

Before running the **export** utility you must ensure that the following tasks are completed:

■ Execution of the script CATEXP.SQL or CATALOG.SQL.

■ Sufficient disk or tape storage space is available to create the export dump file.

■ Users must possess the appropriate privileges to perform the export operation.

You should run the CATALOG.SQL script when you create a database. This script automatically runs CATEXP.SQL. The CATEXP.SQL script assigns necessary privileges to the EXP_FULL_DATABASE and IMP_FULL_DATABASE roles. As a DBA, you need these two roles to do a full database export and import. Users possessing these two roles are known as *privileged users*.

NOTE
To use the **export** utility, you must have been granted the CREATE SESSION privilege on the database.

Export Modes

There are four modes in which you can export data using the **export** utility. These four modes are explained in the following sections:

Table Mode

In the *table export mode,* you can use the TABLES parameter to export selected tables in the database. By specifying this mode, you can perform an export of one or more table segments. This mode is used when you need to transfer an object to a different database user, either in the same database or another database, or to perform a backup of the object.

NOTE
You need privileges to export any objects of another user.

User Mode

In the *user export mode,* you can use the OWNER parameter to export objects owned by users in the database. The user mode enables you to export all objects belonging to a user's schema. Privileged users can export all the objects belonging to the schemas of a specified set of users.

Full Database Mode

In the *full database export mode,* you must use the FULL=YES option to perform an export of an entire database of objects. The objects belonging to the SYS schema are excluded because these objects would be present in the database where the import needs to be performed.

Tablespace Mode

In the *tablespace export mode,* you can move a tablespace of an Oracle database and then plug it into another Oracle database. This feature is well known as *transportable tablespaces.* Transporting a tablespace requires you to perform an export of only the database information stored in the data dictionary (metadata) and then physically copying the data files associated with the tablespace to the destination. This is a faster way of relocating data.

Table 18-1 shows the objects exported for the four export modes.

Table Mode	User Mode	Full Database Mode	Tablespace Mode
Analyze tables/statistics	Table mode +	User mode +	Analyze tables/statistics
Auditing information	Analyze cluster	Application contexts	B-tree, bitmap, domain, functional indexes
B-tree, bitmap, domain functional indexes	Cluster definitions	Default roles	Cluster definitions
Column and table comments	Database links	Directory aliases	Column and table comments
External tables (without data)	Dimensions	Password history	Indexes owned by users other than table owner
Indexes owned by users other than table owner (privileged users only)	Foreign function libraries	Postinstance actions and objects	Nested table data
Nested table data	Index types	Profiles	Object grants
Object grants (only for tables and indexes)	Java resources and classes	Public synonyms	Object type definitions used by table
Object-type definitions used by table	Job queues	Resource costs	Post-table actions
Post-table actions	Object types	Role grants	Post-table procedural actions and objects
Post-table procedural actions and objects	Operators	Roles	Pretable actions

TABLE 18-1. *Modes of Export*

Table Mode	User Mode	Full Database Mode	Tablespace Mode
Pretable actions	Postschema procedural actions and objects	Rollback segment definitions	Pretable procedural actions
Pretable procedural actions	Preschema procedural objects and actions	System privilege grants	Security policies for table
Referential integrity constraints	Private synonyms	Tablespace definitions	Table constraints (primary, unique, and check)
Security policies for table	Procedural objects	Tablespace quotas	Table definitions
Table constraints (primary, unique, and check)	Refresh groups	User definitions	Triggers
Table data	Sequence numbers	User proxies	
Table definitions	Snapshot logs		
Triggers	Snapshots and materialized views		
	User views		
	User-stored procedures, packages, and functions		

TABLE 18-1. *Modes of Export (Continued)*

Methods of export are:

Conventional Path Export and Direct Path Export

You can export table data by one of two methods, the conventional path export or the direct path export.

The *conventional path export* uses the SQL SELECT statements to extract data from the tables that use the buffer cache and evaluating buffer cache. The **export** utility uses the conventional path by default to perform an export operation. The *direct path export* uses only the buffer cache (skips the evaluating buffer cache) and writes directly to the export file on disk. You need to use the parameter DIRECT=Y to do a direct path export.

NOTE
The direct path export is faster when compared to the conventional path.

Import Concepts and Structures

The **import** utility enables you to import data from an export dump file into an Oracle database. Before running the **import** utility, you must ensure that the following tasks are achieved:

- Execution of the script CATEXP.SQL or CATALOG.SQL that assigns proper privileges to the IMP_FULL_DATABASE role.

- Verifying that the user possesses appropriate privileges to perform the import operation.

Import Modes

There are four modes in which you can import data using the **import** utility. These four modes are explained in the following sections:

Table Mode

In the *table import mode*, you must specify the TABLES parameter to import specified tables from an export dump file, which was generated using the table export mode, user export mode, or the full database export mode. A privileged user can perform an import of tables that belong to another user.

User Mode

In the *user import mode*, you must use the FROMUSER and TOUSER parameters to perform an import of the entire schema objects, which belong to another user. Only privileged users can import all objects in the schemas of a specified set of users.

Full Database Mode

In the full *database import mode,* you must specify the FULL=YES option to import the entire database objects from an export dump file to the Oracle database. Only privileged users can import in this mode.

Tablespace Mode

In the *tablespace import mode,* you can plug a tablespace into a database. Only a privileged user with SYSDBA privileges can move a set of tablespaces from one Oracle database to another.

Import Process Sequence

While performing an import of a table, the export file is read and the table and its corresponding data are created, as shown in the following sequence:

- The type definitions that are related with the table objects are imported.

- *New* tables are created. These tables are termed as *new* because they are new to the Oracle server.

- The data is then imported into the tables.

- The table index structure is built.

TIP
You can save a considerable amount of time by specifying the parameter INDEXES= N, which would not build the indexes as part of the import process. This will limit the number of rollback segments required to support the import operation. This parameter would enhance the rate at which the import is performed. You will need to manually build the indexes after the import has completed.

- The triggers are imported, and the integrity constraints are enabled on new tables. The order in which you import tables may be important if you do not import all the objects that a user owns.

- Finally the bitmap, functional, and domain indexes are created.

A List of Export
and Import Parameters

Table 18-2 lists the parameters, which can be defined while using the **export** and **import** utilities through the command line.

Parameter	Default Value	Description
USERID	None	The username/password of the user performing the export or import. Optionally, you can specify the @connect_string clause for Oracle Net to perform export or import operations on a remote database.
BUFFER	OS dependent	The size in bytes of the buffer used to fetch or transport data rows. If zero is specified, or if the table contains LONG data, only one row is fetched at a time. Note: The BUFFER parameter applies only to conventional path export or import. It has no effect on a direct path export or import.
FILE	expdat.dmp	The name of the binary output file created by export at the OS level. Oracle9i export supports multiple export files, and the **import** utility can read from multiple export files. This is also the name of the default import file.
GRANTS	Yes	A flag to indicate whether to export or import grants.
INDEXES	Yes	A flag to indicate whether to export or import indexes.
SKIP_UNUSABLE_ INDEXES	No	This parameter specifies whether or not import must skip building indexes that were set to the Index Unusable state. This parameter applies only to the **import** utility.

TABLE 18-2. *Description of Export and Import Parameters*

Parameter	Default Value	Description
INDEXFILE	Undefined	This parameter specifies a file where all the index-creation statements must be directed to rather than the index being created in the database. None of the database objects are imported. This parameter applies only to the **import** utility.
TRIGGERS	Yes	A flag to indicate whether to export or import triggers.
ROWS	Yes	A flag to indicate whether to export or import rows in the tables. If set to NO, table rows are not imported.
CONSTRAINTS	Yes	A flag to indicate whether to export or import constraints.
COMPRESS	Yes	A flag to indicate whether to compress table data into one extent upon import. This parameter must be specified during export only. You can use this parameter to reorganize a table. In case of large object (LOB) data, compression will not take place.
SHOW	No	A flag to indicate whether to list only the contents of the export file. This would result in the import of the table data, object creation, and database modification not to be performed. This parameter applies only to the **import** utility.
IGNORE	Yes	A flag to indicate whether to ignore errors if the object already exists during import. This parameter applies only to the **import** utility.
FULL	No	A flag to indicate whether to export or import the entire database.

TABLE 18-2.   *Description of Export and Import Parameters (Continued)*

Parameter	Default Value	Description
COMMIT	No	A flag to indicate whether to commit after each array insert. By default, import commits after loading each table. This parameter only applies to the **import** utility.
COMPILE	Yes	This parameter specifies whether or not import must compile packages, procedures, and functions as they are created.
OWNER	Undefined	A list of usernames with objects that are exported. Specify OWNER=(*userlist*) to export in user mode. This parameter should be used only with the **export** utility.
FROMUSER	Undefined	A list of usernames with objects that are exported. This parameter only applies to the **import** utility.
TOUSER	Undefined	A list of usernames to whom data is imported. This parameter only applies to the **import** utility.
TABLES	None	A list of table names and their partition and subpartition names to export or import. Specify TABLES=(*tablelist*) to export or import in table mode.
RECORDLENGTH	OS dependent	The length in bytes of the file record. You can use this parameter to specify the size of the export or import I/O buffer.
PARFILE	Undefined	The name of a parameter file that contains one or more parameters that can be used for exports or imports.

TABLE 18-2.   *Description of Export and Import Parameters (Continued)*

Parameter	Default Value	Description
CONSISTENT	No	Specifies whether or not export uses the SET TRANSACTION READ ONLY statement to ensure that the data is consistent to a single point in time and does not change during the execution of the export command. This parameter applies only to the **export** utility.
DIRECT	No	Specifies whether you use direct path or conventional path export. This parameter applies only to the **export** utility.
DESTROY	No	The parameter specifies whether or not the existing data files that are available at the OS must be reused to constitute the database. If DESTROY=YES, the parameter would delete all the data in the existing files and reuse them. This parameter applies only to the **import** utility.
FEEDBACK	Zero	Specifies that the export or import operation should display a progress meter in the form of a dot for *n* number of rows exported or imported.
HELP	No	Displays a help message with descriptions of the export or import parameters.
LOG	None	Specifies a filename to receive informational and error messages.
QUERY	None	This parameter enables you to select a subset of rows from a set of tables when doing a table mode export.

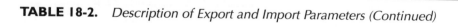

TABLE 18-2. *Description of Export and Import Parameters (Continued)*

Parameter	Default Value	Description
STATISTICS		Specifies the type of database optimizer statistics to generate when the exported data is imported. During export, the default value is ESTIMATE. During import, the various options that can be used are ALWAYS, NONE, SAFE, and RECALCULATE.
TABLESPACES	None	This parameter enables you to export a list of the tablespaces from a database into the export file. This parameter also enables you to import a list of tablespaces from the export file.
TRANSPORT_TABLESPACE	No	When this parameter is set to YES, it enables the export of transportable tablespace metadata. This parameter should be set to YES to import transportable tablespace metadata from an export dump file.
DATAFILES	None	This parameter is used to specify a list of data files while importing a tablespace. This parameter applies only to the **import** utility.
TTS_OWNERS	Undefined	This parameter specifies the list of the users who own the data in the transportable tablespace set. This parameter applies only to the **import** utility.
TTS_FULL_CHECK	FALSE	If the value of this parameter is set to TRUE, then export verifies that a tablespace recovery set has no dependencies on objects outside the recovery set, and vice versa. This parameter applies only to the **export** utility.

TABLE 18-2. *Description of Export and Import Parameters (Continued)*

Parameter	Default Value	Description
VOLSIZE		This parameter enables you to specify the maximum number of bytes in an export or import file on each volume of tape.
FLASHBACK_SCN	None	This parameter enables you to specify the SCN that export will use to enable flashback.
FLASHBACK_TIME	None	This parameter enables you to specify the time to find the SCN that most closely matches it.
RESUMABLE	No	This parameter is used to enable and disable resumable space allocation. If this parameter is not set to YES, then the associated parameters RESUMABLE_NAME and RESUMABLE_TIMEOUT cannot be used.
RESUMABLE_NAME	'User USERNAME (USERID), Session SESSIONID, Instance INSTANCEID'	The value for this parameter identifies the statement that is resumable. This value is a user-defined text string that can be viewed from the dictionary views USER_RESUMABLE or DBA_RESUMABLE. These views indicate a specific resumable statement that has been suspended.
RESUMABLE_TIMEOUT	7,200 seconds	The value specified for this parameter indicates the time period during which an error must be fixed or else the execution will be aborted.
FILESIZE	OS dependent	This parameter specifies the maximum dump file size. Export supports writing to multiple export files, and import can read from multiple export files. While importing, you must use this parameter for import to identify the maximum dump file size.

TABLE 18-2. *Description of Export and Import Parameters (Continued)*

NOTE
Tablespace point-in-time recovery is only available in versions Oracle8 and higher. Direct path export is available in versions Oracle 7.3 and higher.

The export parameter BUFFER applies only to conventional path exports. You must use the RECORDLENGTH parameter to specify the size of the buffer that export uses for writing to the export dump file. In versions of export earlier than 8.1.5, you could not perform an export for tables containing objects and LOBs using the direct path export. This behavior has been changed. The tables with rows that contain LOBs will now be exported using the conventional path, even if the direct path method was specified. These conventional path tables are managed by import, which constitutes the direct path dump files.

Methods to Invoke Export and Import

Export and import can be invoked using different methods. These different methods for invoking the **export** and **import** utilities are described in the following section:

Command Line

You can perform an export and import of objects by using the command line executables and specifying the appropriate parameters. To use the export and import utilities, you should use the following syntax:

```
EXP USERID=username/password PARAMETER=(value1, value2, ...valuen)
IMP USERID=username/password PARAMETER=(value1, value2, ...valuen)
```

NOTE
The number of parameters specified at the command prompt cannot exceed the maximum length of a command line on the system.

Interactive Export Prompts

If using the interactive method, the **export** and **import** utilities prompt you for the value of each parameter:

```
EXP username/password
IMP username/password
```

NOTE
The complete functionality of the **export** *and* **import**
utilities cannot be used when using the interactive
mode.

Parameter Files

If you use the parameter file method, you can specify all valid parameters and their
values in a file. This is known as the *parameter file*. Storing parameters in a file
enables you to easily modify or reuse the file for different export and import
operations. The parameter files can be created using any flat file text editor. You
should use the following syntax when using the parameter file method:

```
EXP USERID=username/password PARFILE=filename
IMP USERID=username/password PARFILE=filename
```

*[handwritten: path   Admin\ BSPA \scripts\ export
\ BSPA_exp_par.par .]*

A sample parameter file is shown here:

```
# This is a parameter file to perform
# a full database Export.
FULL=y
FILE=dbexpdump.dmp
LOG=dbexpdump.log
INDEXES=y
CONSISTENT=y
```

Perform Export and Import Operations

Export and import can be performed with various modes as described in the
previous section. The procedures for performing export and import operations in
these various modes are described in the following section.

Table Mode Export/Import Operation

In this section, we show examples of various modes of export and/or import. A table
mode export is shown in the following code:

```
C:\>EXP USERID=system/manager FILE=ormtest.dmp LOG=ormtest.log
TABLES=scott.ormtest ROWS=y

Export: Release 9.0.1.0.0 - Beta on Sat Oct 20 19:41:00 2001
(c) Copyright 2001 Oracle Corporation.  All rights reserved.
```

```
Connected to: Oracle9i Enterprise Edition Release 9.0.1.0.0 - Beta
With the Partitioning option
JServer Release 9.0.1.0.0 - Beta
Export done in WE8MSWIN1252 character set and AL16UTF16 NCHAR character set
About to export specified tables via Conventional Path ...
Current user changed to SCOTT
. . exporting table                          ORMTEST          3 rows exported
Export terminated successfully without warnings.
```

To perform a table-level import, you can use the following command line options:

```
C:\>IMP USERID=system/manager FILE=ormtest.dmp LOG=ormtest.log
FROMUSER=scott TOUSER=steve

Import: Release 9.0.1.0.0 - Beta on Sat Oct 20 19:47:05 2001
(c) Copyright 2001 Oracle Corporation.  All rights reserved.
Connected to: Oracle9i Enterprise Edition Release 9.0.1.0.0 - Beta
With the Partitioning option
JServer Release 9.0.1.0.0 - Beta
Export file created by EXPORT:V09.00.01 via conventional path
import done in WE8MSWIN1252 character set and AL16UTF16 NCHAR character set
. importing SCOTT's objects into STEVE
. . importing table                        "ORMTEST"          3 rows imported
Import terminated successfully without warnings.
```

Table Export Using the QUERY Parameter

The QUERY parameter must be specified if you want to select a set of rows from tables during export:

```
C:\EXP scott/tiger FILE=exp.dmp LOG=exp.log TABLES=emp_cat,division
QUERY="""where job='SUPPORT ENG' and sal<55000"""
```

In the previous example, the QUERY option enables the **export** utility to export rows from both EMP_CAT and DIVISION tables that match the query.

User Mode Export/Import Operation

To perform a user-level export, use the following command line options:

```
C:\>EXP USERID=system/manager FILE=ormtest.dmp LOG=ormtest.log OWNER=scott
```

```
Connected to: Oracle9i Enterprise Edition Release 9.0.1.0.0 - Beta
With the Partitioning option
```

```
JServer Release 9.0.1.0.0 - Beta
Export done in WE8MSWIN1252 character set and AL16UTF16 NCHAR character set
About to export specified users ...
. exporting pre-schema procedural objects and actions
. exporting foreign function library names for user SCOTT
. exporting object type definitions for user SCOTT
About to export SCOTT's objects ...
. exporting database links
. exporting sequence numbers
. exporting cluster definitions
. about to export SCOTT's tables via Conventional Path ...
. . exporting table                          ORMTEST          3 rows exported
. exporting synonyms
. exporting views
. exporting stored procedures
. exporting operators
. exporting referential integrity constraints
. exporting triggers
. exporting indextypes
. exporting bitmap, functional and extensible indexes
. exporting posttables actions
. exporting materialized views
. exporting snapshot logs
. exporting job queues
. exporting refresh groups and children
. exporting dimensions
. exporting post-schema procedural objects and actions
. exporting statistics
Export terminated successfully without warnings.
```

You can import the entire objects to another user, which were initially exported as a part of user-level export operation. To perform a user-level import, use the following command line options:

```
C:\>IMP USERID=system/manager FILE=ormtest.dmp LOG=ormtest.log
FROMUSER=scott TOUSER=steve

Import: Release 9.0.1.0.0 - Beta on Sat Oct 20 20:18:42 2001
(c) Copyright 2001 Oracle Corporation.  All rights reserved.
Connected to: Oracle9i Enterprise Edition Release 9.0.1.0.0 - Beta
With the Partitioning option
JServer Release 9.0.1.0.0 - Beta
Export file created by EXPORT:V09.00.01 via conventional path
import done in WE8MSWIN1252 character set and AL16UTF16 NCHAR character set
. importing SCOTT's objects into STEVE
.. importing table                          "ORMTEST"          3 rows imported
Import terminated successfully without warnings.
```

Full Database Export/Import Operation

The following export procedure assumes that you don't want any changes made to the database while taking a full database export, so the database will be shut down and started in RESTRICT mode before taking the full database export. The steps to perform a full database export are listed in the following procedure:

1. Shut down any applications or third-party tools running on top of Oracle, and then shut down the database as shown:

```
SQL> SHUTDOWN IMMEDIATE
```

2. To restrict users from accessing the database, start up the database with the *restrict* option by using the command

```
SQL> STARTUP RESTRICT OPEN
```

3. Perform the full database export using the following export command. A partial output is shown:

```
C:\>EXP USERID=system/manager FILE=fulldb.dmp LOG=fulldb.log FULL=y
COMPRESS=y BUFFER=10000000

Export: Release 9.0.1.0.0 - Beta on Sun Oct 21 13:14:18 2001
(c) Copyright 2001 Oracle Corporation.  All rights reserved.
Connected to: Oracle9i Enterprise Edition Release 9.0.1.0.0 - Beta
With the Partitioning option
JServer Release 9.0.1.0.0 - Beta
Export done in WE8MSWIN1252 character set and AL16UTF16 NCHAR
character set
About to export specified users ...
. exporting pre-schema procedural objects and actions
. exporting foreign function library names for user SYSTEM
. exporting object type definitions for user SYSTEM
About to export SYSTEM's objects ...
...

. exporting post-schema procedural objects and actions
. exporting statistics
Export terminated successfully without warnings.
```

4. Use the following command to give the users access to the database again:

```
SQL> ALTER SYSTEM DISABLE RESTRICTED SESSION;
```

Oracle also provides a GUI tool called *data management* along with the Oracle Enterprise Manager. This enables you to use the export, import, and SQL*Loader with a graphical wizard interface.

To perform an import of the full database, you must create a new database having a SYSTEM tablespace and a nondefault system-managed undo tablespace. You can then use the following command line options to perform a full database import:

```
C:\>IMP USERID=system/manager FILE=fulldb.dmp LOG=fulldbimp.log
BUFFER=10000000 FULL=Y
```

NOTE
Prior to importing the full database, you must ensure that the directory structure of the target database is similar to that of the source database.

Tablespace Mode Export/Import Operation

Tablespace mode export enables you to move a subset of an Oracle database and plug it into another Oracle database. Moving data via transportable tablespaces can be much faster than performing either an export/import of the same data, because transporting a tablespace requires the copying of data files and integrating the database schema information into the data dictionary. You can also use transportable tablespaces to move index data, thereby avoiding index rebuilds. Before transporting tablespaces between databases, you should make the set of tablespaces read-only. This is because no transaction should alter the data in the tablespace. If the tablespace is not set to read-only mode and if you try to export the tablespace to another database, you will receive the following error:

```
EXP-00008: ORACLE error 29335 encountered
ORA-29335: tablespace 'DATA_TS' is not read only
ORA-06512: at "SYS.DBMS_PLUGTS", line 411
ORA-06512: at line 1
EXP-00000: Export terminated unsuccessfully
```

The following commands show how to transport a tablespace from one database to another using the tablespace export method:

```
C:\EXP USERID='sys/sys as sysdba' TRANSPORT_TABLESPACE=y
TABLESPACES=data_ts FILE=datats.dmp  LOG=datats.log
```

NOTE
You must connect 'AS SYSDBA' while performing a tablespace-level export to successfully perform the import operation.

During tablespace export, the **export** utility records the database schema changes from the data dictionary regarding the tablespace. It will not export any rows from the tablespace. Once the export is over, you should copy the data files that belong to the tablespace(s) and the export dump file to the destination database and plug in using the **import** utility as shown in the following code:

```
C:\IMP TRANSPORT_TABLESPACE=y DATAFILES='c:\lob\data1' TABLESPACES=data_ts
TTS_OWNERS=prod FROMUSER=prod TOUSER=scott FILE=c:\lob\datats.dmp
LOG=data.log
```

Tablespace mode export is helpful in the following situations:

- Feeding data from Online Transaction Processing (OLTP) systems to data warehouse staging systems

- Updating data warehouses and data marts from staging systems

- Loading data marts from central data warehouses

- Archiving OLTP and data warehouse systems efficiently

- Data publishing to internal and external customers

List Guidelines for Using Export and Import

Some of the guidelines that should be followed when using the **export** and **import** utilities are described in the following section.

Exporting LONG and LOB Datatypes

While exporting tables that contain LONG and LOB datatypes, the **export** utility fetches those datatypes in pieces. However, enough memory must be available to hold all of the contents of each row, including the LONG data.

NOTE
All data in a LOB column does not need to be held in memory at the same time. LOB data is loaded and unloaded in pieces.

Exporting BFILE

When you use the **export** utility to back up BFILE columns, export will only record the names and directory aliases referenced by the BFILE columns. BFILE contents will not be recorded in the export file. If you move the database to a location where the old directories cannot be used to access the included files, you must create the directories at the O/S level and copy the BFILE files to the new location.

NLS Considerations

While moving data from one Oracle database, which has a character set that is different from the database where the data must be imported, you must ensure that the data conversion is handled appropriately. You can do this by setting the NLS_LANG environment variable to the character set definition of the database from which the data is being exported. Not setting this correctly could cause unwanted conversions of characters in the data, possibly causing loss of data. In the 8-bit to 8-bit data movement, whether characters are lost depends upon the specifics of the languages used to enter the data. Multibyte-to-multibyte data movement also depends upon the specifics of the multibyte language.

Exporting Remote Databases Using Oracle Net

Oracle enables you to perform export and import on a remote database using Oracle Net service names. In the examples listed in the previous sections, the export operations were performed on the database residing on the local machine. You can modify the same command to perform export on a remote database by supplying the Oracle Net service name in the export command syntax as follows:

```
C:\EXP USERID=system/manager@prod.oramasters.com
PARFILE=c:\utility\fullexp.txt
```

In this case, Oracle uses the Oracle Net service name prod.oramasters.com to log on to the remote database as user SYSTEM and performs export on the remote database. You should note that the export file and log files (export log file, not archived log files) would be generated in the local machine from where you are issuing the export command. Similarly, you can also perform the import operation on the remote machine using the service name. If the service name is not configured for the remote database, you will get the following error message:

```
"EXP-00056: ORACLE error 12560 encountered
ORA-12560: TNS:protocol adapter error
EXP-00222:
System error message 2
 System error message: No such file or directory
EXP-00000: Export terminated unsuccessfully"
```

Filename Specification

When you specify the FILE parameter in the export command, you should not leave any blank space in the file path string, or else the **export** utility returns an error. In some operating systems, your directory name contains spaces. For example in Windows NT, the export file may be placed in c:\program files\users data\expfile. In this case, you have to enclose the full path in the FILE parameter in triple quotes. For example,

```
C:\EXP USERID=system/manager FULL=y CONSTRAINTS=y
FILE="""c:\program files\export filedb.dmp"""
```

Transportable Tablespaces

The following restrictions apply while transporting a tablespace from one database to another:

- You can only transport a set of tablespaces that are *self-contained*. In this context, self-contained means that there are no references from inside the set of tablespaces pointing outside the tablespaces.

- The source and target database must be a homogenous environment. For example, you cannot transport a tablespace from a HP-UX Oracle database to an NT Oracle database.

- The source and target databases must use the same character set.

- You cannot transport a tablespace to a target database in which a tablespace with the same name already exists.

- Currently, transportable tablespaces do not support the following:

  - Materialized views/replication

  - Function-based indexes

  - Scoped REFs

  - 8.0-compatible advanced queues with multiple recipients

QUERY Parameter Restrictions

The QUERY parameter cannot be specified for full, user, or transportable tablespace mode exports. This parameter cannot be specified when using the direct path export (DIRECT=Y). It also cannot be specified for tables with inner-nested tables.

Chapter Questions

1. **Which one of the following statements is incorrect if the export is performed using the following parameters?**

   ```
   C:\>EXP USERID=system/manager FILE=ormtest.dmp LOG=ormtest.log
   TABLES=scott.ormtest ROWS=y
   ```

   A. The table definition would be exported.

   B. The table data would be exported.

   C. The indexes with the data would be exported.

   D. The constraints would be exported.

2. **Which of the following parameters would you use to record the errors that might be generated during the import operation?**

   A. LOG

   B. HELP

   C. BUFFER

   D. PARFILE

   E. INCTYPE

3. **In what order is the table data imported?**

   A. Data imported, indexes built, triggers imported, integrity constraints enabled, table created

   B. Table created, data imported, index built, triggers imported, integrity constraints enabled

   C. Triggers imported, integrity constraints enabled, indexes built, data imported

   D. Data imported, triggers imported, indexes built, integrity constraints enabled

4. **When moving data from one database to another where both the databases have distinct character sets, which parameter should you set in the destination database to ensure that the data conversion is handled properly?**

   A. DIRECT

   B. PARFILE

    C. INCTYPE

    D. NLS_LANG

    E. CONSISTENT

5. **Which one of the following parameters must be specified when exporting objects that have integrity constraints referencing objects that are currently being accessed by other users?**

    A. IGNORE=y

    B. DIRECT=y

    C. CONSISTENT=y

    D. BUFFER=y

6. **What are the advantages of performing logical backups? Choose two.**

    A. Reorganizing tables

    B. Recovering objects by applying redo

    C. Creating a physical backup

    D. Complements performing a closed database physical backup

7. **Which one of the following syntax examples must be used to perform an interactive export?**

    A. EXP USERID=scott/tiger BUFFER=10000000 FILE=user.dmp LOG=user.log

    B. EXP USERID=system/manager BUFFER=10000000 FILE=user.dmp LOG=user.log

    C. EXP BUFFER=10000000 FILE=user.dmp LOG=user.log

    D. EXP scott/tiger

8. **While exporting the tablespace metadata, you encountered the following error:**

```
EXP-00008: ORACLE error 29335 encountered
ORA-29335: tablespace 'DATA_TS' is not read only
ORA-06512: at "SYS.DBMS_PLUGTS", line 411
ORA-06512: at line 1
EXP-00000: Export terminated unsuccessfully
```

What is the cause of the error?

A. The tablespace to be transported is not self-contained.

B. The tablespace to be transported is read-only.

C. The tablespace is read write.

D. The tablespace is offline but not read-only.

9. **Which of the following parameters must be specified to perform the export operation faster?**

A. GRANTS=y

B. DIRECT=y

C. IGNORE=y

D. INDEXES=y

10. **Which of the following scripts must be executed to grant EXP_FULL_DATABASE and IMP_FULL_DATABASE roles to the DBA role?**

A. CATEXP.SQL

B. CATPROC.SQL

C. CATREP.SQL

D. CATEXP_IMP.SQL

E. CATIMP.SQL

Chapter Answers

1. C.   The indexes with the data would be exported.

Explanation   The export operation generates an export dump file containing table definitions, table data, and constraints. It also stores information pertaining to any indexes, but not the index data. The indexes are built while performing the import of the table segment.

2. A.   LOG

Explanation   The import parameter LOG that specifies a filename maintains a log of all the error messages pertaining to the objects that are imported into the database.

3. B. Table created, data imported, index built, triggers imported, integrity constraints enabled

Explanation During an import operation the tables are first created, data is imported, indexes are built, triggers are imported, and, finally, the integrity constraints are enabled.

4. D. NLS_LANG

Explanation While moving data from one Oracle database that has a character set that is different from the destination database, the NLS_LANG parameter should be specified. Set the NLS_LANG environment variable to the character set definition of the database from which the data is being exported.

5. C. CONSISTENT=y

Explanation While performing an export of multiple tables having referential integrity constraints and while the database is open for user access, you must specify the CONSISTENT=y parameter. This parameter enables a read-consistent view of the data for multiple tables. If you specify CONSISTENT=n, each table is exported in separate transactions, which might lead to inconsistency of two or more tables that have referential integrity constraints enabled.

6. A. and D. Reorganizing tables and Compliments performing a closed database physical backup.

Explanation The primary advantage of performing a logical backup is that the table data can be reorganized or defragmented. This would enhance the performance. While reorganizing the table, all data, which is scattered across the table extents, would be located into one huge extent. To disable reorganization, you must set the parameter COMPRESS=n. The logical backups also complement physical database backups and should be part of the backup strategy.

7. D. EXP scott/tiger

Explanation The export prompts you for the value of each parameter when you use the syntax shown in the following code:

```
EXP username/password
```

8. C. The tablespace is read write.

Explanation   If the tablespace is not set to read-only mode and if you try to export the tablespace, you will encounter the previous error. Make the tablespace read-only by executing the following command and then try the operation:

```
SQL> ALTER TABLESPACE ormtest READ ONLY;
Tablespace altered.
```

9. B. DIRECT=y

Explanation   In comparison with the conventional path export, the direct path export is faster. The data is read from disk into the buffer cache, and the rows are directly transferred to the export client without the intermediate evaluation buffer.

10. A. CATEXP.SQL

Explanation   The CATEXP.SQL performs the following tasks in the course of preparing the database for import:

■ Assigns the necessary privileges to the IMP_FULL_DATABASE and EXP_FULL_DATABASE roles.

■ Assigns the IMP_FULL_DATABASE and EXP_FULL_DATABASE to the DBA role.

■ Creates the required data dictionary views.

CHAPTER
19

Loading Data
into a Database

n this chapter, you will learn the concepts and importance of using the SQL*Loader for loading data into a database. You will learn about the loading methods and the various files associated with SQL*Loader. You will also learn to perform basic SQL*Loader operations. This chapter includes the following topics:

- Direct-path insert operations

- SQL*Loader usage

- Loading methods in SQL*Loader

- SQL*Loader files

- Performing basic SQL*Loader operations

- Guidelines for using SQL*Loader and direct load insert

Oracle enables you to insert data in a table segment either using the *conventional path* method or the *direct-path* method. In the conventional path method, Oracle reuses the available free space in the table segment, interleaving newly inserted data with existing data. The server process executes normal inserts in the database buffer cache and then DBWR writes the data blocks to data files. In this method, Oracle abides by the referential integrity constraints defined on the table.

In the direct-path method, Oracle appends the data to the existing table data. The insert operation directly writes data into the data files, bypassing the buffer cache. The available free space existing in the table is not reused, and Oracle ignores all the referential integrity constraints defined for the table segment during the insert. In the direct-path method, the server process itself assembles blocks and then writes them directly to the data files; therefore, the direct-path method is faster when compared to the conventional path method. Direct-path operations can be performed using the INSERT statement or by using Oracle's direct-path loader utility, also known as the SQL*Loader.

Direct-Path Insert Operations

Direct load insert can be implemented either in the *serial mode* or the *parallel DML mode*.

Serial Mode

To load data in the serial mode, you must activate the direct load insert by specifying the APPEND hint either immediately after the INSERT statement or within the subquery. A sample statement is shown as follows:

```
INSERT /*+APPEND */ INTO hruser1.employees (select * from
acctuser1.employees);
```

In direct path insert, Oracle starts inserting data into the table segment from its high-water mark (HWM). Since no blocks are being UPDATED by overwriting the old value, space is not allocated in the SGA for the insert operation. This greatly *No redo logs produced* improves performance. The changes made to the table would be unrecoverable, unless you perform a backup after the insert operation has completed.

Parallel DML Mode

Direct path insert can be performed in the parallel mode by using the following methods:

- Specifying a PARALLEL hint in the INSERT statement as follows:

  ```
  INSERT /*+APPEND */ INTO hruser1.employees
  (select /*+PARALLEL(acctuser1.employees,4)*/ *
   from acctuser1.employees);
  ```

- Specifying the PARALLEL clause while creating or by altering the table.

Prior to performing a transaction, you must initiate parallel DML in your session using the following command:

```
ALTER SESSION [ENABLE| FORCE] PARALLEL DML
```

SQL*Loader Usage

The SQL*Loader utility enables you to load data from external files into Oracle tables. This utility has a powerful data-parsing engine that can retrieve data that is stored in different formats. SQL*Loader provides you with many features, including the following:

- Loading data into multiple tables within a load session
- Specifying the character set of the data
- Performing the load of selective data based on the record values
- Using SQL functions to manipulate data prior to loading
- Generating unique sequential key values to be loaded in the specified columns

- Loading data from various sources like disks, tapes, or named pipes
- Generating error reports (These reports help in troubleshooting.)
- Using of secondary data files for loading LOBs and collections
- Loading data using either the conventional or direct path method

Loading Methods in SQL*Loader

SQL*Loader utility provides you with two methods for loading data into table segments: conventional path load and direct-path load. Both methods are discussed in the following sections.

Conventional-Path Load

During a conventional-path load operation, Oracle executes the SQL INSERT statements to populate the table segments. All of the Oracle tools and applications use this method. During a conventional path load, Oracle competes with all the processes to acquire buffer resources. This can degrade performance. The Oracle database server looks for partially filled blocks or blocks that are empty below the high-water mark of the table and then attempts to update these blocks. This would drastically slow down the loading process when huge data loads are performed.

Conventional-Path Load Advantages

The following are the advantages of using the conventional-path load operations:

- The conventional-path load enables you to access an indexed table simultaneously with the load operation underway.
- The conventional-path load enables you to load data into clustered and unclustered tables.
- You can load relatively small number of records into a large indexed table in conventional-path load. In comparison with the direct-path load, the existing index is copied when it is merged with the new index keys. If the existing index is very large and the number of new keys is very small, then the index copy time can offset the time saved by a direct-path load.
- You can perform a load operation with referential and column-check integrity constraints enabled on the tables. We recommend that a small number of records be loaded rather than a large number of records when the constraints are enabled since it takes a lot of time and resources.

Direct-Path Load

SQL*Loader bypasses the procedure of loading the data into a bind array buffer and passing it to the Oracle database server, a procedure typically performed in the conventional-path load operation. Instead, a direct-path load uses the direct path API to pass the data to be loaded to the load engine in the server. The load engine builds a column array structure from the data passed to it. The direct-path load engine uses the column array structure to format the Oracle data blocks and build the index keys. The newly formatted database blocks are written directly to the database.

Internally, multiple buffers are used for the formatted blocks. While one buffer is being loaded with data, others would be written if asynchronous I/O were available on the system. The overlapping computation mechanism with I/O enhances the load performance. When compared to the conventional-path load, the direct-path load operation is much faster.

Direct-Path Load Advantages

The following are the advantages of using the direct-path load operations:

- The data is loaded into empty blocks. Partial blocks are not used; therefore, *It is faster* *high perf.* no reads need to be performed to find them, and fewer writes are done.

- The SQL INSERT statements are not executed to perform the loads, this reduces the processing of data and enhances performance.

- The direct-path load method uses multiblock asynchronous I/O for performing writes on to the database files.

- While performing a direct-path load, the processes perform their own write I/O instead of using Oracle's buffer cache. This minimizes any contention with other Oracle users.

- The sorted indexes option that is available during direct-path loads enables *minimizes* you to presort data using high-performance sort routines that are native to *oracle* your system or installation. *contention*

- When a table to be loaded is empty, the presorting option eliminates the sort and merge phases of index building. The index is filled in as data arrives.

- During an instance failure you do not require any redo, as redo does not get logged into the redo log files while performing a direct load.

Direct-Path Load Restrictions

To use the direct-path load method, the following conditions must be met:

- The segment in which data is to be loaded must not be a clustered table.

- The tables into which the data is to be loaded must not have any active transactions pending.

NOTE
You must ensure that the table to which the data is being loaded—either using the SQL*Loader or the SQL INSERT (using APPEND hint) command—must not contain any active transactions.

- The SQL*Loader utility and Oracle server should be the same version.

NOTE
During the direct-path load operation, Oracle locks the tables and indexes at the start of the load and releases them when the load is completed.

SQL*Loader Files

The SQL*Loader utility obtains the input from the control file and the data file. The output from the SQL*Loader is then inserted into the Oracle database. There are other output files like the log file, bad file, and the discard file that SQL*Loader generates during the load operation. The interaction between these files and the SQL*Loader utility is depicted in Figure 19-1 and explained in the following sections.

SQL*Loader Control File

The SQL*Loader control file is a text file written in a language that SQL*Loader understands. As the name suggests, the control file instructs the SQL*Loader about the source from where the data can be obtained and the Oracle objects into which the data must be loaded. It also provides the SQL*Loader utility with information about the parsing of data and how to interpret this data. The control file also contains information pertaining to the various other files where the data must be directed to in case of exceptions.

The contents of the SQL*Loader control file include the following:

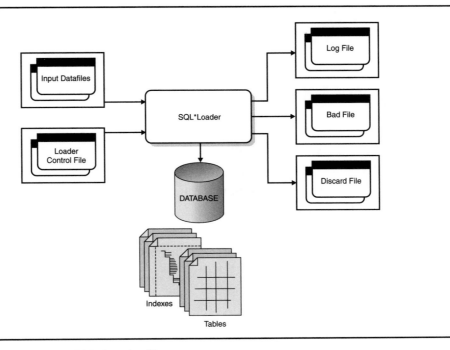

FIGURE 19-1. *SQL*Loader files*

- The LOAD DATA statement informs SQL*Loader that a new data load is starting. If you were continuing a load that had been interrupted before its completion, you must use the CONTINUE_LOAD DATA statement.

- The names of the input data files are specified using the INFILE clause.

- The output files to store bad and discarded records are specified using the BADFILE and DISCARDFILE parameters respectively.

- Arrangement of the physical record in the input data files is different when compared to the logical record. You must include clauses such as CONCATENATE and CONTINUEIF to clearly define a physical record.

- The types of operation you need to perform include the following:

    - **INSERT**   Loads data into an empty table.

    - **APPEND**   Loads data into a table that already has records.

    - **REPLACE**   Loads data into a table after deleting the existing table data.

    - **TRUNCATE**   Loads data into a table after truncating the table data.

- The field specifications, including position, data types, and delimiters condition specifications, by using the INTO TABLE clause.

- Criteria for selecting records to be loaded using the WHEN clause.

- The TRAILING NULLCOLS clause enables SQL*Loader to treat any relatively positioned columns that are not present in the record as null columns.

- Specification of the columns to be loaded.

- The usage of clauses such as RECNUM and SYSDATE and applying SQL functions.

- Column operations, such as trimming and substituting zeros with nulls.

- The SQL*Loader parameters can be specified using the OPTIONS clause. A listing of the SQL*Loader parameters can be found in Table 19-1.

- Storage specifications for temporary segments created during a parallel direct load.

- Other direct load options, such as

    - **REENABLE** Enables constraints.

    - **SORTED_INDEXES** Specifies if data is presorted.

    - **SINGLEROW** Maintains indexes on a row-by-row basis.

    - **UNRECOVERABLE** Suppresses generation of redo.

NOTE
Comments in the control file can be added by prefixing the lines with -- (double hyphens).

You can indicate how the field in the data file must be delimited by specifying a delimiter after specifying the datatype. You can specify a TERMINATED BY clause, or an ENCLOSED BY clause, or both.

NOTE
If both the TERMINATED BY and the ENCLOSED BY clauses are used, then you must first specify the TERMINATED BY clause.

SQL*Loader Data File

SQL*Loader obtains the data from one or more data files (flat files). The location of these files is specified in the control file. The data in the data files is organized as records. These data files can either be in *fixed record* format, *variable record* format, or *stream record* format. The record format can be defined in the INFILE parameter of the control file. The default is the stream record format.

NOTE
*The SQL*Loader utility provides you with the option of specifying the data in the control file itself. In such cases, you must define the INFILE parameter in the control file as INFILE *.*

Bad File

The bad file contains records that were either rejected by SQL*Loader or by the Oracle database server.

SQL*Loader rejects records if the specified input format is invalid. For example, if the second enclosure delimiter is missing or if a delimited field exceeds its maximum length, SQL*Loader rejects the record.

The records that are accepted by SQL*Loader for processing, are forwarded to the Oracle database server for insertion. If this record is termed as invalid due to inconsistent datatypes and constraint violations on the database objects, then these records are also stored in the bad file.

In either of the preceding cases, SQL*Loader generates the bad file that contains all the rejected records. If the bad file is specified using the command prompt parameter BAD or in the control file, then SQL*Loader ensures that all the rejected records are logged into the bad file. The file is not created if there are no bad records and, if the file already exists, then it is overwritten with the same name.

NOTE
On some systems, a new version of the file is created if a file with the same name already exists. Refer to the O/S specific documentation to obtain this information.

Discard File

The records that do not meet the specified load criteria are directed to the discard file. If a discard file is specified and one or more records fail to satisfy all of the WHEN clauses specified in the control file, then they are discarded. If no records are discarded, then the discard file is not generated.

NOTE
The discard file would only contain records that were not inserted into any table in the database.

Log File

A log file stores the detailed summary of the load operation, including the description of any errors that occur. It is created when SQL*Loader begins the execution. If the log file cannot be created, then the execution is terminated.

Parameter File

The parameter file stores all the commonly used command-line parameters. For example, you can specify the following at the command line for performing a load using the SQL*Loader:

```
C:\>SQLLDR PARFILE=sample.par
```

In turn, the parameter file **sample.par** would contain the command-line parameters as follows:

```
USERID=scott/tiger
CONTROL=sample.ctl
LOG=sample.log
DIRECT=true
ERRORS=99
BINDSIZE=100000
```

List of Command-Line Parameters

The SQL*Loader command-line parameters are described here:

USERID	This parameter enables you to specify the Oracle username and password. If the password is not specified, the user will be prompted for the password.
CONTROL	This parameter enables you to specify the control filename.
LOG	This parameter enables you to specify the log filename. The default would be the control file name with the .log as the extension.
BAD	This parameter enables you to specify the bad file. The default would be the control file name with the .bad as the extension.

DATA	This parameter specifies the input data filenames. If the filename is not specified Oracle looks for the file with the control file name and the .dat as the extension.
DISCARD	This parameter enables you to specify the file where Oracle stores all the records that fail to satisfy the WHEN clause.
DISCARDMAX	You can specify the maximum number of discards to allow. By default, all discards would be allowed.
SKIP	You can specify the number of records to skip. This parameter is typically used to continue the load operation after a failure. You can also skip the initial comments and headings specified in the data files.
LOAD	You can specify the number of records to be loaded from the data file.
ERRORS	You can specify the maximum number of bad (rejected) records to allow.
ROWS	This parameter enables you to specify the number of rows in the array to be built before each insert for conventional loads. While performing a direct-path load, this defines the approximate number of rows read from input for each data save.
BINDSIZE	This parameter specifies the maximum size (bytes) of the bind array. The size defined here would override the default size (which is system dependent) and any size determined by ROWS.
DIRECT	If this parameter is set to TRUE, SQL*Loader then uses the direct-path load. It uses the conventional-path load method if set to FALSE.
PARFILE	This parameter specifies the name of the parameter file where all the SQL*Loader parameters are stored.
FILE	This parameter specifies the database file to allocate extents from. It is used only for parallel loads.
COLUMNARRAY ROWS	This parameter enables you to specify the number of rows to allocate for direct path column arrays.
EXTERNAL_TABLE	This parameter instructs the utility whether to load data using the external tables option. The possible values are NOT_USED, GENERATE_ONLY, and EXECUTE.

MULTITHREADING	This parameter can be specified while performing a load operation on a system with more than one CPU. The default value is TRUE on a multi-CPU system and FALSE on single-CPU system.
PARALLEL	This parameter enables you to specify whether direct loads can operate in multiple concurrent sessions to load data into the same table.
READSIZE	This parameter specifies the size (bytes) of the read buffer. You can specify this in conventional-path loads where more data can be read before a commit is required.
RESUMABLE	This parameter is used to enable or disable resumable space allocation. You can only use the RESUMABLE_NAME and RESUMABLE_TIMEOUT if this parameter is set to TRUE.
RESUMABLE_ NAME	This value is a user-defined text string that is inserted in either the USER_RESUMABLE or DBA_RESUMABLE view to help you identify a specific resumable statement that has been suspended.
RESUMABLE_ TIMEOUT	The value of this parameter specifies the time period during which an error must be fixed else the execution of the statement would be aborted. The default is 7,200 seconds.
SILENT	This parameter enables you to suppress the header and feedback messages that normally appear during command-line execution. The possible values are HEADER, FEEDBACK, ERRORS, DISCARDS, PARTITIONS, and ALL.
SKIP_INDEX_ MAINTENANCE	This parameter, when set to TRUE, stops index maintenance for direct-path loads, but does not apply to conventional-path loads.
SKIP_UNUSABLE_ INDEXES	This parameter, when set to TRUE, allows SQL*Loader to load a table with indexes that are in index unusable state prior to beginning the load.
STREAMSIZE	This parameter specifies the size in bytes for the direct path streams.

Performing Basic SQL*Loader Operations

To invoke the SQL*Loader, you must specify certain parameters to establish the session characteristics. The load operations can be initiated by specifying the parameters at the command line as shown here:

```
C:\>SQLLDR CONTROL=dataload1.ctl LOG=dataload1.log BAD=dataload1.bad
DATA=dataload1.dat USERID=scott/tiger ERRORS=99 LOAD=5000 DISCARDMAX=100
DISCARD=dataload1.dis
```

You can also enable the interactive method as follows to specify the parameter values. Note that only limited parameters can be specified when using the interactive method:

```
C:\>SQLLDR scott/tiger [ENTER]
control = case1.ctl
```

Command-line parameters may be specified by either position or keywords. The command-line parameters specified by position follow:

```
C:\>SQLLDR scott/tiger case1.ctl case1.log
```

We explain the procedure of loading data into an Oracle table DEPT using the SQL*Loader in the APPEND mode. The data in this example is available in the control file itself and therefore a data file (.dat) is not specified in the control file. The data fields are terminated by using a comma (,), and some of the field data is enclosed using double quotes (") as shown below in the control file file test1.ctl.

comment

```
-->Filename='test1.ctl'
--Loading data into the DEPT table
LOAD DATA
INFILE *
APPEND INTO TABLE DEPT
FIELDS TERMINATED BY ',' OPTIONALLY ENCLOSED BY '"'
(DEPTNO, DNAME, LOC)
BEGINDATA
91,SALES,"NEW YORK"
92,"PERCHASE",CALIFORNIA
93,"ACCOUNT",NEWJERSY
94,FINANCE,"BOSTON"
99,"SALES",PARIS
```

The following command initiates the loading of data from the control file into the DEPT table that belongs to the ORATEST user:

```
C:\>sqlldr USERID=oratest/oratest CONTROL=c:\sqlldr\test1.ctl
LOG=c:\sqlldr\test1.log
SQL*Loader: Release 9.0.1.0.0 on Wed Oct 24 11:39:57 2001
(c) Copyright 2001 Oracle Corporation.  All rights reserved.
Commit point reached - logical record count 5
```

The preceding message shows a logical record count of 5. Please note that you must verify the outcome of the load operation from the specified log file. The following **test1.log** file contents show that all the five records have been successfully appended to the DEPT table without any data errors.

```
Table DEPT, loaded from every logical record.
Insert option in effect for this table: APPEND

    Column Name                      Position   Len  Term Encl Datatype
------------------------------ ---------- ----- ---- ---- -----------------
----
DEPTNO                               FIRST     *    ,   O(")  CHARACTER
DNAME                                NEXT      *    ,   O(")  CHARACTER
LOC                                  NEXT      *    ,   O(")  CHARACTER

Table DEPT:
  5 Rows successfully loaded.
  0 Rows not loaded due to data errors.
  0 Rows not loaded because all WHEN clauses were failed.
  0 Rows not loaded because all fields were null.
Space allocated for bind array:                  49536 bytes(64 rows)
Read   buffer bytes: 1048576
Total logical records skipped:          0
Total logical records read:             5
Total logical records rejected:         0
Total logical records discarded:        0
Run began on Wed Oct 24 11:39:57 2001
Run ended on Wed Oct 24 11:39:57 2001
Elapsed time was:      00:00:00.06
CPU time was:          00:00:00.04
```

NOTE
Oracle provides you with several case studies illustrating different load options and control file items. We recommend that you review these test

cases that are available in the location $ORACLE_HOME/rdbms/demo on UNIX and %ORACLE_HOME%\rdbms\demo on Windows NT/2000.

Guidelines for Using SQL*Loader and Direct-Load Insert

You should be aware of the following guidelines when using the SQL*Loader to perform data loads:

- Ensure that the tables in which the data is to be loaded already exist in the database. SQL*Loader never creates tables. It only loads data into existing tables that already contain data or are empty.

- To load data into the table segments, a user must have the INSERT and DELETE privileges on the objects.

- You must use the parameter file to store all the commonly used SQL*Loader command-line parameters instead of specifying them at the command line. This enables you to reuse the settings.

- In the direct-path load, the indexes are unusable until the load completes, unlike the conventional-path load.

- When configuring the control file, you must be aware of the following:

  - The syntax is of free-format and the statements can extend over multiple lines.

  - The commands are not case sensitive; strings enclosed in single or double quotation marks are taken literally, including case.

  - You can add comments in the control file using the -- (double hyphens). If the data is contained in the control file then you must not provide any comment in the data section; this would be treated as data rather than a comment. Comments in this data section are not supported.

  - The CONSTANT keyword has special meaning to SQL*Loader and is therefore a reserved word. Do not use the word CONSTANT as a name for any tables or columns.

  - Use a data file to store physical records if large amount of data is to be loaded rather than using the control file. This also enables you to reuse the control file for several load sessions, with minor changes.

- Pre-allocating space based on the expected data volume prevents dynamic allocation of extents during the load and improves the speed of the load.

- When direct loads are used, temporary segments are used to generate indexes for the new data.

- When parallel direct loads, you can specify the location of the temporary segments used for inserting data. For each load session, specify a different database file to archive maximum performance.

NOTE
In Oracle9i, SQL*Loader supports loading of BLOB, CLOB, NLOB, and BFILE datatypes. LOBs can either store specified values, they can be null, or they can be empty.

You should be aware of the following guidelines when using the direct path insert operations to perform data loads:

- The logging of redo and undo information can be disabled while performing direct-path load using the INSERT statement. This is unlikely in the case of conventional load insert operations, since the operations tend to reuse the free space available for a segment and maintain referential integrity associated with table segment.

- You can create the new table and then insert into it, or you can use the CREATE TABLE . . . AS SELECT statement. By creating the table using the CREATE TABLE statement and then using the direct-path insert, you update any indexes defined on the target table during the insert operation. But if you use the CREATE TABLE . . . AS SELECT statement to create a table, then this method does not update any indexes, as they are not defined.

- While performing a parallel direct path insert, if any errors occur during the index update, all the statements are rolled back. This is not the case when errors occur during parallel direct path load, where these indexes may be marked as UNUSABLE at the end of the load.

NOTE
The direct load insert operations only support the subquery syntax of the INSERT statement and not the VALUES clause.

Chapter Questions

1. **When is it appropriate to use direct path insert to load data into a table segment? Choose any two.**

   A. When the data must be copied from one table into another within the same database by bypassing the buffer cache

   B. When you want to recover table data after a media failure

   C. When you want to load data into a table even after an index update has failed

   D. When you want to access an indexed table during the load operation

   E. When you do not want other records in the same table to be simultaneously modified by users

2. **Which of the following SQL*Loader parameters enables you to load a specified number of records stored in the data file?**

   A. ROWS

   B. SKIP

   C. LOAD

   D. BINDSIZE

3. **Which SQL*Loader file records information pertaining to any failures that occurred during the load operation?**

   A. Bad file

   B. Discard file

   C. Log file

   D. Control file

4. **When does Oracle direct records into the discard file?**

   A. The records are rejected by SQL*Loader due to invalid input format.

   B. The records are rejected by the Oracle server due to constraint violations.

    C. The records are rejected from being loaded into one table since they do not satisfy the WHEN clause, but are loaded into the secondary table specified in the control file.

    D. The records are rejected from being loaded into all the tables since they do not satisfy the WHEN clause.

5. Which of the SQL*Loader files can be used to specify the data that is to be loaded into the database? Choose two.

    A. Parameter file

    B. Control file

    C. Log file

    D. Data file

6. Which operation requires the table segment to be empty when loading data using the SQL*Loader?

    A. INSERT

    B. REPLACE

    C. APPEND

    D. TRUNCATE

7. Which parameter allows SQL*Loader to load data into a table with the indexes in the *unusable* state, prior to the load operation?

    A. INDEXES

    B. SKIP_INDEX_MAINTENANCE

    C. SKIP_UNUSABLE_INDEXES

    D. RESUMABLE

    E. INDEXES_UNUSABLE

8. If the TERMINATED BY and the ENCLOSED BY clauses are to be specified, then in which sequence must you specify the clauses?

    A. First TERMINATED BY and then ENCLOSED BY

    B. First ENCLOSED BY and then TERMINATED BY

C. Both the parameters can be specified in any sequence.

D. Both the parameters cannot be specified at once.

9. **Which of the following statements is true about configuring a SQL*Loader control file?**

   A. The statements in the control file can extend to multiple lines.

   B. The commands in the control file are case sensitive.

   C. Comments in the control file cannot be specified.

   D. The CONSTANT keyword can be used while specifying the column names of the table.

10. **Which one of the following SQL*Loader parameters would you use to restrict the maximum number of rejected records if the WHEN condition is not met?**

    A. DISCARD

    B. SKIP

    C. DISCARD_MAX

    D. REJECT_MAX

Chapter Answers

1. A.   When the data must be copied from one table into another within the same database by bypassing the buffer cache

   E.   When you do not want other records in the same table to be simultaneously modified by users

Explanation   Direct path insert enables you to copy data from one table to another table within the same database. It speeds up the insert operation, bypassing the buffer cache and writing the data directly in the database file. Data is loaded above the high-water mark defined for the table segment. During the direct-path load operation, Oracle locks the tables and indexes at the start of the load and releases them when the load is completed.

2. C.   LOAD

Explanation   The LOAD parameter enables you to specify the number of records to be loaded from the data file into the table segment. Note that the SKIP parameter defines the number of records to skip during the load.

3. C.   Log file

Explanation   Oracle stores the detailed history of the load operation that was performed using SQL*Loader utility in the log file. If the log file is not specified, then Oracle generates a log file with the same name as the control file but with the .log extension.

4. D.   The records are rejected from being loaded into all the tables since they do not satisfy the WHEN clause.

Explanation   The records rejected by SQL*Loader due to invalid formats and the Oracle server due to inconsistent datatypes and constraint violations are stored in the bad file. The records that are rejected from being loaded into any tables, since they do not satisfy the WHEN clause, are directed into the discard file.

5. B.   Control file

D.   Data file

Explanation   You can specify the data either by using a separate data file or by including it in the control file. If you are using the control file to specify the data, then you must start including the data after the BEGINDATA command. Note that any comments below the command would be treated as data and not as a comment, since Oracle does not support comments to be included in the data section.

6. A.   INSERT

Explanation   The INSERT option can be specified in the control file to load data into an empty table segment. When you use INSERT option, the table must be empty. The APPEND option must be specified to load data into a table that already contains records. The REPLACE option must be specified to load data into a table after deleting the table data. The TRUNCATE option must be specified to load data into a table after truncating the table data.

7. C.   SKIP_UNUSABLE_INDEXES

Explanation   If the SKIP_UNUSABLE_INDEXES parameter is set to TRUE, SQL*Loader loads data into a table with its indexes in Index Unusable state prior to beginning the load.

8. A.   First TERMINATED BY and then ENCLOSED BY

Explanation   If TERMINATED BY and the ENCLOSED BY clauses are used, then you must first specify the TERMINATED BY clause. A sample control file with the data that includes both the parameters is shown in the section titled "SQL*Loader basic operation" in this chapter.

9. A.   The statements in the control file can extend to multiple lines.

Explanation   The syntax is of free-format and the statements in the control file can extend multiple lines. Also, the commands are not case sensitive, but strings enclosed in single or double quotation marks are taken literally, including cases. Comments can be specified in the control file but not in the BEGINDATA section. SQL*Loader treats CONSTANT as a keyword and Oracle recommends that you do not use it as a column name.

10. C.   DISCARD_MAX

Explanation   The DISCARD_MAX parameter specifies the maximum number of discards allowed by SQL*Loader. By default all discards would be allowed. If the value specified by this parameter is reached, SQL*Loader terminates the load. Note that records that are entered into any table in the database will not be entered into the discard file. The DISCARD parameter enables you to specify the file where Oracle stores all the records that fail to satisfy the WHEN clause.

PART

III

Test Yourself: Oracle9i DBA Practice Exams

CHAPTER
20

Practice Exams for OCP
DBA II Fundamentals

e have included two full-length practice exams in this chapter. Each practice exam consists of 64 questions that cover the areas of Oracle Networking and Oracle Backup and Recovery as part of the OCP DBA II Fundamentals exam. If you have studied this guide and gone over the questions and answers at the end of each chapter, you are ready to take these exams.

You should give yourself 90 minutes for each exam. Time yourself, and take the entire exam in one sitting. Do not peek at the answers or look at the preceding chapters. Remember, only a practice test can tell how well you are utilizing your time in the exam. This will help you to gauge your readiness for taking the OCP exam. We suggest that after taking the first exam, you review your answers carefully and study the chapters relating to the questions that were answered incorrectly. Take the second exam after sufficient preparation. If you answer more than 75 percent of the questions correctly, you are ready to take the actual exam.

We have included some tips and suggestions on test taking strategies in the Introduction of this guide. Read it carefully before taking the exam.

If you are ready to start, take a deep breath, relax, and start reading the first question. Good luck.

Full-Length Examination I

1. **Lopez, a DBA, operates her database in NOARCHIVELOG mode. Due to a disk crash she has lost all the database files. All the other disks were made functional except the disk where the control file resided. Which of the following two steps must she complete before opening the database for user operations? (Choose two.)**

   A. Relocate all data files and the control file to a different disk.

   B. Restore data files, and redo log files to the default location and the control file to the new location.

   C. Edit the initialization parameter file to reflect the new location of the control file.

   D. Rename the database and start up in NOMOUNT mode.

   E. Create a new database and reenter the data.

2. **You are using RMAN to recover a data file associated with the UNDO tablespace that contains active segments. What must be the status of the database to complete this operation successfully?**

   A. OPEN

   B. NOMOUNT

C. MOUNT

D. CLOSED

3. **Elizabeth is a DBA managing a database operating in ARCHIVELOG mode for a Fortune 2000 company. An Oracle user accidentally dropped an object in the database. To perform recovery until a specified time in the past, she restored the entire database on to a test instance. Which type of recovery is she performing?**

   A. Data file

   B. Tablespace

   C. Database

   D. Complete

   E. Incomplete

4. **Daniel has recovered the database by performing a database point-in-time recovery using RMAN. He has opened the database using the OPEN RESETLOGS DATABASE command. What is the next step he needs to take to safeguard his database?**

   A. Back up the entire archive log files generated hereafter, because the database backup was already performed before the occurrence of reset logs.

   B. Perform a whole database backup using RMAN.

   C. Back up only the control file using RMAN.

   D. RMAN automatically performs a backup after resetting the logs and does not require any DBA intervention.

5. **Which one of the following statements is incorrect with respect to RMAN's CROSSCHECK command?**

   A. RMAN crosschecks the availability of the backup sets by verifying the information stored in its repository with the backup sets that are physically available.

   B. It identifies the backup sets or image copies that are either corrupted or have been accidentally deleted.

   C. RMAN automatically deletes information pertaining to the image copy from the repository if it is physically not available.

   D. It updates the non-availability of the files by updating the information in the recovery catalog with the appropriate status.

6. **Which one of the following RMAN views must you query to view the code of an existing stored script in the recovery catalog?**

    A. RC_STORED_SCRIPT

    B. RC_STORED_SCRIPT_CODE

    C. RC_STORED_SCRIPT_LINE

    D. RC_SOURCE_SCRIPT

7. **Which one of the following roles must be granted to a user to perform a full database import?**

    A. CONNECT

    B. IMP_FULL_DATABASE

    C. FULL_EXPORT_PRIVS

    D. RESOURCE

    E. FULL_IMPORT_PRIVS

8. **Which one of the following statements is incorrect about direct-path insert operations?**

    A. Direct-path insert enables you to copy data from one table to another table within the same database.

    B. It speeds up the insert operation, bypassing the buffer cache.

    C. Direct-path insert can be performed when using the INSERT INTO . . . SELECT statement.

    D. Direct-path insert can be implemented either in the serial mode or the parallel DML mode.

    E. To load data using the serial mode, you must activate the direct-path insert by specifying the SERIAL hint.

9. **Which one of the following options enables a user to get authenticated through a single password instead of using multiple passwords?**

    A. Wallet Manager

    B. Radius

    C. Oracle Internet Directory

    D. None of the above

10. **Which one of the following components is not part of the two-tier architecture but is introduced in the N-tier architecture?**

    A. Protocol

    B. Adapter

    C. Agent

    D. Network

11. **Which Oracle background process is responsible for providing information about the instance name associated with the service handlers and services to the listener?**

    A. PMON

    B. SMON

    C. LMON

    D. CKPT

12. **You are configuring the host naming method for an Oracle9*i* database. Which one of the following options is appopriate when you are configuring the global database name to register with the listener that is running on the default TCP/IP port?**

    A. Manually edit and configure the **sqlnet.ora** file.

    B. Manually edit and configure the **tnsnames.ora** file.

    C. It is automatically registered with the listener.

    D. None of the above

13. **Which one of the following parameters can be set to configure dispatchers during startup?**

    A. IP address and db_name

    B. Port number and db_name

    C. IP address and port number

    D. None of the above

14. **A user accidentally drops a very important table. What kind of failure just occurred?**

    A. Statement failure

    B. Process failure

C. Instance failure

D. Human error

15. Which Oracle background process is responsible for writing the redo entries from the redo log buffers to the redo log files?

    A. PMON

    B. SMON

    C. LGWR

    D. DBW*n*

    E. ARC*n*

16. What are the implications of operating the database in NOARCHIVELOG mode?

    A. The database can be completely recovered to the point of failure.

    B. Online recovery can be performed.

    C. No recovery can be performed; you can only perform a simple restore of the database.

    D. Incomplete recovery until a specified SCN can be performed.

17. Which one of the following statements is true while taking tablespace backups using RMAN?

    A. You need to make the tablespace offline.

    B. You need to keep the tablespace in backup mode explicitly.

    C. RMAN generates extra redo information during online backups when compared with user-managed online backups.

    D. RMAN does not require the tablespace to be in backup mode.

18. Vladimir manages a database that is operating in NOARCHIVELOG mode. Which one of the following options should he include in his backup strategy?

    A. Whole database backup while the database is open

    B. Whole database backup after the database is gracefully closed

    C. Can only perform logical backups

    D. Cannot perform any backups in this mode

19. Which one of the following options must be used with the RMAN's COPY command to avoid data block verification while creating an image copy?

    A. NOVERIFY

    B. NOCHECK

    C. NOCHECKSUM

    D. NOTEST

    E. NOINSPECTION

20. Stephanie is a DBA who performs online backups of the database, with the database operating in ARCHIVELOG mode. Due to a media failure she lost the SYSTEM tablespace data files. What must she do to recover the data files?

    A. Take the tablespace offline, restore the lost file, and issue the RECOVER DATAFILE command.

    B. Shut down the database, restore all the Oracle files, and open the database with the RESETLOGS option.

    C. Shut down the database, restore the lost file, mount the database, and recover the database.

    D. Take the tablespace offline, restore the lost file, and issue the RECOVER TABLESPACE command.

21. Which one of the following RMAN commands is equivalent to the SQL statement shown as follows?

    ```
    SQL> ALTER DATABASE RENAME FILE 'c:\old.dbf' TO 'd:\new.dbf';
    ```

    A. RENAME

    B. CHANGE

    C. CATALOG

    D. SWITCH

22. Prior to performing an incomplete database recovery, what is the most important task that you are supposed to perform as a DBA?

    A. Perform a full backup.

    B. Open the database in NOMOUNT mode.

    C. Restore the control files.

    D. Restore the archived redo log files.

23. Michael has performed an incomplete recovery using RMAN. After completing the recover UNTIL log sequence operation, he issued the following command:

```
RMAN> OPEN RESETLOGS DATABASE;
```

Which one of the following sequence of actions does RMAN follow?

A. Full resync complete
Database registered in recovery catalog
Starting full resync of recovery catalog
Database opened

B. Database opened
Database registered in recovery catalog
Starting full resync of recovery catalog
Full resync complete

C. Database opened
Starting full resync of recovery catalog
Full resync complete
Database registered in recovery catalog

D. Database opened
Full resync complete
Database registered in recovery catalog
Starting full resync of recovery catalog

24. Which one of the following views must you query from the recovery catalog database to obtain information about the backup sets that were created using RMAN?

A. V$BACKUPSET

B. RC_DATABASE

C. V$BACKUP_SET

D. RC_BACKUP_SET

25. Which one of the following events takes place during partial resynchronization of the recovery catalog?

A. Information related to redo log switches is updated

B. Information related to previously backed up archived redo log files is updated

C. Information related to undo segments is updated

D. Information related to new backups is updated

26. **Which one of the following export modes must be used to export specific table partitions?**

   A. Full database mode

   B. User mode

   C. Transportable tablespace mode

   D. Table mode

27. **In which one of the following loading methods does SQL*Loader compete with the other processes to acquire buffer resources?**

   A. Conventional path load

   B. Distributed path load

   C. Direct path load

   D. None of the above

28. **Martinez works as an Oracle DBA for a Fortune 500 company. What is the easiest solution that you would recommend to him for configuring and managing a huge distributed heterogeneous Oracle network?**

   A. Client side configuration files

   B. Server side configuration files

   C. Lightweight Directory Access Protocol (LDAP)

   D. None of the above

29. **What is the significance of specifying *net_service_name* in the following SQL*Plus command?**

   ```
   SQL> CONNECT username/password@net_service_name
   ```

   A. To pass the local address

   B. To pass the host descriptor

   C. To pass the destination address

   D. To pass the dispatcher address

30. **Which one of the following statements is true?**

   A. The request queue and response queue are common for all the dispatchers.

   B. The request queue is common, and the response queue is different for all the dispatchers.

    C. The request queue is different, and the response queue is common for all the dispatchers.

    D. The request queue and response queue are different for all the dispatchers.

31. **Which one of the following statements about the TNSPING utility is correct?**

    A. It helps you to determine whether or not the Oracle database is running.

    B. It requires the username and password to check the connectivity of the service.

    C. It does not require the username and password to check the connectivity of the service.

    D. It establishes a session with the database and checks the connectivity of the service.

32. Chris, a DBA, while performing maintenance tasks accidentally drops a very important table. What is the best method available for Chris to recover this table if he is aware of the time when the table was dropped?

    A. Point-in-time recovery

    B. Tablespace point-in-time recovery

    C. Cancel-based recovery

    D. Change-based recovery

33. Which Oracle background process frees SGA resources that were allocated to a user process that failed?

    A. PMON

    B. SMON

    C. CKPT

    D. LGWR

    E. ARC*n*

34. Which initialization parameter can be used to specify the minimum number of destinations that Oracle should successfully archive to, before overwriting the online log files?

    A. LOG_ARCHIVE_SUCCEED_MIN_DEST

    B. LOG_ARCHIVE_DEST_MIN_SUCCEED

C. LOG_ARCHIVE_SUCCEED_DEST_MIN

D. LOG_ARCHIVE_MIN_SUCCEED_DEST

35. **Which one of the following tablespaces cannot be excluded from a backup while using the RMAN command CONFIGURE EXCLUDE FOR TABLESPACE?**

    A. TOOLS

    B. USERS

    C. SYSTEM

    D. INDX

36. **Jeremy works as a database consultant for a Fortune 500 company. He has been performing backups of the data files using O/S commands. Jeremy has switched to RMAN to perform regular backups of the database. Which one of the following commands must he issue for RMAN to recognize the previously backed up files?**

    A. COPY DATAFILE

    B. CHANGE DATAFILECOPY

    C. CATALOG DATAFILECOPY

    D. CATALOG BACKUPFILES

37. **Assume that you need to restore and recover a database that's operating in ARCHIVELOG mode. The archive log files available for recovery start from log sequence 150 to 211. If the archived log files with sequence numbers 155, 156, and 159 are corrupted, then until which log sequence can you recover the database?**

    A. 156

    B. 160

    C. 154

    D. 155

38. **Which one of the following views would you query to obtain information about data files that need recovery?**

    A. V$DATAFILE

    B. V$DATAFILE_COPY

    C. V$DATAFILE_HEADER

    D. V$DATAFILE_RECOVERY

39. Jim is an Oracle user working on an inventory control application. He updates the data of an application on a daily basis. One day he updated the wrong data, which resulted in logical corruption of the data. If you have to rollback the database, which type of recovery method would you recommend?

    A. Incomplete recovery in ARCHIVELOG mode

    B. Incomplete recovery in NOARCHIVELOG mode

    C. Complete recovery in ARCHIVELOG mode

    D. Complete recovery in NOARCHIVELOG mode

40. Which one of the following statements is correct regarding RMAN's CHANGE . . . UNCATALOG command?

    A. It physically deletes the specified backup set or image copies from the operating system (OS).

    B. It removes the records of the specified backup sets and image copies from the catalog and updates the control file records status to DELETED.

    C. It does not delete the records from recovery catalog but only marks it as DELETED.

    D. It removes specified backup sets and image copies physically from its location and updates the control file records status to DELETED.

41. Which one of the following commands must be issued to remove a stored script from the recovery catalog?

    A. DELETE SCRIPT

    B. ERASE SCRIPT

    C. REMOVE SCRIPT

    D. UNCATALOG SCRIPT

42. Which one of the following statements is incorrect with respect to the QUERY parameter of the export utility?

    A. It cannot be specified for full database export mode.

    B. It can be used in conjunction with direct path export.

C. It cannot be specified for tables with inner nested tables.

D. It cannot be specified with transportable tablespaces.

43. **Which one of the following files contains records that are rejected by SQL*Loader due to invalid input format?**

   A. Log

   B. Discard

   C. Bad

   D. Control

   E. Parameter file

44. **Which one of the following statements is incorrect about Oracle Net?**

   A. Oracle Net provides the facility of data conversion between two national language character sets.

   B. Oracle Net should be located on each machine in a two-tier network architecture.

   C. The data conversion with the Oracle Net is invisible to the user and to the application.

   D. Oracle Net supports SPX/IPX network protocol with Oracle9*i*.

45. **What are the different protocols used for accessing the Oracle database over the Web? (Choose two.)**

   A. HTTP

   B. TCP/IP

   C. SPX/IPX

   D. Named server pipes

   E. All of the above

46. **Which command of the listener control utility provides you the ability to load all the updates dynamically, thereby eliminating the need for stopping and restarting the listener?**

   A. START

   B. SERVICES

C. RELOAD

D. SET

47. **What must you do to solve the following Oracle error?**

    `ORA-12533:TNS:illegal ADDRESS parameters.`

    A. Check the settings for the net service name.

    B. Check the listener status.

    C. Verify the **tnsnames.ora** file and ensure that there are no multiple copies of the **tnsnames.ora** and **sqlnet.ora** files.

    D. Verify the database status.

48. **What happens when you execute the following statement?**

    `SQL> ALTER SYSTEM SHUTDOWN IMMEDIATE 'D011';`

    A. The dispatcher D011 is shut down and then restarted.

    B. The dispatcher D011 terminates all new connections.

    C. The dispatcher D011 terminates new and existing connections.

    D. The database D011 is shut down.

49. **Which one of the following statements is true about the LogMiner utility?**

    A. LogMiner can be used for media recovery.

    B. LogMiner can be used for instance recovery.

    C. LogMiner generates SQL_REDO as well as SQL_UNDO with primary key information.

    D. LogMiner can be used by Oracle for log recovery.

50. **Where does Oracle store the parse tree information and the execution plan for a SQL statement?**

    A. Database buffer cache

    B. Redo log buffers

    C. Data dictionary cache

    D. Library cache

    E. Large pool area

51. **Which initialization parameter enables you to turn on automatic archiving for the database?**

    A. LOG_ARCHIVE_START

    B. LOG_ARCHIVE_AUTO

    C. ARCHIVE_LOG_START

    D. ARCHIVE_LOG_LIST

52. **Assume that automatic channel allocation feature has already been configured using RMAN. What happens on execution of the following script?**

    ```
    RMAN>RUN
    {
         ALLOCATE CHANNEL C1 DEVICE TYPE disk;
         BACKUP DATABASE;
    }
    ```

    A. Automatic allocation overrides the manual channel allocation.

    B. Manual allocation overrides the automatic channel allocation.

    C. RMAN allocates two channels because both manual and automatic channel allocations are defined.

    D. RMAN returns an error because both cannot be used at a given point.

53. **Beth manages an Oracle 9*i* database. While performing an online backup, the database crashed due to a media failure. She kept her five tablespaces in backup mode, and each tablespace had several data files. Which one of the following statements is most appropriate to use for taking the tablespaces out of backup mode?**

    A. ALTER TABLESPACE END BACKUP

    B. ALTER DATABASE DATAFILE END BACKUP

    C. ALTER DATABASE END BACKUP

    D. RECOVER DATABASE

54. **Which one of the following views would you query to obtain information regarding corrupt blocks that were detected during the creation of an image copy?**

    A. V$COPY_CORRUPTION

    B. V$RECOVERY_PROGRESS

    C. V$MARKED_CORRUPTION

    D. V$BACKUP_CORRUPTION

55. What is the primary advantage of multiplexing the online redo log files?

    A. To consume more storage space

    B. To enable faster archiving of the log files

    C. To enable Oracle to perform circular writes on the log files

    D. To protect the database from a single point of failure

56. Due to a media failure, all the members that are part of an online redo log group are lost. Under what conditions can you still recover the database without data loss?

    A. The lost redo log group is the CURRENT group.

    B. The lost redo log group has already been archived.

    C. The lost redo log group is not the CURRENT group but has not yet been archived.

    D. You cannot perform recovery when all the members associated with an online redo log group are lost.

57. You are configuring the listener using the Oracle Net Manager. What information is required for configuring the SID_LIST parameter?

    A. Protocol, host, port, and IP address

    B. Protocol, host, global database name, and Oracle Home

    C. Global database name, Oracle Home, and SID

    D. Protocol, host, and port

    E. Prompts the user to enter a new name after the execution of the RUN block

58. What is the significance of using the command SET NEWNAME in the script shown in the following code?

```
Run
  {
  allocate channel c1 type disk;
  set newname for datafile 8 to 'c:\datafiles\users01.dbf';
  restore datafile 8;
  switch datafile 8;
  recover datafile 'c:\datafiles\users01.dbf';
  sql 'Alter database open';
  }
```

A. Renames the data file in the RUN block

B. Control file is updated with the new location specified in the RUN block

C. Specifies a new location in the RUN block where the data file needs to be restored

D. Prompts the user to enter a new name after the execution of the RUN block

59. The following types of incomplete recovery methods require that your database operate in ARCHIVELOG mode, except one. Which one is it?

A. Cancel-based recovery

B. Tablespace point-in-time recovery

C. Recovery, by simply restoring the full offline backup

D. Change-based recovery

60. Which of the following statements is incorrect regarding the occurrence of a checkpoint?

A. A checkpoint is triggered if the database is closed gracefully.

B. A checkpoint is triggered if a user commits a transaction.

C. A checkpoint is triggered if a log switch occurs.

D. A checkpoint is triggered for a tablespace if the tablespace is set to begin backup mode.

61. What is the most important action a DBA must perform after changing the database from NOARCHIVELOG TO ARCHIVELOG?

A. Performing a full database backup

B. Normally shutting down and restarting the database

C. Manually switching the log files

D. Performing a full database logical backup

62. Which one of the following statements enables the control file AUTOBACKUP feature?

A. RMAN>CONTROLFILE AUTO BACKUP;

B. RMAN>CONFIGURE CONTROLFILE AUTOBACKUP ON;

C. RMAN>CONFIGURE CONTROLFILE AUTO ON;

D. RMAN>CONFIGURE CONTROLFILE BACKUP AUTO;

63. What is the output of the following query?

```
SQL> SELECT status FROM v$datafile_header;
```

A. Displays whether or not a data file needs media recovery

B. Displays whether the data file is either online or offline

C. Displays whether the online data file is fuzzy or not

D. Displays a NULL if the information in the data file header is successfully validated

64. Which one of the following options would you use with RMAN to back up archive log files along with other files?

A. ENABLE ARCHIVELOG

B. ADD ARCHIVELOG

C. INCLUDE ARCHIVELOG

D. PLUS ARCHIVELOG

Full-Length Examination II

1. Which one of the following parameters when specified determines the maximum number of the files that can be stored in each backup set?

A. MAXSETSIZE

B. FILESPERSET

C. BACKUPPERSET

D. FILESPERBACKUP

2. What must you do after the completion of copying the data files while performing online database backup?

A. Shut down the database gracefully and restart.

B. Execute the ALTER SYSTEM SWITCH LOGFILE command and copy the archive log files since the beginning of online backup.

C. Execute the ALTER SYSTEM CHECKPOINT command.

D. Back up the online redo log files.

3. While performing a restore of the entire database, the control file was restored to a non-default location. Which one of the following files must be updated for recognizing the new control file location?

   A. Trace file

   B. Password file

   C. Alert log file

   D. Initialization file

   E. Data file

4. When a recovery is performed using RMAN, what is it called?

   A. User-managed recovery

   B. Server-managed recovery

   C. System-managed recovery

   D. Database-managed recovery

5. As a result of a media failure, the current online redo log group is corrupted. The database crashes, as the current online group is inaccessible. Which type of incomplete recovery are you most likely to perform?

   A. Cancel-based

   B. Recovery using a backup control file

   C. Time-based

   D. Change-based

6. The following RMAN script enables you to perform database point-in-time recovery. Examine the script and choose the correct sequence in which the steps must be executed.

```
RMAN> RUN
 {
 1.   SET UNTIL TIME '12-OCT-2001 15:20:00';
 2.   sql "ALTER SESSION SET NLS_DATE_FORMAT=''DD-MON-YYYY HH24:MI:SS''";
 3.   RECOVER DATABASE;
 4.   RESTORE DATABASE;
  }
```

   A. 4,3,1,2

   B. 2,1,4,3

C. 3,4,1,2

D. 1,3,2,4

E. 2,1,3,4

7. If you CROSSCHECK the backup piece that was previously marked as EXPIRED but is now available, what would the status of this backup piece be in the RMAN repository?

   A. EXPIRED

   B. AVAILABLE

   C. UNAVAILABLE

   D. ACCESSIBLE

8. Which one of the following options of the export utility enables data to be directly transferred to the client without the intermediate evaluation buffer?

   A. GRANTS=N

   B. DIRECT=Y

   C. IGNORE=Y

   D. DIRECT=N

   E. CONVENTIONAL=Y

9. Which one of the following files contains records that do not meet the specified load criteria in the SQL*Loader control file?

   A. Log file

   B. Discard file

   C. Parameter file

   D. Bad file

10. When can you perform a database backup using RMAN if the database is in ARCHIVELOG mode? (Choose three.)

    A. NOMOUNT

    B. CLOSED

    C. MOUNT

    D. OPEN

    E. RESTRICTED SESSION

11. **Which one of the following parameters defines the location where the control file trace is generated?**

    A. BACKGROUND_DUMP_DEST

    B. CORE_DUMP_DEST

    C. USER_DUMP_DEST

    D. TRACE_DUMP_DEST

12. **Lisa is a database consultant for a Fortune 2000 company. The database that she manages operates in ARCHIVELOG mode. Due to a media failure she loses a non-system data file for which she has no backups. What conditions must be met for the recovery of the non-system data file? (Choose two.)**

    A. She must have the current or a backup control file, which was created after the data file was created.

    B. She only needs all the online redo log files.

    C. She must have all the archived redo log files and online log files since the creation of the data file.

    D. She only needs all the archived redo log files.

13. **Ryan is a DBA who uses RMAN to perform backup and recovery operations. Due to a media failure the user10.dbf data file was lost. Which one of the following commands must he use at the RMAN prompt, to copy the data files from the backup location to their default location before performing recovery operations?**

    A. RECOVER

    B. REINSTATE

    C. ALLOCATE

    D. RESTORE

14. **Which of the following user-managed recovery options enable you to do incomplete recovery? (Choose three.)**

    A. Complete-based

    B. Time-based

    C. Sequence-based

    D. Change-based

E. Data file-based

F. Cancel-based

15. **Which one of the following statements is incorrect in reference to the RESTORE optimization feature?**

   A. RMAN checks the data file headers during restoration.

   B. RMAN will not restore all the files but only those that have not yet been restored or those not correctly restored.

   C. RMAN does not verify individual data blocks for corruption.

   D. RMAN checks the entire data file and the header during restoration.

16. **Which one of the following RMAN commands is used to register the database files with the repository that were backed up using O/S commands?**

   A. CHANGE

   B. CATALOG

   C. CROSSCHECK

   D. SWITCH

17. **What happens if the REGISTER DATABASE command is issued? (Choose two.)**

   A. RMAN identifies the target database with its unique database identifier.

   B. RMAN creates records in the recovery catalog that store information about the target database.

   C. RMAN performs a partial resynchronization of the recovery catalog.

   D. RMAN creates a separate schema for the database.

18. **Which one of the following conditions must be met in order to transport a tablespace from one database to another?**

   A. Tablespaces need not be self-contained.

   B. The source and the target database must use the same character set.

   C. The source and target database must have different database block sizes.

   D. The objects in the tablespace can have referential integrity constraints defined on other tablespace objects.

19. Listed in the following are parameters that constitute a sample parameter file for the SQL*Loader utility. Which one of the following parameter values is erroneous?

    A. USERID=scott/tiger

    B. CONTROL=sample.ctl

    C. LOG=sample.log

    D. DIRECT=on

    E. ERRORS=99

    F. BINDSIZE=100000

20. Which one of the following packages maintains information in the recovery catalog?

    A. DBMS_RCVMAN

    B. DBMS_RMAN

    C. DBMS_RCVCAT

    D. DBMS_CATPROC

21. Which one of the following Oracle components or products must be installed and configured to enable the secure communications between the client and the server over the network?

    A. Security server

    B. Intelligent agent

    C. Connection Manager

    D. Advanced network option

22. Which one of the following environment variables specifies a non-default location for the listener configuration file?

    A. LSN_ADMIN

    B. TNS_ADMIN

    C. ADMIN_TSN

    D. TSN_ADMIN

23. **You want to prioritize the local naming method over the host naming method. Which one of the following entries in the sqlnet.ora file will enable this?**

    A. NAMES.DIRECTORY_PATH=(TNSNAMES, HOSTNAME)

    B. SQLNET.DIRECTORY_PATH=(TNSNAMES, HOSTNAME)

    C. NAMES.DIRECTORY_PATH=(HOSTNAME, TNSNAME)

    D. SQLNET.DIRECTORY_PATH=(HOSTNAME, TNSNAME)

    E. None of the above

24. **How can you change the SERVICE parameter in the shared server environment?**

    A. Use the ALTER DATABASE command to change the value.

    B. Use the ALTER SYSTEM command to change the value in the running database instance.

    C. Change the parameter in the **listener.ora** file, and reload the listener.

    D. Shut down the database, change the parameter in the **init.ora** file, and restart the database.

25. **Bob executes an UPDATE statement using SQL*Plus. Oracle returns an invalid syntax error. What kind of failure has Bob experienced?**

    A. Statement failure

    B. Instance failure

    C. Application failure

    D. Media failure

26. **Which Oracle process is responsible for archiving the online redo log files when the automatic archiving feature is enabled in ARCHIVELOG mode?**

    A. SMON

    B. PMON

    C. ARC*n*

    D. DBW*n*

    E. LGWR

27. **As a DBA, what is the first step you need to take to configure the database to operate in ARCHIVELOG mode, if high availability is a major factor?**

  A. Shut down the database with the ABORT priority and then edit the **init.ora** file.

  B. Shut down the database using either the NORMAL, TRANSACTIONAL, or IMMEDIATE priority and then edit the **init.ora** file.

  C. Edit the **init.ora** file to specify the parameters related to archiving before shutting down the database.

  D. Issue the ALTER DATABASE ARCHIVELOG statement to enable archiving without shutting down the database.

28. **What is the middle-tier in an n-tier application called?**

  A. Adapter

  B. Agent

  C. Protocol

  D. Router

29. **What is the significance of using the NEXT option in the following statement?**

```
SQL> ALTER SYSTEM ARCHIVE LOG NEXT;
```

  A. It archives the current online redo log group.

  B. It archives all the unarchived redo log groups.

  C. It archives the oldest unarchived online redo log group that is not current.

  D. The statement fails to execute because the number of the redo log group is not specified.

30. **Which Oracle background process is responsible for coalescing free space in the dictionary-managed tablespaces?**

  A. SMON

  B. PMON

  C. DBW*n*

  D. LGWR

  E. ARCn

31. Among the listed recovery method types, which recovery requires the DBA to explicitly issue a recovery command?

A. Crash recovery

B. Thread recovery

C. Media recovery

D. Instance recovery

32. What is the result of issuing the following command?

```
SQL> ALTER SYSTEM SET SHARED_SERVERS=0;
```

A. It disables the shared server.

B. All the existing connections will be terminated immediately.

C. The database will be restarted.

D. The minimum number of shared server processes will be run.

33. Which one of the following listener control utility commands must you use to check if the listener is refusing any connection requests for a database?

A. TRACE

B. SERVICES

C. SHOW

D. RELOAD

34. The following are the partial contents of the listener.ora configuration file:

```
(SID_DESC=
  (GLOBAL_DBNAME=support.oramasters.com)
  (ORACLE_HOME=/usr/oracle)
  (PROGRAM=extproc)
  (SID_NAME=support)
)
```

What does the value 'support.oramasters.com' for the parameter GLOBAL_DBNAME represent?

A. Instance name and database domain name

B. Service name and database domain name

C. Database name and database domain name

D. None of the above

35. **Which one of the following statements is not true about the listener process?**

   A. It is responsible for detecting and routing incoming requests from the clients.

   B. It spawns a new process or redirects the request to an existing process.

   C. It is not possible to use a release 9.0 listener with previous versions of the Oracle database.

   D. A listener is configured with one or more listening protocol addresses.

36. **Which one of the following statements is incorrect in reference to the Connection Manager?**

   A. It enables the propagation of requests to either the intermediate destination or to the destination server.

   B. It enables the clients to take advantage of its advanced capabilities such as connection multiplexing, access control, and protocol conversion.

   C. CMAN can filter connections based on origin, destination, or database service names.

   D. Multiplexing using the Connection Manager is not available for TCP/IP.

37. **What is the default value for the initialization parameter CONTROL_FILE_RECORD_KEEP_TIME?**

   A. One day

   B. Five days

   C. Seven days

   D. Nine days

   E. Ten days

38. **Which one of the following statements is not true about the application Web server?**

   A. The browser on the client uses HTTP to communicate with a Web server to make a connection request.

   B. The application on the application web server uses Oracle Net to communicate with the database server.

   C. The HTTP protocol is used for communicating between the Web browser and the application Web server.

    D. TCP/IP protocol can be used for communicating between the application and the Web server.

    E. None of the above

39. Which of the following values can be specified for the parameter TRACE_LEVEL_*listener_name*? (Choose two.)

    A. SUPPORT

    B. HISTORY

    C. HIGH

    D. USER

    E. LOW

40. Which one of the following configuration files can be used to implement the host naming method?

    A. tnsnames.ora, sqlnet.ora, host.ora

    B. host.ora, tnsnames.ora

    C. sqlnet.ora, tnsnames.ora

    D. sqlnet.ora, names.ora

    E. sqlnet.ora

41. Which one of the following views will help determine the number of shared servers that are currently running on a host?

    A. V$SHARED_SERVER_MONITOR

    B. V$SHARED_SERVER

    C. V$QUEUE

    D. V$DISPATCHER

42. The buffers in the database buffer cache that are currently being accessed by a server process are referred to as

    A. Pinned buffers

    B. Reuse buffers

    C. Free buffers

    D. Dirty buffers

43. **What is the maximum number of archiver processes that can be started during the instance startup?**

    A. One

    B. Five

    C. Seven

    D. Ten

44. **Which protocol has to be adopted for secure access to the database over the Internet?**

    A. LDAP

    B. SSL

    C. Radius

    D. All of the above

45. **Which one of the following commands can you use to display whether or not the automatic archiving feature is enabled?**

    A. ARCHIVE LOG NEXT

    B. ARCHIVE LOG STATUS

    C. ARCHIVE LOG LIST

    D. ARCHIVE LOG REPORT

46. **Which Oracle database file stores the log history and the archived log metadata?**

    A. Redo log files

    B. Control files

    C. Data files

    D. Archived log files

47. **You have been recruited to manage a large Oracle database for a Fortune 500 company. What would be your plan of action to verify that the backup and recovery strategy that was outlined by the previous DBA?**

    A. You build and test a new backup and recovery strategy.

    B. You assume that it has been already tested.

C. You test the existing backup and recovery strategy.

D. You should advise the management to hire people to build a new strategy because this is not part of a DBA's job.

48. **Which one of the following commands must you execute at the listener control prompt to stop the default listener service?**

   A. SHUTDOWN

   B. QUIT

   C. STOP

   D. EXIT

49. **Ann uses a very small sized target database. She uses RMAN with the target database control file as its repository to perform backup and recovery operation. What must she do to protect the control file against media failure?**

   A. She must use pre-compiled scripts for backup and recovery.

   B. She must often issue the RESYNC CATALOG command.

   C. She must maintain multiple copies of the control file.

   D. She must replicate the database objects.

50. **The initialization parameter LOG_CHECKPOINT_INTERVAL is defined in which of the following units?**

   A. Oracle blocks

   B. Time interval in days

   C. O/S blocks

   D. Time interval in seconds

51. **Which of the files are affected when the following statement is issued?**

   ```
   RMAN> CONFIGURE DATAFILE BACKUP COPIES FOR DEVICE TYPE sbt TO 3;
   ```

   A. Data files and the current control file

   B. Only for the online redo log files

   C. Archived redo logs, current control files, and the data files

   D. Data files and archived redo logs

52. Which one of the following SQL*Loader files contain information about the data source and to which of the schema objects the data must be loaded?

A. Log file

B. Bad file

C. Discard file

D. Parameter file

E. Control file

53. Assume that the AUTOBACKUP feature for the control file is enabled. What happens if you issue the following statement?

```
RMAN> BACKUP TABLESPACE tools INCLUDE CURRENT CONTROLFILE;
```

A. RMAN overrides the AUTOBACKUP feature and creates only one backup copy of the control file along with the backup of the tablespace TOOLS.

B. RMAN prioritizes AUTOBACKUP and overrides it the explicit inclusion of the control file.

C. RMAN generates two control file backups.

D. The command fails to execute.

54. Which of the following dynamic performance views are populated if corruption is detected during the execution of the BACKUP, BACKUP . . . VALIDATE or the COPY command at the RMAN prompt? (Choose two.)

A. V$BACKUP_CORRUPTION

B. V$BACKUP_ERROR

C. V$COPY_CORRUPTION

D. V$COPY_ERROR

55. Under which of the following cases would you need to open the database using the RESETLOGS option? (Choose three.)

A. All the data files were restored and incomplete recovery was performed.

B. Complete recovery of a lost non-system data file was performed with the current control file.

C. Complete recovery was performed using a backup control file.

D. Incomplete recovery was performed using a backup control file.

E. Complete recovery of a SYSTEM data file using the current control file.

56. Which one of the following RMAN commands would ensure that the backup sets and image copies conform to the configured retention policy?

    A. CHANGE . . . . KEEP

    B. CHANGE . . . . NOKEEP

    C. CHANGE . . . . AVAILABLE

    D. CHANGE . . . . UNCATALOG

57. Corey is working as a DBA for a Fortune 2000 company. He uses RMAN to perform backup and recovery operations. He has performed a structural change to the target database by adding a new log group. Which one of the following commands enables him to update this information in the recovery catalog?

    A. REGISTER DATABASE

    B. RESYNC CATALOG

    C. OPEN RESETLOGS DATABASE

    D. RESET DATABASE

    E. PARTIAL RESYNC CATALOG

58. James is an Oracle user. He wants to export database objects from another user's schema. Which role must be granted to him for his operation to be successful?

    A. IMP_FULL_DATABASE

    B. RESOURCE

    C. CONNECT

    D. EXP_FULL_DATABASE

59. While performing an online database backup, Raj encountered a database crash. To obtain the information about the tablespaces currently in backup mode, which one of the following dynamic performance views must he query?

    A. V$TABLESPACE

    B. V$DATAFILE

    C. V$BACKUP

    D. V$BGPROCESS

60. Which one of the following views displays information about archived logs that are stored in a backup set?

    A. V$BACKUP_REDOLOG

    B. V$BACKUP_DATAFILE

    C. V$BACKUP_SET

    D. V$BACKUP_PIECE

61. You have issued the following commands to perform recovery of the database:

```
SQL> SET AUTORECOVERY ON
SQL> RECOVER DATABASE;
```

    While performing recovery, which portion of the database can the Oracle database users access?

    A. Objects not affected by the recovery operation

    B. All tablespaces not affected by the recovery operation

    C. Read-only tablespaces

    D. Any data files not being recovered

    E. Database is inaccessible

62. Which one of the following lines would cause the RMAN script to fail?

    A. `run{`

    B. `allocate channel c1 type disk;`

    C. `sql 'ALTER TABLESPACE users OFFLINE IMMEDIATE';`

    D. `set newname for datafile 8 to 'd:\oracle\oradata\oemdb\users01.dbf';`

    E. `restore tablespace users;`

    F. `switch datafile 8;`

    G. `recover tablespace;`

    H. `sql 'ALTER TABLESPACE users ONLINE';`

    I. `}`

63. Paul administers a database operating in ARCHIVELOG mode. The database has two redo log groups. Redo log group 1 cannot be archived because it is corrupted. This is delaying the group from being overwritten. Which one of the following statements must Paul issue to temporarily solve his problem?

A. ALTER SYSTEM ACTIVE LOGFILE GROUP 1;

B. ALTER DATABASE CLEAR UNARCHIVED LOGFILE GROUP 1;

C. ALTER DATABASE CLEAR GROUP 1 UNARCHIVED;

D. RECOVER LOGFILE GROUP 1;

64. Which of the following statements is true about the SPFILE? (Choose two.)

A. It maintains information regarding initialization parameters in a text file, which can be edited.

B. It must be created using the CREATE SPFILE command.

C. It eliminates the need to manually update the initialization parameters in the init.ora file.

D. It makes the **init.ora** file unusable.

Answers to Full-Length Examination I

1. B.   Restore data files, and redo log files to the default location and the control file to the new location.

C.   Edit the initialization parameter file to reflect the new location of the control file.

Explanation   When a media failure occurs and you need to restore a database file to a new location, you should use O/S commands to move the file, mount the instance, and use the ALTER DATABASE RENAME FILE command to update the control file. If you moved a control file, you need to update the parameter file with the new location of the control file before the instance can be started.

2. C.   MOUNT

Explanation   You can perform recovery of a non-system data file without active rollback segments with the database mounted or opened. However, to recover a SYSTEM data file or any data file containing an active rollback segment, you must MOUNT (but not OPEN it) the database and then perform the recovery operations.

3. E.   Incomplete

Explanation   The database is restored to a time prior to the time of failure when you perform an incomplete recovery of a database in ARCHIVELOG mode. Oracle provides various methods for incomplete recovery like cancel-based, time-based, and change-based.

4. B. Perform a whole database backup using RMAN.

Explanation RMAN does not enable you to perform any recovery using backups that were performed prior to the RESETLOGS operation. It is recommended that you take a whole database backup after resetting the online redo log sequence.

5. C. RMAN automatically deletes information pertaining to the image copy from the repository if it is physically not available.

Explanation The RMAN's CROSSCHECK command updates the status of a backup file in the repository as EXPIRED if the file is not physically available.

6. C. RC_STORED_SCRIPT_LINE

Explanation RMAN enables you to obtain the code of an existing stored scriptthat is created using the RMAN CREATE SCRIPT command by querying the RC_STORED_SCRIPT_LINE. You can obtain the names of all the stored scripts, which are associated with a particular database through the view RC_STORED_SCRIPT.

7. B. IMP_FULL_DATABASE

Explanation Any user performing an entire database export and import must have the EXP_FULL_DATABASE and IMP_FULL_DATABASE roles, respectively. By default the IMP_FULL_DATABASE role is assigned to the DBA role. Granting the DBA role thereby enables the user to import the full database from an export dump file.

8. E. To load data using the serial mode, you must activate the direct path insert by specifying the SERIAL hint.

Explanation To load data using the serial mode, you must specify the APPEND hint in the SQL statement.

9. A. Wallet Manager

Explanation The user only needs to remember one password, which opens the wallet to access his or her credentials. Wallet Manage is used to authenticate the user to multiple services.

10. C. Agent

Explanation The Agents are introduced for the N-tier architecture. They provide scalability, translation, and intelligent agent services.

11. A. PMON

Explanation Before forwarding a client request to a database server, the listener determines if a database service and its service handlers are available through a service registration. The background process PMON is responsible for providing this information to the listener. This enables the listener to direct the client requests to the appropriate service.

12. C. It is automatically registered with the listener.

Explanation In Oracle9*i*, the information about the database is automatically registered with the listener and includes the global database name. For earlier releases of Oracle, you would need to configure the listener to register the database information by editing the **listener.ora** file manually.

13. C. IP address and port number

Explanation During the dispatcher startup, you can configure it to start with an IP address and port number.

14. D. Human error

Explanation This kind of failure is termed as human error. Human errors are a leading cause of failures and data corruption, for example, an accidental operation performed by a user such as deleting table rows or dropping a table.

15. C. LGWR

Explanation: In the Oracle background process, LGWR writes redo entries from the redo log buffers to the redo log files. The LGWR process performs the write operation if one of the following conditions is met:

- Whenever a COMMIT occurs
- Whenever a timeout of three seconds occurs
- Whenever the redo log buffer is one-third full
- Whenever the DBW*n* process signals the LGWR to perform a write operation

16. C. No recovery can be performed; you can only perform a simple restore of the database.

Explanation If the database is operating in NOARCHIVELOG mode, then you must regularly perform an offline database backup. In case of a media failure, which may result in the loss of one or more files, the only option available would be to restore the entire database from the last whole database backup. Note that all the data that has been entered since the last backup would be lost.

17. D.   RMAN does not require the tablespace to be in backup mode.

Explanation   When using RMAN to perform a backup of the online tablespaces, it is not required to keep the online tablespaces in backup mode. RMAN does not generate extra redo during online backups when compared with user-managed online backups.

18. B.   Whole database backup after the database is gracefully closed.

Explanation   When the database operates in NOARCHIVELOG mode, you can only perform a whole database backup after you shut down the database gracefully. Note that if you perform a whole database backup after shutting down the database with the ABORT option, then the backup is treated as invalid by Oracle.

19. C.   NOCHECKSUM

Explanation   The NOCHECKSUM option is used for avoiding data block verification during the process of making image copies. This in turn will speed up the copy process.

20. C.   Shut down the database, restore the lost file, mount the database, and recover the database.

Explanation   When the SYSTEM tablespace requires recovery, the database must be closed when the files are recovered. For a SYSTEM data file, you can't do online recovery because the SYSTEM data files can never be taken offline. You must use O/S commands to restore the corrupt or missing files. You can then mount the database and issue the RECOVER command for recovery.

21. D.   SWITCH

Explanation   The RMAN's SWITCH command performs the equivalent function of the ALTER DATABASE RENAME FILE statement.

22. A.   Perform a full backup.

Explanation   To avoid human errors during incomplete recovery, Oracle recommends that you take a full backup of the database after you shut down. After you take a full backup, restore the data files using O/S commands, start an instance and mount the database, recover the database, and open the database with the RESETLOGS option.

23 B.   Database opened
       Database registered in recovery catalog
       Starting full resync of recovery catalog
       Full resync complete

Explanation   Whenever you open the database with the RESETLOGS option after an incomplete recovery of the database, RMAN initially opens the database and registers the new incarnation of the database in the recovery catalog. It then performs a full resynchronization of the recovery catalog.

24. D. RC_BACKUP_SET

Explanation The RC_BACKUP_SET view can be queried from the recovery catalog to obtain information about the backup sets that were created using RMAN.

25. D. Information related to new backups is updated

Explanation Options A and C are applicable only during full resynchronization of the recovery catalog. As part of a partial resynchronization, RMAN reads the target database's control file to update changed information mostly related to new backups and new archived redo logs generated.

26. D. Table mode

Explanation Partition level export enables you to export one or more specified partitions or subpartitions within a table. Full database, user, and transportable tablespace mode exports do not support partition level export; only table mode export allows specific partitions to be exported.

27. A. Conventional path load

Explanation During conventional path load, Oracle has to compete with all the processes to acquire buffer resources. In contrast, the direct path loading feature reduces overhead and speeds the loading process by directly writing to the data file blocks.

28. C. Lightweight Directory Access Protocol (LDAP)

Explanation Support of LDAP-compliant directory servers provides a centralized vehicle for managing and configuring a distributed Oracle network. The directory can act as a central repository for all data on database network components, policies (user and corporate), user authentication, and security.

29. C. To pass the Destination address

Explanation Net service name is an alias that stores the information about the listener location through a protocol address along with service name. The service name is typically the global database name, which comprises of the database name and the database domain name.

30. B. The request queue is common, and the response queue is different for all the dispatchers.

Explanation There is only one request queue for all the dispatchers, and the dispatcher will pick up the request from it and service the request. It then places it to the corresponding response queue.

31. C.   It does not require the username and password to check the connectivity of the service.

Explanation   The TNSPING utility enables you to check for connectivity of a database service without specifying any username and password.

32. A.   Point-in-time recovery

Explanation   Point-in-time recovery (PITR) is to perform recovery on the database until a specified time. It is widely used to overcome human errors and physical corruptions. Oracle supports various incomplete recovery commands to overcome human errors.

33. A.   PMON

Explanation   If a user process abnormally terminates, the background process PMON frees resources occupied by the failed process. Note that the PMON process rolls back any uncommitted transactions associated with the user process.

34. D.   LOG_ARCHIVE_MIN_SUCCEED_DEST

Explanation   The initialization parameter LOG_ARCHIVE_MIN_SUCCEED_DEST defines the minimum number of destinations that Oracle should successfully archive to before overwriting the online log files. You can define the value for this parameter from 1 to 10. If LOG_ARCHIVE_MIN_SUCCEED_DEST is set to less than the number of destinations in which the MANDATORY option is chosen, then the value in LOG_ARCHIVE_MIN_SUCCEED_DEST is ignored. If the value set is to greater than the specified mandatory destinations, then some of the optional destinations are treated as mandatory.

35. C.   SYSTEM

Explanation   You cannot exclude the SYSTEM tablespace using the CONFIGURE EXCLUDE FOR TABLESPACE command when performing a whole database backup.

36. C.   CATALOG DATAFILECOPY

Explanation   The data files that are backed up using the O/S commands or O/S utilities are similar to those that are generated by using the RMAN's COPY command. The O/S files are not recognized by RMAN until you catalog these files. To catalog these files you must execute the CATALOG command at the RMAN prompt.

37. C.   154

Explanation   Media recovery requires applying of archived log files. All the archive and online log files since the backup was performed are required for complete recovery. If one of the archived logs is missing or corrupt, you can only recover until the previous archived log in the sequence.

38. C.   V$DATAFILE_HEADER

Explanation   The V$DATAFILE_HEADER dynamic performance view displays information about data files that need recovery. The RECOVER column displays whether or not the file needs media recovery.

39. A.   Incomplete recovery in ARCHIVELOG mode

Explanation   A database that operates in NOARCHIVELOG mode can only be recovered to the last full backup. To recover the database until a specified log sequence, a time, or until change, you will need to perform incomplete recovery, which is only possible in ARCHIVELOG mode.

40. B.   It removes the records of the specified backup sets and image copies from the catalog and updates the control file records status to DELETED

Explanation   RMAN's CHANGE . . . UNCATALOG command removes the records of the specified backup sets and image copies from the catalog and updates the control file record status to DELETED.

41. A.   DELETE SCRIPT

Explanation: In order to delete an existing script you must use the DELETE SCRIPT command and specify the name of the script, as shown in the following code:

```
RMAN> DELETE SCRIPT Full_backup;
```

42. B.   It can be used in conjunction with direct path export.

Explanation   The QUERY parameter cannot be specified for full, user, or transportable tablespace mode exports. This parameter cannot be specified when using the direct path export (DIRECT=Y). It also cannot be specified for tables with inner nested tables.

43. C.   Bad

Explanation   The bad file is created after execution of the SQL*Loader if the records are either rejected by SQL*Loader or by the Oracle database server. SQL*Loader rejects records if the specified input format is invalid.

44. D.   Oracle Net supports SPX/IPX network protocol with Oracle 9*i*.

Explanation   Note that SPX/IPX will no longer be supported with Oracle9*i*.

45. A.   HTTP

   B.   TCP/IP

Explanation   The browser on the client uses HTTP to communicate with the web server, thereby making a connection request where HTTP is carried by the TCP transport layer.

46. C.   RELOAD

Explanation   Oracle provides you the ability to load all the updates dynamically, thereby eliminating the need for stopping and restarting the listener by using the RELOAD command.

47. A.   Check the settings for the net service name.

Explanation   This error occurs when the protocol specific parameters in the ADDRESS section of the designated connect descriptor is incorrect. To resolve this error you must verify the settings for the net service name.

48. C.   The dispatcher D011 terminates new and existing connections.

Explanation   If this statement is executed with the IMMEDIATE keyword, it terminates the existing and any new connections. You can also issue the command without the IMMEDIATE option. In this case, the dispatcher stops accepting new connections immediately but waits for all its users to disconnect and for all the database links to terminate. Then it literally shuts down.

49. C.   LogMiner generates SQL_REDO as well as SQL_UNDO with primary key information.

Explanation   LogMiner generates SQL_REDO as well as SQL_UNDO with primary key information to help you undo the changes. The LogMiner utility provides you with the ability to audit user operations and recover data if lost due to accidental operations.

50. D.   Library cache

Explanation   Oracle stores the parse tree information and the execution plan for a SQL statement in the library cache. The library cache is part of the shared pool area of the SGA.

51. A.   LOG_ARCHIVE_START

Explanation   The parameter LOG_ARCHIVE_START enables automatic archiving. If you don't enable this parameter, you can still turn on the database to ARCHIVELOG mode, but the database will be in manual ARCHIVELOG mode. If you forget to turn this parameter on in the **init.ora** file, you can enable automatic archiving at session level by using the ARCHIVE LOG START command after you open the database.

52. B.   Manual allocation overrides the automatic channel allocation.

Explanation   Manual channel allocation in a RUN block overrides the automatic channel allocation settings. Therefore, automatic and manual channels cannot be defined and used at the same time.

53. C.   ALTER DATABASE END BACKUP

Explanation   This command is especially useful when several tablespaces have been placed in backup modes. Executing the ALTER DATABASE END BACKUP command once takes all the tablespaces out of the backup mode. In previous releases of Oracle, you had to take each data file out of the backup mode individually or perform media recovery on the database if the database crashed during an online backup.

54. A.   V$COPY_CORRUPTION

Explanation   The dynamic performance view V$COPY_CORRUPTION displays information related to the data file copy corruptions. The CORRUPTION_CHANGE# column of this view displays the change number at which the logical corruption was detected. If the value for this column is set to 0, it indicates that media corruption was detected. If the value for the MARKED_CORRUPT column is set to YES, then it indicates the corruption was detected while performing the image copy of the data file.

55. D.   To protect the database from a single point of failure

Explanation   The contents of the online redo log files are very important to recover data completely during failures. You must multiplex the online redo log files, thereby having redundant copies of the data stored in different drives that are mounted under different controllers. This would help protect the database from a single point of failure.

56. B.   The lost redo log group has already been archived.

Explanation   The loss of one or more online log members could result due to a media failure if multiplexing is not properly done. In such a situation, you can still recover the database with no data loss, provided that the lost redo log group has already been archived.

57. C.   Global database name, Oracle Home, and SID

Explanation   A listener can be configured to support multiple databases. The list of all the databases included in the listener is specified within the SID_LIST_<*listener_name*> parameter. For configuring the SID_LIST parameter in the **listener.ora** file, the components that you need to specify for the databases are the global database name (GLOBAL_DBNAME), Oracle home directory for the database (ORACLE_HOME), and the system identifier (SID).

58. C.   Specifies a new location in the RUN block where the data file needs to be restored.

Explanation   If you run the SET NEWNAME command before you restore a file, then RMAN creates a data file copy with the specified name and location.

59. C.   Recovery by simply restoring the full offline backup

Explanation   The only recovery option available if archiving is not enabled is to do recovery from full offline backups. The other three options are simply variants on complete or incomplete recovery, all of which require archiving to be enabled on your database. Any type of recovery that requires the redo records to be applied using archived redo log files requires that your database operate in ARCHIVELOG mode.

60. B.   A checkpoint is triggered if a user commits a transaction.

Explanation   The checkpoint does not occur if a user commits a transaction. The following conditions apply for a checkpoint to be triggered:

- When a log switch occurs
- When configured through the database initialization parameters LOG_CHECKPOINT_INTERVAL and LOG_CHECKPOINT_TIMEOUT
- When an online database backup begins
- When a tablespace is taken offline with the NORMAL priority
- When the ALTER SYSTEM CHECKPOINT command is issued
- When the database is closed gracefully

61. A.   Performing a full database backup

Explanation   It is recommended that you immediately perform a closed full database backup after switching the database into ARCHIVELOG mode. The previous backups performed while the database was in NOARCHIVELOG mode would not be useful if you need to recover the database from media failures in the future. You can also perform an online database backup but you will run the risk of a media failure until the full database is backed up.

62. B.   RMAN>CONFIGURE CONTROLFILE AUTOBACKUP ON;

Explanation: By default this feature is disabled. If this feature is enabled using this command, RMAN performs the automatic backup of the control file at the following instances:

- After completion of every BACKUP and COPY commands at the RMAN prompt
- After every non-consecutive BACKUP or COPY command within a RUN block

63. B.   Displays whether the data file is either online or offline

Explanation   Displays the status of the data file, which is either ONLINE or OFFLINE. The status information is obtained from the control file. Note that although the V$DATAFILE_HEADER displays information mentioned in the other answers, the question was specific to the output displayed for the STATUS column of this view.

64. D.   PLUS ARCHIVELOG

Explanation   Archived log files can be backed up along with other files by using the PLUS ARCHIVELOG option with the RMAN's BACKUP command.

Answers to Full-Length Examination II

1. B.   FILESPERSET

Explanation   You can specify the maximum number of input files for inclusion in the backup set by specifying the FILESPERSET parameter. For example, if you set the FILESPERSET parameter to 5, then RMAN never includes more than five files in a backup set.

2. B.   Execute the ALTER SYSTEM SWITCH LOGFILE command and copy the archive log files since the beginning of the online backup.

Explanation   The ALTER SYSTEM SWITCH LOGFILE command archives the CURRENT online redo log group. You must execute this command so that the redo generated during online backups can be backed up. The online backup is consistent only when you have all the archived log files.

3. D.   Initialization file

Explanation   The initialization parameter file stores the information about the control file location. During instance startup, Oracle reads the initialization parameter file and locates the control file. If there is any change in the location of the control file, then you must update the initialization parameter CONTROL_FILES with the new location.

4. B.   Server-managed recovery

Explanation   Recovery Manager (RMAN) requires Oracle server sessions to perform recovery operations. Hence it is known as *server-managed recovery*.

5. A.   Cancel-based

Explanation   Cancel-based recovery can be performed when a current online redo log file or all the files of an online redo log group are missing or are corrupt. Cancel-based recovery is used when you apply recovery till then end of a log file. The recovery operations can be terminated at the end of a log file by issuing the CANCEL command.

6. B.   2,1,4,3

Explanation   To perform an incomplete recovery, you must first specify a date format for the specified time using the SQL command in the RUN block. You can then set the time, restore the files, and perform recovery.

7. B.   AVAILABLE

Explanation   If the missing or corrupted image copy or backup piece is replaced with a duplicate copy that is in a good condition, then RMAN modifies the status of the backup piece in the repository to AVAILABLE.

8. B.   DIRECT=Y

Explanation   The direct path export reads data from disk into the buffer cache and the records are then directly transferred to the export client without the intermediate evaluation buffer. Because the direct path export bypasses the evaluating buffer, it is a faster method for performing exports. Data is already in the format that the export requires, thereby avoiding any unnecessary data conversion. The data is then transferred to the export client, which writes the data into the export dump file.

9. B.   Discard file

Explanation   The records that do not meet the specified load criteria are directed to the discard file. If a discard file is specified and one or more records fail to satisfy all of the WHEN clauses specified in the control file, then they are discarded. If no records are discarded then the discard file is not generated.

10. C.   MOUNT

   D.   OPEN

   E.   RESTRICTED SESSION

Explanation   Before executing the BACKUP command, the target database should be in one of the modes specified previously. In such situations, RMAN can either perform a consistent or an inconsistent backup.

11. C.   USER_DUMP_DEST

Explanation   The trace file would be generated in the location defined by the initialization parameter USER_DUMP_DEST on your system.

12. A.   She must have the current or a backup control file, which was created after the data file was created.

   C.   She must have all the archived redo log files and online log files since the creation of the data file.

Explanation   Oracle enables you to recover data files that have no backups only if they belong to the non-system tablespace. Note that you must have all the archived redo log files and online redo log files since the creation of the data file. You must have the current or a backup control file that was created after the data file was created. This means that the control file used during recovery should recognize the data files.

13. D. RESTORE

Explanation   The RESTORE command of RMAN is used to restore the required database files prior to performing recovery operations. You can either specify DATABASE, DATAFILE, or TABLESPACE with the RESTORE command.

14. B. Time-based

D. Change-based

F. Cancel-based

Explanation   In time-based recovery, the recovery session terminates at a specific point in time. Cancel-based recovery terminates whenever the 'CANCEL' option is issued at the recovery prompt. Change-based recovery is terminated at the specified SCN. All these incomplete recovery options enable a DBA to recover the database to a time prior to the failure.

15. D. RMAN checks the entire data file and the header during restoration.

Explanation   The RESTORE optimization feature of RMAN only checks the data file headers and not the entire data file while performing a restore. RMAN restores only those files that have not yet been restored or those that were not correctly restored.

16. B. CATALOG

Explanation   The backup of database files created using O/S commands must be manually restored and recovered. You can, however, register these files with the repository by using RMAN's CATALOG command. The restore and recover operations hereafter would be possible using RMAN.

17. A. RMAN identifies the target database with its unique database identifier.

B. RMAN creates records in the recovery catalog that store information about the target database.

Explanation   After issuing the REGISTER DATABASE command, RMAN identifies the database with a unique database identifier and then creates records in the repository that holds information about the target database. RMAN then performs a full resynchronization with the recovery catalog in which it transfers all pertinent data about the target database from the control file and saves it in the recovery catalog.

18. B.   The source and the target database must use the same character set.

Explanation   The source and target databases must have similar character sets, and the tablespace should be self-contained.

19. D.   DIRECT=on

Explanation   This parameter takes the value of either TRUE or FALSE. If set to FALSE, SQL*Loader uses the conventional path load method.

20. C.   DBMS_RCVCAT

Explanation   RMAN uses the packages DBMS_RCVCAT and DBMS_RCVMAN. These are undocumented packages. The DBMS_RCVCAT package is responsible for maintaining information in the recovery catalog, and the DBMS_RCVMAN is used for querying the recovery catalog or the control file.

21. D.   Advanced network option

Explanation   By installing the Advanced networking option, which is an Oracle Net product, you can enable secure transmissions between the client and the server.

22. B.   TNS_ADMIN

Explanation   The entire listener related configuration is stored in the file called **listener.ora**. The default location of this file is platform specific. You can also relocate the file **listener.ora** to a different destination by specifying the path through the TNS_ADMIN environment variable or by modifying its registry value.

23. A.   NAMES.DIRECTORY_PATH=(TNSNAMES, HOSTNAME)

Explanation   For specifying the order of the naming methods that Oracle Net will use to resolve connect identifiers to the connect descriptors, you will need to set the NAMES.DIRECTORY_PATH parameter in the **sqlnet.ora** file. To configure local naming as the first method, you should change the order defined in the previous parameter.

24. D.   Shut down the database, change the parameter in the **init.ora** file, and restart the database.

Explanation   The SERVICE parameter cannot be changed without restarting the database. You will need to change the parameter in the **init.ora** file and then restart the database.

25. A.   Statement failure

Explanation   A statement failure occurs when there is a logical failure due to a bad SQL statement. A statement failure is defined as the incapability of Oracle to execute an SQL operation. Oracle returns an appropriate error to the user when a statement failure occurs.

26. C.   ARC*n*

Explanation   When the database is operating in ARCHIVELOG mode, the archiving of the redo log files can either be automated or manually performed. If automatic archiving is enabled, then the ARC*n* process is responsible for archiving the online redo log files.

27. C.   Edit the **init.ora** file to specify the parameters related to archiving before shutting down the database.

Explanation   You must edit the initialization file and set the parameter LOG_ARCHIVE_START to TRUE to enable automatic archiving. By editing the **init.ora** file before shutting down the database and mounting it, we save time thereby reducing downtime of the database.

28. B.   Agent

Explanation   The agent (middle tier) also acts as a transaction-processing monitor to balance the load of requests between servers and provides the intelligent agent services.

29. C.   It archives the oldest unarchived online redo log group that is not current.

Explanation   The NEXT option of the ALTER DATABASE ARCHIVE LOG statement instructs the Oracle server to archive the oldest online redo log group that needs archiving.

30. A.   SMON

Explanation   The SMON process is responsible for releasing free space in dictionary-managed tablespaces. SMON also performs instance recovery after an instance failure and cleans up all the temporary segments that are no longer in use.

31. C.   Media recovery

Explanation   All the other recovery methods listed, other than the media recovery, do not require a DBA's intervention during the recovery process. Crash recovery is done when the DBA starts the instance. Instance recovery is done by SMON of another instance. When media failure occurs, the DBA must issue Oracle-specific recovery commands to perform either a complete or incomplete database recovery.

32. A.   It disables the shared server.

Explanation   The ALTER SYSTEM statement, mentioned in the question, when executed, will disable the shared server temporarily until you specify a value that is higher than zero for the parameter SHARED_SERVERS.

33. B.   SERVICES

Explanation   The **lsnrctl** utility can be used to check the status of the listener and also ensure that it is listening for a database. You need to use the **lsnctrl** utility's SERVICES command to check if the listener is refusing any connections.

34. C.   Database name and database domain name

Explanation   The global database name is comprised of the database name and the database domain name. You can obtain the GLOBAL_DBNAME value from the SERVICE_NAMES parameter or from the DB_NAME and DB_DOMAIN parameters in the initialization parameter file.

35. C.   It is not possible to use a release 9.0 listener with previous versions of the Oracle database.

Explanation   A release 9.0 listener is required for an Oracle9*i* database. Previous versions of the listener are not supported for use with an Oracle9*i* database. However, it is possible to use a release 9.0 listener with previous versions of the Oracle database.

36. D.   Multiplexing using the Connection Manager is not available for TCP/IP.

Explanation   Multiplexing can be implemented using the Connection Manager only for the TCP/IP protocol.

37. C.   Seven days

Explanation   The initialization parameter CONTROL_FILE_RECORD_KEEP_TIME specifies the minimum number of days a record must be maintained in the control file before it can be reused. If a low value is specified for this parameter, the records in the control file are overwritten frequently.

38. E.   None of the above

Explanation   All the statements from A to D are true in reference to the way clients access connections when using the application Web server.

39. A.   SUPPORT

   D.   USER

Explanation   The TRACE_LEVEL_*listener_name* parameter turns tracing on or off to a certain specified level. If the parameter is set to OFF, no trace files will be written to the trace destination. The USER value for this parameter will enable user-level tracing. The ADMIN level enables you to trace information related to administration. The SUPPORT level writes the information of the packets transferred and actions taken by the listener process.

40. E.   **sqlnet.ora**

Explanation   The host naming method is mostly preferred for simple networks. To configure host naming as the first method, you must set the NAMES.DIRECTORY_PATH parameter in the **sqlnet.ora** file.

41. B.   V$SHARED_SERVER

Explanation   The V$SHARED_SERVER view displays the detailed information about the shared server processes.

42. A.   Pinned buffers

Explanation   Pinned buffers are part of the database buffer cache's LRU list, which is currently being accessed by the server process. Once the pinned buffers are written and released, they become dirty buffers.

43. D.   Ten

Explanation   You can define the maximum number of archiver processes that will be started during instance startup by using the initialization parameter LOG_ARCHIVE_MAX_PROCESSES. The maximum value for this parameter is 10. If no value is defined for this parameter, then the Oracle starts 1 ARC*n* process by default.

44. B.   SSL

Explanation   SSL is the protocol for network connections over the Internet. It secures Oracle Net connections and other protocols as well, including IIOP connections used with thin clients and Enterprise Java Beans.

45. C.   ARCHIVE LOG LIST

Explanation   To obtain the information about the automatic archiving feature, you must issue the ARCHIVE LOG LIST command at the SQL*Plus prompt. It will show whether the database is in archive log mode or not and also if automatic archiving is enabled. Note that you must possess the system privileges SYSDBA or SYSOPER to use this command. You can also query the V$INSTANCE dynamic performance view, which displays whether or not the automatic archiving feature is enabled. The ARCHIVER column in the V$INSTANCE displays the values STOPPED, STARTED, or FAILED.

46. B.   Control files

Explanation   The control file stores the log history (V$LOG_HISTORY) and the archived log metadata. Apart from this, the control file also stores the information about the database structure and details about the data files, log files, and thread information.

47. C.   You test the existing backup and recovery strategy.

Explanation   The existing backup and recovery strategy should always be checked for validity and consistency. You must test the strategy in a test environment before implementing it on your production database. This avoids any mishap on the production server, which may result in major losses.

48. C.   STOP

Explanation   The listener control utility can be used to administer the listener at the command line. The STOP option with the *listener_name* would enable you to stop the listener. When you do not define any name for listener, Oracle takes the default name as LISTENER.

49. C.   She must maintain multiple copies of the control file.

Explanation   If a control file is used as a repository instead of a recovery catalog, then Ann must ensure the safety of the control file by multiplexing them. The multiple copies must be placed on separate disks, preferably mounted under different controllers.

50. C.   O/S blocks

Explanation   The LOG_CHECKPOINT_INTERVAL must be set to a value that corresponds to the number of O/S blocks. If the value exceeds the actual redo log file size, checkpoints occur only when the logs switch.

51. D.   Data files and archived redo logs

Explanation   The CONFIGURE settings apply only to data files and archived redo log backups. This feature is known as *duplexing*. By default, the value is one copy for each device type.

52. E.   Control file

Explanation   The control file instructs the SQL*Loader about the source from where the data can be obtained and the Oracle objects into which the data must be loaded. It also provides the SQL*Loader utility with information about the parsing of data and how to interpret this data. The control file also contains information pertaining to the various other files where the data must be directed to in case of exceptions.

53. C.   RMAN generates two control file backups.

Explanation   RMAN in this situation creates two control file backups. It first creates the backup set, including the control file in it, and then backs up the control file separately, as part of the AUTOBACKUP.

54. A. V$BACKUP_CORRUPTION

C. V$COPY_CORRUPTION

Explanation The V$BACKUP_CORRUPTION and V$COPY_CORRUPTION dynamic performance views are populated during the execution of the BACKUP, BACKUP . . . VALIDATE, or the COPY commands of RMAN, if corruptions are detected. These views display detailed information about the corrupted blocks that are part of the data file backup sets or image copies. They are populated if physical corruption and logical corruption is detected.

55. A. All the data files were restored and incomplete recovery was performed.

C. Complete recovery was performed using a backup control file.

D. Incomplete recovery was done using a backup control file.

Explanation The database must be opened using the RESETLOGS option after performing an incomplete recovery or if the recovery has been done using a backup control file. To open the database with the RESETLOGS option, all data files must be recovered to the same SCN, and if a backup control file is restored, it must also be recovered to the same SCN. A RESETLOGS operation invalidates all redo in the online logs. Restoring from a whole database backup and then resetting the logs discards the changes to the database made from the time the backup was taken to the time of failure.

56. B. CHANGE . . . . NOKEEP

Explanation For a backup to work in accordance with the configured retention policy, you must use the NOKEEP option either with the CHANGE command or while creating the backup sets or image copies.

57. B. RESYNC CATALOG

Explanation If any structural changes like adding or dropping of tablespaces, data files, log groups, and log members occur on the target database, you must manually resynchronize the recovery catalog by issuing the RESYNC CATALOG command at the RMAN prompt.

58. D. EXP_FULL_DATABASE

Explanation He must be granted the EXP_FULL_DATABASE role or all the privileges contained in this role to export any objects belonging to another user's schema. Users possessing the EXP_FULL_DATABASE role are known as *privileged users*.

59. C. V$BACKUP

Explanation   To view information about data files that are currently in backup mode, you must query the V$BACKUP dynamic performance view. This view displays the file identification number, the current status (ACTIVE, NOT ACTIVE, OFFLINE, NORMAL, or a description of an error), the SCN, and the time when the backup started.

60. A. V$BACKUP_REDOLOG

Explanation   The dynamic performance view V$BACKUP_REDOLOG displays information about archived logs that are stored in a backup set. This information is obtained from the control file.

61. E. Database is inaccessible

Explanation   This RECOVER DATABASE command will recover the entire database. This type of recovery can only be performed only when the database is closed database. This type of recovery is also called *offline recovery*.

62. G. `recover tablespace;`

Explanation   The tablespace name is not given in this statement. The correct syntax for this statement is shown in the following code:

```
Recover tablespace <tablespace specification>;
```

63. B. ALTER DATABASE CLEAR UNARCHIVED LOGFILE GROUP 1;

Explanation   This command must be used when the corrupt redo log group is an online group that has not been archived. This command will clear or re-create the members of group. If this command is issued, the redo log will not be archived, so complete recovery will not be possible until you perform a full database backup after issuing the command.

64. B. It must be created using CREATE SPFILE command.

C. It eliminates the need to manually update the initialization parameters in the **init.ora** file.

Explanation   Oracle9*i* enables you to maintain the initialization parameters in a binary file called the *server parameter file* (SPFILE). The spfile stores the initialization parameters pertaining to the Oracle database server. If you use the spfile, changes to the initialization parameters using the ALTER SYSTEM command persists across the instance shutdown and startup operations, eliminating the need for updating the **init.ora** file manually.

Index

W

INTERNATIONAL CONTACT INFORMATION

AUSTRALIA
McGraw-Hill Book Company Australia Pty. Ltd.
TEL +61-2-9417-9899
FAX +61-2-9417-5687
http://www.mcgraw-hill.com.au
books-it_sydney@mcgraw-hill.com

CANADA
McGraw-Hill Ryerson Ltd.
TEL +905-430-5000
FAX +905-430-5020
http://www.mcgrawhill.ca

**GREECE, MIDDLE EAST,
NORTHERN AFRICA**
McGraw-Hill Hellas
TEL +30-1-656-0990-3-4
FAX +30-1-654-5525

MEXICO (Also serving Latin America)
McGraw-Hill Interamericana Editores S.A. de C.V.
TEL +525-117-1583
FAX +525-117-1589
http://www.mcgraw-hill.com.mx
fernando_castellanos@mcgraw-hill.com

SINGAPORE (Serving Asia)
McGraw-Hill Book Company
TEL +65-863-1580
FAX +65-862-3354
http://www.mcgraw-hill.com.sg
mghasia@mcgraw-hill.com

SOUTH AFRICA
McGraw-Hill South Africa
TEL +27-11-622-7512
FAX +27-11-622-9045
robyn_swanepoel@mcgraw-hill.com

**UNITED KINGDOM & EUROPE
(Excluding Southern Europe)**
McGraw-Hill Publishing Company
TEL +44-1-628-502500
FAX +44-1-628-770224
http://www.mcgraw-hill.co.uk
computing_neurope@mcgraw-hill.com

ALL OTHER INQUIRIES Contact:
Osborne/McGraw-Hill
TEL +1-510-549-6600
FAX +1-510-883-7600
http://www.osborne.com
omg_international@mcgraw-hill.com

Knowledge is power. To which we say,

crank up the power.

Are you ready for a power surge?

Accelerate your career—become an **Oracle Certified Professional (OCP)**. With Oracle's cutting-edge *Instructor-Led Training*, *Technology-Based Training*, and this *guide*, you can prepare for certification faster than ever. Set your own trajectory by logging your personal training plan with us. Go to **http://education.oracle.com/tpb**, where we'll help you pick a training path, select your courses, and track your progress. We'll even send you an email when your courses are offered in your area. If you don't have access to the Web, call us at 1-800-441-3541 (Outside the U.S. call +1-310-335-2403). **Power learning has never been easier.**

Get Your FREE Subscription to *Oracle Magazine*

- Up-to-date information on Oracle Database Server, Oracle Applications, Internet Computing, and tools
- Third-party news and announcements
- Technical articles on Oracle products and operating environments
- Development and administration tips
- Real-world customer stories

Three easy ways to subscribe:

1. Web Visit our Web site at www.oracle.com/oramag/. You'll find a subscription form there, plus much more!

2. Fax Complete the questionnaire on the back of this card and fax the questionnaire side only to **+1.847.647.9735.**

3. Mail Complete the questionnaire on the back of this card and mail it to P.O. Box 1263, Skokie, IL 60076-8263.

If there are other Oracle users at your location who would like to receive their own subscription to *Oracle Magazine*, please photocopy this form and pass it along.

☐ YES! Please send me a FREE subscription to *Oracle Magazine*.   ☐ NO

To receive a free bimonthly subscription to *Oracle Magazine*, you must fill out the entire card, sign it, and date it (incomplete cards cannot be processed or acknowledged). You can also fax your application to +1.847.647.9735. Or subscribe at our Web site at www.oracle.com/oramag

SIGNATURE (REQUIRED)	X		DATE	

NAME	TITLE
COMPANY	TELEPHONE
ADDRESS	FAX NUMBER
CITY	STATE	POSTAL CODE/ZIP CODE
COUNTRY	E-MAIL ADDRESS

☐ From time to time, Oracle Publishing allows our partners exclusive access to our e-mail addresses for special promotions and announcements. To be included in this program, please check this box.

You must answer all eight questions below

1 What is the primary business activity of your firm at this location? *(check only one)*
- ☐ 03 Communications
- ☐ 04 Consulting, Training
- ☐ 06 Data Processing
- ☐ 07 Education
- ☐ 08 Engineering
- ☐ 09 Financial Services
- ☐ 10 Government—Federal, Local, State, Other
- ☐ 11 Government—Military
- ☐ 12 Health Care
- ☐ 13 Manufacturing—Aerospace, Defense
- ☐ 14 Manufacturing—Computer Hardware
- ☐ 15 Manufacturing—Noncomputer Products
- ☐ 17 Research & Development
- ☐ 19 Retailing, Wholesaling, Distribution
- ☐ 20 Software Development
- ☐ 21 Systems Integration, VAR, VAD, OEM
- ☐ 22 Transportation
- ☐ 23 Utilities (Electric, Gas, Sanitation)
- ☐ 98 Other Business and Services
- _____

2 Which of the following best describes your job function? *(check only one)*
CORPORATE MANAGEMENT/STAFF
- ☐ 01 Executive Management (President, Chair, CEO, CFO, Owner, Partner, Principal)
- ☐ 02 Finance/Administrative Management (VP/Director/ Manager/Controller, Purchasing, Administration)
- ☐ 03 Sales/Marketing Management (VP/Director/Manager)
- ☐ 04 Computer Systems/Operations Management (CIO/VP/Director/ Manager MIS, Operations)

IS/IT STAFF
- ☐ 07 Systems Development/ Programming Management
- ☐ 08 Systems Development/ Programming Staff
- ☐ 09 Consulting
- ☐ 10 DBA/Systems Administrator
- ☐ 11 Education/Training
- ☐ 14 Technical Support Director/ Manager
- ☐ 16 Other Technical Management/Staff
- ☐ 98 Other _____

3 What is your current primary operating platform? *(check all that apply)*
- ☐ 01 DEC UNIX
- ☐ 02 DEC VAX VMS
- ☐ 03 Java
- ☐ 04 HP UNIX
- ☐ 05 IBM AIX
- ☐ 06 IBM UNIX
- ☐ 07 Macintosh
- ☐ 09 MS-DOS
- ☐ 10 MVS
- ☐ 11 NetWare
- ☐ 12 Network Computing
- ☐ 13 OpenVMS
- ☐ 14 SCO UNIX
- ☐ 24 Sequent DYNIX/ptx
- ☐ 15 Sun Solaris/SunOS
- ☐ 16 SVR4
- ☐ 18 UnixWare
- ☐ 20 Windows
- ☐ 21 Windows NT
- ☐ 23 Other UNIX _____
- 99 ☐ **None of the above**

4 Do you evaluate, specify, recommend, or authorize the purchase of any of the following? *(check all that apply)*
- ☐ 01 Hardware
- ☐ 02 Software
- ☐ 03 Application Development Tools
- ☐ 04 Database Products
- ☐ 05 Internet or Intranet Products
- 99 ☐ **None of the above**

5 In your job, do you use or plan to purchase any of the following products or services? *(check all that apply)*
SOFTWARE
- ☐ 01 Business Graphics
- ☐ 02 CAD/CAE/CAM
- ☐ 03 CASE
- ☐ 05 Communications
- ☐ 06 Database Management
- ☐ 07 File Management
- ☐ 08 Finance
- ☐ 09 Java
- ☐ 10 Materials Resource Planning
- ☐ 11 Multimedia Authoring
- ☐ 12 Networking
- ☐ 13 Office Automation
- ☐ 14 Order Entry/Inventory Control
- ☐ 15 Programming
- ☐ 16 Project Management

- ☐ 17 Scientific and Engineering
- ☐ 18 Spreadsheets
- ☐ 19 Systems Management
- ☐ 20 Workflow
HARDWARE
- ☐ 21 Macintosh
- ☐ 22 Mainframe
- ☐ 23 Massively Parallel Processing
- ☐ 24 Minicomputer
- ☐ 25 PC
- ☐ 26 Network Computer
- ☐ 28 Symmetric Multiprocessing
- ☐ 29 Workstation
PERIPHERALS
- ☐ 30 Bridges/Routers/Hubs/Gateways
- ☐ 31 CD-ROM Drives
- ☐ 32 Disk Drives/Subsystems
- ☐ 33 Modems
- ☐ 34 Tape Drives/Subsystems
- ☐ 35 Video Boards/Multimedia
SERVICES
- ☐ 37 Consulting
- ☐ 38 Education/Training
- ☐ 39 Maintenance
- ☐ 40 Online Database Services
- ☐ 41 Support
- ☐ 36 Technology-Based Training
- ☐ 98 Other
- 99 ☐ **None of the above**

6 What Oracle products are in use at your site? *(check all that apply)*
SERVER/SOFTWARE
- ☐ 01 Oracle8
- ☐ 30 Oracle8i
- ☐ 31 Oracle8i Lite
- ☐ 02 Oracle7
- ☐ 03 Oracle Application Server
- ☐ 04 Oracle Data Mart Suites
- ☐ 05 Oracle Internet Commerce Server
- ☐ 32 Oracle interMedia
- ☐ 33 Oracle JServer
- ☐ 07 Oracle Lite
- ☐ 08 Oracle Payment Server
- ☐ 11 Oracle Video Server
TOOLS
- ☐ 13 Oracle Designer
- ☐ 14 Oracle Developer
- ☐ 54 Oracle Discoverer
- ☐ 53 Oracle Express
- ☐ 51 Oracle JDeveloper
- ☐ 52 Oracle Reports
- ☐ 50 Oracle WebDB
- ☐ 55 Oracle Workflow
ORACLE APPLICATIONS
- ☐ 17 Oracle Automotive

- ☐ 35 Oracle Business Intelligence System
- ☐ 19 Oracle Consumer Packaged Goods
- ☐ 39 Oracle E-Commerce
- ☐ 18 Oracle Energy
- ☐ 20 Oracle Financials
- ☐ 28 Oracle Front Office
- ☐ 21 Oracle Human Resources
- ☐ 37 Oracle Internet Procurement
- ☐ 22 Oracle Manufacturing
- ☐ 40 Oracle Process Manufacturing
- ☐ 23 Oracle Projects
- ☐ 34 Oracle Retail
- ☐ 29 Oracle Self-Service Web Applications
- ☐ 38 Oracle Strategic Enterprise Management
- ☐ 25 Oracle Supply Chain Management
- ☐ 36 Oracle Tutor
- ☐ 41 Oracle Travel Management
ORACLE SERVICES
- ☐ 61 Oracle Consulting
- ☐ 62 Oracle Education
- ☐ 60 Oracle Support
- ☐ 98 Other _____
- 99 ☐ **None of the above**

7 What other database products are in use at your site? *(check all that apply)*
- ☐ 01 Access
- ☐ 02 Baan
- ☐ 03 dbase
- ☐ 04 Gupta
- ☐ 05 IBM DB2
- ☐ 06 Informix
- ☐ 07 Ingres
- ☐ 08 Microsoft Access
- ☐ 09 Microsoft SQL Server
- ☐ 10 PeopleSoft
- ☐ 11 Progress
- ☐ 12 SAP
- ☐ 13 Sybase
- ☐ 14 VSAM
- ☐ 98 Other _____
- 99 ☐ **None of the above**

8 During the next 12 months, how much do you anticipate your organization will spend on computer hardware, software, peripherals, and services for your location? *(check only one)*
- ☐ 01 Less than $10,000
- ☐ 02 $10,000 to $49,999
- ☐ 03 $50,000 to $99,999
- ☐ 04 $100,000 to $499,999
- ☐ 05 $500,000 to $999,999
- ☐ 06 $1,000,000 and over

If there are other Oracle users at your location who would like to receive a free subscription to *Oracle Magazine*, please photocopy this form and pass it along, or contact Customer Service at +1.847.647.9630

Form 5

OPRESS

About the BeachFrontQuizzer™ CD-ROM

BeachFrontQuizzer provides interactive certification exams to help you prepare for certification. With the enclosed CD, you can test your knowledge of the topics covered in this book with more than 175 multiple choice questions.

Installation

To install BeachFrontQuizzer:

1. **Insert the CD-ROM in your CD-ROM drive.**

2. **Follow the Setup steps in the displayed Installation Wizard. (When the Setup is finished, you may immediately begin using BeachFrontQuizzer.)**

3. **To begin using BeachFrontQuizzer, enter the 12-digit license key number of the exam you want to take:**

    OCP Oracle9*i* Database Fundamentals II Exam   419859487222

Study Sessions

BeachFrontQuizzer tests your knowledge as you learn about new subjects through interactive quiz sessions. Study Session Questions are selected from a single database for each session, dependent on the subcategory selected and the number of times each question has been previously answered correctly. In this way, questions you have answered correctly are not repeated until you have answered all the new questions. Questions that you have missed previously will reappear in later sessions and keep coming back to haunt you until you get the question correct. In addition, you can track your progress by displaying the number of questions you have answered with the Historical Analysis option. You can reset the progress tracking by clicking on the Clear History button. Each time a question is presented the answers are randomized so you will memorize a pattern or letter that goes with the question. You will start to memorize the correct answer that goes with the question concept.

Practice Exams

For advanced users, BeachFrontQuizzer also provides Simulated and Adaptive certification exams. Questions are chosen at random from the database. The Simulated Exam presents a specific number of questions directly related to the real exam. After you finish the exam, BeachFrontQuizzer displays your score and the passing score required for the test. You may display the exam results of this specific exam from this menu. You may review each question and display the correct answer.

 NOTE
For further details of the feature functionality of this BeachFrontQuizzer software, consult the online instructions by choosing Contents from the BeachFrontQuizzer Help menu.

Technical Support

If you experience technical difficulties, please call (888) 992-3131. Outside the United States call (281) 992-3131. Or, you may e-mail **bfquiz@swbell.net**.

ORACLE SOFTWARE LICENSE AGREEMENT

YOU SHOULD CAREFULLY READ THE FOLLOWING TERMS AND CONDITIONS BEFORE BREAKING THE SEAL ON THE DISC ENVELOPE. AMONG OTHER THINGS, THIS AGREEMENT LICENSES THE ENCLOSED SOFTWARE TO YOU AND CONTAINS WARRANTY AND LIABILITY DISCLAIMERS. BY USING THE DISC AND/OR INSTALLING THE SOFTWARE, YOU ARE ACCEPTING AND AGREEING TO THE TERMS AND CONDITIONS OF THIS AGREEMENT. IF YOU DO NOT AGREE TO THE TERMS OF THIS AGREEMENT, DO NOT BREAK THE SEAL OR USE THE DISC. YOU SHOULD PROMPTLY RETURN THE PACKAGE UNOPENED.

LICENSE: ORACLE CORPORATION ("ORACLE") GRANTS END USER ("YOU" OR "YOUR") A NON-EXCLUSIVE, NON-TRANSFERABLE DEVELOPMENT ONLY LIMITED USE LICENSE TO USE THE ENCLOSED SOFTWARE AND DOCUMENTATION ("SOFTWARE") SUBJECT TO THE TERMS AND CONDITIONS, INCLUDING USE RESTRICTIONS, SPECIFIED BELOW.

You shall have the right to use the Software (a) only in object code form, (b) for development purposes only in the indicated operating environment for a single developer (one person) on a single computer, (c) solely with the publication with which the Software is included, and (d) solely for Your personal use and as a single user.

You are prohibited from and shall not (a) transfer, sell, sublicense, assign or otherwise convey the Software, (b) timeshare, rent or market the Software, (c) use the Software for or as part of a service bureau, and/or (d) distribute the Software in whole or in part. Any attempt to transfer, sell, sublicense, assign or otherwise convey any of the rights, duties or obligations hereunder is void. You are prohibited from and shall not use the Software for internal data processing operations, processing data of a third party or for any commercial or production use. If You desire to use the Software for any use other than the development use allowed under this Agreement, You must contact Oracle, or an authorized Oracle reseller, to obtain the appropriate licenses. You are prohibited from and shall not cause or permit the reverse engineering, disassembly, decompilation, modification or creation of derivative works based on the Software. You are prohibited from and shall not copy or duplicate the Software except as follows: You may make one copy of the Software in machine readable form solely for back-up purposes. No other copies shall be made without Oracle's prior written consent. You are prohibited from and shall not: (a) remove any product identification, copyright notices, or other notices or proprietary restrictions from the Software, or (b) run any benchmark tests with or of the Software. This Agreement does not authorize You to use any Oracle name, trademark or logo.

COPYRIGHT/OWNERSHIP OF SOFTWARE: The Software is the confidential and proprietary product of Oracle and is protected by copyright and other intellectual property laws. You acquire only the right to use the Software and do not acquire any rights, express or implied, in the Software or media containing the Software other than those specified in this Agreement. Oracle, or its licensor, shall at all times, including but not limited to after termination of this Agreement, retain all rights, title, interest, including intellectual property rights, in the Software and media.

WARRANTY DISCLAIMER: THE SOFTWARE IS PROVIDED "AS IS" AND ORACLE SPECIFICALLY DISCLAIMS ALL WARRANTIES OF ANY KIND, EITHER EXPRESS OR IMPLIED, INCLUDING, BUT NOT LIMITED TO, THE IMPLIED WARRANTIES OF MERCHANTABILITY, SATISFACTORY QUALITY AND FITNESS FOR A PARTICULAR PURPOSE. ORACLE DOES NOT WARRANT, GUARANTEE OR MAKE ANY REPRESENTATIONS REGARDING THE USE, OR THE RESULTS OF THE USE, OF THE SOFTWARE IN TERMS OF CORRECTNESS, ACCURACY, RELIABILITY, CURRENTNESS OR OTHERWISE, AND DOES

NOT WARRANT THAT THE OPERATION OF THE SOFTWARE WILL BE UNINTERRUPTED OR ERROR FREE. ORACLE EXPRESSLY DISCLAIMS ALL WARRANTIES NOT STATED HEREIN. NO ORAL OR WRITTEN INFORMATION OR ADVICE GIVEN BY ORACLE OR OTHERS SHALL CREATE A WARRANTY OR IN ANY WAY INCREASE THE SCOPE OF THIS LICENSE, AND YOU MAY NOT RELY ON ANY SUCH INFORMATION OR ADVICE.

LIMITATION OF LIABILITY: IN NO EVENT SHALL ORACLE OR ITS LICENSORS BE LIABLE FOR ANY DIRECT, INDIRECT, INCIDENTAL, SPECIAL OR CONSEQUENTIAL DAMAGES, OR DAMAGES FOR LOSS OF PROFITS, REVENUE, DATA OR DATA USE, INCURRED BY YOU OR ANY THIRD PARTY, WHETHER IN AN ACTION IN CONTRACT OR TORT, EVEN IF ORACLE AND/OR ITS LICENSORS HAVE BEEN ADVISED OF THE POSSIBILITY OF SUCH DAMAGES. SOME JURISDICTIONS DO NOT ALLOW THE EXCLUSION OF IMPLIED WARRANTIES OR LIMITATION OR EXCLUSION OF LIABILITY FOR INCIDENTAL OR CONSEQUENTIAL DAMAGES SO THE ABOVE EXCLUSIONS AND LIMITATION MAY NOT APPLY TO YOU.

TERMINATION: You may terminate this license at any time by discontinuing use of and destroying the Software together with any copies in any form. This license will also terminate if You fail to comply with any term or condition of this Agreement. Upon termination of the license, You agree to discontinue use of and destroy the Software together with any copies in any form. The Warranty Disclaimer, Limitation of Liability, and Export Administration sections of this Agreement shall survive termination of this Agreement.

NO TECHNICAL SUPPORT: Oracle is not obligated to provide and this Agreement does not entitle You to any updates or upgrades to, or any technical support or phone support for, the Software.

EXPORT ADMINISTRATION: You acknowledge that the Software, including technical data, is subject to United States export control laws, including the United States Export Administration Act and its associated regulations, and may be subject to export or import regulations in other countries. You agree to comply fully with all laws and regulations of the United States and other countries ("Export Laws") to assure that neither the Software, nor any direct products thereof, are (a) exported, directly or indirectly, in violation of Export Laws, either to countries or nationals that are subject to United States export restrictions or to any end user who has been prohibited from participating in the Unites States export transactions by any federal agency of the United States government; or (b) intended to be used for any purposes prohibited by the Export Laws, including, without limitation, nuclear, chemical or biological weapons proliferation. You acknowledge that the Software may include technical data subject to export and re-export restrictions imposed by United States law.

RESTRICTED RIGHTS: The Software is provided with Restricted Rights. Use, duplication or disclosure of the Software by the United State government is subject to the restrictions set forth in the Rights in Technical Data and Computer Software Clauses in DFARS 252.227-7013(c)(1)(ii) and FAR 52.227-19(c)(2) as applicable. Manufacturer is Oracle Corporation, 500 Oracle Parkway, Redwood City, CA 94065.

MISCELLANEOUS: This Agreement and all related actions thereto shall be governed by California law. Oracle may audit Your use of the Software. If any provision of this Agreement is held to be invalid or unenforceable, the remaining provisions of this Agreement will remain in full force.

YOU ACKNOWLEDGE THAT YOU HAVE READ THIS AGREEMENT, UNDERSTAND IT, AND AGREE TO BE BOUND BY ITS TERMS AND CONDITIONS. YOU FURTHER AGREE THAT IT IS THE COMPLETE AND EXCLUSIVE STATEMENT OF THE AGREEMENT BETWEEN ORACLE AND YOU.

Oracle is a registered trademark of Oracle Corporation.